I0759520

The Character Sketch as Philosophy

THE CHARACTER SKETCH AS PHILOSOPHY

Manners, Mores, Types

KATIE EBNER-LANDY

HARVARD UNIVERSITY PRESS
Cambridge, Massachusetts
London, England
2025

Printed in the United States of America

First printing

EU GPSR Authorised Representative
LOGOS EUROPE,
9 rue Nicolas Poussin,
17000, LA ROCHELLE, France
E-mail: Contact@logoseurope.eu

Library of Congress Cataloging-in-Publication Data

Names: Ebner-Landy, Katie, author.
Title: The character sketch as philosophy : manners, mores, types / Katie Ebner-Landy.
Description: Cambridge, Massachusetts : Harvard University Press, [2025] | Includes bibliographical references and index.
Identifiers: LCCN 2025004349 (print) | LCCN 2025004350 (ebook) | ISBN 9780674294127 (cloth) | ISBN 9780674302075 (epub) | ISBN 9780674302082 (pdf)
Subjects: LCSH: Character. | Character sketches. | Characters and characteristics. | Theophrastus. Characters.
Classification: LCC BJ1531 .E26 2025 (print) | LCC BJ1531 (ebook)
LC record available at https://lccn.loc.gov/2025004349
LC ebook record available at https://lccn.loc.gov/2025004350

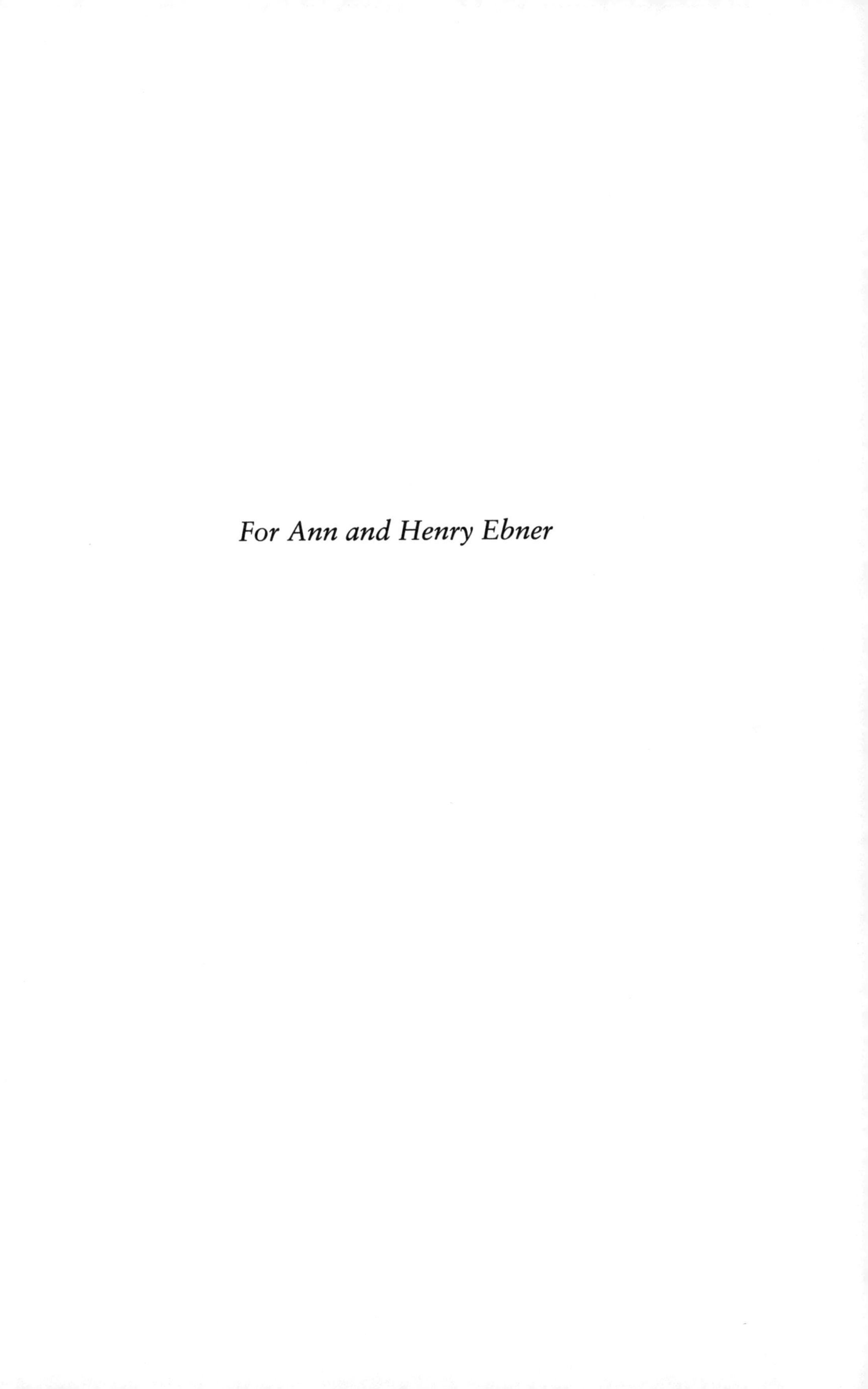

For Ann and Henry Ebner

Contents

Note on Conventions

Classical sources. All classical names, works, and places cited in the endnotes follow the conventions outlined by the *Oxford Classical Dictionary*, 4th ed. (Oxford: Oxford University Press, 2012). In the main text, I generally translate classical titles into English for ease of reading (unless the Latin title is more familiar) and refer to ancient writers in their single-name style.

French sources. I generally translate titles of French sources into English. Original titles are used in the endnotes.

Early modern and modern names. I have changed back into the vernacular the classical versions of the names that early modern humanists gave themselves. This is not to say that I revert to their given names but to the vernacular equivalent of the classical names they had chosen. For example, I use Angelo Poliziano rather than Angelo Ambrogini or Angelus Politianus. I similarly leave names of later writers in the vernacular—György, not Georg Lukács, for example—unless citing a source where an editor has chosen otherwise.

Gender. In my own writing, I use gender-inclusive language, such as substituting "person" for "man," wherever possible. I do not, however, change references to gender within quotations by other writers. Neither do I shift the emphasis in my analysis of their work when it seems that by "man" they meant "man" and not "person."

Transcriptions. In general, I preserve original spelling, capitalization, and punctuation in my transcriptions of early modern texts. But I expand contractions, lower raised letters, resolve ligatures, correct obvious typographical errors, remove diacritical marks in Latin, and swap *u* and *v* where necessary. I reduce the italicization common in early-modern printed texts, and I allow myself to substitute lowercase initial letters to upper and vice versa.

Translations. When quoting from sources in languages other than English, unless noted, all translations are my own. If noted, a first cited translation should be taken to carry across each reference of a given source. I include original language in the endnotes where scholarly editions are not easily available or where it seems useful to the reader.

The Character Sketch as Philosophy

Introduction

At the heart of moral philosophy, and at the center of political attempts to shape the ordinary behaviors of citizens, lies an unexpected form: the Theophrastan character. This form gets its name from the Hellenistic philosopher Theophrastus (c. 370–287 BCE), who studied under Aristotle, and perhaps Plato, and lived in a moment of tremendous political upheaval and philosophical innovation.[1] Born in Lesbos into a family of laundry workers, Theophrastus died in his eighties in Athens, having founded the art of botany and having succeeded Aristotle as leader of the Peripatetic school at the Lyceum. Theophrastus was born Tyrtamus, only later gaining the name by which we know him now—a name that literally means "divine speaker" (from *theo,* "divine," and *phrazein,* "to speak") and that is said to have been given to him by Aristotle, "on account of his graceful style."[2] Theophrastus was famous throughout antiquity for his metaphysics, his classification of plants, and his investigation into empirical phenomena as wide ranging as odors, dizziness, fire, and juice. Of the few texts of his that remain today, one is a small work that came to be known as the *Characters.*[3] This curious text, the focus of our story, had an enormous influence that stretched across the centuries, from Hellenistic Greece to early modern Europe.

Theophrastus's short text sketched thirty different types of men, each defined by a particular vice—from "bad timing" to "absent-mindedness" to "idle chatter"—and described through an account of their behavior. As these three titles hint, Theophrastus's set of vices are not glamorous vices, vices that make tragedies, vices that present clear problems like Envy or Lust. Free from any theological baggage, they are only linked together by the special quality of being *ordinary*: these are social sins that we commit at the scale of the everyday. Here is the Man with Bad Timing, the *akairos*:

> The Man with Bad Timing is the sort who goes up to someone who is busy and asks his advice. He sings love songs to his girlfriend when she has a fever. (. . .) He shows up to give testimony after the case has already been decided. If he's a guest at a wedding, he launches into a tirade against women. When a man has just returned from a long journey, he invites him to go for a walk. (. . .) After people have listened and understand, he stands up to explain all over again. (. . .) When he is on an arbitration board he exacerbates the dispute, when what both sides desire is a reconciliation. When he wants to dance, he grabs a partner who is still sober.[4]

This sketch shows us the Man with Bad Timing in a range of circumstances. We encounter him in somewhere like the street, in a domestic scene with his girlfriend, in court, at a wedding, in dialogue with a tired man, at a public meeting (a political deliberation, perhaps, or philosophical conversation), and at a dance. The sketch itself operates as a kind of mechanism, or mathematical function, composed of phrases that position this type in one situation after another and describe his similar responses. Underlying each situation is a particular disposition: an overarching incapacity to recognize the needs of a given moment and adapt one's actions accordingly.

This pattern can be seen in each sentence's structure. Each phrase begins with a clause that sets up an expected action in response to a situation. Seeing a busy man should lead to avoiding him; meeting a weary traveler, to comforting him; attending a wedding, to participating in the celebration of romance. But these expectations are swiftly undercut with another clause, showing how the type fails to meet its demands. When the Man with Bad Timing sees the busy passerby, he not only fails to avoid him but decides to go up to him and stop him for advice. And, in the few cases when the sentences begin with the Man with Bad Timing seemingly doing something fitting for a situation, such as singing love songs to his girlfriend (a classic trope of Greek lyric poetry), Theophrastus is quick to show that the type has misjudged the moment. If the *akairos* has good intentions, these are matched with little to no sensitivity as to when they should be realized. This quality has bad outcomes for other people: a frustrated hurried pedestrian, a suffering girlfriend, two irreconciled parties in an arbitration dispute, and, if we consider the high importance of witnesses in Athenian courts, a potential misjudgment of a case.

The sketches of other vices in Theophrastus's collection follow a similar formula. Each one begins with an abstract definition of a quality (e.g., "Rumormongering is the invention of untrue reports and events"), moves into a meticulous description of someone who exemplifies this quality, focusing on their habitual, quotidian actions ("The Rumor-monger is the sort who . . ."), and often ends either with a warning for the reader to avoid people like this or with a reflection on the kind of life led by the person in question ("I wonder what such people hope to gain from their rumormongering; not only do they tell lies, they also end up no better for it").[5] While it seems that the sketches were compiled through the close observation of many different people who embody their vice, they are written strictly in the third-person singular. No sketch is longer than fifteen sentences. Each vice is described from afar, with the sketches rarely considering a type's motivations or intentions. There is no other system beyond this three-part formula of unquestioned statement, detailed description, and final judgement: no reasoning, explanation, argument, or rebuttal. That is, apart from an inauthentic moralizing Proem, added around the fourth or fifth century CE by an unknown Roman author, which introduces the *Characters* by suggesting that it contains not only vices but corresponding virtues and that it has been written in the belief that future generations "will be better if such writings are bequeathed to them, which they can use as a guide in choosing to associate with and become close to the finest men, so as not to fall short of their standard."[6] It is in the pairing of the Proem's tantalizing claim that the *Characters* is an ethical guide with the fact that the *Characters* today reads like observational comedy that we find our story.

The *Characters* is a very small book with a very large influence. It was read, translated, adapted, and transformed across early modern and Enlightenment Europe, first in Latin, and then in a range of vernacular languages, including English, French, German, Italian, Spanish, and Russian.[7] The *Characters* inspired a highly popular genre of character-writing in the seventeenth century, which extended far beyond depicting ordinary vices to describing all kinds of people, places, and things: button-makers of Amsterdam, Bowle-Alleys, battles, and French beaus. Theophrastus's short text also had an influence on the writing of characters of nations (culminating in works of political philosophy by Montesquieu and Hume), played a role in developing the construction of literary character in the early modern novel, and, by offering a descriptive form in which to classify social, national, and professional types, has been understood as foundational for the development of the human sciences.[8]

The pages that follow describe the entanglement of the Theophrastan sketch with moral and political objectives: how, projected beyond its original context into early modern Europe, across a period of around 300 years, one set of readers after another imagined these descriptions of types to have a series of notable implications. Indeed, the anonymous Roman writer of the Proem was not alone in picking up on an ethical intention to the *Characters*. Rather, the early modern translators and adapters of the *Characters* had similar instincts about this text's purpose, sensing that these sketches had a morally and politically formative role to play. This is visible in the decision made by Willibald Pirckheimer, the German humanist and patron of Albrecht Dürer, to use Theophrastus's text as a piece of political propaganda in the aftermath of the 1520s German Peasants' War. It is also apparent in how both royalists and revolutionaries, on opposite sides of the English Civil War, used the character sketch as a means of sharing knowledge of their political opponents. A Renaissance tradition of interpreting and adapting a text by a little-known—or even "lost," according to one recent biography—Greek philosopher thus finds itself entangled with questions about the development of moral philosophy and the relationship between politics and literary description.[9]

Across the early modern period, readers saw character sketches as vehicles of knowledge and as a means to transform people's habitual actions: claims that aligned character sketches with philosophy and gave them an important political function. It was in the middle of the eighteenth century that both of these notions started to weather: a point at which the description of characters started to lose its status as a central part of moral philosophy and began to stop being treated as an adequate means to know a person, place, or thing. We still live, this book claims, somewhat in the shadow of that moment, an epochal break in which philosophy moved away from painting pictures toward finding principles and in which knowledge could no longer anchor itself to the description of appearances alone.

This eighteenth-century shift is brought into striking clarity in the work of the Scottish philosopher David Hume. In the opening of his *Enquiry concerning Human Understanding,* published in 1748, Hume sets out two methods of writing philosophy: an "easy and obvious" mode, which he associates with character-writing, and an "accurate and abstract" alternative, which involves a search for principles.[10] In Hume's view, the former had predominated for much too long. Grouping together the Roman rhetorician Cicero, the bestselling seventeenth-century French moralist Jean de La Bruyère, and the English playwright and essayist Joseph Addison, Hume argues that these easy and obvious moral philosophers have proved much more popular than their accurate and abstract competitors:

> The Fame of *Cicero* flourishes at present; but that of *Aristotle* is utterly decay'd. *La Bruyere* passes the Seas, and still encreases in Renown: But the glory of *Malebranche* is confin'd to his own Nation, and to his own Age. And *Addison,* perhaps, will be read with pleasure, when *Locke* shall be entirely forgotten.[11]

The world, Hume thought, has for too long preferred the easy and the obvious manner of writing moral philosophy. People are reading Cicero, enjoying new translations of La Bruyère, and will profit from Addison in years to come. Aristotle, on the other hand, has been left languishing, Malebranche untranslated, and Locke on the dusty path to being forgotten. With the easy and obvious philosophers linked together by their penchant for placing "opposite Characters in a proper contrast," Hume positions character-writing as one of two standard manners of writing moral philosophy.[12] Unlike the early modern writers who preceded him, however, Hume no longer thought this a sufficient manner in which to philosophize. He instead proposes an alternative mode that remains the most recognizable way of writing philosophy today.

By turning back before Hume, this book aims to provide an understanding of what moral philosophy once was and what kinds of texts political thought once encompassed. The Theophrastan tradition, it claims, shows us a lost vision of moral philosophy in which the literary description of social mores, behavioral habits, and quotidian actions was key—a tradition in which moral philosophy and what we now call literature were not distinct. This book further exposes an understanding of politics in which the hopes to shape civic behavior, and provide knowledge of society, centrally involved the writing and reading of typical, often vicious, figures. In both cases, it proposes that these apertures can speak to the present moment by offering us new ways of thinking about what philosophy might become and new sensitivities to the kinds of texts that have political import. This old manner of writing philosophy directed toward depicting manners, it argues, should warrant our attention once again. Even though character sketches continue to populate our own moment—consider our descriptions of experts, hoarders, snobs, and mansplainers—they are no longer seen as holding much philosophical weight. This book turns to a tradition that saw character sketches differently, a tradition that began in ancient Greece, stretched through the European Renaissance, and lasted up until the mid-eighteenth century.

The recovery of this unusual interpretative model in the Theophrastan tradition represents a striking departure from the two best-known classical treatments of aesthetic spectatorship. These early modern readers' sense that bad characters can induce good behavior is a clear reversal of the Platonic concern that by watching bad characters in the theater, we risk imitating them.[13] Their use of the character sketch as a means to provide knowledge of the social world also goes beyond the circumscribed role Aristotle gives character in his *Poetics*: an aspect of tragedy that he thought was less important than narrative.[14] In the Theophrastan tradition, it is not good characters who are entrusted to do moral work, nor is it the progress of a narrative, in which a hero suffers a misfortune and provokes an audience's pity and fear.[15] Here moral instruction is found in bad examples, and knowledge is gained through the description of typical characters, in texts free from narrative, without insight into a character's interiority, and that do not require the provocation of emotion. Authors can show us the bad, the cruel, and the ugly, without any poetic justice, psychological depth, or comeuppance—and still promise to help us become good.

The Original Purpose of the *Characters*

The intention of Theophrastus's short text has been fiercely debated, with three major kinds of purposes having been proposed: that it is a work of ethics, rhetoric, or comedy.[16] The scholars who have argued for an ethical intention have used the similarities between the *Characters* and Aristotle's *Nicomachean Ethics* to suggest that Theophrastus decided to illustrate certain vicious attributes that Aristotle outlined. Those who have proposed that the *Characters* is a work of rhetoric, in contrast, think that it would have been used to teach students of law how to vilify their opponents in court. Those who call for an association between the *Characters* and comedy have alternatively positioned the text as a dramatic handbook used to inspire playwrights.

If, however, we look closer at the Man with Bad Timing, the *akairos,* we can start to see another possibility—that the original purpose of *Characters* lies within the realm of politics. The Man with Bad Timing is characterized by his lack of *kairos,* a notion that was central to Greek ethical and political life. *Kairos* was the knack of seizing the moment, or recognizing an "opening" or "opportunity," and approaching it with "due measure."[17] It was a key concept for both Plato and Aristotle and a topic to which Theophrastus himself dedicated a political treatise: *Politics in Accordance with Circumstances* (*Politika pros tous kairous*).[18] The word comes from archery, denoting the vulnerable aperture at which an arrow should aim as a mark or target: *kairos* is the place on the body you strike to mortally wound.[19] From this beginning, *kairos* gained its more metaphorical meanings, given that an archer's shot, as historian Joanne Paul elegantly writes, "requires not only accuracy, but also the right amount of power—neither too much nor too little—in order to pass successfully through the opening."[20] Plato's good statesman is accordingly someone who knows "when it is the right time to begin and set in motion the most important things in cities and when it is the wrong time"; Aristotle's sense of practical wisdom, or *phronesis,* is similarly based on being able to realize one's intentions at the right moment.[21] Theophrastus's choice to sketch a type who systematically lacks this important quality then takes on more of a political key: a man lacking *kairos* is a man who would be a bad statesman, according to Plato, and would lack one of the virtues essential to be a good citizen, according to Aristotle. This is a sketch of a person who lacks the necessary qualities to participate in public life.

Part of this type's failure to register the needs of the moment involves his failure to register the needs of the people within it. We have seen how the Man with Bad Timing is insensitive to his girlfriend's fever, the desires of the guests at a wedding, or the interests of a group in conversation, parties in court, or someone at a dance. In this, the *akairos* is not alone, but he finds his insensitivity mirrored by the other vices that populate the collection. Each of the other characters possess qualities that can be reduced to a similar problem: from the Absentminded Man, who lacks the perceptive capacities to act appropriately toward others; to the Idle Chatterer, whose monologic nature prevents smooth conversation; to the Shameless Man, who threatens the social norms that bind communities together, with his absence of decorum. This insensitivity can also be found in the one party-political character in the collection, the Oligarch, whose dogmatic preferences prevent him from adequately adapting his arguments to suit a changing political context. If Athenian democracy rests on what Jacques Derrida calls a "community of friends," we might think that these characters, in not taking other people's needs seriously, threaten not only the social bonds between citizens but the possibility of democracy itself.[22]

The *akairos* thus provides a route—one of many, as we shall see—into understanding the political meaning of the collection as a whole. It nudges us to see how the text is intimately tied up with instilling virtues in Athenian citizens: by teaching them how to avoid the vices that could threaten political stability. As this book argues, Theophrastus's collection belonged to a wave of Hellenistic writing interested in what has been described as "virtue politics."[23] Where previous scholarship has shown that rhetoric and public oratory were used to inspire Athenian virtue politics, I propose that Theophrastus's literary description of types played an equivalent role. To understand the *Characters* in these terms is to arrive at a new sense of its original purpose. It is this interpretation of Theophrastus's text that is picked up on, again and again, in the *Characters*' early modern reception.

Approaching the Theophrastan Tradition

The Theophrastan character is not a new phenomenon: this book does not claim to have unearthed it from the teeming morass of European intellectual history. It promises instead to recover, and closely examine, the ways in which it was interpreted by a set of sixteenth- to eighteenth-century readers and writers. In this way, it departs from and seeks to complement prior accounts of the early modern and modern afterlives of the Theophrastan character. There are two existing monographs on the Theophrastan character sketch by Benjamin Boyce and J. W. Smeed, dissertations by Michael Mangan and Kristin Hay Jensen, and a large oeuvre of works on character by the Dutch scholar Louis van Delft. Boyce, Smeed, and Magnan are concerned with the Theophrastan character's development as a literary genre—how this form affected drama and the novel, how its style evolved over time, and what literary techniques writers used to express character.[24] Van Delft's numerous studies on character-writing are more situated in the history of ideas, unfolding a broad story about the status of character in the early modern period.[25]

In this book, however, I aim to prioritize exactly how early modern readers understood the function and value of Theophrastus's text as it was repeatedly translated and adapted in different contexts.[26] In other words, I am most interested in what writers were doing when translating or adapting the *Characters*—in how they used texts to carry out specific purposes within the world. In this, I derive my methodology partly from Quentin Skinner's writings on methods of interpretation in the history of political thought.[27] Following both Ludwig Wittgenstein and J. L. Austin, Skinner encouraged historians to consider words as "deeds," or "tools," and therefore to find a means of "recovering what the agent may have been *doing* in saying what was said."[28] I embrace these methodological orientations in a consideration of the history of a literary form. My question is therefore what people wanted to achieve by writing, translating, or adapting characters.

In asking what a series of authors were attempting to do in using a strange and unfamiliar literary genre—the character sketch—this book aims to flesh out what it might mean to consider something like the intention of a literary form from within the framework of the so-called Cambridge school. This is a question of what the choice of a specific literary form connoted, what kinds of tasks it was thought to be able to perform in a given moment, and why an author may have chosen it. It is also an examination of whether the repeated use of a literary form, for a specific kind of intention, loads it with a performative meaning. This book combines history and literary criticism, then, in a way that departs from Skinner's own work at this intersection.[29] It poses the intentional question at the foundation of the Cambridge school in relation to a literary genre—asking what authors, translators, and adapters intended by publishing these texts—and further investigates the changing intentions behind the form of character-writing over a circumscribed period of history.[30]

That said, the form of the character sketch frustrates many of the tools developed by the Cambridge school. It is frequently anonymous, and it was inspired by an original text notoriously ambiguous as to its purpose. The more localized methods that I have deployed to answer my overarching questions respond to this difficulty by pairing tools familiar to the history of philosophy and intellectual history with close reading. As the book is in part a reception history, and in part the history of a form of writing, the methods of reception studies I use to trace the first Latin translations must be supplemented by these other strategies. My own intellectual roots stand between literary and historical ways of thinking: one method that aims to "treat texts as particular objects" and thinks "about literature across wide spans of time and space" and another that attends "to the ways in which vocabularies change and persist through time, as they are tested and transformed by their usage at specific historical junctures."[31] I take these descriptions from Colin Burrow, in whose account of his own intellectual background I found something of myself.

I conclude this section with some more pedestrian methodological comments. This book is not intended to be encyclopedic but rather to offer an account of how the character sketch was repeatedly seen as a way of doing moral philosophy and providing political knowledge. First, a word on geography. The *Characters* was translated and adapted all over Europe. As my book cannot possibly cover all these editions, I have instead taken a dual approach. The early chapters go broad, ranging across time and place: ancient Athens, fifteenth-century Italy, and sixteenth-century Germany and France. In this way, I aim to spotlight the diverse range of arguments made about the text's moral and political purchase. The later chapters then narrow in on the adaptations in seventeenth-century England and France. Here, I intend instead to analyze and compare the two early modern nations in which vernacular character-writing took off.

Though there are many traditions of how to write characters in the early modern period, and many typical characters that end up in plays, novels, poems, and sermons (to name only a few genres), this book is focused on collections of characters, and single characters, that stand separate to other literary casing.[32] In a large chapter of *The Theophrastan Character,* Boyce describes the "native background" of character-writing in England before the first English vernacular adaptation of the *Characters* appears in 1608. This chapter encompasses the typical characters found in medieval allegories, estates literature, writings on the seven deadly sins, early drama, commonplace florilegia, and experiments in early prose fiction.[33] In this book, however, I leave that expansive tradition aside in order to isolate what people thought the character sketch could do on its own. This is an attempt to shield the character from other literary variables so that the study can singularly ask what a writer thought a character was doing, rather than asking both what a writer thought a drama was doing, for example, and how, within that drama, a particular character sketch was intended to work.[34]

How then to spot a Theophrastan character? Since this book covers the translations and adaptations of the Theophrastan character, as it evolved over the course of centuries, attempting to reach a limited definition of this moving object risks prejudicing the investigation from the outset. Rather than approaching the archives with a set of fixed rules, I locate Theophrastan characters through their "family resemblances."[35] The overlapping and crisscrossing features of this family include the brevity of a sketch; its composition in the third person; its presentation from afar, without detailing the character's motivations; the inclusion of a title with a definite article, making an individual a type ("*The* Rumor-monger"); and the description of a type's quotidian actions, as something like a snapshot. Not all the character sketches selected in this study have all these features. Rather, the possession of a subset has served as a guiding principle of selection. While several of these features can present a means of distinguishing the character sketch from adjacent genres—such as the exemplary life, with its extraordinary actions, or the historical portrait, with its focus on a known individual—over the course of this history, distinctions between these genres do not prove watertight.

The *Characters*, and character-writing, are frequently likened to images: from icons, to paintings, to snapshots. But in early modern Europe, it is in fact rare to see translations or adaptations of the *Characters* accompanied by actual images, and especially images of types.[36] (One explanation for this puzzling fact might lie in the fact that these sketches are intensely interested in speech. Unlike allegories of the cardinal sins, each recognizable by a single symbol, the Theophrastan characters are typified by their habits of conversation.)[37] While this book thinks deeply about the likenesses that character writers drew between their form and the visual arts, almost all the sketches that appear in its pages do so only within the written word.

The Arguments of This Book

This book contains three major arguments. First, I argue that writers were drawn to character sketches again and again over the centuries because they saw this form as a persuasive, and often novel, way of effecting behavioral change and providing a guide to a changing social sphere. The Theophrastan model of the character sketch, with its Greek pedigree, its freestanding form (one could write a character sketch without having to master any other literary genre), and its apparent status as at once timeless and contemporary, universal and particular, proved highly conducive to these ends.

Second, I propose that the function of early modern character-writing underwent a trajectory of change between the sixteenth and eighteenth centuries, as assumptions about the Theophrastan characters shifted. Character-writing, in its ancient context, was a means to instill a set of virtues that Theophrastus thought citizens needed to possess in order to achieve civic harmony. It was also, as we will see, a means to psychologize certain political perspectives and thereby refuse them their rational due. As the genre of character-writing took off in sixteenth- and seventeenth-century Europe, a whole host of translators, religious writers, polemicists, occasional writers, and moral philosophers became interested in using the form for a variety of reasons, not dissimilar to these older purposes, that also had moral and political implications. These early modern writers used the character to inspire virtue by portraits of vices, to implicitly instruct behavior, to reveal people in the social world, and to provoke a reader to adopt a set of religious practices and beliefs. Through this process, the character became associated with reforming actions and providing knowledge. Animating these interpretations were a series of assumptions that were present in the sixteenth century but began to be challenged toward the end of the seventeenth century and certainly in the eighteenth century. In the earlier period, character writers took for granted the idea that the Theophrastan characters were timeless, the possibility of reforming oneself by reforming one's actions alone, and the notion that an impressionistic account of how someone appears is a valid form of knowledge. By the eighteenth century, these assumptions were no longer widespread: portraits of Athenian manners were considered past, not present; moral reform required soul searching alongside sketches; and new character sketches were required to depict not just behavior but motives, to be a real guide to the social world. The character sketch thus felt the effects of broader changes in intellectual history: changes to the notion of character, changes to the theory of mind, and changes to the theory of art.[38]

The third argument concerns the end of this tradition in the mid-eighteenth century. It claims that Hume directly engaged with the Theophrastan tradition and elaborated an argument to deny it philosophical relevance and status. This comes in part from Hume's concern about the status of a genre that was uninterested in determining the principles of character—such as what character might be or where it might come from—in preference for sketching existing character types as they appear to the uninformed observer. Hume's distinction has the effect of separating out two methods of writing: one likened to anatomy and the other to painting. Just as the Rhine and the Rhone, to use one of Hume's own metaphors, are two rivers that come from the same spring, these two methods of writing are two streams that find a shared source in the mountain of moral philosophy.[39] Though both are driven by an attempt to grasp reality, they follow two different inclinations that end up creating two different courses, eventually discharging in seas that we now respectively call "philosophy" and "literature."[40] While from the perspective of the sea, we cannot see these two rivers' single spring, by training our eyes on Hume, we get somewhere close to its origin.

This account complicates the story that Richard Rorty tells about the changing function of philosophy in eighteenth-century Europe, which focuses not on Hume but Kant. Rorty suggests that this moment represents a major turning point in the direction of Western thought, from which, he argues, it has not diverged.[41] In Rorty's view, Kant was responsible for moving philosophy away from speculative metaphysics, and toward epistemology, in order to distinguish philosophy from physics by making it the epistemological foundation of the natural sciences. By centering Hume, rather than Kant, this book offers a story about how eighteenth-century philosophy not only wishes to distinguish itself from physics but also from what we consider literature. Rorty's interest in narrating this intellectual history came from his dissatisfaction with the present state of philosophy. He longed for a kind of philosophy that has a closer relationship with poets, novelists, and psychologists than with natural scientists, that is more interested in shaping a reader's actions than providing a truthful account of a given phenomenon. It is by returning to the Theophrastan tradition, this book proposes, that we can catch a glimpse of precisely this alternative mode of philosophy: one that existed before Hume foreclosed it. The history of the character sketch, I ultimately suggest, tells us something about the division of disciplines and spotlights a moment in which literary description had a different kind of status as both behavioral reform and knowledge. This, in turn, should nudge us to rethink the kinds of texts we can take as having political or philosophical seriousness.

Of course, a critic might justifiably ask if we can really say that sketching Theophrastan characters ended with Hume. What about Charles Dickens's *Sketches by Boz* (1833–1836), or William Makepeace Thackeray's 1848 *Book of Snobs*, or George Eliot's own *Impressions of Theophrastus Such* (1879), her brilliant, experimental final work? What about the Victorian wave of writing sketches of the working class, such as Henry Mayhew's 1851 *London Labour and the London Poor*? Or even the few collections of characters that have extended into the twentieth century, such as Elias Canetti's absurdist 1974 *Earwitnes: Fifty Characters*?

My claim here is not, however, that Hume represented the end of the Theophrastan character sketch. Rather, I argue that after Hume, character-writing was no longer considered de facto as a third way of writing moral philosophy or as a vehicle for knowledge. In these later collections, the character is a work designed to please, with the potential to instruct or reform; it is entertainment that may have some informational properties. The emphasis is on pleasure, rather than reform or knowledge. Smeed, whose study covers these later character collections, is clear that in eighteenth-century Britain, Vienna, and Germany, the notion of the character as a vehicle for moral "improvement" clearly "loses ground."[42] By the twentieth century, he concludes, the character sketch had become a "form of minor importance, associated with the past and, perhaps, no longer thought fit for the serious portrayal of human nature."[43] The use of the character as a vehicle of social knowledge follows a similar trajectory. Consider, for example, the sociological sketches popular in the nineteenth century. Though newspapers like *Punch* did use sketches to inform the reading public of working conditions, Smeed notes that there was a growing feeling that "the realities of people's lives can be best communicated either through their own words or in the form of generalized surveys backed up by graphs and statistics."[44] This is why Mayhew's *London Poor* posed such a problem for the continuation of the character sketch, he argues, as it allowed "actual poor people" to "speak for themselves."[45]

This sense that "the realities of people's lives" could no longer be gained via sketch might be further observed in the changing methods of the emergent human sciences. To take one example: when Alexis de Tocqueville, positioning himself as a revived La Bruyère, decided to write a portrait of the "democratic man" in his *Democracy in America* (1835), he felt the need to pair it with an analysis of the democratic society in which this type is made, complete with a depiction of its institutions, "dogmas," and laws.[46] This literary description of social mores needed to be matched, that is, with an account of their underlying "principles." This balance has set a precedent for how Theophrastan types now appear in sociology, from their emergence in Georg Simmel's early twentieth-century "social types" ("The Stranger," "The Adventurer," "The Poor," "The Miser and the Spendthrift") through to works such as William H. Whyte's *The Organization Man* (1956), Nels Anderson's portrait of *The Hobo* (1961), Richard Sennett's "flexible self" (1998), and Thomas Nail's recent *The Figure of the Migrant* (2015).[47] All these texts refuse to settle for depiction alone. In the places where painting remains a means to knowledge, we might say, it can no longer be separated from anatomy.

The Character Sketch and the Disciplines

The principal field in which the book is firmly situated is intellectual history: that mixed discipline that so often generates bewilderment in its name. It is, to borrow a phrase, the study of *why* people thought *what* they thought *when* they thought it: a motto that shapes how I have navigated this study from the outset.[48] From the early modern humanists to Hume, character-writing was considered a standard method of writing philosophy. To think about character-writing in these terms, I suggest, is to expand existing accounts of early modern virtue politics and to expose the ethical and political heft of this form for both its writers and its readers.[49]

But especially given that the character sketch sits at the crossroads of philosophy, literature, and the social sciences, this book also seeks to reach beyond ongoing conversations within history. One of its ultimate aims is to provide a defense of the tradition of moral philosophy as "painting" that Hume decries: placing sketches of types, "striking Observations and Instances from common life," and visions of alluring examples on par with the anatomical style of working from first principles that still characterizes much philosophical research.[50] This might be understood as a call for ethics to be tied back to *ethos*, for moral philosophy to find its roots again in mores, and for both subfields to renew their interest in the work of their description. Indeed, the Theophrastan tradition is a historical goldmine for someone convinced by Cora Diamond's arguments that moral philosophers should more closely attend to the "texture of life," and, in particular, to things like "manners, habits, styles of utterance, dress"—as opposed to focusing squarely on topics like "action and choice."[51] The character sketch defeats our expectations of what *counts* as a philosophical work, something that, as Diamond puts it, Wittgenstein thought was "all a philosopher should do."[52] What would it mean, the book asks, to reincorporate literary texts back into the philosophical canon, to place La Bruyère alongside Descartes?

In relation to literary studies, meanwhile, this book might be positioned as something of a prequel to Deidre Lynch's *The Economy of Character,* which sets out on a related mission to examine how "eighteenth-century writers and readers *used* the characters in their books."[53] My account, animated by a similar spirit of inquiry, identifies the assumptions that earlier sixteenth- and seventeenth-century writers held about how readers would respond to particular imaginary creations.[54] Moreover, I aim to more broadly connect some moves in contemporary literary theory to this much older interpretative discourse to show that certain current arguments actually have a Theophrastan flavor. Unlike the postmodern moment, which either denied the existence of character or thought of it, as Hélène Cixous did, as part of the "machine of repression," literary studies has brought character back and has come to celebrate it as a major part of how we engage with literature.[55] "Some of the most interesting and inventive academic criticism of the past twenty years has violated the taboo on character talk," wrote Evan Kindley in 2021 in the *New York Review of Books*.[56] Two of the best contemporary taboo breakers are Rita Felski and Blakey Vermuele, both of whom make humanist arguments that could have walked out a Latin preface to Theophrastus.[57] Characters, Felski thinks, have the ability to "inspire emulation and adaptation, irritation and dislike."[58] Fictional types, Vermuele says, provide "a tool to think with, a path through the thicket, a shorthand, a satirical device, a rule of thumb, a way to sit home in our chairs and work it all out."[59] My book suggests that there is a historical pedigree to claims like these: one whose classical ancestor is not Plato, or Aristotle, but their successor, Theophrastus.

Finally, in relation to the social sciences, the Theophrastan tradition offers a long history of the social type: a powerful tool for the sociologist looking to understand economic, cultural, and social relations.[60] More normatively, this book aims to continue the project begun by Judith Shklar in her *Ordinary Vices,* a work inspired in part by Theophrastus.[61] For Shklar, ordinary vices "pose complicated puzzles for liberal democrats."[62] With their commitment to a private sphere free from political intervention, liberal democrats may easily think that the qualities of cruelty, hypocrisy, snobbery, betrayal, and misanthropy stand outside their purview. This, Shklar argues, is a mistake, as the habits of character that make us good citizens are developed in both public and private arenas—something that Theophrastus and his imitators understood well. This book takes Shklar's argument a step further forward. How, it asks, have people historically understood this process of character formation to work? It does so by focusing on one strategy: sketches of types. Here, it speaks to both old and new debates within political theory about the public role of aesthetics. This debate has often focused on how storytelling, and especially novels, can help us better understand the public sphere and engage with others within it.[63] These pages expand the political import of literature to incorporate the description of typical characters. This trains our attention on the ever-expanding cast of Theophrastan characters that populate our everyday speech, are peppered throughout our media, and are used to parcel out our political life—a way of speaking, writing, and thinking that does not seem to be disappearing anytime soon.

∻ ∻ ∻

Chapter 1 of this book introduces the Theophrastan *Characters* more fully in their own Hellenistic context, setting them in dialogue with Theophrastus's other works, as well as with Plato and Aristotle, and offering an account of Theophrastus's life that shows him to be more interested in politics than previously thought. It argues for the status of his *Characters* as a work of Athenian virtue politics by examining the role of *kairos* in the collection and by focusing on the character of the Oligarch.

The early modern reception of the *Characters* began in a Latin republic of letters. As traced in Chapter 2, it encompassed the many sixteenth-century Latin translations of the *Characters* published across Europe, from Vienna to Venice and from Leipzig to Lyon. Turning to the dedication letters, book-bindings, prefaces, prolegomena, and paratexts of these editions, the chapter uncovers a set of diverse explanations for how to find moral instruction in bad examples—an interpretative tradition that positions character-writing as having a significant status in the realm of moral philosophy.

Following the popularity of the Latin editions in the sixteenth century, the Theophrastan tradition gradually moved into the vernacular and also largely shifted from translations to adaptations. Character-writing boomed in this period, with over 1,000 characters printed in English from 1608–1700, making this one of the most popular prose forms of the century.[64] This literary trend was sparked by the first two major English adaptations of the *Characters*: Bishop Joseph Hall's 1608 *Characters of Vertues and Vices* and the collection of character sketches adjoined to the murdered courtier Thomas Overbury's posthumous poem, *A Wife* (1614). These two texts, the subjects of Chapter 3, introduce new facets to the moral reading of Theophrastus, which entangle character-writing with neo-Stoic, and even republican, ideas.

Alongside these two collections, a different approach to character-writing took root in seventeenth-century England. In the white heat of the English Civil War—a conflict obsessed with trying to read "the characters of man's heart," as Thomas Hobbes puts it—character-writing came to serve as a tool for social discovery with the emergence of new social types and the need to determine who they were and whether they could be trusted.[65] Chapter 4 examines the functions of the figures penned in this period, which include Puritans, Roundheads, Independents, and Agitators. Their authors were now no longer people who saw themselves as moral philosophers. They were polemicists, scribblers, and political actors, and they often wished to remain anonymous. These types were too factional and too precise to serve as models for who not to be, for how not to behave. Their new function was providing social discernment, helping the reader to discover someone's nature.

While the Civil War played a major role in shaping the nature of character-writing in England, the Fronde—which caused upheaval in France at roughly the same time—did not have the same effect. As Chapter 5 shows, across the Channel, the character retained an older, more moral function. La Bruyère, Theophrastus's most famous imitator, felt the need to modify the character's moral promise. He came to feel that he could not trust any attempt to shape a reader's behavior through the depiction of vices alone, without any reflection on motives and intentions. This led him to both translate and update the *Characters,* newly promising an insight into the "Vices of the mind," "the interior part of Man," and "the principle" of each character's "Villany and Folly" in his own sketches of the manners of contemporary France.[66]

La Bruyère's desire to look behind appearances into explanatory motivations or "principles," and to distance the sketch from the direct shaping of action, was taken a step further by Hume in 1748. Hume was a Francophile, a profound admirer of La Bruyère, and someone with an interest in the Theophrastan tradition. Hume, however, felt the need to distance himself from the moral approaches to characters, no longer convinced that character-writing could be a valid means of moral philosophy. His *First Enquiry* is the key text for this story, which unfolds in Chapter 6. Hume's methodological move has two important legacies. It contributes to the separation of literature from philosophy: framing character-writing as an unnatural form in which to philosophize. It also affirms a language of principles to think about other kinds of character, above all characters of nations. This, as we will see, was a step that encouraged more schematic approaches to questions of race. Where the early modern Theophrastan character sketch surprisingly had little to say about race, Hume's move away from sketching characters to explain differences, in the language of "principles," represents a key component of race's systematization in European philosophy.[67]

In an epilogue, the book lays out how we might begin to take on board the insights of the Theophrastan tradition today. It asks what it would mean to consider these flat, typical characters seriously, in spite of their lack of interiority and their freestanding form.[68] This is not another prompt for us to dwell on rich, novelistic characters, such as Anna Karenina or Maggie Verver, or on characters who experience tumultuous life events, like Antigone or Billy Budd—all of whom have already found their way into major works of philosophy.[69] Instead, the Theophrastan tradition entreats us to take a closer look at ordinary social figures in the twenty-first century, amid the revivals of both Platonic and Aristotelian arguments about literature's ethical and epistemic potential. Neoplatonic arguments can be found in contemporary fears that readers or viewers will imitate representations of bad actions or bad characters: consider, for example, contemporary debates about the ethics of pornography and violent video games.[70] Neo-Aristotelian arguments, meanwhile, continue to reaffirm that the sight of suffering literary characters can help train readers into good citizens by provoking their compassion and training their imaginative capacities.[71]

The Theophrastan tradition offers two different kinds of arguments: one focused on the idea that bad characters provoke good actions and another on their possible epistemic status.[72] Ultimately, I want to probe how this interpretative mode might apply to the Theophrastan types that proliferate in our own public sphere. The epilogue entreats us to ask what is really happening when we use these categories and to examine what we might learn from these figures and what effects they might produce. Do character types provide a kind of knowledge by giving names to aspects of the social world? Do they reassure us with the serenity of diagnosis? Do they change how we engage with other people or ourselves? Or do they mischaracterize and blame and refuse us the dignity of transformation?

To be sure, another history of the Theophrastan tradition might bracket it as a discrete phenomenon in which people thought sketches could do moral and political work, until they did not. I conceive of this book's history a little differently, guided by Rorty's instinct that tracing the path philosophy took in the mid-eighteenth century is a means to tell a story about what philosophy might become again today. Where the theoretical and the descriptive parts of this book meet is in the question about whether Hume was *right* to think that characters in themselves should not be considered as part of moral philosophy. While it is obvious that, as Smeed says, people have long felt that "the realities of people's lives" require something beyond literary description, one of this book's aims is to suggest that we are living in a moment that may have gone too far the other way.

In tracing the trajectory of the Theophrastan tradition, I seek to draw our attention to a set of assumptions that ground the way it was interpreted over time. Changes in these assumptions spelled the transformation and subsequent decline of this way of reading. These changes involve new doubts about the epistemic status of a genre unconcerned with underlying inner principles and a gradual shift away from the political language of civic virtue toward an understanding of the moral domain as a site of self-reflection, intentions, and motives.[73] My tentative contention is that our moment may operate with a set of conceptual assumptions that are again receptive to a Theophrastan way of thinking.[74] I want to suggest that recovering this history might make particular sense in a modernity that confers veracity to immediate, observed phenomena; is highly concerned about the ethics of ordinary civic behaviors; and—perhaps due to both factors—increasingly sees literary description as having significant performative moral effects.[75] A modernity that is experiencing an "ethical turn" in the study of literature, and in which it is no longer possible to say, as literary critic Guido Mazzoni did in 2011, that today "those who criticize Walter Siti, Michel Houellebecq, or Jonathan Littell with moralistic arguments position themselves in the intellectual rear guard."[76] What could it mean, then, to attempt to recover aspects of a Theophrastan aesthetic today—to use the insights of this model to think about the present?

1

The *Characters* as Virtue Politics

Theophrastus's *Characters* is, as translator Jeffrey Rusten puts it, "a pleasant little book for the casual reader, but an enormously difficult one for the scholar."[1] Its pleasantness lies in its portrayal of ordinary vices through brief examples of the daily habits of a man who embodies each quality in question. Its difficulty lies in its complex manuscript tradition, "perhaps the most corrupt among classical Greek authors," its debatable date (it is now thought to have been written progressively between 335 and 309 BCE), and the ambiguity around its purpose and function.[2] A recent article on the question of the intention behind Theophrastus's *Characters* indeed describes the search for its original purpose as the "history of an enigma": a riddle that has puzzled generations of scholars and split them into three main camps, respectively aligning the text with rhetoric, comedy, and ethics.[3] A closer look at Theophrastus's life and works—both the extant treatises and the fragments and paraphrases that have been recently collected—exposes, however, an alternative possibility: that Theophrastus wrote the *Characters* to engage with Athenian politics.

To determine the purpose of the *Characters,* scholars have turned to the works of Theophrastus's teacher Aristotle and to those of his student, the comic playwright Menander. They have pointed out the intertextual echoes of Aristotle's *Rhetoric* and *Ethics* in individual sketches, positing that the *Characters* shares the *Rhetoric*'s interest in depicting the kinds of audiences to whom aspiring orators should learn to appeal. Relatedly, they have questioned how Theophrastus's choice of vices compares to Aristotle's classificatory scheme of positive and negative attributes, which stand on either side of "the virtuous mean" that Aristotle considered the basis of good conduct.[4] Scholars have also examined the text's relationship with the *Tractatus Coislinianus,* the ancient Greek treatise on comedy authored by either Aristotle or Theophrastus, observing how the *Tractatus*'s lists of typically comic attributes, along with the titles of Greek comedies, can be found in the names of Theophrastus's figures.[5]

This intertextual scholarship on the *Characters* is not, however, complete. It has left most of Theophrastus's extensive corpus untouched, from the works that seem most immediately relevant (his treatises on rhetoric, ethics, and comedy) to his political writing, metaphysics, epistemology, and natural philosophy. In the account written by the ancient Greek biographer Diogenes Laertius, Theophrastus's entire body of work amounts to 232,808 lines, distributed among 225 works both esoteric and exoteric, written for students and for a popular audience.[6] This corpus spans treatises on physics and friendship, on juices and jokes, on syllogisms and sweat. Less than 10 percent of this work survives. In addition to the *Characters,* only a small number of other texts are extant in their entirety: two treatises on botany, one treatise on the senses, a work of *Metaphysics,* and several short treatises on human physiology and particular topics in the natural world. While many other works have not survived the passage of time, traces of them can be found in fragments, in their discussion by other authors, and sometimes in full paraphrasing. These traces have been recently compiled from their sources in Arabic, Greek, and Latin authors.[7] Pairing the existing and the fragmentary works, we gain a fuller sense of the Theophrastan corpus, from which we can start to discern patterns in the way he approaches a given subject. These patterns will help us solve the riddle of his *Characters.*

The existing intertextual methodology has also obscured another facet of the *Characters*: the peculiarity of the social world that it depicts and the fact that it contains only one explicitly political sketch. Theophrastus's set of thirty types all have something striking in common: they are all male, all rich, and all from Athens. They also contain one party-political type within their ranks, an Oligarch. Thus far, none of the proffered explanations of the text's intentions have accounted for these demographic details, nor have they considered what the presence of this political figure might mean. This is in part because Theophrastus has long been thought to be a reclusive and scholastic philosopher who was relatively uninterested in participating in public life and who generally inclined toward oligarchy and monarchy, rather than democracy.[8] Given his presumed support of oligarchy, it is surprising that scholars have not questioned why Theophrastus satirized only this political position—a distinctive choice, given that character sketches of political constitutions usually came in a number of varieties, as in book 8 of Plato's *Republic* or Aristotle's *Politics*. Recently, however, significant pressure has been put on this biographical orthodoxy. In the words of the historian Robin Lane Fox, a number of details from Theophrastus's life "warn us against making [him] too monarchic or oligarchic figure."[9] Above all, perhaps, is the possibility that on two occasions in his late thirties, Theophrastus worked to liberate his native town of Eresus from tyrants in favor of a democracy.[10]

These revisions to Theophrastus's biography encourage us to return to the many political texts that Theophrastus is said to have written, which evince continual interest in issues of kingship, governance, and *kairos*, and are substantial enough to qualify him as a political philosopher.[11] The *Characters*, this chapter argues, should be read with just such a political edge—one that does not necessarily assume his praise of oligarchy or monarchy.[12] This text should be seen not as a comic or rhetorical handbook, or as a continuation of Aristotle's *Ethics*, but as a work that participates in what Ryan Balot has called "virtue politics."[13] In this, the *Characters* is indicative of a moment in which ethics and politics were not thought of as distinct. Indeed, for the Athenians, a prerequisite for political participation was personal and civic virtue: good judgment, loyalty, and identification with the common good. This ideology was upheld by a number of different texts in the Hellenistic world; this chapter proposes that we should consider the *Characters* as one of them. The *Characters* partook in this tradition, I argue, by ridiculing people who possess qualities prejudicial to virtue politics, from oligarchic (or authoritarian) tendencies to an inability to suit their actions to the right moment and respect the *kairos*.[14]

The retrieval of a political intention for these sketches should not only change how we consider the purpose of the *Characters*. It also holds significant implications for our understanding of ancient approaches to character. The political implications of character sketches were an aspect of poetics over which Plato and Aristotle were significantly at odds. The character sketch is the one kind of poetry that Plato's *Republic* allows in the ideal city, provided that these character sketches portray morally upstanding citizens, rather than characters of vice.[15] In the *Poetics,* in contrast, Aristotle wishes to reduce the dramatic importance of character, rendering it less essential to tragedy than the progress of action.[16] By exploiting the political importance of sketches of *bad* types, Theophrastus positions himself somewhere between these two arguments: recognizing the power of the character, unlike Aristotle, but thinking that *bad* characters could have positive effects, unlike Plato. The *Characters,* seen in dialogue with these philosophers (one, and perhaps both, of whom were Theophrastus's teachers), thus constitutes an intervention into ancient aesthetics, one that implicitly valorizes the character sketch of vice for its normative political potential.

Theophrastus's Life and Politics

A first step toward reframing the *Characters* as a political text must involve examining the assumptions about—and recent reevaluations of—Theophrastus's own life and political outlook. Theophrastus was born around 370 BCE in Eresus, a city on the Southwest of the island of Lesbos, an island so near what is currently Turkey, but what was then the Persian Empire, that its outline can be seen from the shores of Ayvalık, a town on the Turkish coast. When Theophrastus was born, Eresus was a democracy under Athenian influence and had recently become a member of the Second Athenian League, a confederation headed by Athens designed to protect its members from the joint threats of the Persian Empire and Sparta.[17] When Theophrastus was fifteen, the Athenian League broke down and the island was left open to be conquered by another great power.[18] In less than a year, Eresus was controlled by Persia, which installed three rulers: Apollodorus and his brothers Hermon and Heraeus, who came to be known as tyrants. They ruled the island from when Theophrastus was fifteen until he was thirty-six.[19]

In the interim, Theophrastus became interested in philosophy. In his youth, he had attended lectures in Eresus by a philosopher called

Alcippus.[20] In his late teens or early twenties, it is possible that Theophrastus decided to sail to Athens, where Plato's Academy had been running for over thirty years.[21] The students who would have been studying at the Academy in that period included Aristotle as well as the mathematician and philosopher Xenocrates. In 346, when Theophrastus was twenty-three, Plato died, and the Academy was handed to Plato's nephew.

Aristotle and Xenocrates then left Athens for Atarneus, a town opposite Lesbos where there was a small Academic community.[22] Bequeathed a place to stay in the neighboring town of Assos, Aristotle and Xenocrates "spent their time in philosophy, meeting together in a courtyard."[23] In Assos, Aristotle married Pythias, and two or three years later, he left for Mytilene in Lesbos.[24] The biographers who think that Theophrastus was not with Aristotle already (either journeying with him from Athens or meeting him in Assos) maintain that they met here.[25] In Mytilene, Aristotle spent his time studying marine biology, conducting research that he would later formulate into his works on animals.[26] It seems likely that Theophrastus complemented this program of study, observing and classifying plants, in preparation for his two major botanical works, *Historia plantarum* and *De causis plantarum,* and empirically recording marine life for his own biological treatise, *On Fish*. Aristotle is then thought to have returned home to his native city of Stagira until summoned in 343 by Philip II of Macedon to teach his son Alexander.[27] Most biographers of Theophrastus suggest that he accompanied Aristotle to Philip's court.[28] The two stayed there for around nine years until they went to Athens together in 334.[29]

On two occasions during this period, in 334 and 332, Plutarch argues that Theophrastus "twice delivered" Eresus "from tyrants." These actions replaced two different sets of pro-Persian rulers (the first of which were Apollodorus, Hermon, and Heraeus) with democrats favorable to Macedonian interests.[30] Most accounts of Theophrastus's life do not mention his participation in these two liberation struggles, and scholars have dismissed Plutarch's claim in part because it has seemed impossible that Theophrastus could have gone all the way back to Eresus from Mieza, and then again from Athens, to help his city.[31] However, we have reason to reconsider the evidence. A closer look at the context of Plutarch's remarks suggests that Theophrastus may have supported these struggles from afar. Plutarch makes his claim about Theophrastus in the context of defending philosophers who undertook political action on behalf of their *patria*. This is not, Plutarch clarifies, a question of listing slayers of tyrants, champions of battle, advisors of kings, leaders of people, or martyrs for just causes: actions that would have required Theophrastus to be in Eresus in person. Rather, Plutarch means those who "took ship in his country's interests, went on an embassy, or expended a sum of money," interventions that could easily have been carried out remotely.[32] Theophrastus could have "delivered" Eresus from tyrants in one of these ways, above all by going on "an embassy" to his pupil Alexander. In this case, Theophrastus could have lobbied Alexander to help Eresus while they were both in Mieza in 334 before Alexander set out for Asia. Two years later, when Theophrastus was in Athens, he could have sent Alexander a letter urging the same.

While in Athens, Theophrastus studied and taught at the Lyceum, the philosophical school that Aristotle established. The first decade that Aristotle and Theophrastus were there was a time of relative calm. Up until 324, Alexander the Great ruled Athens under a restored and stable democracy led by Lycurgus.[33] But after Lycurgus's death in 324, and Alexander's the year later, the city started to shake.[34] Athens eventually exploded in mass revolt against Alexander's regent in 322, generating a wave of anti-Macedonian feeling that forced Aristotle to flee the city.[35] Aristotle died in exile, leaving his school to Theophrastus. Today, a mural in the National and Kapodistrian University of Athens, which represents a swathe of figures from ancient Greece, gestures to this succession. It depicts Aristotle teaching his successor Theophrastus (and Theophrastus's own successor Strato), how to dissect a goose (Figure 1.1): an emblem of the practices of observation and documentation that characterized the Peripatetic school at the Lyceum.[36] Theophrastus was forty-eight when he became head of the Lyceum, and he held this position for over thirty-five years before he died in his late eighties. Over the course of his tenure, he lectured over 2,000 students, who are thought to have included Menander and Demetrius of Phalerum.[37]

After 322, Hellenistic Athens existed in a state of major political turbulence, swinging between regime and revolt, oligarchy and democracy.[38] The mass uprising of 322 was suppressed, and a Macedonian garrison installed a new oligarchic constitution in Athens led by Phocion and Demades. This regime lasted until 318, which heralded a yearlong democratic revival.[39] In 317, Demetrius of Phalerum then installed another oligarchy before Athenian democracy was again restored in 307.[40] Theophrastus experienced firsthand the consequences of this political instability. At fifty-one, he was prosecuted for impiety under the revived Athenian democracy of 318. Then, at sixty-three, after the fall of Demetrius, Theophrastus had to flee Athens when a law subjected philosophical schools to state control on the grounds of their antidemocratic leanings and collusion with Macedon.[41] Somehow, perhaps due to his popularity, Theophrastus managed to get off lightly on both occasions. He was "so highly valued at Athens" that "when Agnonides ventured to prosecute him

FIGURE 1.1. Mural painting of Aristotle, Theophrastus, and Strato (left to right), by Eduard Lebiedzki, after a design by Karl Rahl. Detail from the eastern part of the frieze in the main building of the National and Kapodistrian University of Athens, c. 1888. *Credit:* Georges Prevelakis.

for impiety, the prosecutor himself narrowly escaped punishment." Moreover, one year after his banishment, Theophrastus was recalled to Athens and the man who promulgated the law was subsequently penalized.[42] In the words of the ancient Greek biographer Diogenes Laertius, "The Athenians repealed the law, fined Sophocles five talents, and voted the recall of the philosophers, in order that Theophrastus also might return and live there as before."[43]

The fact that a democracy twice prosecuted Theophrastus has encouraged commentators to suggest that Theophrastus held non-democratic political views. Further support for this argument comes from indications that Theophrastus was close to his former student, the oligarch Demetrius, who helped Theophrastus acquire a garden of his own (something difficult for a foreigner in Athens), and from his reported proximity to monarchs, such as Cassander, who went on to hold the kingship of Macedonia from 305 to 297.[44] Scholars have paired these details with the fact that Theophrastus is thought to have written four treatises on kingship, including one dedicated to Cassander himself.[45]

This argument has, however, been recently compromised on a number of fronts. Theophrastus's possible actions in Eresus have strengthened his democratic credentials, as they suggest an active rejection of tyranny in preference for democracy, at least when he was in his late thirties. This coheres with a number of critical comments that Theophrastus is reported to have made on certain tyrants, now collected in his full corpus.[46] A more nuanced attitude toward Theophrastus's views on democracy is further indicated by the circumstances of his trial, which reveal his popularity. This was an attitude that continued after his death in circa 287. As Diogenes Laertius reports it, Theophrastus was dignified by the whole of Athens "out of respect," escorting "his bier on foot."[47]

Relatedly, there are details that suggest we should complicate our approach to Theophrastus's presumed support for both monarchy and oligarchy. Lane Fox has exposed a tradition indicating that Theophrastus was hostile to Cassander, a possibility bolstered by the fact that his authorship of the treatise *To Cassander on Kingship* was called into question in antiquity.[48] Theophrastus's remaining works on kingship may even have been directed toward alerting readers to its possible descent into tyranny, following similar arguments made by Aristotle in his *Politics*.[49] For Aristotle, there can be good kinds of kingship and bad kinds: the former were *basileia* and the latter *monarchia*. It seems that Theophrastus might have upheld this schema on the basis of a report that his *On Kingship* (*Peri basileias*) criticizes the tyranny of Hiero, a Greek ruler of Syracuse.[50] While it would make sense for Theophrastus to write about tyranny in a work entitled *Peri monarchias,* dedicated to discussing *bad* kingship, the fact that he does so in a treatise on *good* kingship is worthy of note. Could Theophrastus have here been indicating that even the good kind of kingship might turn sour? Skepticism can also be applied to the notion that Theophrastus was a supporter of oligarchy. Luiza Fizzarotti has recently argued that Theophrastus likely wrote a work entitled *On the Choice of Magistrates*: a guide to elected public officials. If she is right, Theophrastus would be the author of an anti-oligarchic warning that "a simple property qualification is a poor standard for evaluating prospective magistrates."[51]

For these reasons, we cannot continue to operate on the assumption that Theophrastus was simply "a friend of kings and oligarchs."[52] Rather, these details paint a much more nuanced picture of Theophrastus's politics, one befitting his long life and the turbulent political contexts that it spanned. This complexity coheres with what we know about one of Theophrastus's final actions. On the delicate matter of his will, Theophrastus decided to hedge his bets: leaving one copy to Demetrius Poliorcotes, an agent of oligarchic Macedon, and the other to the democracy's top general, Olympiodorus.[53] Theophrastus himself seems to have been no stranger to balancing different political attitudes at various points across his life, and perhaps even at the same time. Framed by this more nuanced account of Theophrastus's life and politics, the political facets of his *Characters* become less curious and more coherent.

The *Characters*

The title that Diogenes Laertius lists for this text is *ethikoi charakteres,* "character traits"—with *ethos* meaning "character" and *charakteres* meaning "traits."[54] The word *charakter* in Greek derives from *charax,* a "pointed stake" that was used to mark distinguishable traits on objects (like the imprint of a face or a number on a coin) and people: for example, in the branding of slaves with the name of their proprietors or the tattooing on female prisoners of war.[55] In Old Comedy, the word *charakter* had already been used to refer to how a nation engraves physical traits on its inhabitants. By the Hellenistic period, it had come to also mean "distinctive nature" or "style."[56] Theophrastus, however, does not use the word *charakter* or *charakteres* once in the body of the text. Nor does he use it elsewhere in his existing corpus. Instead, when he describes the distinctive "traits" of animals, plants, or other phenomena of the living world, he uses *ethos* and its Greek synonyms *ideos, phusis,* and *tropos*—words that also appear, unlike *charakter,* in the body of this treatise.[57]

The text is split into thirty chapters, each introduced with a one-word character trait (for example, the trait of "Absentmindedness"). Each trait is then elaborated with a sketch of a person who embodies this vice, through the repeated formula—as Rusten puts it—"the X man is the sort who . . ."[58] The Absentminded Man, for example,

> is the sort who, when he has made a calculation with an abacus and determined the total, asks the person sitting by him, "What's the answer?" If he is a defendant, and intends to appear in court, he forgets and goes to the country. If he's in the audience at the theatre, he falls asleep and is left behind alone. If he eats too much and gets up at night to go to the toilet, he is bitten by his neighbor's dog.
>
> When he's received something and put it away himself, he looks for it and can't find it. If it's reported to him that one of his friends has died, so he should attend the funeral, he makes a sad face and says weepingly, "Let's hope it's for the best!" He is apt to ask for a receipt when he receives money that is owed to him. If it is winter, he quarrels with his slave because he didn't buy cucumbers.
>
> When he forces his children to practice wrestling and running, he drives them to exhaustion. When he is cooking himself bean-soup in the field, he adds salt to the pot twice, and makes it inedible.[59]

While the Absentminded Man's behavior is particular to each situation, all his actions are linked by the form of his underlying disposition. In this sketch, his disposition is an essential forgetfulness, a lack of wherewithal, and an overarching incapacity to recognize the needs of a given moment and adapt his behavior accordingly. Although we only hear the voice of the Absentminded Man, this quality creates problems both for himself and for others. It leads to inedible soup, exhausted children, and, presumably, a very frustrated slave. While his disposition is presented as having a kind of internal logic, it is not clear what motivates it, what its end or *telos* might be. This is a point that, as we shall see, proves important in evaluating the purpose of the collection.

In each of these aspects, the character of "Absentmindedness" is like the Man with Bad Timing, whom we met in the introduction. Both are representative of the rest of Theophrastus's collection. The other twenty-nine vices are structured around a similar set of scenes: observing a type's actions rather than providing insight into his thoughts or intentions. Indeed, very rarely is any explanation provided for why these characters behave as they do.[60] These other sketches may all be thought of as "ordinary vices," to borrow Judith Shklar's phrase, "the sort of conduct we all expect, nothing spectacular or unusual."[61] Shklar says that what she has learned from Theophrastus is his style, his art of putting "characteristics in familiar settings" and telling a "story about what happens to them in the diverse but common encounters that are likely to occur there."[62] But what she has also adopted from him—even if her chosen parent for this aspect of her work is Montaigne—is a focus on vices that are commonplace and familiar. The full set of vices in Theophrastus's *Characters* is as follows:[63]

1. Irony (*eironeia*)
2. Flattery (*kolakeia*)
3. Idle Chatter (*adoleschia*)
4. Provinciality (*agroikia*)
5. Obsequiousness (*areskeia*)
6. Senselessness (*aponoia*)
7. Garrulity (*lalia*)
8. Rumormongering (*logopoiia*)
9. Shamelessness (*anaischuntia*)
10. Penny-Pinching (*mikrologia*)
11. Repulsiveness (*bdeluria*)
12. Bad Timing (*akairia*)
13. Overzealousness (*periergia*)
14. Absentmindedness (*anaisthesia*)
15. Self-Centeredness (*authadeia*)
16. Superstition (*deisdaimonia*)
17. Ingratitude (*mempsimoiria*)
18. Mistrust (*apistia*)
19. Squalor (*duschereia*)
20. Disagreeableness (*aedia*)
21. Petty Ambition (*mikrophilotimia*)
22. Illiberality (*aneleutheria*)
23. Boasting (*alazoneia*)
24. Arrogance (*huperephania*)
25. Cowardice (*deilia*)
26. Oligarchy (*oligarchia*)
27. Late Learning (*opismathia*)
28. Slander (*kakologia*)
29. Friendship of Villains (*philoponeria*)
30. Profiteering (*aischrokerdeia*)

In Theophrastus's fourth-century context, each of these vices would have been rich with significance. Irony, *eironeia* (1), in the *Characters,* is the quality of dissimulating, deviously pretending, or being disingenuous, something that in the sketch leads to forms of disengagement from social obligation, and other kinds of noncommitment.[64] It was an attribute discussed in both ethical and comedic literature. Aristotle situates *eironeia,* understood as self-deprecation, as the opposite extreme to boastfulness in his *Ethics,* bracketing a virtuous mean of truthfulness, and the *Tractatus Coislinianus* considers irony a characteristic belonging to one of the stock characters of comedy.[65] Flattery, *kolakeia* (2), or servile behavior to a patron, is a vice that also holds comic and ethical connotations: it furnished the titles for plays by Menander and Eupolis and was included in Aristotle's *Ethics* in relation to the virtuous mean of *philia,* or friendliness.[66] Idle Chatter, *adoleschia* (3), is discussion about topics not considered worthy by other people. Aristotle treats it as a vice on several occasions, and the *Tractatus* considers it a comedic tactic.[67] Provinciality, *agroikia* (4), provides titles for dramas by playwrights Anaxandrides, Antiphanes, Menander, and Philemon describing the sight of rustic behavior from the urbane perspective of those in the city.[68] Obsequiousness, *areskeia* (5), is different from Flattery (2) as it concerns servile behavior directed toward everyone, not just one's patron.

Senselessness, as *aponoia* (6), is a concept not included in Aristotle's *Ethics,* being more familiar to the polemics of the orators.[69] Garrulity, *lalia* (7), is different from Idle Chatter (3) in that this character talks to everyone in abundance, not just to one person. Rumormongering, *logopoiia* (8), is another quality commonly found in Attic oratory, describing the fabrication and spreading of tales. Shamelessness, *anaischuntia* (9), in the *Characters,* is a shamelessness that only pertains to money—whether that is stinginess or greed—following the association Aristotle made between the two in his *Rhetoric.*[70] (In Aristotle's *Ethics,* shamelessness is also the extreme for the virtue of modesty, with its opposite being bashfulness.)[71] Penny-Pinching, *mikrologia* (10), describes a character who is protective over his property: he is, in the words of Rusten, "not concerned with taking from others but making sure no one takes from him."[72]

Repulsiveness, *bdeluria* (11), is a common term used to vilify opponents by both orators and Aristophanes, with the orator Demosthenes deploying it to describe his worst enemies. In the *Characters,* it typifies the qualities of being "indecent, disruptive, crude, discourteous, over-familiar, tactless, tasteless, tiresome."[73] Bad Timing, *akairia* (12), is a failure to obey *kairos,* presenting a man whose "actions do not suit the circumstances."[74] Overzealousness, *periergia* (13), is the quality of someone who "does not know when to stop."[75] Absentmindedness, *anaisthesia* (14), which simply means "insensitivity" (as in "anesthetic"), describes a loss of judgment, or sense, that leads to unsuitable behavior.[76] It is the quality of lacking sense perception or *aesthesis*—the origin of the word *aesthetics.* Self-Centeredness, *authadeia* (15), describes someone "who lives without regard for others, on whom he looks down" (as Aristotle puts it in his *Ethics*).[77]

Superstition, *deisidaimonia* (16), means "fear of the gods." This vice provides the title of another play by Menander. In a Peripatetic ethical treatise, it also served as an excess to the virtuous mean of piety, with the other extreme being atheism.[78] Ingratitude, *mempsimoiria* (17), literally means finding fault with one's "lot or share (*moira*)."[79] Its earliest recorded instance is by the Athenian lawmaker Solon, who condemned the "rich and poor, who are not satisfied with what he has allotted them" after he had given the Athenians their constitution.[80] It is also the title of a comedy by Antidotus. Mistrust, *apistia* (18), is a vice "fueled by a specific fear—loss of money or property"—and titles another one of Menander's plays.[81] Squalor, *duschereia* (19), is "physical repulsiveness causing offence or disgust," covering offensive features of the body and extending to inappropriate behavior more generally.[82] Disagreeableness, *aedia* (20), is the creation of "annoyance and inconvenience," describing someone who speaks without tact or good taste and does so by virtue of being "insensitive or indifferent to the feelings of others."[83]

Petty Ambition, *mikrophilotimia* (21), is a word only found here, meaning the desire or love of small honors. Although Aristotle describes no vice that is "fully comparable" to this one, he is careful to underline that the magnanimous man is someone who rejects all honors that come from "petty achievements."[84] Illiberality, *aneleutheria* (22), is the vice of wealthy stinginess. In his *Ethics,* Aristotle considered this vice in his discussion of the virtuous mean between giving and getting: illiberality describes someone who has an excess in getting but is deficient in giving, "a wealthy man who falls short of what he owes himself and others."[85] Boastfulness, *alazoneia* (23), essentially refers to "being an imposter": a quality that defines one of the *Tractatus*'s other stock characters of comedy and that Aristotle's *Ethics* describes as the opposite of irony, in relation to the virtuous mean of truth.[86] Arrogance, *huperephania* (24), is a quality "often associated with hubris," where hubris plays out in physical action and *huperephania* in habits of mind.[87] Cowardice, *deilia* (25), is described in Aristotle's *Ethics* in relation to the virtuous mean of courage: a person exhibiting this vice "fears the wrong things in the wrong manner at the wrong time."[88]

Oligarchy, *oligarchia* (26), is a type of government more than a trait of character, but the two had been interlinked by Plato, with his "sketches of human types who respond to kinds of government" in the *Republic,* and by the Athenian political orators.[89] As a character trait, it signals someone who believes excellence lies in wealth and who is "anti-democratic," and it represents, as we know, the one party-political caricature.[90] Late Learning, *opsimathia* (27), is the vice of the elderly who act like the young, a vice that appears in Old Comedy.[91] Slander, *kakologia* (28), is someone who takes "a perverse pleasure in speaking ill," a vice that faced legal sanction in Athens.[92] Friendship of Villains, *philoponeria* (29), refers to a character who supports people in trouble: scholars are divided on whether this means the underprivileged or those who are "morally deficient."[93] Lastly, Profiteering, *aischrokerdeia* (30), describes someone who takes advantage of those close to him for a small profit by claiming more than he needs and who avoids expenditure, refusing to give presents and charging people inappropriately—qualities shared by the Avaricious Man whom Aristotle describes in his *Ethics.*[94]

These ordinary Theophrastan vices exhibit several key similarities and patterns, already apparent even in this brief outline. There are, for example, eight characters that cohere with aspects of Aristotle's *Ethics*; nine that have links with ancient comedy; three that are frequent terms used in Athenian rhetoric; and one, the Oligarch, with an overt connection to politics. There are also four characters that deal with varieties of being stingy with money, and in the text as a whole, there are "almost thirty references to credit operations."[95] All these characters are men, operating in a male world that corresponds to Theophrastus's own. This choice is striking, nonetheless, given that there was an ancient tradition of female caricature and that the vice of Superstition was typically associated with women.[96] It is also notable that all these characters are old, with Theophrastus, unlike Aristotle in his *Rhetoric,* not once extending his caricatures to the young.[97]

The setting for these old, male characters seems unmistakably to be "the Athens of the last few decades of the fourth century."[98] Half the types, as has been observed, mention one or more slaves, but this would allow them to occupy a wide range of class statuses.[99] While a number of characters clearly "belong in the upper reaches of the Athenian social pyramid"—as either *hippeis* (cavalry) or liturgists—the set as a whole spans a vast "slave-owning spectrum," which at its lowest end includes characters who own "roughly 5 acres and a cow."[100] Theophrastus himself would have been at the upper end of this spectrum, with a will that "reveals ownership of even more slaves" than any of his characters.[101]

To date, the primary method that scholars have used to approach the *Characters* has been intertextual: focusing on how Theophrastus's choice and presentation of vices fit into existing ancient discourses. This kind of analysis has exposed the *Characters*' relationship to texts by Theophrastus's teachers, successors, and contemporaries—above all, Aristotle. Given the paucity of Theophrastan texts readily available, this scholarship has rarely placed the *Characters* in dialogue with Theophrastus's other treatises. On the basis of this methodology, scholars have understood the intention of the *Characters* in terms of ethics, comedy, and rhetoric. Alongside this intertextual approach, classicists have highlighted how Theophrastus's choice of personas reveals a particular kind of social world, peopled by old, male, slave-owning Athenians. This analysis depends instead on an understanding of the *Characters* as a cultural document within a sociohistorical context.[102]

My aim is to bring these two methods together: to take both the intellectual echoes and the sociological details seriously. But I do so with both a wider range of Aristotelian texts in mind and with the good fortune of having the recent collation of a much larger body of Theophrastan texts to hand. This impressive collation poses some problems for the existing arguments about the rhetorical, comic, and ethical intentions of the *Characters* and leads me to think that an alternative intention should be called for instead: one that frames the *Characters* as partaking in virtue politics.

Reevaluating the *Characters* as Rhetoric, Comedy, and Ethics

First, however, let us turn to the three major purposes that have been assigned to the *Characters*: that it is a work of rhetoric, comedy, or ethics. Some scholars have also argued that because the collection is so fragmentary and piecemeal, it might instead be a miscellany of some kind or even preparatory lecture notes. Placed in dialogue with Theophrastus's broader corpus, and the sociological details in the *Characters* itself, each proposition, on its own, falls short of answering key questions about the structure, contents, and style of this text.

RHETORIC

Those who claim a rhetorical purpose for the *Characters* generally propose that it teaches students how to vilify others in court. This argument is grounded in the fact that character sketching was "an important weapon" within legal rhetoric.[103] Cicero, Quintilian, Suetonius, and the *Rhetorica ad Herennium* describe the rhetorical power of character-writing under the titles *notationes, characterismoi,* or *ethologias,* sometimes pointing to Theophrastus's *Characters* as its progenitor.[104] In addition, "every single medieval manuscript which contains [the *Characters*] is derived from collections of treatises on rhetoric (whose central authors were [Greek rhetoricians] Hermogenes and Aphthonius)," betraying a classification of the *Characters* as rhetoric that is thought to have occurred by the ninth century but potentially earlier.[105] Quintilian notes some of Theophrastus's continuations of Aristotle's *Rhetoric.* For example, like Aristotle, Theophrastus distinguished between epideictic, deliberative, and judicial rhetoric—rhetoric that, in Quintilian's words, is concerned with "praise and blame"; with public deliberation and verdicts; and with producing an effect on its listeners, or "display."[106] The *Characters* might then be examples of epideictic rhetoric, showing a means by which to blame an individual.

This argument for the text's rhetorical intention is further grounded in its links to Aristotle's *Rhetoric*, in particular to his discussion of *ethos*. Aristotle argues that rhetoric relies on three elements: *ethos*, *pathos* (emotion), and *logos* (reasoning).[107] What Aristotle means by *ethos* is twofold.[108] First, that the speaker should shape their own character so that they seem to their audience to possess *phronesis*, *arete* (virtue), and *eunoia* (goodwill).[109] Second, that they should work to understand the character of the audience to whom they are speaking so that they can ensure their discourse appeals to this audience's desires and interests.[110] To respond to this latter requirement, Aristotle provides sketches of several characters, who differ on the basis of their emotions, habits, ages, fortunes, and the types of government under which they live. In Aristotle's view, this last quality shapes the "ends" people want in their own lives, to which a speaker should appeal. In a democracy, for example, people will want liberty; in an oligarchy, wealth.[111]

Aristotle's depiction of this second kind of *ethos* has been said to bear resemblances to the *Characters*. Classicist William W. Fortenbaugh and Rusten both note that the *Characters* is reminiscent of the technique of *ethopoeia* Aristotle uses to depict the old and the young in his *Rhetoric*: the rhetorical practice of sketching their characters, from the words "to produce" (*poiein*) and "character" (*ethos*).[112] There are, however, even deeper similarities to be noticed between the two texts. This was not simply a case of two philosophers using a shared technique. Rather, Theophrastus borrows several particular qualities from Aristotle's depiction of the old. Aristotle mentions five qualities of the old that Theophrastus uses for the titles of his vices: Character 18, "Mistrust," *apistia*; Character 22, "Lack of Generosity," *aneleutheria*; Character 25, "Cowardice," *deilia*; Character 9, "Shamelessness," *anaischuntia*; and Character 3, "Idle Chatter," *adoleschia*.[113] Aristotle's sense of the *ethos* of the wealthy provides a further point of direct comparison as he outlines that they are "arrogant" with the same word that Theophrastus uses for his Character 24, "Arrogance": *huperephania*.[114] The *Characters* could then be embodying examples of the *ethos* of the old, examples of older types to whom the student of rhetoric should learn to appeal.

However, even if Theophrastus perhaps used these sections of Aristotle's *Rhetoric* to characterize the old and wealthy men that he describes, a rhetorical explanation on the basis of Aristotelian *ethos* on its own is wanting: the *Characters* lacks an analysis for *why* these types behave as they do, preventing a speaker from appealing to the "ends" that animate their behavior. Very rarely does Theophrastus provide a sense of a character type's intention, or motive. If the text has a rhetorical purpose, it seems more likely to lie in providing examples of how to write character sketches designed for students to copy and imitate. This, however, does raise the question of why Theophrastus has only chosen to depict vices and further does not explain why all these characters share sociological characteristics or why Theophrastus included a sketch of an Oligarch.

A rhetorical reading of the text further would not seem to accord with Theophrastus's own stated rhetorical commitments elsewhere. The treatises that Theophrastus is reputed to have written on rhetoric include *On the Art of Rhetoric, On Kinds of Rhetorical Arts, Precepts, On Invention, On Example, On the Maxim, On Praise, On Slander,* and *On Statement and Narration*—all of which have been lost. From the few traces of these works that survive and have now been brought together, it is clear that Theophrastus also developed Aristotle's *Rhetoric* in new directions, above all in terms of style. Theophrastus was commended by Cicero for having "written not only better but also much more on these matters than all the teachers of speaking" and by Quintilian for being "accustomed fearlessly to dissent from [Aristotle]."[115] Rhetoric, for Cicero, requires language in "pure and good Latin," "expressed clearly and simply," which considers "what is appropriate": three Aristotelian virtues of style.[116] It also, however, must incorporate "the one thing missing" from Aristotle's system, a quality that "Theophrastus numbers fourth among the virtues of a speech: that ornamentation [which is] pleasant and abundant."[117] While Theophrastus emphasizes the need for "pleasant and abundant" rhetorical ornament, the *Characters* is written in a simple, unadorned style—so simple that it seemed to classical scholar Giorgio Pasquali that it could be lecture notes. To be sure, if the *Characters* is a propaedeutic for rhetoric, it would not need to be completely faithful to all aspects of Theophrastus's rhetorical theory. But, nonetheless, it seems strange not to have something of Theophrastus's signature rhetorical virtue present.

The rhetorical reading does not then seem either to fit within the framework of Theophrastus's own rhetorical commitments or to help us clarify the sociological and political details in the collection. Let us now turn to the comic proposition to see if it can help explain these details.

COMEDY

A second major explanation of the intention behind the *Characters* asserts that it has a relationship to comedy. Because three characters are mentioned as features of comedy in the *Tractatus,* because six characters furnish the titles of several plays of Old and New Comedy, and simply because so many of the sketches are funny, it has been argued that the *Characters* is either a kind of comic handbook of figures for playwrights to use, or that it is a work of poetics, illustrating the importance of the construction of character within drama by providing a set of examples.[118] On this latter point, the commentator Graziano Ranocchia argues that by focusing on character, the *Characters* took up the challenge of developing a theory of one of the six components of tragic drama outlined in Aristotle's *Poetics*—plot, character, diction, thought, spectacle, and lyric poetry—on which the Peripatetic authors had not yet focused.[119]

The comic argument certainly deals with the problem of the characters' lack of motives for their actions. In Aristotle's *Poetics,* we only understand a character, and therefore their motives, through the plot of a drama, in which we see a character's active choices, "what kinds of thing an agent chooses or rejects."[120] It is then possible that the motives of the Theophrastan characters would only become clear once these types were projected into plays. There are, however, other issues that remain. On the one hand, if we see the *Characters* as a handbook designed for playwrights, we might ask whether Theophrastus would have thought that playwrights would need to come to him for their examples.[121] Although both Old and New Comedy clearly influenced Theophrastus, this does not mean that Theophrastus intended to influence the playwrights in turn. On the other hand, if we see the *Characters* as a comic addendum to Aristotle's *Poetics,* we must confront the issue that Aristotle's six definitional elements of tragedy (plot, character, diction, thought, spectacle, and lyric poetry) may not also hold for comedy, making a work on comic character less likely to fill a Peripatetic gap.

Once we turn to Theophrastus's fragments on poetics, a number of more pressing problems emerge. Theophrastus's poetic works include *On the Ludicrous, On the Art of Poetry, On Style, On Comedy, On Meters,* and *In Reply to Aeschylus.* These treatises continue several Aristotelian commitments and reveal a particular emphasis on comedy and prose. In *The Art of Grammar,* the Latin grammarian Diomedes provides a set of definitions that Theophrastus gave of tragedy, comedy, satyric drama, and mimes, which has led some scholars to suggest that it was in fact Theophrastus who initiated the separation of dramatic genres into these categories.[122] According to Diomedes, Theophrastus understood tragedy as "a crisis of heroic fortune."[123] This puzzling phrase seems to mean something close to Aristotle's definition of tragedy as a reversal in fortune for people of heroic stature, people who are "superior to existing humans."[124] Comedy, on the other hand, is defined as "a story of private affairs involving no danger," differing from tragedy because it does not deal with "kings" or "generals" but "humble and private figures."[125] Contrary to Fortenbaugh's comment that Theophrastus omits "reference to worthless individuals" in his definition of comedy, Theophrastus here maintains an Aristotelian delineation of the two genres partly on the basis of the class of the characters depicted (even if he gives additional emphasis to comedy also being "a story of private affairs").[126] Satyric drama is like comedy in this regard, as it does not deal with "heroes or kings but satyrs," brought out to humor the audience "in the midst of tragic and serious matters."[127] The mime is similarly defined as an irreverent and often licentious "imitation of any speech and movement (. . .) encompassing things permitted and things forbidden."[128]

The *Characters* fits uneasily with Theophrastus's description of comedy as focused on the "private affairs" of "humble people." While clearly fulfilling the former quality, his sketches do not so adequately fulfill the latter, as they collectively present a class spectrum that stretches all the way to the upper reaches of Athenian society. The characters represented are not humble enough to be comedic, nor do they suffer a reversal of fortune that would allow them to be tragic. They also do not seem to fit into the other dramatic genres that Theophrastus is credited with having delineated: they are not licentious enough to be mimes or serious enough to be satyric drama, which relies on humor punctuating tragic matters.

The fact that they do not fit into Theophrastus's own system of dramatic classification perhaps here signals that the *Characters* is not an unclassified species of artistic prose but something else entirely. This perspective is further corroborated by Theophrastus's own views on prose, as paraphrased in Cicero's *De oratore*. There, Cicero comments that Theophrastus thinks prose "ought to be rhythmical not in a rigid but in a rather loose way," or in other words, that it should share one of the qualities typically designated for poetry.[129] The *Characters* is therefore not only dramatically unclassifiable, in Theophrastus's own system, but also not written in the kind of rhythmic prose that Theophrastus himself admired and advocated.

Finally, an understanding of the *Characters* in relation to comedy also does not help explain the sociological uniformity of its sketches in terms of age, gender, class, and place, nor does it explain Theophrastus's decision to depict a political figure. We turn, then, finally to the possibility that an ethical explanation may shed light on these matters.

ETHICS

The claim that the *Characters* is in some way ethical rests on the connection between this text and Aristotle's two major works of ethics, and in particular on the importance that Aristotle gives to the cultivation of virtuous character. For Aristotle, gaining a virtuous moral character is the result of a process of training oneself into a posture or disposition, a *hexis,* from which one can make wise choices that will lead to one's flourishing.[130] *Arete,* or virtue, is the development of an enduring *hexis* that "disposes a person to make good moral choices for the right reasons."[131] A person can develop this *hexis* by practicing good moral actions: "The virtues on the other hand we acquire by first having actually practiced them," Aristotle says, "just as we do the arts."[132] "We become just," in other words, "by doing just acts."[133] For Aristotle, the arena in which we can best carry out these just actions, and therefore train and eventually expose our characters, is that of "social relations and living together and sharing words and actions."[134] It is this framework that leads Aristotle to classify good and bad traits—eight of which are also exemplified in the *Characters*—and to propose the theory of the virtuous mean.

Beyond its borrowing of these character traits, the *Characters* is thought to be close to Aristotle's *Ethics* in two further ways: its clear sense of social relations and actions as the sphere in which a person's character is revealed and its style of portraits, which on occasion seem to extend the style of character sketches found in the *Ethics*.[135] Aristotle's magnanimous man, for example, has "a slow gait, a deep voice and a deliberate utterance," qualities that could have walked out of one of Theophrastus's *Characters*.[136] He is, however, the exception, and of course is a virtuous figure, not a vice. Further support for the ethical argument has been found in the Aristotelian inheritance visible in Theophrastus's works on ethics. Theophrastus wrote numerous works of ethics, several of which dealt with topics treated by Aristotle: *On Emotions, On the Voluntary, On Virtue, On Happiness, On Marriage, On Kindness, On Wealth, On Retribution, On Friendship, On Pleasure,* and *On Drunkenness*. The fragments and paraphrases of these works indicate an important continuation of several Aristotelian tenets, including the importance of education for the cultivation for moral character.[137] The short ethical treatise *On Virtues and Vices,* which exemplifies qualities by listing their many forms of expression and is thought to have been written by scholars in Aristotle's school, would add further support to the ethical case.[138]

The critique of seeing the *Characters* as ethical has been twofold. First, when Theophrastus engages with Aristotelian qualities, he either represents the excess or the deficient versions of certain traits, rather than the virtuous mean, representing a break with this central Aristotelian doctrine.[139] Second, unlike Aristotle's *Ethics,* the *Characters* has no broader analytical framework, no clear grouping or ordering of vices, and no explanation for why individuals take on these vices and act as they do. We might add a third critique: if this was a text intended to instruct virtue, why should all the characters be old Athenian men and include an Oligarch among them? The first criticism can be countered if we contextualize the *Characters* with Theophrastus's other works. Yet like the rhetorical and the comedic, the ethical explanation does little to answer the second and third issues.

To explain Theophrastus's representation of excess or deficiency, several commentators have claimed that the *Characters* could be designed to steer its readers away from these deficient or excessive options though a process of *negative imitation,* training them to avoid the series of thirty vices they see.[140] Traces of a Theophrastan poetics of negative imitation can indeed be found in some of his other writings, including what we know of his lost treatise *On the Ludicrous*. Both Plutarch's *Table Talk* and the *Gnomologium Vaticanum*, a fourteenth-century collection of Greek aphorisms, paraphrase the arguments Theophrastus is thought to have made in this text.[141] In Plutarch's words, for Theophrastus, "a jest is a concealed rebuke for error." This phrasing points to a potentially morally educative potential for jests, through which the person being mocked discovers their wrongdoing.[142] Theophrastus would have had an Aristotelian precedent here, as well as one derived from Plato, both of whom connected laughter to rebuking the ridiculous.[143] With this, the ethical argument could protect itself from the first critique: that these excessive or deficient characters can do moral work without the presence of a virtuous mean.

This enables the ethical reading to be more robust than the previous explanations, which the Theophrastan fragments on rhetorical style and comic poetics call into question. It does, however, still leave two questions hanging in the air. Why, if Theophrastus designed the *Characters* for ethical instruction, did he choose to use such uniform sociological features and to spotlight one political figure? And why, if this is a text that aims to cultivate virtuous character, did Theophrastus leave out the motives for these figures' vicious actions? These questions prompt a turn to a fourth interpretative option, which operates in the space between ethics and politics. To arrive at this interpretation, we need to turn to a set of Theophrastan texts that are rarely brought into discussion: his works of natural philosophy and metaphysics.

The *Characters* as Virtue Politics

Here, then, are four terms for our search for an alternative interpretation for the intention of the *Characters*. It must be an interpretation that first clarifies the sociological details present in the *Characters*, accounting for the uniform depiction of these personality types in terms of their class, age, gender, and location. It must secondly offer a plausible explanation for the one political sketch that none of the proposed intentions thus far incorporate: the Oligarch. It should thirdly account for the direct echoes of Aristotle's *Rhetoric* and of Old and New Comedy, explaining why Theophrastus chose to incorporate these elements into the *Characters*. Finally, it should respond to an issue we have seen troubling each existing interpretation thus far: the fact that these types mostly lack intentions, ends, or motives for their behavior.

Lane Fox's argument that the *Characters* were "born from a new combination: philosophical classification and comic caricature" begins to suggest an alternative that might suit our purposes.[144] Yet while Lane Fox understood that the vices are clearly classified in some way, he did not pursue this possibility further. A serious reading of the *Characters* as "classification" makes intrinsic sense, however, in light of the fact that Theophrastus's natural philosophy—as displayed in numerous other texts—reflects his insatiable drive to categorize and classify. Might the *Characters* be written with the intention to *classify* a particular set of phenomena, in the same way that Theophrastus's botanical works are intended to classify plants? To answer this question, we must turn from Theophrastus's works of rhetoric, poetics, and comedy to his works of natural philosophy and metaphysics instead.

AN EXERCISE IN CLASSIFICATION

The most immediately apparent similarities between the *Characters* and Theophrastus's works of natural philosophy are stylistic in nature. This vast corpus encompasses theories of winds and weather signs, works of biology and botany, and writings on aspects of human physiology such as sweat, fatigue, dizziness, and odors. In his natural philosophy texts, Theophrastus repeatedly deploys a consistent two-stage methodology. First, he discerns and categorizes observed phenomena into species on the basis of similarities in their components, capacities, or effects. This fulfills the way in which Theophrastus's *Metaphysics* defines the task of science as the need "to distinguish what is the same in a plurality of things."[145] Second, he considers how each of these species follows a logic of regularity. The *Characters,* as we will see, is no exception to this approach—although approaching these similarities first requires a more elaborate articulation of the two-stage methodology that undergirds Theophrastus's natural philosophy.

The first stage, classification, comes into its own in Theophrastus's botanical writings (Figure 1.2).[146] In his *Historia plantarum*, a ten-volume encyclopedia that contains examples of different kinds of plants and lists over 550 species, Theophrastus separates plants by distinguishing "their parts, their qualities, the ways in which their life originates, and the course which it follows in each case."[147] Here, he specifies that what he cannot consider in the case of plants are "conduct and activities," qualities that he argues are found in animals instead.[148] What makes Theophrastus, as one recent article put it, "the unsung hero of Western science" is that his descriptions of

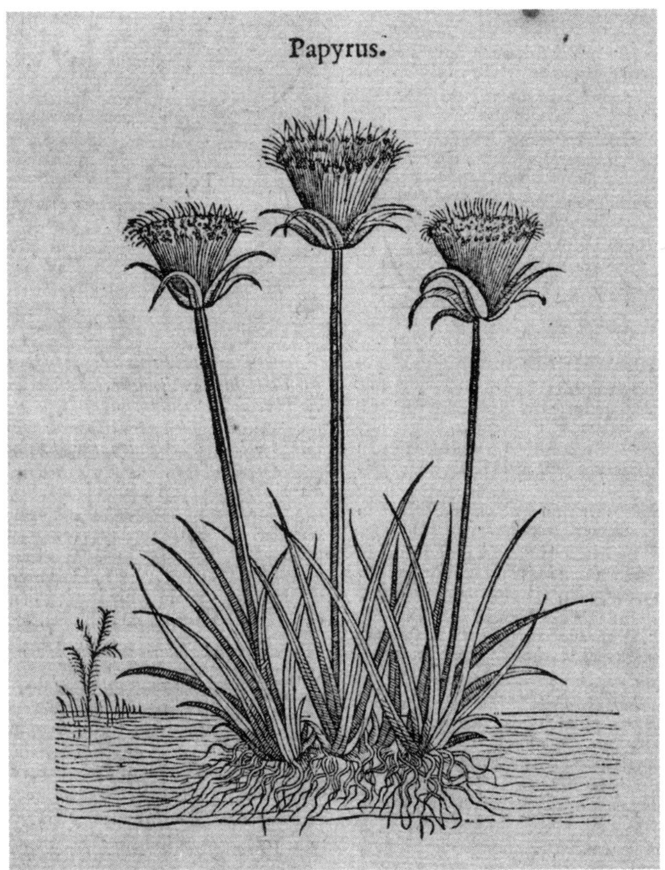

FIGURE 1.2. Illustration of papyrus reeds in Theophrastus's *Historia plantarum*. In Joannes Bodaeus's illustrated 1644 Greek and Latin edition, published in Amsterdam. *Credit:* Gt 44. 130, Houghton Library, Harvard University.

plants are empirical: always derived from close observation.[149] This coheres with what we know of Theophrastus's epistemology, which is said to have outlined an essential role for "sense-perception." As the sixth-century CE Neoplatonist Simplicius wrote, "We must search out the truth about natural principles (starting) from the senses and from what is perceived, obeying Theophrastus."[150]

The second stage, determining the logical regularity of each species, can be found in a number of Theophrastus's miscellaneous works. *On Stones* contrasts two kinds of stone that seem similar by examining how they react when placed in the same circumstances, such as being burned or melted.[151] He then looks for an explanation of this shared effect. The stones that "break and fly into pieces as if they are fighting against being burnt," like pottery, do so because they have lost their moisture, something that "is natural" (*kata logon*).[152] *On Winds,* similarly, argues that "there is a *logical order* as it were for each during which (times) they blow most frequently," that "the stoppages of the winds *occur logically,*" that "it is *according to reason* for this very breeze to come to be."[153] When Theophrastus describes animate phenomena, these regularities are often understood as habitual behaviors. *On Fish,* for example, is an endeavor to make sense of "occurrences or reported occurrences" of peculiar habitual behaviors, such as a fish that "every day makes its bed on the land."[154] Theophrastus, in all these examples, is interested in phenomena that are *kata logon,* that work "according to logical order." This phrase is deployed over fifty times in his corpus, revealing an orientation toward descriptions of "something happening according to some proportion or regularity."[155]

These methodological orientations often inform how Theophrastus structures his material. This is most obvious in his treatise *On Weather Signs*, which describes the various kinds of weather signaled by different natural phenomena. This text is organized under headings that describe the weather predicted by particular signs: "the signs of rain," "the signs of wind," "the signs of storm," and "the signs of fair weather." As commentators have noticed, this structure hinders the treatise from being of "practical use for a farmer, or sailor, where they could easily look up a sign they have just observed in order to determine a prognosis of the weather."[156] Rather, all the signs are placed together, as follows:

> A crow lifting its head while on a rock washed by a wave signals rain; likewise, if it makes frequent dives and flies in circles it signals rain. If a raven in the morning producing many different sounds repeats one of these quickly twice over and shakes its wings to make a whirring sound, it signals rain.[157]

The text's organizational principle thus exposes a commitment not to providing practical information that will help people understand individual phenomena but to grouping phenomena together on the basis of the end state that they predict.

The style of the *Characters* echoes many aspects of this method. Characters, like plants, stones, winds, types of sweat, kinds of fatigue, forms of dizziness, and odors, are separated first on the basis of their observed differences, derived from sensory or empirical impressions. As Theophrastus distinguishes natural phenomena based on differences in their components, capacities, or effects (how they react to particular actions), he seems to similarly distinguish the characters based on their different responses to a given situation. Where *On Stones* distinguishes between stones by asking how they react differently to the process of melting, the *Characters* seems to be guided by a similar—if silent—animating question: how do different types of people react differently to the processes that a day would demand of them? This makes further sense in light of Theophrastus's comment in *Historia plantarum* that one cannot distinguish plants on the basis of "conduct and activities," qualities that are found in the animal world instead. Classifying these Athenians into types would then be equivalent to classifying types of English setter dogs: human differences do not come from the species' shared provenance but from their conduct and activities, much like the differences between a field and a show dog.[158] Each type's behavior is regular, reasonable, and even necessary once their vice has been understood: something that leads Fortenbaugh to describe the figures as possessing "behavioral regularities."[159]

Across Theophrastus's empirical treatises, the logical regularity of the behavior of an animal, plant, or weather system does not always imply that there is a teleology at work, that this regularity must serve some discernible end. This approach is consistent with the approach to teleology that Theophrastus outlines in his *Meta-*

physics. In the words of one scholar, Theophrastus's *Metaphysics* is "the most significant metaphysical text that we possess between the time of Aristotle and the flowering of the new philosophical schools of the Hellenistic period."[160] Though for a long time the significance of Theophrastus's *Metaphysics* was thought to lie in its rebuff of Aristotle, something that "affected his school, costing it in the end the loss of inheritance of its teacher," today, its seems more likely to reside in how Theophrastus clarifies the limits within which Aristotle's teleological explanations are applicable.[161]

For Aristotle, four interrelated causes are needed to explain phenomena.[162] "The material cause," that out of which something is made (e.g., the bronze of a statue); "the formal cause," the form or account of what this material is to become (e.g., the shape of a statue); "the efficient cause," the primary source of change or rest (e.g., the art of casting the statue); and "the final cause," or *telos*: the sake for which the thing is done (e.g., artistic production).[163] In Aristotle's view, the presence of a *final cause* means that it is not a coincidence, for example, that the front teeth of an animal are regularly sharp and their molars broad. They grow, he claims, in this way to best serve biting and chewing food, which is good for the animal's existence and flourishing: its *telos*.[164] "Nature," as he famously puts it on several occasions, "does nothing in vain, for everything by nature is for the sake [*eneka*] of something."[165] But nature, as Aristotle qualifies, only "holds either universally or for the most part."[166] It can make mistakes, and, within the regular workings of mechanical necessity, it can generate superfluities.[167] We must not, as one commentator summarizes, "expect to discover a purpose (a final cause) in all things, seeing that some of them come into being only by necessity in consequence of the existence of others."[168]

Theophrastus picks up on these exceptions in his *Metaphysics*, with the aim to shore up Aristotelian teleology against people who either reject it out of hand or apply it too liberally. "The actual assignment of a formal account to each entity by referring to something for the sake [*eneka*] of which [it happens] in all cases is difficult," he concedes.[169] It is hard, Theophrastus writes, to understand "for the sake of what" (*tinos . . . eneka*) there are tides, breasts for males, discharge for females, the growth of beards on certain animals, the growth of hair in certain places, the growth of enormous horns for deer, and the incredibly short lifespan of a fly.[170] Rather than being for "the better," or being "for the sake of something," Theophrastus instead proposes that these inexplicable phenomena "follow by some necessity" (*ananke*), maintaining that they obey certain laws and needs, but not always those that serve their own interests.[171]

Instead of being subsumed under the general principle that nature does nothing in vain, Theophrastus clarifies that phenomena can occur by "some necessity" outside of a subject's own purview. The silver-fir tree, for example, is easily split not because that helps it in some way but because "the grain is straight"—unlike the olive tree, which breaks easily because it is "crooked and hard."[172] This insistence on a lack of final causality could also apply to Theophrastus's character types, who do not carry out their behaviors for the better and who often do not appear to act for the sake of any clear purpose. Rather, they seem to obey a logical necessity to act according to the directives of their ordinary vice in all aspects of their everyday behavior.[173] A commonalty between human beings and other natural phenomena on this point is made more plausible once we consider how Theophrastus frequently draws links between animals, plants, and human beings: whether that is explaining the differences in the parts of plants by comparing them to animals, through the vocabulary of "muscles" (*ines*), "veins" (*phlebes*), and "flesh" (*sarx*), or emphasizing that there is an affinity (*oikeiotes,* from *oikos,* "household") between human beings and animals.[174] This might help explain that puzzling feature of the *Characters,* the fact that we do not often know *why* Theophrastus's characters behave as they do.[175]

The *Characters* recalls Theophrastus's natural philosophy not only in its methods but also in its presentation and language. Significantly, the *Characters* does not include an index: it does not list a plethora of singular behaviors that a reader could then understand by associating them to a type. Instead, just like *On Weather Signs,* the *Characters* groups examples of similar phenomena (the signs, for example, of "absentmindedness") together in one figure, just like the signs of rain. As we know, the Greek word for "character" does not appear at all in the body of the text, but the words *tropos* and *ethos* do (the former five times, the latter twice). Theophrastus uses both words when considering and systematizing aspects of the natural world. Here, we might ask whether the title that Diogenes Laertius identifies for this text has blinded us to its similarities with other parts of Theophrastus's corpus. It is not surprising that a thinker who was interested in observing similarities across so many domains—who analogized plants to animals and argued that animals have an affinity to humans—embraced a singular methodological approach to such a wide array of phenomena.

But what, exactly, is Theophrastus classifying in the *Characters*? If this text indeed was intended to classify a set of phenomena, what united these phenomena in the first place? One simple answer might be that Theophrastus understood them to be thirty kinds of Athenian vice. Just as he is said to have written a book of *Laws* that catalogued the legislation of "almost all political societies not only of Greece," the *Characters* could be cataloguing the particular vices of one political society: Athens.[176] Yet if the larger corpus of Theophrastan texts helps explain the classificatory ambition of the *Characters* and sheds some light on why Theophrastus may have chosen to generally exclude a type's motives, it has not accounted for the traces of Aristotle's *Rhetoric* and the figures of comedy in the text. Moreover, it has neither clarified the uniform sociological detail—apart from the detail of place—nor the presence of the Oligarch.

THE PROBLEM OF THE OLIGARCH

Let us begin with the Oligarch to see whether a political reading of the text can help us respond to some of these issues. For Aristotle, oligarchy was to be taken with the warning that

> those who enter into office may also be reasonably expected to offer magnificent sacrifices and to erect some public building, so that the common people, participating in the feasts and seeing their city embellished with offerings and buildings, may readily tolerate a continuation of this constitution.[177]

In other words, for oligarchy to be tolerable to citizens, oligarchs must lavishly and generously spend their money on things that will benefit the people.[178] They must also avoid "harming the crowd and banning them from town."[179] Theophrastus's Oligarch, however, does not carry out either of these actions. He spends his money on personal grooming, with his "fingernails expertly trimmed."[180] He criticizes the people's reliance on the generosity of the wealthy, complaining that "the common people show no gratitude; they always follow anyone with a handout or a gift," and asks when he will "be delivered from the deathgrip of being forced to pay for public events and warships."[181] He wishes to "be rid of the rabble and the marketplace" and to instead found a city with fellow oligarchs.[182] Rather than following Aristotle's advice, he seems to do exactly the opposite. In many of these behaviors, the Oligarch is not alone. His stinginess is mirrored in the four other sketches dedicated to this vice: "Shamelessness" (9), "Penny-Pinching" (10), "Illiberality" (22), and "Profiteering" (30). And his hatred of the people finds an echo in the Garrulous Man, who interjects "a condemnation of the masses" into a long-winded story.[183]

The Oligarch is not only stingy but grumbles against democratic institutions and makes no reference to the particularities of Macedonian oligarchy, a quality that has led scholars to place this character as having been written in the democratic Athens of Alexander (335–323).[184] The four characters of stinginess do not exhibit this feature and therefore can be thought to have been written all the way up to 309, in a period that saw two Macedonian oligarchies take power. A desire to critique *bad* oligarchs—either when constrained by a democracy or when left to flourish (or fester)—would account for why, at least in the case of these characters, Theophrastus chose moneyed old men: the kinds of people who would be required to give. What I mean by *bad* oligarchs are oligarchs who do not perform the requisite tasks to make their constitution tolerable and therefore stable. In his *Rhetoric,* as we saw, Aristotle argued that the "end" of oligarchy is wealth.[185] In his *Politics,* he argued that for this constitution to be maintained, oligarchs who want wealth must be encouraged to be generous. By revealing, then, that oligarchic rule does not lead the rich to generosity, Theophrastus seems to mount a critique of oligarchy itself as a type of government that is only rendered stable when the rich are liberal with their fortune. This argument would be supported by the possible critiques of monarchy and oligarchy that we saw in Theophrastus's political writing.

But if Theophrastus was keen to criticize oligarchy, why did he do so by writing the *Characters*? One answer here might be that, just as he did in his will, Theophrastus hedged his bets in his works as well. Rather than upsetting his position in Athens once again, Theophrastus buried a critique of oligarchy in the *Characters*. This would align with his view on comedy that serious rebukes can be hidden in jest. It would also correspond to his reported conception of music that melodies will work their effects more readily if they are implicit. "Souls are more attentive to melodies," the medieval Arabic gnomologium *Siwan al-hikma* (*Depository of Wisdom Literature*) quotes Theophrastus as saying, "when they are concealed than to that which is manifest and whose meaning is apparent to them."[186] In order to render the politics of the *Characters* less dangerous, Theophrastus might have decided to incorporate characters from comedy and to use the *Rhetoric* to produce more accurate presentations of the old. These choices, in other words, would lead readers to focus on the comic or mimetic aspects of the text, leaving its political melody concealed.

The result is a delicate balance between a criticism that remains politically operative but does not force Theophrastus to too readily reveal his hand. But achieving this balance is not the only political role the other characters play.

KAIROS AND VIRTUE POLITICS

The Oligarch's vice is not only his stinginess and his hatred of the people. It is also an inattention to *kairos*: his ability to understand and grasp a moment. This is a quality that is lacking in many of the other characters in the collection.

To begin with the Oligarch. His political positions are fixed: he has developed a set of ideas that he applies no matter the circumstances. Rather than engaging in political debate from an oligarchic perspective—in line with the tradition of oligarchy as a serious political position expressed in Plato's *Republic* and in Aristotle's *Politics*—the Oligarch is oblivious to what a given situation demands. This is a type who is "apt," Theophrastus writes, to speak certain catchphrases, such as "Either they must run the city or we must!"[187] He does not measure when to deploy these slogans but duly rolls them off, no matter what is happening. It is, for example, at midday that he chooses to go out "with his cloak arranged about him" to intone his antidemocratic speeches in the city, when no one is around to hear him.[188]

This point helps to clarify both the sketch of the Oligarch and the collection as a whole. Although Theophrastus certainly had ample material to pillory the radical partisans of democracy in Hellenistic

Athens, as Lane Fox puts it, "unlike the comedians of the post-Periclean decades, Theophrastus, most conspicuously, never pokes fun at the demos."[189] Theophrastus's choice to represent oligarchy as a character type seems, in this light, to betray a further political position: it highlights that oligarchy lends itself to typifying much better than democracy. Theophrastus, in other words, is *characterizing* oligarchy, suggesting that being an oligarch is not an opinion, or political preference, as much as a feature of someone's personality—which encompasses their stated beliefs as much as the cut of their hair ("moderate length"), the trim of their fingernails, and the style of their outer garments.[190] In this sense, the 1950 study of the authoritarian personality by Theodor W. Adorno and his colleagues presents a compelling parallel: fascism, they found, is not a political stance based on a consideration of facts as much as it is a particular psychology—one in which individuals think and act in more rigid ways than individuals who are pro-democracy.[191] This framework opens up one possibility for why Theophrastus did not include a character of the Democrat in the collection: he considered democracy to be less amenable to rigid characterization than oligarchy.[192] Theophrastus may have been inspired by Socrates here, who describes the "manifold" nature of democracy, which could make it harder to represent in a single figure.[193] The democratic man, in Socrates's view, is someone "stuffed with most excellent differences," someone who contains "within himself the greatest number of patterns of constitutions and qualities."[194] The behavior of the Oligarch, in contrast, is predictable and fixed, unable to possess *kairos* and meet the demands of a moment.

In Theophrastus's lifetime, the sculptor Lysippus of Sicyon made a statue of *kairos* that tells us more about the contemporary understanding of the concept. A relief of the statue shows a winged adolescent boy with a strange hairstyle engaged in a precarious balancing act (Figure 1.3). Clearly on the move, with one hand he swings a pair of scales, which he balances on the rounded side of a razor with the other.[195] As the archaeologist Dietrich Boschung puts it, "It is only Kairos' virtuosity" that keeps everything in check.[196] Writing two generations after Lysippus, the ancient Greek epigrammatic poet Posidippus of Pella decided to expose the statue's symbolism and purpose in the form of a dialogue:

A. Why do you hold a razor in your right hand?
B. As a sign to men that I am sharper than any sharp edge.

A. And why does your hair hang over your face?
B. For him who meets me to take me by the forelock.

A. And why, in Heaven's name, is the back of your head bald?
B. Because no one who I have once raced by on my winged feet will now, though he wishes it sore, take hold of me from behind.

A. Why did the artist fashion you?
B. For your sake, stranger, and he set me up in the porch as a lesson.[197]

FIGURE 1.3. Marble relief showing *kairos,* after a lost bronze statue made by Lysippus of Sicyon, for Alexander the Great. Second century CE. *Credit:* © Museo di antichità, Turin, Italy, 86707. By permission of the MiC-Musei Reali.

Together, this litany of symbols—the razor, the winged feet, and the half-shaven head with a lock of hair flowing in front—combine to achieve a singular purpose: to teach passersby to give due reverence to the god of opportunity by recognizing the right thing to do at the right moment. Lysippus's concretization of this abstract notion works as an "example of the ability of the artist to endow abstract concepts (knowledge, ideas) with a concrete form that can be apprehended by the senses."[198] Theophrastus also merits this accolade: penning his figures at precisely the same moment, to precisely the same end.

Theophrastus's interest in *kairos* can be traced across his corpus, and we know that he even dedicated a specific treatise to the issue.[199] *Kairos,* for Theophrastus, was an essential quality to possess in all spheres of politics. In his account of Theophrastus's twenty-four books of *Laws,* Cicero says that Theophrastus was especially drawn to "the changes in the circumstances of a state and the critical moments of time that must be dealt with as the situation demands."[200] *On the Choice of Magistrates,* the text likely authored by Theophrastus, makes a similar argument. It proclaims that political candidates must possess virtue as well as sufficient wealth because people with these qualities "are generally good at perceiving things and are best at recognizing critical moments (*kairos*)."[201]

Theophrastus also thought about *kairos* in terms of quotidian behaviors. According to a paraphrase by the fifth-century CE Macedonian scholar Joannes Stobaeus, Theophrastus understood conversational *kairos* to be a virtue. As "Theophrastus says," Stobaeus recounts, "during meetings one man goes through many things and chatters at length, another says little and not even what is essential, but a third says only what is necessary and so lays hold upon due measure [*ton kairon*]."[202] Indeed, if oligarchy is the only party-political position that prevents the virtue of *kairos,* a number of other characters have dispositions that disturb it in equal measure. We have already encountered one sketch that exemplifies this quality: the Man with Bad Timing, the *akairos.* We have also met the Absentminded Man (*anaisthetos*), whose lack of perceptive capacities (*aisthesis*) prevents him from acting appropriately.[203] The strange character of the Late Learner—who, while riding a horse, "tries to practice fancy horsemanship" and "falls and hurts his head"—is also easier understood once we consider this broader critique of behaviors that are outside of their time.[204]

A version of this inattention to *kairos* can be seen in the broader concern with characters who are "conversational non-cooperators," to borrow the classicist Paul Millett's phrase: people who thwart civic speech instead of furthering it and who are inattentive of the requirements of their surroundings.[205] The Ironic Man tells people who are urgently seeking a meeting with him "to come back later" and "if he is selling something says that he is not, and if he's not, says that he is."[206] The Idle Chatterer speaks nonsense to a man he does not know.[207] The Provincial Man only speaks in the assembly to praise garlic, distrusts his close friends, and reserves his longer conversations for his laborers.[208] The Garrulous Man cannot make a faithful report of what happened in the assembly, busy as he is telling unrelated stories, including his own rhetorical feats, and constantly disrupting common activities with his untimely interventions.[209] His vice poses problems for schoolboys trying to study or wrestle and for guests at a dinner party, as well as jurors trying to reach a verdict. The Rumor-monger does not care about spreading false information.[210] The Arrogant Man "casts his eyes down" in order not to talk to anyone.[211] This, just like saying the wrong thing at the wrong political moment, breaks civic bonds, as it prevents the act of deliberation. Alongside these conversational noncooperators are figures who disrupt the social fabric by their actions. This includes the Superstitious Man, whose fanaticism prevents him from handling the dead and thus fulfilling his social duties.[212] He is a figure, as one commentator writes, whose overbearing piety leads him "to take matters of religion" into his own hands, which may even represent "a potential threat to political stability."[213]

Thus, although the Oligarch is the only explicitly political character in the collection, several other figures share in the ethical defects that would have been thought prejudicial to political cohesion and stability: from his stinginess to his lack of *kairos*. What the *Characters* seems then to be classifying is not only kinds of Athenian vice but kinds of Athenian vice that prevent the smooth running of political society: behaviors that are prejudicial to virtue politics. Just as good political action, for Theophrastus, was predicated upon being able to handle crisis or navigate *kairos*, a good citizen should be able to discern the right kinds of actions, for themselves and for society, no matter the circumstances. These character sketches, then, at once encouraged citizens to adopt a set of specific political virtues and reduced certain political positions to personality traits. Where Balot has argued that the role of political virtue is to be recovered in the "corpus of Attic oratory," Theophrastus's *Characters* indicates that a wider range of texts may have participated in embodying this political language.[214]

The *Characters,* in this case, shows us how written literary description was also used to this political effect: through a kind of negative imitation, as the partisans of the ethical interpretation suggest, pleasantly instructing readers through soft rebuke. And while Balot, alongside other scholars, has argued for the relevance of virtue politics within neo-Aristotelian political theory, Theophrastus's presentation of virtue politics in the *Characters* also has broader significance. Specifically, it exposes an alternative approach to the links between character-writing and ethical or political imperatives—one that sits in between the approaches upheld by Plato and Aristotle.

Implicit Aesthetics

Both Plato and Aristotle offer clear perspectives on character in their respective poetics. In book 3 of the *Republic,* Socrates asks Glaucon if it is "only the poets that we must supervise and compel to embody in their poems the semblance of the good *character* or else not write poetry among us." He answers the question himself in book 10 with the decision that "we can admit no poetry into our city save only hymns to the gods and praises of *good men.*"[215] As these statements imply, Socrates holds that character sketches of vice would be very dangerous for an audience, outlining the risk that impressionable spectators or listeners could imitate the negative actions that they heard or saw. Aristotle's *Poetics,* in contrast, presents character as less important to tragedy than plot (notwithstanding the central role that character plays in Aristotle's *Ethics* and *Politics*). In his words, "Without action there could be no tragedy, but without character there could be."[216]

Martha Nussbaum has convincingly argued that the two philosophers' disagreements over the question of character is a debate with deep sources, which extend all the way to their respective ideas about luck. Plato, Aristotle, and the tragic poets all took part, Nussbaum writes, in "an anxious and rich debate on the ethical role of luck."[217] While Plato and Aristotle were both gripped by the dangers inherent in a contingent human life—the painful consequences of which the tragic poets represented so well—they developed different prescriptions for how an individual should respond. In Plato's works, we find a conception of philosophy that involves developing a *techne*, a human art or science, to protect the individual from the vagaries of chance: a process that involved encouraging a human being to be as self-sufficient as possible. The virtuous man, in this framework, would not let bad luck touch him. Aristotle, however, saw human flourishing, or *eudaimonia*, as inseparable from the condition of living subject to luck: even if becoming close to friends and lovers puts one at risk of losing them, their fleeting presence makes life so worth living that trying to completely protect oneself from the danger of their disappearance necessarily comes at "too high a price."[218] Rather than trying to become immune to luck, Aristotle thought that we should recognize the value of "vulnerable relationships."

Nussbaum argues that these differences on the pressing question of luck shape the two philosophers' aesthetic commitments. It is why Aristotle can prioritize the tragic reversal of fortune as a device that enacts the notion that good people can suffer bad luck. Aristotle's attitude to the problem of luck also shaped his interest in tragic action. If, for Aristotle, "good living" is "good acting" rather than "good character," a coherent poetic form would need to depict someone's actions, rather than represent them statically.[219] Concretely, Nussbaum continues, this led Aristotle to prioritize drama over the character sketch. Rather than adopting the artistic form of showing unchanging virtuous figures, recommended by Socrates for the ideal city, Aristotle was drawn to a literary genre that places an individual in a series of exceptional events beyond their control.

As we have seen in this chapter, this debate seems to spill over into the work of Theophrastus, whose *Characters* offers a midpoint. Theophrastus, like Aristotle and Plato, was writing in a moment that had recently undergone something of an artistic revolution, in which many of the arts, including "vase painting, music, and sculpture," newly evinced a heightened attention to mimesis.[220] Given these circumstances, it is not surprising that Theophrastus, like his philosophical predecessors, became conscious of art's latent ethical and political potential. He developed, however, his own approach to mimesis, one that stands at the intersection of their perspectives. On the one hand, Theophrastus chose to write character sketches: a static form that Socrates praised, which can depict unchangeable virtue. On the other, Theophrastus is thought to have upheld Aristotle's idea that moral character can be perturbed by bad fortune.[221] Theophrastus therefore stands somewhere between a Platonic and an Aristotelian position. He makes more room than Aristotle for the character sketch used without any other philosophical apparatus, to be of ethical and political consequence. Theophrastus's collection suggests that while the character is not a form that tells us about bad luck and flourishing, it can still have public significance. Theophrastus is, however, most interested in representing characters of vice, rather than virtue. In this, Theophrastus upends Socrates's worries about imitation, offering bad examples as anti-models in order to encourage virtue politics.[222]

While this ethical and political approach to character sketching remains implicit in Theophrastus's own work, this was no longer the case by the time the *Characters* arrived in Rome. Sometime in the late imperial period, an anonymous author took it upon themselves to try to spell out the collection's meaning by craftily adjoining moralizing epilogues to several characters, as well as a Proem to introduce the set, in which Theophrastus supposedly lays bare his intention for these sketches. This was how the early modern readers encountered this set of vices, which prompted them in turn to develop a series of explanations for how exactly this process of ethical instruction by bad example should be envisaged.

2

Moral Instruction by Bad Example

THE LATIN TRANSLATIONS

After its composition in Hellenistic Athens, the next thing we know about the *Characters* is that it was read by late Peripatetics. In the third century BCE, there was an adaptation of it by the new head of the Peripatetics, Lyco of Troas, a philosopher from the northwestern Çanakkale province of modern Turkey. In the second century BCE, a further adaptation was written by Aristo of Ceos, a Peripatetic philosopher from the Greek Cycladic island of Kea, who likely succeeded Lyco as leader of the school.[1] The famed historical biographer, Satyrus the Peripatetic, from the Black Sea port city of ancient Callatis, in present-day Romania, was also familiar with the *Characters* (Figure 2.1). Lyco wrote a sketch of a drunkard, Aristo composed one of arrogance, and Satyrus is thought to have written his own treatise entitled *On Characters* (*Peri charakteron*).[2] Satyrus's treatise is reported to have critiqued extravagance, revealing a shift in mores from Theophrastus's satirizing of those who are not generous enough to those who are too generous altogether. It is in this early transmission that the *Characters* is thought to have likely gained its first editorial additions: a series of philosophical definitions of each vice preceding the description of the associated type. "Absentmindedness," for example, now began, "Absentmindedness, to say it in a definition, is slowness of soul in words and deeds."[3] In the first century BCE, the *Characters* was known to Philodemus of Gardara, an Epicurean philosopher born in what is now Jordan, who taught in the Roman town of Herculaneum, near Naples. Philodemus quotes Character 5, "Obsequiousness," in full. This quotation constitutes

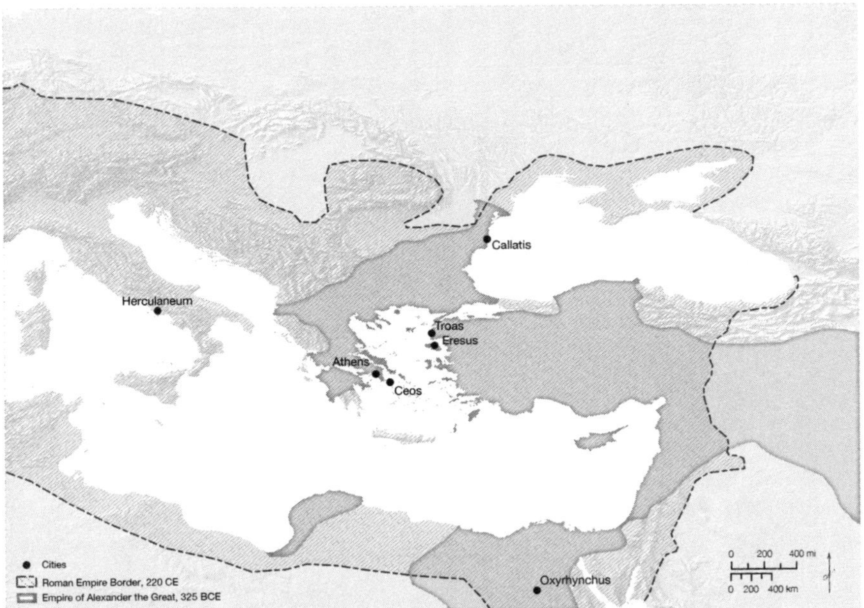

FIGURE 2.1. The posthumous continuation of Theophrastus's project until the third century CE, noting birthplace of imitators or sites of surviving papyri. *Credit:* © Katie Ebner-Landy

one of the two earliest surviving papyrus copies of the *Characters*: a progressively deteriorating roll found in the ruins of Herculaneum.[4] The other papyrus quotes Characters 7 and 8 (Figure 2.2). A later, third-century CE copy, found in an ancient rubbish dump in Al-Bahnasa, or Oxyrhynchus, in Egypt contains shortened versions of Characters 25 and 26.[5]

The *Characters* continued to survive well into the Roman period by virtue of its incorporation into rhetorical instruction. From there, it started to feed into Roman culture more broadly.[6] In the words of one historian, "The success of Theophrastus's *Characters* was part of the more general diffusion of the techniques of the Second Sophistic [60–230 CE]." During this period, figures including *ethopoeia, prosopographia, prosopopeia,* and dialogue took "pride of place among the scholastic *progymnasmata,*" the rudimentary rhetorical exercises given to young students.[7] When sketches from the *Characters* were copied, they came to often be "shortened in transmission" as part of the process of their inclusion in collections of rhetoric.[8] As we saw in the previous chapter, all the medieval manu-

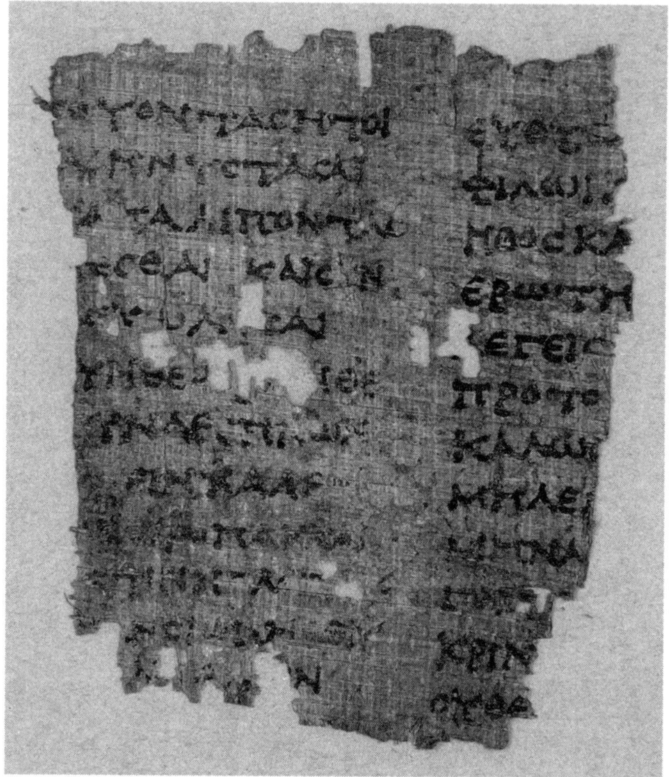

FIGURE 2.2. Papyrus copy of Characters 7 and 8, found in Egypt, 150–100 BCE. *Credit:* Staats- und Universitätsbibliothek Hamburg: P. Hamb. graec. 647.

scripts that contain the *Characters* are collections of treatises on rhetoric, the first existing copies of which date from around the eleventh century.[9] Further east, in the Byzantine empire, we know of at least three scholars who were familiar with the *Characters*. In his commentary on the *Iliad,* the twelfth-century archbishop Eustathius of Thessalonica suggested that Homer could have inspired Theophrastus's technique of character sketching.[10] Eustathius's contemporary, the prolific poet and grammarian John Tzetzes, also made mention of Theophrastus's treatise within the extensive set of commentaries he wrote to his own published letters.[11] Finally, just like the scholars of western Europe, the thirteenth-century Byzantine monk Maximus Planudes decided to include the *Characters* within his collection of manuals of rhetoric, abbreviating and editing the sketches as he went.[12]

At some point in the later Roman Empire, or in early Byzantium, an unknown writer decided to add a Proem that was to dramatically shape the *Characters*' early modern reception.[13] The Proem introduces the *Characters* as providing the answer to a problem. It opens with Theophrastus telling his interlocutor, Polycles, that he has long wondered why, "even though Greece lies under the same sky, and all Greeks are educated in the same way, it happens that we do not have the same composition of character [*taxis ton tropon*]."[14] Clearly a good reader of Theophrastus's natural philosophy, with its interest in separating and classifying natural phenomena, this unknown writer positions Theophrastus as a coherent thinker, asking how it is that one soil, which only produces a limited variety of plants, has nurtured so many different kinds of people. After long observation, the Proem continues, Theophrastus has found the answer to this question: there are men who are "good [*agathoi*] and bad [*phauloi*]," two "classes of character" that separate and distinguish individuals who share the same education and climate.[15] With this phrase, the Proem introduces the idea that there was once a set of virtues penned to match Theophrastus's vices. Having come to this conclusion, the Theophrastus of the Proem states that he feels he "ought to write" about how these two categories of men "normally behave in their lives."[16]

The Proem's explanation of the *Characters*' ambition does not, however, end here. Rather, the Proem proposes that these sketches serve a moral function, in addition to this more epistemological purpose. By reading the *Characters,* Theophrastus says, both his and Polycles's sons will somehow be made "better."[17] The Proem outlines two ways in which this instruction will work. Their sons should first use this text as "a guide" (*paradeigmata*) to navigate which kind of people they should solicit and which they should avoid so that they can learn "to associate with and become close to the finest men." By mixing with these people, their sons will then secondly develop an understanding of how not to "fall short" (*katadeesteroi*) of their standards: they will learn from others how to be excellent themselves.[18] The Proem thus presents the *Characters* as a set of models for how to ensure that one chooses to associate with people who are virtuous and as a key to how to become virtuous oneself. In other words, it outlines a morally instructive as well as an empirically clarifying purpose for the text: the *Characters* will not only reveal the two distinct classes of men it has observed, but it will do so in order to teach its readers how to associate with the best men and therefore how to become good. This moral reading is compounded by a set of epilogues added to several characters, perhaps also by this unknown writer, that highlight how readers should mobilize these portraits for their own good.[19] "Men like this you must flee at top speed if you want to stay unscathed," now reads the conclusion to the sketch of the Idle Chatterer, as "it is hard to stand people who don't care whether you are busy or free."[20]

As the medieval manuscript tradition preserved both the Proem and the epilogues, a series of early modern Latin translators and editors approached Theophrastus's work with this moral intention in mind.[21] But the Proem left these editors with a difficult task on their hands. How to make sense of these moralizing claims, given that the *Characters* only contained a set of vices without corresponding virtues? How to frame this text as a guide to associating with "the finest men" from these portraits of their opposites? And how to give these ordinary vices, each represented by what might have seemed like figures from farce, ancient comedy, *commedia dell'arte*, or carnival plays, the solemn dignity the Proem conferred on them?[22] From Vienna to Nuremberg, Basel to Venice, Paris to Leipzig, Frankfurt to Lyon, editors and translators came up with their own explanations for precisely how Theophrastus's ordinary vices would work the Proem's claimed moral effects. These editors and translators' arguments are instrumental in explaining why, across sixteenth-century Europe, the *Characters* became so extraordinarily popular to edit or translate. "The printing presses," declares the preface to the thirteenth printed edition of the *Characters* that had been published that century, "began to be fired up by this little work" that was designed to "refine uneducated and roughhewn morals" and "investigate the natures of virtues and vices."[23] This chapter is concerned with this striking ethical reading of the *Characters*, an interpretative tradition that is first seen in print in 1517 and concludes with the brilliant philologist Isaac Casaubon's celebrated editions at the turn of the century.

This ethical interpretative tradition of the *Characters* has not, however, been studied in detail, as literary historians and classicists have both preferred to focus on Casaubon's magisterial editions, rather than on those that preceded them.[24] In both Boyce's and Smeed's major studies on the literary impact of the *Characters,* when discussion turns to the Latin reception, only Casaubon's editions are given detailed consideration. The classicist James Diggle, in his account of the early printed copies of the *Characters,* similarly skates over the editions before Casaubon's, citing their philological inadequacy.[25] Donald Beecher writes that that the sixteenth-century editions of the *Characters* were in fact read "principally as a philological challenge," a point echoed by the literary historian Richard Squibbs in his affirmation that "earlier manuscript and print works containing some of the Theophrastan characters were studied mainly for philological purposes."[26]

But if we look closely at the many editions before Casaubon's, we find a rich story in which a set of humanists developed three distinct arguments about how bad examples of ordinary vices could teach readers how to behave. For the fifteenth-century Italian humanist Lapo da Castiglionchio the Younger, the *Characters* shows us how to discern other people's natures in order to better manage them. For Willibald Pirckheimer, the Nuremberg philologist, patron, and friend of Albrecht Dürer, the *Characters* provides a novel means of social control and a vehicle for corrective self-reflection. For Leonhard Lycius and Frédéric Morel, Theophrastus's collection is a pedagogical device for encouraging children to avoid adopting bad habits. In their focus on vice, each of these answers turns the usual humanist emphasis on the imitation of virtue on its head: indeed, each one considers portraits of typical ugly behaviors to be just as important as the popular tradition of writing exemplary lives. In developing their arguments, these humanists were responding to the tricky problem posed by the Proem. It is in the prefaces, dedication letters, and other paratexts of their editions of the *Characters* that we find their surprising solutions. Taken as a cohesive set, the Latin editions of the *Characters* not only present a "philological challenge" but also offer the reader a challenge that is distinctly moral. This chapter homes in on the editions with the richest prefatory material, though this moral reading can also be found in more minor details, as we will see.

If the Proem ignited its readers to approach the *Characters* with these particular moralizing intentions in mind, encouraging them to mine portraits of men with bad timing for signs of instruction and revelation, several other factors helped fan the flames. These readers were aware that Theophrastus was Aristotle's successor at the Lyceum—"leader of the Peripatetics after Aristotle" as one title proudly claims—and, in several cases, that he was an important botanist, metaphysician, and philosopher of the senses in his own right.[27] They were often also further familiar with the study of character as an important part of ancient philosophy, as Aristotle's *Ethics* had made its way into Latin translation long before.[28] Armed with this context, these Latin editors and translators retained additional grounds on which to base a reading of the *Characters* as providing moral guidance. This did mean, however, that they needed to justify how exactly these bad examples might serve the end of helping transform a reader's actions for the better. It is in these justifications that we find a curious aesthetic: one of moral instruction by bad example.

Lapo: Managing Other People

The first Latin translator to rise to the challenge of the Proem was Lapo da Castiglionchio the Younger, whose circa 1435 manuscript translation of Theophrastus's text (complete with the Proem and Characters 1–15) was printed in Vienna in July 1517, edited by the humanist Johannes Gremper.[29] This Vienna edition is the text's *editio princeps*—both in terms of primacy and influence—not Willibald Pirckheimer's 1527 edition, as has often been claimed.[30] It contains a set of prefaces that emphasize the moral use of the text and specifically direct the reader to see the *Characters* as a means of perfecting the art of government.

It is not clear exactly where Gremper came across Lapo's manuscript, but it would not have been out of place in his collection of ancient texts—one of which he had acquired from the Hungarian King Vladislaus II, who had granted Gremper access to the renowned Hungarian library, the *Bibliotheca Corviniana,* when Gremper visited the court as part of a diplomatic mission.[31] Lapo's translation is prefaced by Gremper's own dedication to Andrea del

Burgo (an ambassador to the king of Hungary and Bohemia) and a poem by the humanist Philip von Grundel (Figure 2.3).[32] Of the three, Grundel is the first to alert the reader to the moral use of Theophrastus's *Characters*. Aware that Theophrastus's work on botany had already been translated into Latin and recently printed, Grundel ventures a striking comparison.[33] The *Characters* "has been torn out of the underworld itself" and given a "gift of Latinity," to rival Cicero, he explains,

> So that following the advice of this man, by whose teaching
> We already sow and study green plants correctly,
> We may identify and uproot with swift art
> The lupin that is harmful to the soul, the fruits of the darnel
> That choke the sacred crop of virtues, and the heavy burdock.[34]

The *Characters* here becomes a moral version of Theophrastus's works on botany: teaching the reader "to identify and uproot" not bad plants—the poisonous lupin, the darnel weed, and the prickly burdock—but bad people. And Grundel's choice of plants here is not arbitrary. Theophrastus's *Historia plantarum* describes how the lupin "does not admit of cultivation" and how wheat and barley "degenerate and change" into darnel weed.[35] Taking this comparison all the way through the poem, with a further pun on "fruitfulness," Grundel concludes by entreating the reader to peruse "this little book, whoever you are, / And its fruitfulness, novelty and style will please."[36] While Grundel's poem gives a moral valence to the text, it leaves the reader with the question of how exactly to follow Theophrastus's "advice." Are we to use Theophrastus to identify bad qualities in ourselves or in others? Should we be practicing an "emotional horticulture" to control our own dangerous passions or a political horticulture to control for the dangerous passions of other people?[37] Gremper's subsequent dedicatory letter does not really help answer this question. More concerned with flattering Burgo than with elucidating the text, all that Gremper gives the reader in the way of explanation is that just as the *Characters* was "born of much practical experience of things," it would be an especially apt gift for an ambassador, who is "most expert in diverse affairs."[38] This leaves the real work of explaining the *Characters*' precise moral claim to Lapo.

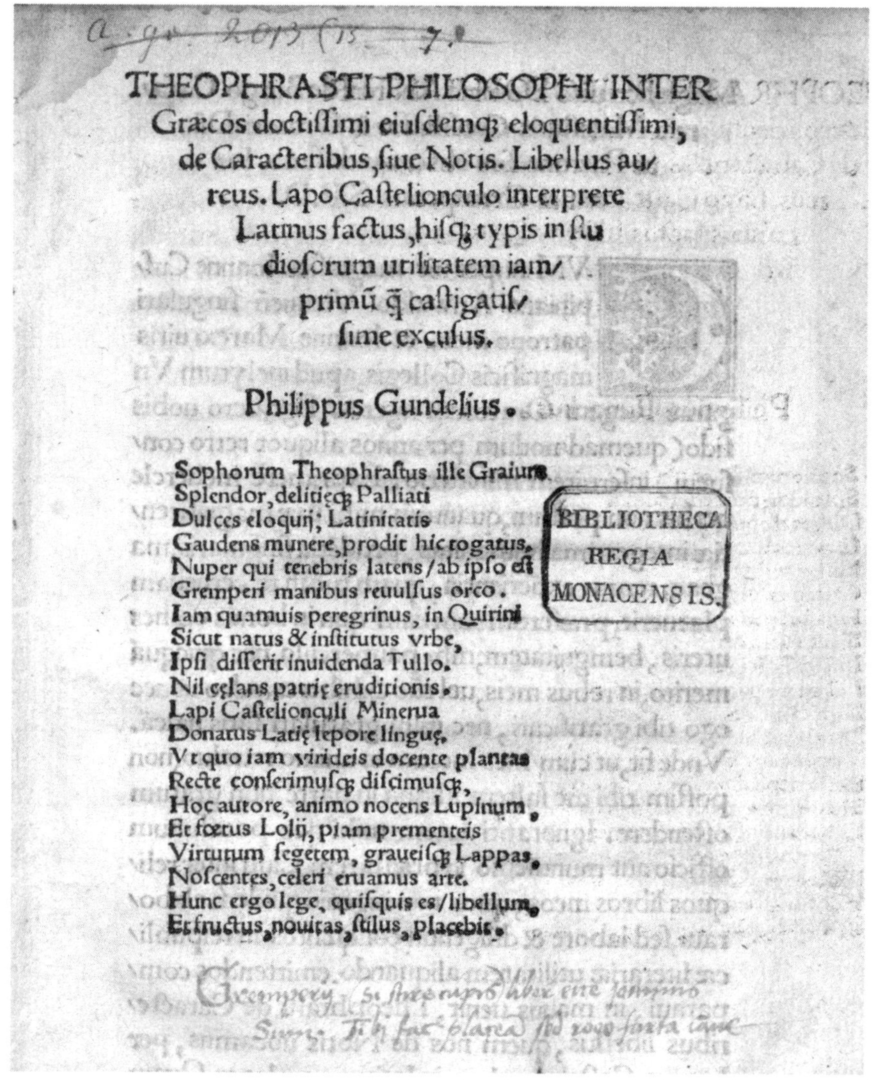

THEOPHRASTI PHILOSOPHI INTER
Græcos doctiſſimi eiuſdemq; eloquentiſſimi,
de Caracteribus, ſiue Notis. Libellus au/
reus. Lapo Caſtelionculo interprete
Latinus factus, hiſq; typis in ſtu
dioſorum utilitatem iam/
primũ q̃ caſtigatiſ/
ſime excuſus.

Philippus Gundelius.

Sophorum Theophraſtus ille Graium
Splendor, delitięq; Palliati
Dulces eloquij; Latinitatis
Gaudens munere, prodit hic rogatus,
Nuper qui tenebris latens / ab ipſo eſt
Gremperi manibus reuulſus orco.
Iam quamuis peregrinus, in Quirini
Sicut natus & inſtitutus vrbe,
Ipſi diſſerit inuidenda Tullo.
Nil cęlans patrię eruditionis.
Lapi Caſtelionculi Minerua
Donatus Latię lepore linguę,
Vt quo iam virideis docente plantas
Recte conſerimuſq; diſcimuſq;,
Hoc autore, animo nocens Lupinum,
Et foetus Lolij, piam prementeis
Virtutum ſegetem, graueiſq; Lappas,
Noſcentes, celeri eruamus arte.
Hunc ergo lege, quiſquis es / libellum,
Et fructus, nouitas, ſtilus, placebit.

FIGURE 2.3. Philip von Grundel's prefatory poem to the 1517 *editio princeps* of the *Characters*. *Credit:* Bayerische Staatsbibliothek München, A.gr.b.1276, A1r.

Lapo's dedication seems to be addressed to the Paduan humanist Francesco dal Legname, a fifteenth-century Papal chamberlain.[39] Lapo begins by justifying his choice to work on a Greek text. Greek writers, rather than Latin writers, Lapo claims, "better and more copiously pursued" topics "concerned with the direction and governance of the republic, the administration of private affairs (. . .) the education of children, the restraining of desire, and the moral instruction of men."[40] Lapo argues that Theophrastus's book of *Characters*, billed as having been written by a "very distinguished philosopher," is a clear representative of this kind of work.[41] In it, he continues,

> very many vices are collected and are so variously, distinctly, urbanely, and elegantly expressed that the light of the teaching of Aristotle (of which he was a follower) clearly appears in him. Wherefore (unless you chance to disdain it) I think that you can reap from it a large amount of advantage—for what could be more useful or more fitting for someone like you who is in charge of administering the most important affairs, and wishes to do so with dignity, than to grasp certain signs and marks by which he could distinguish the souls of men, their varied and multiple natures, and control them with intelligence and wisdom?[42]

With this, Lapo establishes the *Characters* as having a number of fundamental qualities. He declares it to be a text that collects only "vices" (contra to the Proem), he associates it with moral philosophy through a methodological connection with Aristotle, and he indicates that it is a work from which "a large amount of advantage" can be derived.

Lapo's decision to closely associate Theophrastus with philosophy, and in particular with Aristotle's method, was a choice also made by many later editors, who repeatedly printed the *Characters* together with Aristotle's works and other ancient philosophical writing. Claude Auberi's 1582 Basel edition sandwiches the *Characters* between Aristotle's *Nicomachean Ethics* and selections of Pythagoras collected under the title *Fragmenta Ethica*.[43] A 1584 Frankfurt edition similarly places the *Characters* in a Greek volume of Aristotle's *Opera*. And in 1589, the *Characters* became one of four works extracted in the *Thesaurus philosophiae moralis*, a treasury of moral philosophy, alongside Cebes's *Table* (a likely pseudonymous dialogue written in the first century BCE or CE in which an old man explains an allegorical painting of vices and virtues to a group of young people); Epictetus's *Enchiridion*, or "handbook" (a second-century CE Stoic manual of ethical advice); and, again, the Pythagorean *Fragmenta Ethica*.[44]

Lapo's argument about the utility of the book was to prove more singular. He proposes that the *Characters* exposes "certain signs and marks" through which its reader can learn to "distinguish" other people, understand their natures, and thus "control them" (*moderari*) with "intelligence and wisdom." Lapo clarifies that this work will particularly interest those who, in his elusive phrase, are "in charge of the administration of the most important affairs." At first sight, this compliment may seem conventional, fitting into humanist strategies of flattery, such as Angelo Poliziano's hope that Lorenzo de Medici will "find a patch of time" in the midst of his occupations to dedicate himself to reading the *Enchiridion*.[45] However, Lapo is not here excusing himself for impeding on dal Legname's busy schedule but suggesting that the *Characters* may help dal Legname better operate within it. This is a tactical choice worthy of mention. Lapo's description of those who are "in charge of the administration of the most important affairs" seems to refer to people who, like dal Legname, encounter people of all different types, whose qualities they are entrusted to discern. The *Characters*, Lapo hopes, is a text that not only will help its readers recognize the vices of others but, on the basis of this recognition, learn how to better engage with them. As Lapo concludes, "For as no one could excel in any art, if he does not know the use of the tools that he needs," no prince can excel "if he has not deeply and excellently scrutinized those men, whom he uses like instruments to get things done."[46] It is through "this little book," Lapo promises, that dal Legname will learn how to do so.[47] To be able to understand the men at his disposal, to work out whom he should use as a tool or instrument, dal Legname needs Theophrastus.

In this way, Lapo's reading extends an aspect of the moralizing purpose established for the *Characters* in the Proem, which positions Theophrastus's text as a guide to the social world. This aspect of the *Characters* coheres with the Italian Renaissance's interest in texts (ancient and modern) that provide a means of navigating the daily practice of social relations.[48] Rather than suggesting that this guide will help the reader to get close to men of the finest sort—a reading that would depend on the representation of virtue—Lapo here inverts the power dynamic, positioning the *Characters* as advice to a man of the finest sort about how to best deal with those around him who are not good. If both readings imagine the *Characters* as a text that helps its reader better judge others, only Lapo's version requires bad examples alone to do so. While Lapo's argument shares with the Proem a similar scaffold and structure, it also differs in its aim: rather than presenting the *Characters* as a text that can transform the reader's virtue, he positions it as a text that can transform the reader's ability to handle other people's vice. The later Latin translators, however, would shift away from this emphasis on reacting to other people's behavior. Instead, they came to focus more directly on the question of fashioning one's own. Stephen Greenblatt's famous argument about self-fashioning as a process of shaping one's own "consistent mode of perceiving and behaving," while not applicable to Lapo's edition, would become central in the editions that followed.[49]

Pirckheimer: Self-Correction

A second and rather different approach to the transformative effects of the *Characters* emerged in the next Latin translation to appear: Pirckheimer's 1527 edition, published in the newly Lutheran Nuremberg. This edition presents the *Characters* as a vehicle for self-reflection and correction of the reader's own behavior.

Pirckheimer had received a Greek manuscript of the *Characters,* including the Proem and the first fifteen sketches, from Gianfrancesco Pico della Mirandola (the nephew of the more famous Giovanni) in September 1515.[50] Gianfrancesco wrote to Pirckheimer explaining that he hoped to use the *Characters* to redeem "the debt" he owed him. This followed a conversation that the two men had enjoyed the year before in Innsbruck about Gianfrancesco's *De reformandis moribus oratio,* a discourse Gianfrancesco intended to address to Pope Leo X on the need for ecclesiastical reform.[51] Though we do not know precisely what "debt" Gianfrancesco has in mind, there is a symmetry between the gift of the *Characters* and Pico's text about reforming actions. Several years later, a connection between the *Characters* and the improving of mores became very clear to Pirckheimer when he decided to send his edition of Theophrastus's text to Albrecht Dürer, explaining how it could help remedy people's corrupt customs.

Pirckheimer and Dürer were very close. Having become neighbors in the 1490s, they developed a relationship that some say was like one between servant and master, artist and patron, subject and lord.[52] Others have described it as one in which Pirckheimer "combined the roles of surrogate father, tutor of classical mythology, door-opening mentor, and something like dorm-mate."[53] In 1506, Dürer wrote to Pirckheimer, saying, "I have no other friend on earth like you." After Dürer died in April 1528, Pirckheimer confided to Johann Tschertte that "with Dürer, I have truly lost the best friend I had on earth."[54] Dürer made several portraits of his friend, including a silverpoint sketch of Pirckheimer laughing in 1503—which has an erotic Greek phrase scratched into it, written in Pirckheimer's hand—as well as a more sober engraving of Pirckheimer in furs in 1524.[55] While exchanges of gifts and goods were common between these two friends, with Pirckheimer asking Dürer to pick him up precious stones, Greek manuscripts, and birds' feathers while the artist was in Venice, this was the only occasion on which Pirckheimer gave Dürer a book.[56] Why was it this Greek text that he decided to dedicate to Dürer? What purpose did he want his new Latin translation to serve, and why did he choose to send it at this moment in time—so many years after he had received the *Characters* as a gift from Gianfrancesco? These questions, for the most part, remain unanswered.[57] Tentative responses, however, lie embedded within the text of the dedication.[58] In recovering them, we find an alternative reading of how Theophrastus's sketches of vice might have moral import.

Pirckheimer's dedication begins by describing Theophrastus as having depicted "human feelings."[59] Although the "feelings" that Theophrastus represents do not correspond, as we know, to the more dramatic capital vices, Pirckheimer insists on taking them very seriously. These feelings, according to Pirckheimer, are held in "the deepest recesses of the heart" and are kept there, "most of the time," through law and education.[60] They only "erupt" from their concealment if they have "occasion to do so," and this occasion is when "the fear of lawgivers and pedagogues, by which they have long been constrained and suppressed has been removed." At this point, vices burst out into the light of day "and show themselves openly." This sentence contains within it an argument of political philosophy—that the fear of the law and educators is needed to keep vices at bay. But it is also a contemporary political comment, as for Pirckheimer, "the age we live in makes clear beyond all others" that this philosophical principle is "wholly true." The problem of "the age we live in," Pirckheimer clarifies, is that "an excess of freedom" has produced "an excess of contempt," that people are no longer afraid of "lawgivers and pedagogues" and are now therefore contemptuously showing their vices "openly."[61] This new lack of submission to authority means, as Pirckheimer's dedication continues, that when lawgivers and pedagogues preach the truth, they are ignored rather than obeyed. The result is that "everywhere the truth is preached, yet at the same time what truth demands is least performed, just as if the kingdom of God were better brought about by mere words than by works."[62]

This comparison betrays Pirckheimer's preference for salvation by "works" (i.e., good actions) rather than by "mere words," exposing his "disillusionment," as Jeffrey Ashcroft describes, "with the failure (. . .) of the Lutheran reformation to improve personal and social morality."[63] While, for Luther, salvation is "instilled in us without our works by grace alone," Pirckheimer here reveals his belief that works were still needed to achieve salvation and that preaching was not enough to bring it about.[64] Pirckheimer had hosted Luther at his house in 1518 and had even been included in the excommunication bull against Luther in 1521. Yet by the time he wrote this dedication six years later, he had begun to disavow the Reform. This major change is sometimes attributed to his problems with Luther's rejection of free will, sometimes to Luther's position on the Eucharist, and sometimes to the major disturbance of the Peasants' War (1524–1525).[65]

Ashcroft's note on Pirckheimer's disenchantment with Lutheranism concludes by directing the reader to a letter that Pirckheimer sent to Johann Tschertte in the autumn of 1530. Here, Ashcroft argues, the theme is "expressed again more forcibly."[66] In this letter, Pirckheimer mentions again the gap between preaching and performance, complaining to Tschertte about "how far apart the Lutherans' words are from their works" and clarifying the importance of works for salvation. "Yet I know full well," Pirckheimer writes, "that each and every one shall receive reward according to his works, for it is not in our words but in our works that the strength of our faith is manifest."[67] The major revelation of this letter, however, lies in Pirckheimer's narration of the precise events that led him to this conclusion:

> The common man has had the Gospel taught him in a way that makes him think that all goods should be equally divided, and truly, if it had not been for Providence and armed force, there would have been a general looting, as indeed did happen in many places.[68]

Pirckheimer here betrays not only a general disillusionment with Lutheranism but a particular concern with the connection between Lutheranism and the Peasants' War, perceiving that the new way in which the Gospel was being taught was partly responsible for the uprising.[69] If we can read back into the dedication of 1527 the context that Pirckheimer makes explicit in this very similar letter of 1530, its reference to an "excess of contempt" seems to gesture to the political commotion of the Peasants' War: a war that had finished two years earlier, in which the Nuremberg council played a key role, and that was spoken about frequently in terms of looting—notably by Luther, in his 1525 tract "Against the Robbing and Murdering Hordes of Peasants."

The urgency of Pirckheimer's decision to send the *Characters* to Dürer in 1527 then seems a little clearer. Pirckheimer lived through the uprising, perceiving it to be an outbreak of disobedience and a fearlessness of the peasants toward authority: a concern echoed in Luther's analysis that "they have sworn to be true and faithful, submissive and obedient . . . they are breaking this obedience" (and later in Engels's notion that the war released a previous "old habit of submission inherited from generation to generation").[70] Pirckheimer understood that preaching was not reforming morality but encouraging what he saw as vice. For this reason, he was looking for an alternative approach to moral education, one that would transform people's actions, not only their beliefs. His options for what this alternative could be were, however, limited. He did not think that the swarm of vices that concerned him could be stopped by lawgivers preaching "the truth" as these lawgivers no longer commanded any authority or inspired any fear. Nor did he think that these vices could be tempered by personal criticism of particular behavior, as "we are all now so sensitive that no one can bear to hear his vices reproved."[71]

This is where Theophrastus's *Characters* comes in. "Nothing," Pirckheimer says, would be "more useful" for a person who is too sensitive to criticism than reading the kinds of book of which the *Characters* is the "most excellent" example.[72] The *Characters*, he thought, could reform morals where preaching and critique could not by virtue of two of its qualities. First, it operates by delighting rather than admonishing its readers: a text "suffused with acid wit" that "frolics most playfully about the heart," it does not need to rely on the now-absent political emotion of fear.[73] Second, it encourages a process of corrective self-reflection that indirectly takes place while reading, avoiding any pointed reproach or critique. The political context and purpose of this text helps make some sense of the later editorial decision by Melchior Goldast, who, when reprinting it in 1610, classified the *Characters* within the section of Pirckheimer's work entitled "Politica."[74]

The *Characters* is the kind of book, as Pirckheimer continues, "in which each of us can contemplate the condition of his own soul as if in a mirror, and by contemplating improve it."[75] These sketches of vice depict characters who you can, tellingly in our contemporary expression, "see yourself in," inviting readers to identify with the vices and then, by a process of contemplation, to rid themselves of those vices that they feel they share. Just as you correct aspects of your body when contemplating your reflection in a mirror, Pirckheimer hopes that the reader will correct aspects of their soul when reading and contemplating a text that is like a mirror.[76] This introduces an unusual aesthetic process for what happens when a reader encounters images of vice. Pirckheimer did not believe that seeing the embodiment of these vices would give readers license to carry them out, as Plato had feared.[77] Nor did he believe that these vices had to come to bad ends so that readers would avoid them for the sake of escaping similar consequences in their own lives. Rather, he saw the *Characters* as initiating a process of moral instruction through a mechanism of negative imitation: where a reader identifies with a character and then decides to avoid the very behavior that made them similar to this character in the first place.[78]

This inverts an aesthetic that was ubiquitous across the newly Lutheran cities: seeing art as the provision of good moral examples to imitate. As Gerald Strauss puts it, in the newly reformed towns of the 1520s, moral indoctrination by good example was not only common but a "matter of urgency."[79] If Luther did not think that "works" would achieve salvation, he did think that man was free to choose to follow "the righteousness of the civil and moral law," and it was often to these precepts that this indoctrination tended.[80] Texts of all genres were published with characters that showed "exemplary qualities in every life situation," civil, moral, and familial.[81] Commentaries on classical texts were equally produced to highlight when characters displayed Protestant virtues, with Telemachus, for instance, being read as "an example of a child's most pious duty, the obedience and reverence he owes to his father."[82]

In Strauss's judgment, the only artistic form used by the Lutherans that succeeded in this endeavor was the drama, while the novels, with "their stilted and preachy tone and their cloying sentimentality, rob them of all verisimilitude."[83] Pirckheimer's approach to the *Characters*, then, seems to have emerged from this Lutheran reformer tradition, even if it daringly reversed its central tenet by highlighting the moral use of characters of ordinary vice rather than virtue. But by showing us ourselves "as if in a mirror," the *Characters* would have excelled the reformers' images and texts in its degree of mimesis, all the while holding the same potential for "the alteration of the human personality."[84] Pirckheimer's play with the Lutheran aesthetic of moral exemplarity did not, however, prevent Lutherans from picking up the *Characters*. In fact, all but two of the century's subsequent editions were published in Protestant cities or by editors affiliated with the Reformation.[85] One explanation for this may simply be the well-understood connection between Lutheranism and the currents of German classical scholarship, as exemplified in figures such as Philipp Melanchthon, Andreas Osiander, Wolfgang Capito, and Jacob Wimpfeling.[86] But it could also be the case that these editors found the *Characters* to fit into discourses of exemplarity, which could be made supple enough to incorporate negative imitation, as Pirckheimer intuited.

If this goes some way to explain why Pirckheimer decided to print an edition of this Greek text in 1527, it does not yet shed light on why he thought to send it to Dürer. A sense of Pirckheimer's aims here can be found in two moments of the dedication, where he hints at how much the sketches in the *Characters* are like written images, and intimates that Dürer will be tempted to draw versions of them himself. Pirckheimer opens by saying that he is giving

Dürer this little book because "you who excel in the art of painting would perceive how skilfully the old and wise Theophrastus was able to depict human feelings," a linking together of Dürer and Theophrastus's respective arts.[87] Pirckheimer returns to this point at the end of the dedication, where he asks Dürer to "be so kind as to accept this graphic picture which Theophrastus has penned." He clarifies that "if you are not able to imitate it with your own brush, then at least turn it over diligently in your mind."[88] By phrasing his request in this way, Pirckheimer seems to presume that Dürer will necessarily try to imitate Theophrastus with his "own brush," the only question being whether or not he will succeed.

This implicit invitation for Dürer to make images of this text—perhaps to accompany Pirckheimer's translation—furnishes a possible explanation of the link between the dedication's argument about the ethical value of the *Characters* and its addressee.[89] Dürer had previously illustrated Pirckheimer's Latin translation of Horapollo's *Hieroglyphica,* so this request would have had a precedent.[90] Moreover, the subject of the *Characters* was not so different from the allegories that Dürer was used to engraving or the popular types that Pirckheimer knew Dürer often copied from instructive playing cards, which themselves delineated people into clearly identifiable types.[91] Dürer's own "Discourse on Aesthetics" in the third of his *Four Books of Human Proportion* (posthumously published by Pirckheimer in 1528 but written progressively in the early 1520s) is much occupied with discussions of character and type.[92] For Dürer, there are twenty-six basic human types, and familiarity with these categories, alongside consistent geometrical principles, will allow an artist to portray whatever is in front of them: a sitter old or young, black or white, weak or strong, choleric or kind.[93] In his view, strong people, for example, "have a hard stamp like lions," a comment that harks back to the Greek etymology of "character."[94]

Pirckheimer thus seems to have had good reason to suspect that the *Characters* would interest Dürer. And if Dürer had created a set of Theophrastan images, they would have appealed to a public who had otherwise been left unconvinced by admonishing preachers.[95] In fact, they might even have had a larger reach than the text itself. The power of images was something that Nuremberg officials understood well, having banned all images of Luther in 1524 in the knowledge that political persuasiveness on a large scale lay more in printed pictures than it did in words.[96]

Having received the *Characters* seven months before he died, Dürer sadly did not leave any trace of an attempt at sketching a Theophrastan vice, preventing Pirckheimer from achieving this ambition. In his last months, Dürer instead spent his time painting society figures and returning to older religious imagery: his only listed images from this period are titled *A Headdress of a Nuremberg Lady, Christ Bearing the Cross,* and *Anvil of the Heart.* But if it was a decision, and not simply fate, that led Dürer to ignore Pirckheimer's proposition, we might find an explanation in the ethical import with which Pirckheimer presented the *Characters.* Dürer had spent his career distancing himself from an ethical approach to art as a careful strategy in a moment of censure and iconoclasm. In a 1513 draft to the introduction of his *Handbook on Painting,* Dürer expressed the view that art is outside of moral categories: just as a sword can be used "for judgement or for murder," art can be used for good or for bad.[97] He reiterated this perspective in the dedication to his later *Human Proportion,* affirming that "there is no idolatry in this art," as "no one is so mad as to worship wood, stone, metal or paint."[98] Art, for Dürer, contains neither the divine or the morally good, the devilish or the bad—a position that presented him with a solid defense against iconoclasm. If there is no essentially good or divine art, there is no essentially bad or diabolical art either. Dürer might have feared agreeing to Pirckheimer's notion that paintings of character types may work some moral or political effects, seeing it as a perverse agreement to the censorship of works that do not fit into this category.

Whatever the reason for this absence in art history, it is perhaps in part this failure to secure his alternative approach to moral reform that explains why, by 1530, Pirckheimer decided to return to a politics of fear. In his conclusion to his letter to Tschertte, he concludes that when dealing with "the common man," who has been led astray by preachers, now "nothing will avail but fear and tight defense."[99] His approach to the *Characters* nevertheless offers a strikingly original argument about how these images of vice might curiously help a set of readers learn how to become better.

Lycius and Morel: Preemptive Pedagogy

The third approach to explaining how this set of vices might instruct and inform a reader's behavior is found in two editions by Leonhard Lycius and Frédéric Morel, respectively published in Leipzig in 1561 and Paris in 1583. These two editions, far apart in time and location, resonate with one another by virtue of their shared reliance on a story taken from Spartan history to explain their understanding of the intention underlying Theophrastus's text. Both position Theophrastus's text as playing a role in the moral education of children by teaching them to laugh at the sight of vices so that they themselves will avoid adopting them in the future. Unlike Pirckheimer, they do not see the *Characters* as an attempt to correct vices that children already share with these figures; rather, they understand this text as an effort to prevent children from developing those vices in the future. And unlike Lapo, Lycius and Morel are more concerned about fashioning attributes of the reader's own self than about instructing readers on how to engage with others.

The title page of Lycius's 1561 edition bears a moral maxim by the first-century BCE Latin writer Publilius Syrus, "The wise man uses another's fault to correct his own."[100] Lycius goes on to make clear in his subsequent dedication to Gottfried Camerarius, the fifteen-year-old son of the Protestant philologist Joachim Camerarius (who himself had written a preface for a Greek edition of the *Characters* in 1541), that this maxim especially pertains to the instruction of children. Lycius begins by arguing that those who best deserve "the republic's gratitude" are those who devote their time to the education of children, "because children are not only taken in and reared for their parents but also for their country."[101] Indeed, primary schools (*ludi literarii*) should be seen as a "sort of seedbed for outstanding men who are conducive to the health of the community."[102] This makes it imperative for children to be given the best education, and Theophrastus's text, Lycius argues, offers a prime means of doing so. Through its use of examples, the *Characters* can illustrate moral lessons while arousing "emotions [*motus*] in hearers and pupils."[103] Moreover, by using examples that are not historical but "widely applicable," Theophrastus can be sure to imbue "the tender minds of children with good opinions and honorable morals," showing them characteristics and traits that they would recognize.[104] Theophrastus can do so, without risking that people will imitate the bad behavior of his types, via "some marvelous and divine regulation [*praescriptio*] of the mind," whereby once "the ugliness of moral deficiency has been seen," the reader will understand the "reason for virtue and integrity better."[105] The visual language here, in the "sight" of moral "ugliness," suggests that Lycius, like Pirckheimer, understood the *Characters* to be like images. This association would not have been unfamiliar by the mid-sixteenth century, given the growing use of emblem books for moral instruction: books that combined moral mottos with visual representations as a means of both "striking the eye and stimulating the mind."[106] This trend began with the Milanese jurist Andrea Alciato's *Emblematum libellus* in 1531, a book that was soon widely copied by many other authors.

Lycius's understanding of the moral importance of images comes to the fore in the example he chooses to better clarify this cognitive operation: "Clement of Alexandria is recommending that method of honorable instruction (. . .) in his *Paedagogus* where he teaches that 'Images [*eikones*] and models [*hupodeigmata*] are the largest part of the correct education.'"[107] This text

> uses the well-known example of the Spartans, who, renowned for the great attention that they used to pay to the education of children, wished that a part of this would be when they would take their children to see young slaves who were obliged by their masters to get drunk on wine, so that—on seeing the disorderly behavior brought on by their drunkenness—children would be educated to hate this vice and thereafter live with more moderation and sobriety.[108]

The educative notion here is that free Spartan boys, once introduced to wine through the ugly sight of "disorderly behavior" to which it can lead, will avoid the temptation of alcohol in the future, associating this vice with shame and slavery rather than freedom and pleasure. It is also no accident that the helots were forced to provide this moral lesson, rather than other freeborn boys; as members of a perceived lower social category, they would be all the less able to serve as positive paragons to imitate. The valence given to the representation of this behavior is also significant: if the helots were to seem to be enjoying themselves when drunk, the moral instruction that the sight of them is supposed to furnish would be lost. For this educative process to work, it seems essential not only that the helots' drunken behavior is "disorderly" but also that the young boys observing it are completely sober: they must watch this spectacle unfold without sharing in any aspect of the vice that produced it.

To make the Theophrastan parallel: young readers, like Gottfried, will perceive vices through their embodiment in Theophrastus's text. They will then observe that if they possessed these vices themselves, they would be ripe for ridicule, and so they will try to avoid adopting them in the future. This insistence on the *Characters*' capacity to instruct young men clearly follows the indication in the Proem that it was originally meant for Theophrastus's and Polycles's sons, an especially relevant point given the dedicatee of Lycius's translation.[109] The imagined young male readership remains constant across these contexts, something that mirrors Theophrastus's own choice of male figures. Lycius concludes his dedicatory letter as follows, complete with an intriguing suspicion about the Proem's authenticity: "It seemed right to me to procure this little book—devoted by the author (either Theophrastus or some other) to schoolboy studies (. . .)—once again for free-born children, and indeed most of all for you, dearest Gottfried."[110]

Morel's 1583 Paris edition imagines the moral instruction of the *Characters* to work in a similar way. Immediately following his Latin translation of twenty-three sketches, Morel includes a Latin translation of a comment found in his copy manuscript. He annotates this in the margin with the conjecture that it is perhaps by Polycles, the man to whom the Proem is addressed.[111] In this comment, a speaker worries about what to do with this text. "O Theophrastus," the comment begins, as it is so "difficult to catch sight of pure people," and so easy to be infected by the habits of those who are vicious, it seems that only two options remain as a means to stay upright.[112] Either one must hide away from other people, "and stay out of the light," like Timon the misanthrope, or one must chance the possibility of social contamination and risk the subsequent "alienation from virtue."[113] Both of these options, however, seem equally bad. Morel uses this complaint as a springboard for a response, which he presents in the form of an apologetic poem "in the name of Theophrastus":[114]

> You should remember the advice I gave in the Proem:
> These marks of vice can help young people,
> As it was useful once for boys born in Sparta
> To often see helots drunk on pure wine.
> Nor am I advising to avoid the eyes of men but crimes of all kinds.
> In this way you will not be like Timon, but you will be wise.[115]

With this, Morel hopes to show that the *Characters* does not place the reader in the kind of bind that the speaker describes. If the reader carefully consults the Proem, they will learn that this is a text designed to instruct young people by showing them the ridiculous sight of vice: a sight most similar to the spectacle of "helots drunk on pure wine." Bearing this in mind, young people will not need to take the extraordinary measure of misanthropy, as Timon did, or worry that other people's vices will rub off on them, but can gain moral instruction, and even wisdom. Though Morel does not directly address the risk of a reader catching vices from these sketches, he may have chosen the example of the helots to do some of this work for him, on the same presumption that freeborn boys could not be infected by their perceived social inferiors.[116] A second poem to the reader adds a further compliment to Theophrastus's text, proclaiming its deftness in combining the comic and the ethical: "Away with nimble-tongued mockers, of no seriousness, / Unimpaired is the seriousness from Lesbos, mixed with jokes."[117]

Taken together, Lycius and Morel offer one new way of understanding the moral interest of the *Characters*. Not only do they newly emphasize the way in which the *Characters* is designed to instruct the young, accommodating Theophrastus's text into the broader project of humanist pedagogy, but they also outline the importance of making the vices seem unattractive, ridiculous, or shameful, and furnish a sense that this text is designed to correct vices one might have in the future, rather than those one already shares. For Morel, this justifies printing a book of vices that some might worry will provoke more danger than it promises to heal.

Casaubon: Moral Instruction by Vice and Virtue

It is in Isaac Casaubon's influential translations—published in Lyon at the end of the century, in 1592 and 1599—that we start to see a fundamental break with several patterns evident in the Latin editions (Figure 2.4). The second of these newly incorporated five further characters (24–28), which were brought to Casaubon's attention by his friend Marquard Freher, through a manuscript in the Palatine Library in Heidelberg.[118] Casaubon worked on Theophrastus's *Characters* for over twenty years, a laborious and organic process of continual "reading, revising, and expanding" the text.[119] This was an act of philological devotion that reveals, as historian Richard Calis writes, "the intimate bond that Casaubon" forged "with his ancient philosopher."[120] One can catch a glimpse of this devotion by looking at the few inserted pages Casaubon added to his first edition to the *Characters,* containing the five new sketches. These are prefaced by Casaubon's own signature, alongside a signal of his gratitude expressed in the Hebrew phrase "Praise to God, Creator of the Universe" (Figure 2.5).[121]

Casaubon's careful study of Theophrastus's prose enabled him to clarify Greek terms that were previously seen as nonsensical. In this Casaubon worked "like a great philological laser," as Anthony Grafton and Joanna Weinberg memorably comment.[122] It was no surprise that Casaubon even impressed the towering philologist Joseph Justus Scaliger, who wrote to him to tell him how much he admired his Theophrastus.[123] This interest in Casaubon's approach to editing the *Characters* is more than understandable, given its extensiveness, erudition, and sheer brilliance. Yet it also has overshadowed the way in which Casaubon innovates not only on the scholarly methods needed to interpret Theophrastus's Greek but also on the prior moral approaches to the intent of this little book. Grafton and Weinberg, for example, seem to credit Casaubon with offering the first moral reading of the text, where, as we know, this reading was simply one of many.[124] This is not, however, to minimize Casaubon's status as an original reader of Theophrastus. Rather, in his extensive prefatory material, Casaubon hazards, for the first time, two moral approaches to the text that newly rely on the representation of both vice and virtue. One of these adumbrates an argument for both negative and positive exemplarity, and the

1

ΘΕΟΦΡΑΣΤΟΥ ΗΘΙ-
κοὶ χαρακτῆρες.

THEOPHRASTI CHA-
racteres Ethici,

ſiue,

Morum deſcriptiones.

ISAACO CASAVBONO
INTERPRETE.

SÆPE equidem iam antè quum hac de re attentius cogitare cœpiſſem, miratus ſum : ſed nec mirari fortaſſe deſinã, quid cauſę ſit cur quum Græcia omnis eidem cælo ſubiecta ſit, quum etiam Græci omnes eodem modo inſtituantur, non omnes tamen iiſdem moribus

ΗΔΗ μὲν καὶ πρότερον πολλάκις ἐπιστήσας τὴν διάνοιαν, ἐθαύμασα, ἴσως δὲ οὐδὲ παύσομαι θαυμάζων, τί δήποτε τῆς Ἑλλάδος ὑπὸ τὸμ αὐτὸμ ἀέρα κειμένης, καὶ πάντωμ τῶμ Ἑλλήνωμ ὁμοίως παιδευομένωμ, συμβέβηκεν ἡμῖμ οὐ τὴν αὐτὴν τάξιμ τῶμ

A

FIGURE 2.4. The Proem, in Casaubon's 1599 Greek and Latin facing-page edition of the *Characters*. *Credit:* Bayerische Staatsbibliothek München, A.gr.b.3228, A1r.

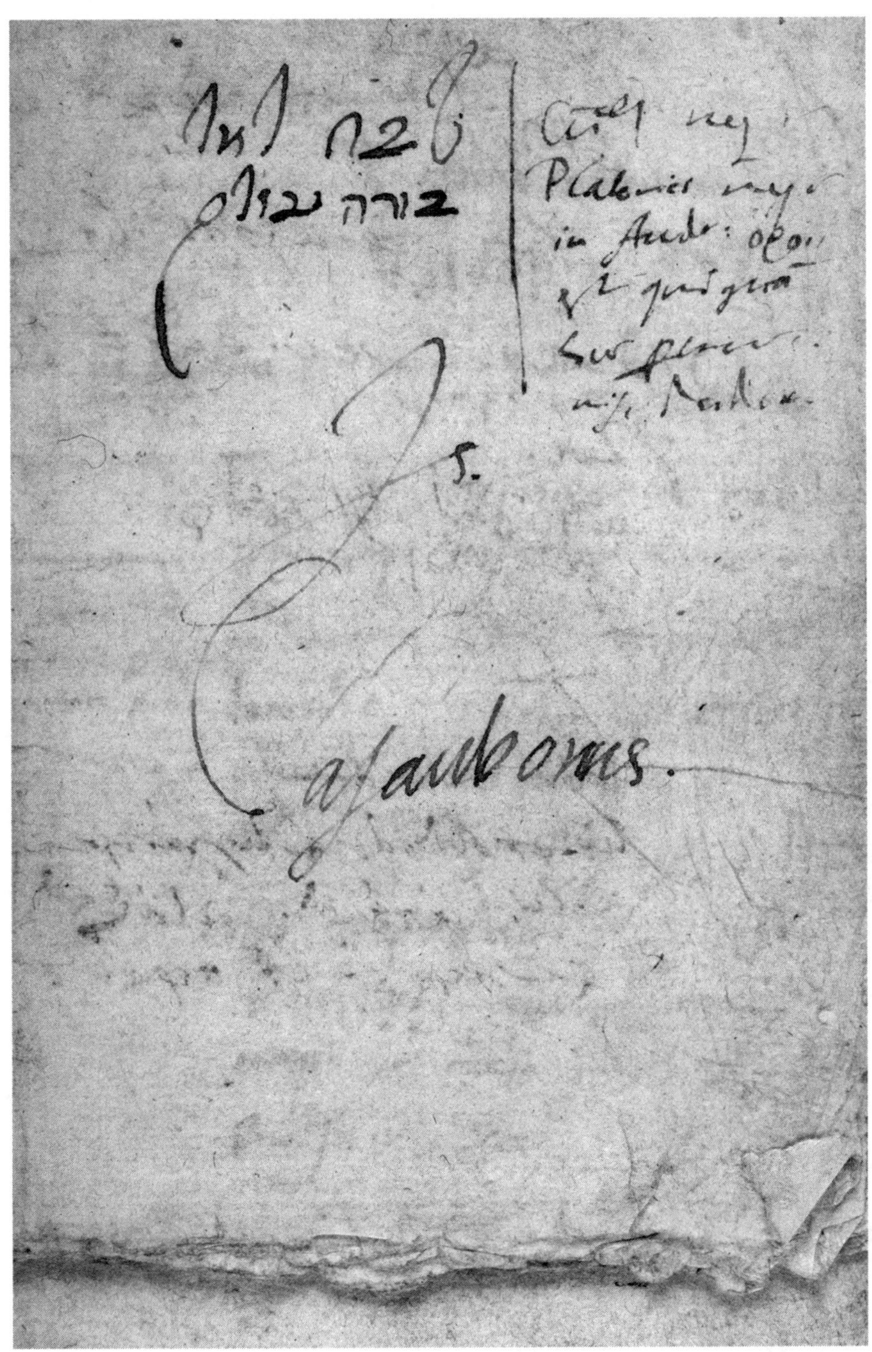

FIGURE 2.5. The opening page to the manuscript insert that Casaubon added to his 1592 edition of the *Characters*. *Credit:* British Library Collection, 525.a.10, after f. 89. © The British Library Board.

other introduces the idea that Theophrastus's sketches provide a kind of moral knowledge through mimesis.

Just like the earlier Latin translators, Casaubon maintains that the *Characters* is a work interested in improving behavior. Character-writing, he begins in his dedication to Nicolas Brûlart de Sillery and Henri IV of France, is the third and "most elegant" way that the ancients had of instructing mores, along with dogmatic philosophy and exhortatory paraenesis.[125] What is special about character-writing as a method of moral instruction is how it proposes to teach ethics through "a description of the way men endowed with this or that virtue or vice tend 'as such' to behave."[126] By providing these descriptions of behavior, Casaubon argues in the Prolegomena, "Theophrastus wanted to lead us [*praeire*] (. . .) to live a straight and honest life," a goal that could not be "more worthy of a philosopher."[127] One of the meanings of the verb *praeire* is "to dictate a formula to someone who must repeat it," providing a striking image, as Marc Escola notes, for how Casaubon thinks the *Characters* works on its reader.[128] If Theophrastus is providing the reader with characters in the same way a tutor gives a student formulas to be repeated, he is in some way intending the reader to copy what they see, making these sketches "veritable models of behavior."[129] In this, Casaubon believed, Theophrastus found a means to extend one of Plato's arguments. "Nor is it far-fetched to suppose," Casaubon writes, that Theophrastus sought out "a means by which he could display both the most beautiful appearance of virtue, and also the shameful appearance and ugliness of vices," having "learned from Plato that virtue would arouse wonderful desires for itself if discerned by the eyes."[130]

Casaubon makes even clearer how this mechanism of readerly imitation is to work when he discusses the relationship between the *Characters* and the genres of poetry, philosophy, and history. What is unique about the *Characters,* in Casaubon's view, is its position as an "intermediate genre between the writings of philosophers and poets."[131] For Casaubon, the philosopher, "dealing with virtue and vice, tells us to follow one and avoid the other."[132] "The poet and the historian," on the other hand, "do not deal with vices and virtues in the abstract, nor are they concerned with their nature or their origin."[133] Instead, they

> consider the men who are endowed with these virtues or vices: by describing the actions and customary behavior of these two groups, they provide us with examples of those whom we should imitate, and those whom we should avoid, inviting us implicitly to look closely at human life and follow the example of others.[134]

To be "an intermediate genre" between philosophy and poetry is therefore to exist between one genre concerned with abstractly promoting virtue and dismissing vice, and another concerned with displaying good and bad moral examples, for readers to follow or flee. If the former accounts for the *Characters*' intention and the latter explains its method—highlighting the way in which this form renders the abstract particular—together they describe a text with a collection of good and bad examples that aim, by encouraging imitation or avoidance, to shape a reader's behavior.

This is the first moralizing approach to the *Characters* that Casaubon outlines. He then continues, through a discussion of mimesis, to elaborate a second way in which the *Characters* is aligned with moral philosophy. Casaubon argues that it is the text's relationship with mimesis that accounts for why the *Characters* is a mixed genre between philosophy and poetry rather than philosophy and history. Despite their shared task of providing particular examples for imitation, the "great and profound difference between the historian and the poet," he continues, following book 9 of Aristotle's *Poetics*, is that "the former simply tells the facts as they happened" whereas the latter can narrate things that "may have taken place."[135] The relationship here with mimesis is that the poet's freedom from the past brings with it one new constraint: by virtue of dealing with the possible, the poet must work to make the possible seem like it really took place. The poet, Casaubon continues, must therefore provide "an acceptable image" of all they create, a demand that makes them "a *mimetes*, an imitator, as Plato also says."[136]

Casaubon emphasizes two ways in which the *Characters* betrays this degree of poetic mimesis. He describes the *Characters* through visual language: they are "images of mores" (*imagines morum*), "ethical icons" (*eikones ethon*), and "images of daily life" (*imagines vitae quotidianae*), a phrase he attributes to Cicero.[137] Casaubon also repeatedly compares the work to a mirror, using this metaphor differently from how Pirckheimer deployed it. "The mores of men had been described in the original state of this work," Casaubon argues, "in such a way that one could, in one part, contemplate as in a mirror the brilliance and most beautiful face of virtue and, in the other part, become aware of the ugliness and inappropriateness of vices."[138] Where Pirckheimer's dedication asserts that the reader will see the condition of their own soul and "by contemplating improve it," Casaubon claims that what they will see in the mirror of the *Characters* is virtue and vice in and of themselves. "The work was in fact a sort of portrait, or mirror," Casaubon continues, "in which the distinctive features of each of the virtues and vices could be distinguished and highlighted."[139] This idea that the *Characters* reveals the nature of virtue and vice undergirds Casaubon's second moral approach, which is less oriented toward shaping a reader's actions than toward furnishing them with a kind of knowledge of mores.[140]

By emphasizing how the *Characters* provides models for the kinds of behaviors "to be followed" as well as "to be avoided," and a faithful exposure of virtue and vice, Casaubon introduces a different understanding of the text's purpose, distinct from those offered by previous editors. Casaubon's two approaches are more closely inspired by the Proem's double pledge to provide both moral guidance and clarificatory knowledge, and just like the Proem, both approaches are predicated on having a text that contains virtues as well as vices. Casaubon's innovation here is that, unlike the previous editors, he does not attempt to provide an argument for how these bad examples alone can produce these effects. Instead, he asserts that the virtues must have been present in the text's original state. "Unfortunately," he says, "the best part of the work has been lost, for the part that concerned virtues is now completely lacking."[141]

In a final discussion in the Prolegomena about the meaning of the title of the *Characters,* Casaubon lays the groundwork for one further rupture with the sixteenth-century tradition: he associates the ancient practice of character-writing not only with ethics but with rhetoric and satire. Here, he connects the *Characters* with what Cicero calls *notatio* and what the Greeks called *ethopoeia,* an essential part of the orator's tool kit. He further points to how sketches in the style of Theophrastus can be found in Greek and Roman satire, particularly in Varro. Having begun lecturing on the

Roman satirist Persius around 1591, in preparation for his landmark edition of 1605, complete with its companion piece on Greek and Roman satire, Casaubon was no stranger to this tradition.[142] Casaubon did not choose to place his edition of the *Characters* with texts of moral philosophy, as the earlier sixteenth-century editors did, but instead with a section from the *Rhetorica ad Herennium* on the practice of *notatio*, and a poem from Horace's *Satires* describing a garrulous man's character.[143] These further connections also draw on two associations that had been building over the century. Namely, the rhetorical power of vividness, or *enargeia*, and the valorization of a classical aesthetic grounded on the idea of showing rather than telling, summarized in Horace's dictum that poetry is like painting: *ut pictura poesis.*[144] For these Latin translators, character sketches were a means of writing as vivid, and hence as memorable, as the metaphors that constitute poetry's verbal pictures.

Several aspects of Casaubon's break with the earlier editions had significant and lasting impact. Casaubon's insistence on the loss of corresponding virtues was picked up by the satirist and bishop Joseph Hall, who decided to add characters of virtue to his English adaptation of Casaubon's edition of the text. Hall's edition, bringing character-writing into the vernacular, in turn inspired a wave of characters in English, French, and German, several of which included virtues.[145] Since Casaubon's edition became the standard translation of the *Characters* over the centuries—"reprinted more than thirty times before 1800," as Charles B. Schmitt details—the connections that he drew with rhetoric and satire also both left their mark.[146] By 1659, the anonymous editor of a new preface to Casaubon's edition acknowledged that it was no longer sufficient to think of Theophrastus only as a moral philosopher but that the work "also provides no small use for the rhetorician, in so far as they too are concerned with customs."[147] This association with rhetoric revived the Roman classification of the *Characters,* which, as we have seen, remains a debated original intention for the Greek text. The impact is no less strong in relation to satire, with a recent introduction to satire describing how Casaubon's edition of Theophrastus "stimulated the development of a new satirical form which was to become popular across Europe for some two centuries, and whose effects continue to the present."[148]

But it is the moral import with which Casaubon, and the editors before him, endowed the *Characters* that is most surprising today. A sense that the *Characters* teaches us how to "control" other people's natures with "intelligence and wisdom," as Lapo thought; that it helps us see the ordinary vices we share with characters so that we can learn to improve them, as Pirckheimer suggested; that it ridicules behaviors sufficiently so we refuse to adopt them, as Lycius and Morel outlined; and that it stands, as Casaubon felt, as an intermediate genre between philosophy and poetry, providing examples of vice to be avoided and virtue to be imitated, as well as furnishing knowledge of moral qualities through mimesis.

The Moral Landscape

Ultimately, these moral approaches to the *Characters*—although they differed in many of their particulars—all depended on a series of four assumptions shared by the editors and translators of the Latin editions. It was these assumptions that made possible their belief that this short text offered political guidance and moral wisdom. And it was these assumptions that vernacular developments in the reception of the *Characters,* and character-writing, would come to challenge in the following centuries.

The first assumption is that Theophrastus's types could be found in contemporary society: they are not distant, historical portraits but figures that are universal and accurately described. This notion is found across the translations. Pirckheimer, for example, notes that Theophrastus shows "human feelings" (*humanae affectiones*): a choice of phrase that insists we do not see Theophrastus's *Characters* as historically specific but as being applicable to humanity in general. These ancient Athenians are no different from the sixteenth-century Germans. Similarly, in his Prolegomena, Casaubon positions Theophrastus as describing "men who are endowed with these virtues or vices" and as inviting readers to look closely at "human life" (*vitae hominum*) and follow its examples. These particular models of Athenian men are understood as types of human life as such, carrying out "customary behavior" that seems to last through the ages.

John Healey's first English translation of the *Characters,* published in London in 1616, also insists on the universality of its types. In his dedicatory letter to William Earl of Pembroke, Healey explains that Theophrastus "very lively and sharpely described those deformed vices which flourished in his time, but raigne in ours."[149] Healey is able to recognize Theophrastan characters in the people he knows not only because Theophrastus has accessed the kinds of vices that exist through time but because Theophrastus has described them with *enargeia*. These portraits are "lively" and "sharp," bringing to life the people they describe. The assumption that Theophrastus writes accurate descriptions of living people is necessary for establishing the ease with which the *Characters* can provide a form of moral instruction. It prevents the work from being read as an antiquated document describing the people of Athens and instead encourages the sense that it is a realistic description of people with whom its readers are familiar.[150] It can therefore warn readers not to fall into these types of behavior, which themselves seem both past and present.

The second assumption at work in the placement of the *Characters* as moral instruction is that there is a close relationship between reading about the actions of other people and shaping your own. This attitude coheres with an early Renaissance practice of adapting ancient texts to serve pragmatic ends, something that Lisa Jardine and Anthony Grafton found long ago in Gabriel Harvey's reading of Livy, which highlights examples in Livy for Harvey's patrons to adapt into political maneuvers.[151] Since then, a growing number of scholars have shown how, in the early modern world, imaginative writing served not only political but also ethical objectives. Enrica Zanin has described Renaissance literature as a kind of "self-help," in which readers were invited to "use" books rather than "read" them and in which there was no functional opposition between practical books and reading for pleasure.[152] David A. Lines has given an extensive account of the surprising sources in which this moral "use" was found. "Expressions of Renaissance ethics," he writes, "often lurk in extremely diverse formats and genres," from aphorisms to essays, allegories to dialogues, short stories to plays.[153] And Ann Moss, working from Erasmus's 1512 advice on how to make a commonplace book, has described the humanist method of reading as a means of ensuring morals are "stored and ready for use."[154] Humanist reading involved a way of thinking closely tied to "application."[155] The sixteenth-century reception of the *Charac-*

ters slots right into this framework. We see this in the prefatory materials to the translations, as much as in its editorial packaging. It is perhaps most evident in the decision to insert the *Characters* into the 1589 *Thesaurus philosophiae moralis,* a tiny volume designed to provide practical examples of moral precepts, which invites the reader to search for a moral quality—where O, for example, lists "Obscenitas," "Obscenitas fugienda," and "Obsequium"—and follow the pagination to a series of examples of the quality in question.[156]

Colin Burrow has also recently traced the importance of application in early modern writing: its capacity to generate other writing, a practice of what he calls "formal imitation" ubiquitous in English sixteenth- and seventeenth-century poetry, by which a "quasi-Platonic Form of an author might be imitated in new words which were suitable for new times."[157] While François Rigolot finds a "crisis of exemplarity" present in the Renaissance, due to how "the appeal of mimesis (. . .) greatly problematized the reception of ancient models," the mimetic nature of Theophrastus's *Characters* seems to have been able to extend its exemplary appeal.[158] The capacity of Theophrastus's *Characters* to provide moral instruction, then, is also keyed to a combination of discursive contexts around questions of reading, imitation, adaptation, and mimesis. Just as the *Characters* was thought to encourage negative imitation in its readers, it was imitated by translators in "new words," in order to render its insights about "human feelings" widely understood.[159]

A third assumption held by these translations is equally important in explaining the moral valence that they accorded to Theophrastus's text. All of them assume that the way we behave is who we are, that no self exists separate from the actions that an individual carries out. Casaubon makes this assumption clear when he recounts the etymology of the word "character," in an addition to the Prolegomena of his 1599 edition. Casaubon here focuses in particular on the Hebrew derivation, where variants of the Hebrew words *teva' / tava'* (טבע) mean "character," "nature," and "stamp."[160] For Casaubon, these three meanings indicate that there is a close proximity between your "stamp"—your external appearance, your habits, your behavior—and your "character" or "nature." As he writes, "The true character of each thing—its true image—is the one that best expresses its nature. For that reason, the Hebrew philosophers" use similar words for "nature," "character," and "stamp."[161]

This approach is coherent with one dominant Renaissance vision of moral philosophy, which understood virtue as "theatrical," or performative (where *performing* virtuous actions was equivalent to *being* virtuous) and saw no issue with including descriptions of customs as part of moral philosophy.[162] Indeed, as one scholar succinctly puts it, the Latin *philosophia moralis* was "directly connected to the Latin *mos* and *mores,* which referred to behavioral habits and customs."[163] The philosophical underpinnings of this vision are both Aristotelian and Ciceronian: two authors foundational to what Tuck has called the "old humanism" present in the Renaissance and whom, as we have seen, are both frequently referenced in editions of the *Characters.*[164] This vision draws, in particular, on Aristotle's notion of *hexis,* or *habitus* in Latin, an approach to moral philosophy that focuses on forming moral character through ordinary actions, as well as on Cicero's emphasis on citizens cultivating virtues to serve the republic.[165]

I say that this older humanism represents "one" Renaissance vision of moral philosophy, given the contemporaneous and growing influence of a competing "new humanism" in the work of Niccolò Machiavelli. In the early sixteenth century, Machiavelli had started to cleave apart being and seeming by arguing, to cite just one example, that the wise ruler need only to "appear" (*parere*) to have good qualities rather than actually possess them.[166] For them, this kind of dissimulation, or *dissimulatio*—the word the Latin editors often used to translate Theophrastus's first vice of "Irony"—was not a vice but a necessary virtue.[167] The older humanists did not allow for this space between what you were perceived to be and what you were. Their assumption that performing good actions equated to being good enabled them to think that a reader would be able to morally improve by avoiding the habitual behaviors of Theophrastan sketches.

The final assumption foundational to framing the *Characters* as a text of moral instruction is that there is no contradiction in this text being at once comic and instructive. Both Pirckheimer and Morel, for example, understood the *Characters* as a text that delights and instructs. Similarly, Casaubon notes in his dedicatory epistle that the teaching of morals is the most useful part of philosophy and that character-writing is a particularly beautiful way of doing so. These translators never deride the *Characters* for being too comic or too literary to be moral. Instead, they see these as qualities that go hand in hand with this text's philosophical import. In this, the translators stand in line with their century's approach to laughter.

The century of Erasmus and Rabelais, as one critic puts it, was a period "marked by the rehabilitation of laughter."[168] In the Renaissance, writes another, the comic was endowed "with new force and meaning."[169] This force was often moral, with laughter being newly theorized as a popular form of mockery, reproach, and reproval, something evidenced by the many new descriptions of laughter coined in the period, from "taunting" (1529) to "jeering" (1553) to "bantering" (1677).[170] The potentially corrective aspect of laughter offered a place for it within moral philosophy that humanists were keen to explore, asking questions about when laughter is legitimate and when it oversteps the mark. There are discussions of laughter in several sixteenth-century Italian treatises on civil conversation, including Baldassare's Castiglione's 1528 *Book of the Courtier*, Giovanni della Casa's 1558 *Galateo*, and Stefano Guazzo's 1574 *Civil Conversation*.[171] They do not see laughter as a carnivalesque means of turning the world upside down: the roaring and subversive guffaws of the people and against their princes so treasured by Mikhail Bakhtin.[172] In these treatises, laughter is more often a subtle, gentlemanly means to entrench social norms by chastising those who break them.[173]

The *Characters* would fit right into this latter category. In particular, as the humanists interested in this kind of laughter borrowed ideas from Aristotle about the pleasure of laughing at the ridiculous, as well as notions favored by the Roman rhetoricians, who specified that only certain kinds of blemishes could be mocked: ones that stood, like the ordinary vices in the *Characters*, between "outstanding wickedness" and "outstanding wretchedness."[174] A number of Renaissance theorists of laughter were especially drawn to justify laughing at miserly, vain, and self-regarding old men, as well as other figures who act "beyond measure"—many of whom are also favored by Theophrastus.[175] Beneath these accounts of laughter lay the moralizing hope that, after being ridiculed, these misbehaving characters will learn how to comport themselves better and thus help preserve the shared goods of sociability, civility, and decorum. As Giovanni della Casa wonderfully writes,

> Men fear wild beasts but have no fear of smaller animals such as mosquitoes or flies; still, because these insects are constant pests, men complain about them more often. Similarly, most people hate unpleasant and bothersome people as much as, if not more than, evil ones.[176]

When laughter came to be understood as a decisive means to correct these bothersome quotidian vices, the comic and the moral could sit hand in hand. And so, the *Characters,* with its pleasant ridiculing of old men, boasters, and misers, who do not respect the *kairos,* could easily be accorded philosophic significance in the sixteenth century. It is this fourth assumption that enables the *Characters* to serve as a text of moral instruction in this period.

These sixteenth-century translations of Theophrastus reveal a moral landscape that both gave rise to renewed interest in the *Characters* and justified how sketches of vice could improve their readers. In this landscape, there was no fixed distinction between aesthetics and ethics, or a person's nature and the behavior they displayed. It was a landscape in which types of people were imagined to be universal rather than specific to their moment in time and in which Theophrastus's *Characters* was seen to be true, somehow, to life. Perhaps most importantly, it was a landscape of imitation, avoidance, and examples, of the good and the bad. In the following century, however, some of these assumptions would begin to falter.

3

Early Modern Stoics

TWO ENGLISH ADAPTATIONS

In 1604, Theophrastus's *Characters* arrived in Oxford. But, when it did so, it was only printed in ancient Greek, without an introduction or letter of dedication, and designed to instruct translation, with the facing pages to each character sketch left blank.[1] This could have been the end of the story of the *Characters* in England, as a tricky scholastic exercise for students of classics. This, however, was not to be the case. Instead, character-writing became a frame through which the literate English of the seventeenth century saw and comprehended their period's major political events and dramas. The success of character-writing in the period is not, however, down to translations of Theophrastus's text but to the many adaptations. No less than 1,000 characters were printed in English from 1608 to 1700.[2] In these new collections of sketches, old types were adapted, updated, or simply dropped, and new characters were added: characters of virtues, professions, religions, political perspectives, nationalities, and places.

This chapter, the first of two on the English reception, focuses on the two earliest adaptations of the *Characters*: Joseph Hall's 1608 *Characters of Vertues and Vices* and an expansive, miscellaneous, and multiauthored text that has come to be known as the Overburian *Characters*, first published in 1614. Though the *Characters* had been translated into German in 1606, vernacular adaptations in German did not really take off until the eighteenth century, something that J. W. Smeed chalks up to a hiatus caused by the Thirty Years' War.[3] Likewise with the Italian translation of 1620, which might instead come down to how its Baroque translator, Ansaldo

Cebà, used his dedicatory preface not to extol the moral virtues of the *Characters* but rather to critique its "pomp."[4] The 1613 French translation, on the other hand, provoked a great wave of highly moral seventeenth-century character-writing, which I discuss in chapter 5.

Back in England, sometime before 1608, the ecumenical Calvinist Joseph Hall (1574–1656), chaplain to the Prince of Wales, later bishop of Exeter and Norwich, read Casaubon's Latin editions of Theophrastus.[5] Hall found himself particularly taken by two aspects of Casaubon's magisterial editions: Casaubon's idea that character-writing could be a novel and persuasive means of writing moral philosophy and Casaubon's intriguing suggestion that Theophrastus's thirty vices must be missing a corresponding set of virtues. When Hall decided to embark on his own moralizing adaptation of Theophrastus—having already published a number of works on religion, satire, and Stoic philosophy—he ran with Casaubon's suggestion and took the opportunity to add his own set of virtues, as well as some reworked vices. In Hall's *Characters of Vertues and Vices,* Theophrastus's name is nowhere to be found. Instead, new portraits of "The Wise Man," "An Honest Man," and "The True Friend" rub shoulders with "The Slothfull" and "The Envious," as well as with more recognizable Theophrastan sketches of "The Hypocrite" and "The Superstitious." Where the language of virtue and vice had never been far from the *Characters*—present in the spurious Proem and in the Latin commentaries—until Hall it remained in the prefatory material. Through these additions, Hall introduced the possibility of using Theophrastus's *Characters* not as a basis for faithful translation but for freer and freer adaptation—which in turn grounded new possibilities for a genre of character-writing, allowing it to become a malleable literary form used to describe the contemporary world.

To be sure, there was already a native tradition of character-writing in late sixteenth- and early seventeenth-century England. In 1599, a number of indications suggest that both Philip Sidney and Ben Jonson knew of Theophrastus's original text in Greek or Latin. John Hoskins, when recommending Sidney's pastoral romance *Arcadia* to a young lawyer as an example of excellent prose style, says that Sidney "had much helpe out of *Theophrasti imagines.*"[6] Writing that same year, William Scott also acknowledges Sidney's indebtedness to the *Characters,* praising the poetic creation of consistent "notes or *characters* (as after Theophrastus they may be called)."[7] And, while Benjamin Boyce argues that the induction to Ben Jonson's 1599 *Every Man out of His Humor* only includes "a set of near-Characters," by 1605, Jonson is credited with including the "first tangible allusions" to the *Characters* in *Volpone.*[8] This allusion occurs in a scene in which the character Peregrine reads Sir Politick Would-Be's diary, coming across the note, "A rat hath gnawn my spur leathers; notwithstanding, I put on new and did go forth; but first I threw three beans over the threshold."[9] This is a reference to Theophrastus's Superstitious Man, who, if a weasel runs across his path, will not proceed on his journey until "he has thrown three stones over the road."[10]

Non-Theophrastan character sketches and the rhetorical tool of *ethopoeia* have an equally long English history.[11] Examples of *ethopoeia* can be found in mid-sixteenth-century rhetorical manuals, character sketches appear in the writings of Thomas Nashe and Thomas Lodge and across medieval literature, and in 1605, Francis Bacon spoke of the need for moral philosophers to provide "sound and true distributions and descriptions of the several characters and tempers of mens Natures and dispositions."[12] However, before Hall, there was not yet a vernacular tradition of writing books of character sketches, which stood on their own, that were not included in a pastoral or a play. Before Hall, neither was there yet the assumption that it was possible to adapt Theophrastus's model to suit contemporary mores.

It is not, however, only the fact of Hall's adaptation that holds importance but the particular angle of adaptation that he chose. Consistent with his professional and confessional commitments, one part of Hall's manipulation of Theophrastus involved making what was once ancient Greek newly Christian, giving the secular form of character-writing a religious aspect. The text's Christian commitments emerge in the way Hall frames the collection in his paratexts, in his choice of which new virtues to depict, as well as which new vices to castigate. The other part of Hall's approach to Theophrastus comes from a different tradition entirely: Stoicism.

Roman Stoicism had been known in western Europe for many centuries.[13] Seneca and Cicero circulated widely in the Middle Ages, and it is even a "*déformation professionnelle*" in early modern history, as Jill Kraye observes, to locate the beginning of the Renaissance with Petrarch's fourteenth-century rediscovery of Cicero's *Letters to Atticus*.[14] By the sixteenth century, many new texts had been made available in Latin and in the vernacular—from Epictetus to Diogenes Laertius—and a broader corpus of Stoic ideas started to be read, admired, and critiqued by northern Europeans, as well as those further south.[15] These Stoic ideas included the valorization of self-mastery, independence, constancy, and tranquility.[16] What was later called neo-Stoicism emerged in 1584 with the publication of the Dutch humanist Justus Lipsius's *De constantia in publicis malis*: a text that, for the first time, provided a systematic treatment of Stoic philosophy, argued for its political salience, and explained its compatibility with Christianity.[17] This was a move followed by Guillaume Du Vair in his vernacular *Philosophie morale des Stoïques* (1594). In the words of Thomas James, translating Du Vair into English in 1598, "no kinde of philosophie is more profitable and nearer approaching unto Christianitie than the philosophie of the Stoicks."[18] Hall is firmly situated in this neo-Stoic tradition—a term that I use to mean the combination of Stoicism and Christianity—even if there are important differences to be drawn between his approach and Lipsius's.[19]

Hall's *Characters of Vertues and Vices* makes his neo-Stoic commitments manifest. In his adaptation of Theophrastus, he chooses to depict characters who balance Stoic and Christian philosophies. His vices castigate types who lack requisite Stoic virtues, such as "The Unconstant." His virtues, on the other hand, praise those who possess them, like "The Wise Man" who desires to know nothing more than "most and first himselfe."[20] But they also praise figures like "The Faithfull Man" who has "a cleane soule, fit to lodge God in."[21] Just as Hall's move to adapt and update the *Characters* rather than simply translate them left a legacy, his decision to infuse neo-Stoicism into character-writing also had a profound effect. In this case, it came to inform a more subtle kind of moral instruction present in the brilliant Overburian adaptation that succeeded his own.

The Overburian collection gets its name from the courtier Sir Thomas Overbury (bap. 1581–1613), who was murdered in what one literary historian has called the early seventeenth century's "most notorious scandal" and what another has described as "the nearest we can come to Jacobean noir."[22] The scandal implicated the lover of King James VI and I, Robert Carr, and his divorcée wife Frances Howard, who both allegedly killed Overbury in the Tower of London. Posthumously, Overbury had a poem of his published by the London bookseller Lawrence Lisle, entitled *A Wyfe, Now a Widowe*.[23] Overbury's name did not initially appear with his poem until it came repackaged with twenty-two "witty characters" in a second edition published later that year. A few of these characters were by Overbury, but many were by other writers and found their place in a larger volume alongside "conceited newes" and a number of response pieces and elegies.[24] In 1614 alone, Overbury's poem reached five issues, and by 1632, the volume was in its fifteenth edition, having expanded and ballooned into a collection of diverse writings by a range of mostly anonymous authors, including over eighty characters, several recipes for mountebanks, and an increasing number of the fictive forms of domestic and foreign news. The few shadowy authors of this collection who have been identified to date are John Webster, Thomas Dekker, John Stephens, John Cook, and John Ford.[25] Their sketches moved beyond the convention of depicting characters named after vices or virtues and instead began to also describe social types. One copy of the 1632 edition includes a handwritten contents page that runs from "A Wife" to "an affected Traveller" to "A braggadocio Welchman" later added by a judicious reader (Figure 3.1). Overbury's best-selling initial poem, as one scholar puts it, "did more to launch the vogue for characters and character books in the first half of the seventeenth century than any other single literary work."[26] The text continued to be frequently reissued in new editions: a scrawl in the 1632 copy attests that a 1753 edition was "The Last."[27]

On the basis of its portrayals of socio-professional characters, the Overburian volume has made its way into scholarship as the proto-scientific beginning of a qualitative documentation of the social world. In Louis van Delft's view, it is an anthropological mapping of seventeenth-century society, an idea echoed by Donald A. Beecher, who comments that the volume provides "a portrait of London as a sociological memory theatre."[28] For Élisabeth Soubrenie, in this volume we similarly find an experience of reading that transformed "into a society game."[29] Critics have further

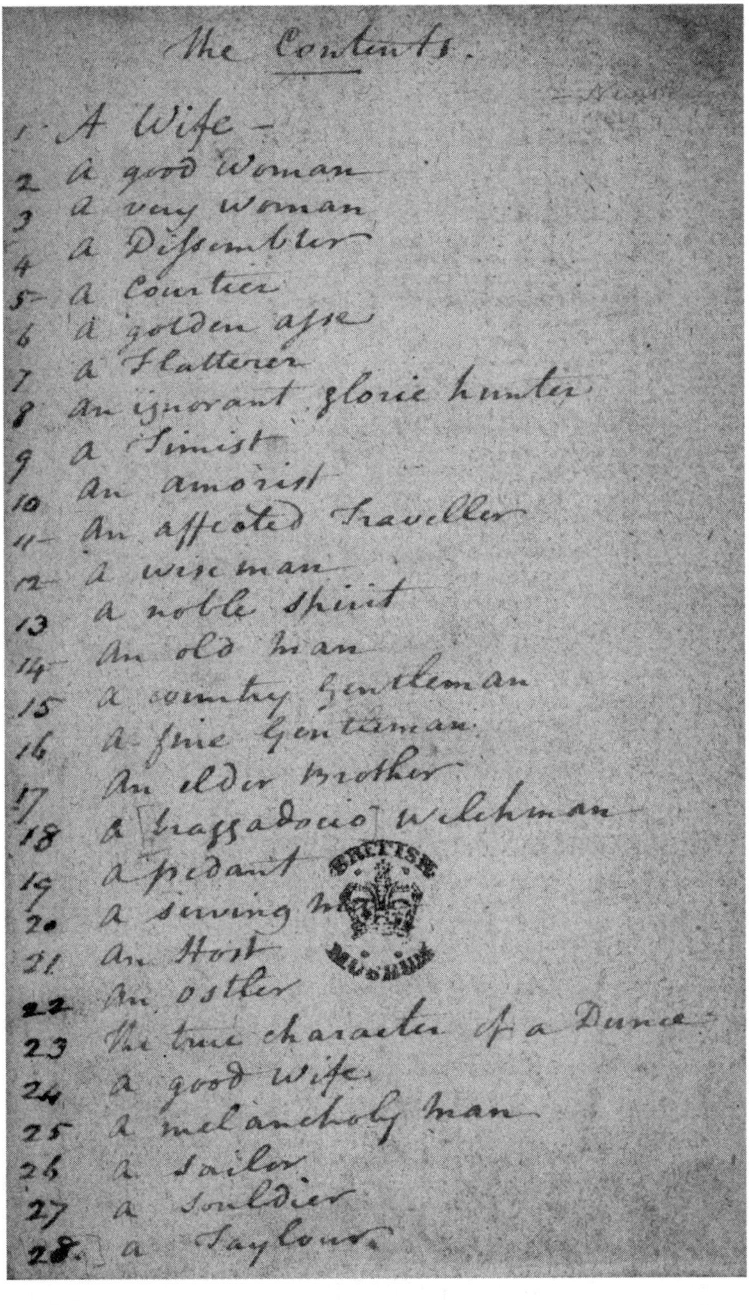

The Contents.

1 A Wife –
2 a good Woman
3 a very Woman
4 a Dissembler
5 a Courtier
6 a golden asse
7 a Flatterer
8 an ignorant glorie hunter
9 a Timist
10 an amorist
11 an affected traveller
12 a wise man
13 a noble spirit
14 an old man
15 a country Gentleman
16 a fine Gentleman
17 an elder brother
18 a [braggadocio] Welchman
19 a pedant
20 a serving man
21 an Host
22 an ostler
23 the true character of a Dunce
24 a good Wife
25 a melancholy man
26 a Sailor
27 a Souldier
28 a Taylour

FIGURE 3.1. *The "Conceited newes" of Sir Thomas Overbury* (London, 1632), with manuscript notes by Thomas Park and William Ford. This contents page enumerating the sketches was added to this edition. It looks like it was written by Park. *Credit:* British Library Collection, 1078.a.15, W2r. © The British Library Board.

claimed that the Overburian collection marks a shift into a new way of conceiving of this genre. Beecher comments that the "Overburians (. . .) discovered a gallery of idiosyncratic social types, whereas their predecessors had discovered a theater of the venial and deadly sins," and Eliane Cuvelier writes that Overbury is a key figure in the move away from allegory in the development of character in English literature.[30] Where Hall penned a work "with a clear didactic purpose," a "purely social Character," as Richard McCabe says, is thought to have been written by Overbury and his successors.[31]

It is undoubtedly true that the Overburian *Characters* depict a whole new range of social types and thereby shift character-writing away from sketching figures housed under abstract qualities, like "Patience" or "Honestie," to depicting people shaped by their professions and status. However, a clear boundary between the moral and the social need not be erected. In fact, the innovation of the Overburian set lies precisely in how it remains invested in moral instruction, just like the sixteenth-century translations before it and just like Hall's own *Characters of Vertues and Vices*. Its acuity is that it uses social types to do so: making what was once explicit and didactic now implicit and insinuating. Taking its cue from Hall, the Overburian collection finds myriad ways to instill Stoic virtues in the reader. By remaining alert to the neo-Stoic emphasis we saw in Hall, and by situating Overbury's original poem in the dramatic circumstances in which it was written, the collection's moral intent becomes evident. And this is not something only to be found, as McCabe later concedes, in the Overburian virtuous figures of the "Wise Man" and "Reverend Judge" but in figures as innocuous and quotidian as "A Button-Maker of Amsterdam."[32] This has so far been overlooked in the criticism, preventing us from seeing how writing society characters in the seventeenth century became a more covert means to encourage readers to change their behavior.

Stoicism, with its emphasis on independence and self-mastery, was not only an ethical framework but was associated with two diametrically opposite approaches to politics. On the one hand, the way in which Stoicism valorized independence meant that it came to be linked with the politics of republicanism. On the other, the way in which Stoicism valorized self-mastery grounded a politics not of political participation but of retreat. Where Hall is squarely in the latter camp, the Overburian collection often spills over into the former: setting a precedent for using character-writing to grapple with contemporary politics.

To better clarify the link between Stoicism and republicanism, one might simply comment that it is only a short distance from believing in the importance of being one's own master to believing that this kind of personal freedom could only be achieved in a state free from mastery. It is important, however, to stress that in late sixteenth- and early seventeenth-century England, there were different kinds of republicanism at play. There was a moderate "monarchical republicanism," the conviction "that it was necessary to control the powers of the crown" through a coterie of virtuous counsellors, who would work to ensure that the monarch acted within the limits of the law.[33] This was a republicanism that could work alongside monarchy. It prioritized the importance of a "mixed constitution," in which Parliament stood alongside kings and queens, and it emphasized the practical participation of citizens in the life of politics.[34] As Mark Goldie has shown, early modern England in fact lived and breathed this kind of republicanism, given that "large numbers of people undertook the self-management of their local communities."[35]

There was also, however, also a more radical republicanism on the horizon. In the words of one literary historian, "As the possibility that monarchy could ever realize the values of a 'commonwealth' came to seem more remote, 'commonwealth' or 'republic' became more and more firmly identified with non-monarchical government."[36] This antimonarchical republicanism emphasized that living under the arbitrary power of the king constitutes a kind of dependence, as it means living under "a power capable of interfering with our activities without having to consider our interests."[37] The influence of Roman authors on radical republican politics even meant that someone like Thomas Hobbes could go on to think, as one historian summarizes, "that it was mainly the influence of classical authors that was to be blamed for the Civil War."[38]

Standing at odds with this republican uptake of Stoic tenets was a politics, as Quentin Skinner succinctly puts it, of "*mastering your self* as opposed to *being your own master.*"[39] Associated with the contemplative life, with retreating into what Isaiah Berlin called "the inner citadel," this second interpretation of Stoicism saw an engagement with the world as too full of compromise to be worth one's while.[40] Instead of valorizing the forum, the whirl of Parliament, or different kinds of local responsibilities, it opts for "the seclusion of one's own home" and other spaces in which "it is possible to live for or belong to oneself."[41] Where republicanism foregrounds the assertion of an individual's will, a Stoic emphasis on retreat rather underlines its withdrawal. It is a politics that flourishes when the external world, as Berlin continues, "has proved exceptionally arid, cruel, or unjust."[42] It tells the individual to prioritize self-preservation in an unruly universe.

Though Hall's neo-Stoic framework grounds his sense of the importance of the *vita contemplativa,* in the hands of the Overburians, it is more open to encouraging political participation and includes a hint of republicanism. It is the entry of Stoicism that therefore provides the final aspect of Hall's legacy: a mixing of character-writing and a philosophy of self-mastery that filtered into the Overburian collection. In the process, character-writing became a subtle tool to encourage its readers into developing not only virtuous behaviors but also virtuous political perspectives. It is this inheritance that allowed the form to become an important and unique tool during the English Revolution, where it served as a vehicle of social and political knowledge.[43] This chapter lays the groundwork for how this happened. The movement it traces begins in 1608 with Hall's approach to character-writing as a means of neo-Stoic instruction and runs through the Overburian characters, which direct the form to related imperatives while relishing the pleasure of societal description and embodying a different approach to politics. In the history of character-writing, the movement of this chapter traces one clear arc: from explicit to implicit reform.

Joseph Hall

Historians have pointed to how Hall's *Characters* is religious in its intention, use, and effect: how it finds a conceptual basis in allegory and was principally designed as "a useful collection for preachers."[44] This has been paired with a more general move to situate Hall as "the leading Neo-Stoic of the seventeenth century," its "most thoroughgoing" representative.[45] In Richard McCabe's account, this is in part due to Hall's choice of form. The plain and terse Senecan prose style in Hall's early works—a style that prioritizes meaning over ornament and is pithy and aphoristic—is what, McCabe argues, led to Hall being called "the English Seneca."[46] Hall, in another critic's account, "talked about prose style in the same terms he used for fine clothes: he felt that excess ornament and elaboration were wicked."[47] One argument of this chapter is that neo-Stoicism is visible in Hall's adaptation of Theophrastus not just in terms of its form but in terms of the kinds of qualities he chooses to praise and denigrate. Unlocking the neo-Stoic qualities of Hall's adaptation requires an examination of the paratexts to his *Characters of Vertues and Vices* and of the specific virtues and vices that Hall chose for his collection.

Joseph Hall was educated at Emmanuel College, Cambridge, recently founded to provide a place to train candidates for the ministry in "uncompromisingly Protestant principles," as Arnold Davenport comments.[48] Hall was elected a Fellow at twenty-one and took an MA a year later. At twenty-three, he published the first part of a satirical work, *Virgidemiarum*: the first collection published in England of formal verse satires on the Latin model, which projected Hall into prominence within the literary world.[49] Hall boldly opened this work with the grand ambition to be the first "English Satyrist," and a year after it was published, the author and ecclesiastic Francis Meres confirmed that Hall had more than achieved this aim.[50] But, the following summer, in June 1599, *Virgidemiarum* was banned and burned alongside a number of other works of satire and polemic in a major act of censorship by the archbishop of Canterbury and the bishop of London directed against social criticism.[51] Hall's "private connections," as William Jones argues, seem to be what managed to get him off the hook soon after.[52] Hall's father had been deputy to the Earl of Huntington, and by 1599, Hall himself had started his training for the clergy and so had a direct line to church officials. After this complication was resolved, Hall took up a post as the rector of Hawstead in Suffolk in 1601 and married in 1603.

In 1605, Hall traveled to the Netherlands, availing himself of the opportunity to enter into theological debate with the Jesuit order. That same year, he published a first collection of *Medita-*

tions and Vowes, which shares much with his *Characters.* It contains sketches of "an ambitious man" and "a faithfull man," investigates the "causes of ingratitude"—a vice explored in his *Characters*—and advocates self-knowledge, a quality that provides the collection's central theme.[53] This volume was followed in 1606 by *Heaven upon Earth, or of True Peace and Tranquilitie of Mind,* an examination of the relationship between Senecan philosophy and Christian morality. Hall's *Arte of Divine Meditation* was published that same year: a work that introduced Continental methods of contemplation to English readers and became one of the most popular Protestant devotional texts of the first half of the century. Hall complemented these moral pieces with the anonymous printing of a work of Latin satire, *Mundus alter et idem* (1605), a dystopian journey to the Antipodes, which Jonathan Swift later used as a model for his *Gulliver's Travels.*[54] After his return from the Netherlands, at thirty-three, Hall was appointed chaplain to Prince Henry and simultaneously offered the donative of Waltham Holy Cross in Essex. A year later, he decided to pen his *Characters of Vertues and Vices*: pairing fifteen vices with nine new virtues (later expanded to eleven) (Figure 3.2).[55] The body of work that preceded this shows his profound interest in brief forms—with many of Hall's resolves, as one commentator describes, "so brief as to suggest epigrams or moral maxims"—and a keen desire to effect moral improvement.[56]

PRINTERS AND PARATEXTS: CHRISTIANIZING THE GREEKS

Hall outlines the moral work that he imagines his comparison of virtues and vices to carry out in "A Premonition of the Title and Use of Characters." Here, he likens his *Characters* to moral philosophy, indicates that character-writing is a unique and new form of moral instruction, and suggests that it can have a plethora of ethical effects. Hall begins his "Premonition" by emphasizing that the Greek text on which he has based his adaptation is like a work of seventeenth-century theology. "The Divines of the olde Heathens," he says, "were their Morall Philosophers": a chiasmus presenting a structural equivalence between the new seventeenth-century ecclesiastic and the ancient moral philosopher.[57] This effort at rendering

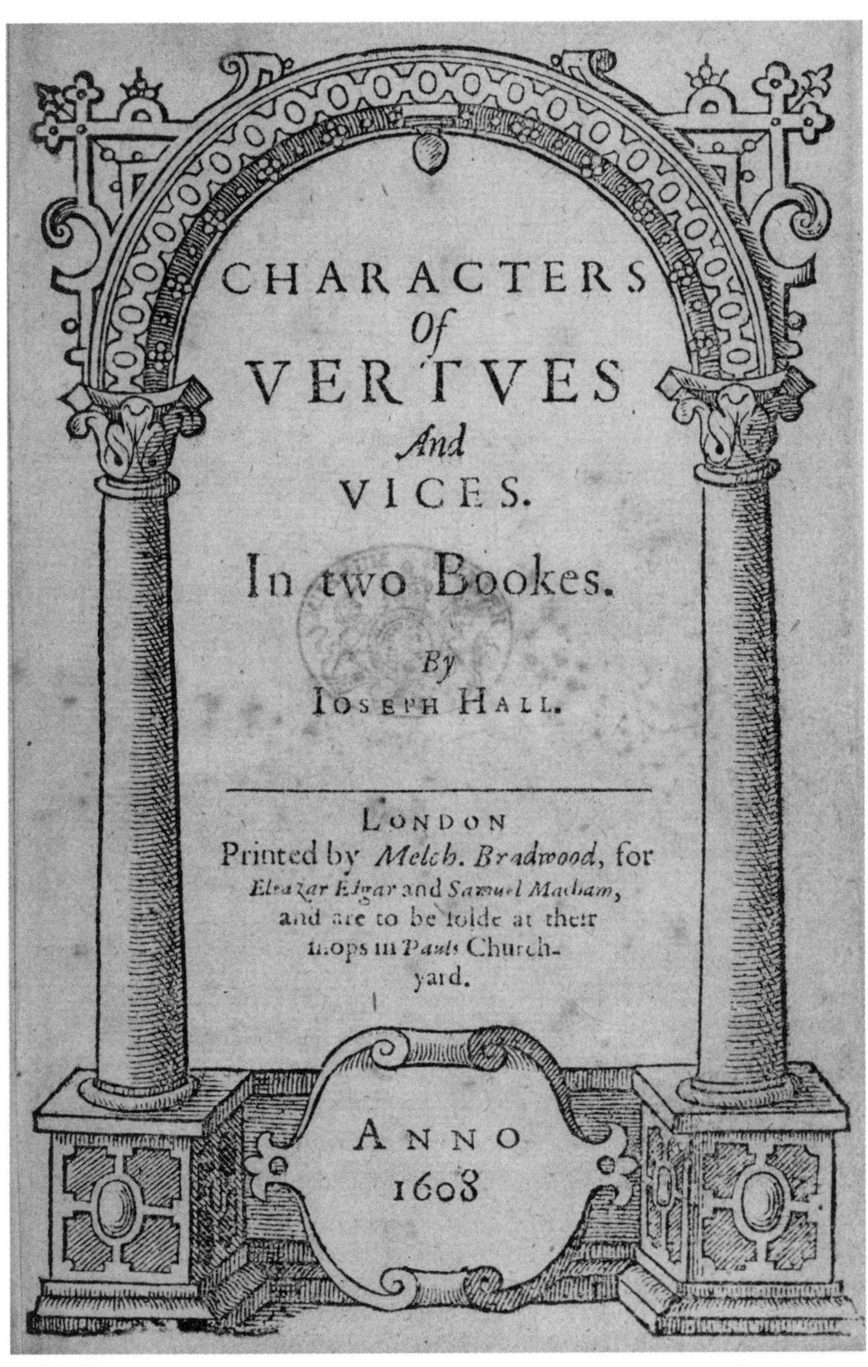

CHARACTERS
Of
VERTVES
And
VICES.

In two Bookes.

By
IOSEPH HALL.

LONDON
Printed by *Melch. Bradwood*, for
Eleazar Edgar and *Samuel Macham*,
and are to be solde at their
shops in *Pauls* Church-
yard.

ANNO
1608

FIGURE 3.2. Frontispiece to Joseph Hall's 1608 *Characters of Vertues and Vices*. *Credit:* British Library Collection, C.122.c.28. © The British Library Board.

the two moral systems compatible continues in what follows. These ancient moral philosophers

> received the Acts of an inbred law, in the Sinai of Nature, and delivered them with manie expositions to the multitude: These were the Overseers of maners, Correctors of vices, Directors of lives, Doctors of vertue, which yet taught their people the body of their naturall Divinitie, not after one manner.[58]

Hall uses the language of nature to describe the process of ancient moral instruction, not only in the image of the "Sinai of Nature" and the description of "naturall Divinitie" but also in the idea of an "inbred" law (meaning "innate, native, inherent by nature"). In this way, Hall is able to gesture to a depth of connection between the concerns of the ancients and the moderns by virtue of their shared trust in natural law.[59] This creates a fundamental connection between the "Heathen" and the Christian, a link emphasized through the continuation of a chiastic structure, projecting the Greeks into a Judeo-Christian topography. The Greeks received the "Acts" of their laws in "the Sinai of Nature," just as the Jews received the Ten Commandments in the Sinai desert.[60] Across the three stages of religious knowledge—nature, law, and scripture—the ancients and the moderns are elided. In a context in which a work on characters of virtue and vice may well invoke associations with the seven deadly sins, with their anchoring in Catholic practice, Hall's mention of the Decalogue would further reassure readers of the Protestant nature of this work of moral reform.[61]

After establishing this similarity, Hall outlines a major difference between ancient moral philosophers and contemporary divines. While the Greeks share with contemporary divines the social and structural functions of being the "Overseers of manners" and "Doctors of vertue," they teach their "naturall Divinity" "not after one manner, but with manie expositions." He continues,

> While some spent themselves in deepe discourses of humane felicitie, and the way to it in common; others thought best to applie the generall precepts of goodnesse or decencie, to particular conditions and persons. A third sort in a meane course betwixt the two other, and compounded of them both, bestowed their time in drawing out the

> true lineaments of every vertue and vice, so lively, that those who saw the medals, might know the face: which Art they significantly termed Charactery.[62]

Of the three ways that the Greek moral philosophers used to instruct morality—discussions about how to collectively achieve human happiness, the application of general moral principles to specific situations, and the writing of characters of virtue and vice—it is the third that is most attractive to Hall. This third approach of "Charactery" consists in "drawing out" the details of each virtue and vice and describing their "true lineaments": a process of depicting embodied qualities, drawn faces, rather than focusing on abstract notions or ideas. As a result of their "lively" descriptions—descriptions that achieve *enargeia,* that extreme vividness that the sixteenth-century English rhetoricians found in Roman rhetoric and had begun to celebrate—these mimetic character sketches would teach the reader how to recognize virtues and vices when they encountered them in person.[63] From seeing the "medals" of these qualities, the representations of these faces (as stamped into a medal or coin, the "seal" from which the etymology of the Greek word for "character" derives), the reader could then recognize them in real faces.

Much of this argument borrows from Casaubon's edition. In Casaubon's words, "There was, however, a third way in which morals were taught, and this was called Characterising," and, as we have observed, Casaubon too drew attention to the idea of the character as a "seal."[64] Hall also borrows from Casaubon the notion that the *Characters* are particularly imagistic. While McCabe notices the connections between Hall's preface and Casaubon's prolegomena, he does not consider Hall's plagiarism of the division of philosophy into three species that Casaubon develops in the dedication.

It would have been highly politic for Hall to borrow so much from Casaubon. This was the classical scholar preferred by King James, the man whom the monarch had attempted to lure to Scotland, before Henri IV's assassination in 1610 forced him to accept an invitation to the English court instead.[65] By working from his edition, Hall could foreground how much he shared with this scholar, not only in his learning but perhaps also in his politics. James's interest in Casaubon, historian Adriana McCrea has argued, lay in his lack of public ambition. The brilliant philologist—whose death revealed that he had famously developed a supplementary bladder due to his "sedentary habits, and inattention to the calls of nature"—was no scholar-strategist, like Francis Bacon, but someone who dedicated his life to scholarship.[66] In contrast to humanists who wanted to use classical texts to inspire political action on the part of citizens, or to take up that action themselves, James felt he could be safe with Casaubon. Hall's decision to engage with Casaubon's treasured project of Theophrastan character-writing may well have been a means to suggest that James could also be safe with Hall, who espoused a Stoicism not of engagement but of retreat.

Returning to the dedication, in Hall's view, we must recover this third way of morality, compounded in part from "discourses" about the common good and in part from the application of general precepts to particular situations, due to its particularly effective nature. This kind of moral instruction is "more likely to prevaile" not only because it is visual but because it works through pleasure, insinuating its lessons without the reader realizing these lessons are being received. Referring to Horatian ideas of the unity of profit and pleasure, Hall argues that in Charactery, "the grosse conceit is led on with pleasure, and informed while it feeles nothing but delight."[67] While "Charactery" creates writings that are like "so many speaking pictures, or living images"—writings so realistic in their descriptions that they seem like images—they should not be thought to be crude or basic: "If pictures have beene accounted the books of idiots," Hall argues, "beholde heere the benefit of an image without the offence."[68] Hall thought that with this route to moral instruction, "the ruder multitude might even by their sense learne to know vertue, and discerne what to detest," imagining that "this worke shall save the labour of exhorting, and disswasion." Here, he picks up on a similar function of the *Characters* to the one that Pirckheimer had outlined.[69] Given the long tradition of interpreting the *Characters* as moral in the sixteenth century, it does not therefore seem accurate to say, as McCabe does, that "Casaubon's work had the effect of transforming the Greek characters into a moral tract, and to a large extent Hall simply followed in his wake."

These written images of characters avoid being only a book "for idiots" because they provide the concrete "benefit" of moral instruction. The moral instruction that Hall believes to be latent in his *Characters* is imagined as a tripartite process. First, readers will learn the true nature of virtue and vice, "to know vertue, and discerne what to detest." Second, readers will rid themselves of their own vices that they may not have before realized were vices at all: "thou shalt hence abjure those vices, which before thou thoughtest not ill-favoured." Third, they will "fall in love with any of these goodly faces of virtue" and go on to practice new virtues themselves. As is clear, the new presence of the virtues is central to this operation. Both by adding these virtues, and then by showing them without reservation—here are "Vertue and Vice strip't naked to the open view"—Hall can invite the reader to choose which way of life is more attractive: "See now whether shall finde more suiters," ends the first book of his *Characters*.[70] This phrase reveals that the simple sight of virtue or vice stripped "naked" will be enough to change a reader's behavior: that the reason why "Vertue is not loved enough," is "because shee is not seene," that "Vice loseth much detestation, because her uglinesse is secret."[71] If it is true that virtue is not loved because people do not know what it is like and vice is practiced because people do not know how bad it is, all that would need to happen for moral instruction to be effective would be a simple act of representation. In Hall's words, "What need we more than to discover these two to the world?"[72] Where Hall's *Virgidemiarum* was critiqued for providing "largely negative" satire, by including the virtues, Hall's *Characters* did something different. As Hall himself wrote in an epistle of 1608, in this work he had "both censured and directed."[73]

Just as the "Premonition" indicates this relationship between Hall's *Characters* and moral instruction and its discussion of "Divines" points to how this instruction works in a religious framework, Hall's choice of Eleazar Edgar and Samuel Macham as his publishers also signals its confessional commitments. Edgar, as Fredson Bowers notes, was "a publisher dealing principally in theological works," and Macham regularly published Hall's theological pieces, including a text Hall wrote on divine meditation in 1606 and his 1608 sermon *Pharisaisme and Christianitie*.[74] Unlike the Continental readers of Latin before them, who were picking up Theophrastus's *Characters* in volumes bound together with other ancient philosophers, the first readers of an adapted version of the *Characters* in English would have found it in a context that was more Christian than "Heathen." This religious quality would be made all the more evident when the *Characters* was reprinted in 1621 as part of a new edition of Hall's *Meditations and Vowes*. Moreover, the new title of Hall's popular volume, which ran to five editions in 1608 alone, would place it alongside the many other works of Christian morality concerning the perfection of virtue and the avoidance of vice that were published in early seventeenth-century London, including those that specifically catalogued and compared capital sins with cardinal virtues.[75] In the years leading up to 1608, these included the printing of *The Seven Soveraigne Medicines and Salves, to be Diligently Applied to the Seven Deadly Wounds and Sores* (1603), the English translation of Fulvio Androzzi's *Certaine Devout Considerations of Frequenting the Blessed Sacrament* [. . .] *Composed for the Benefit of such as Seeke to attain the Perfection of Vertue* (1606), and the anonymous *Two Guides to a Good Life, The Anathomy of Sinne and the Genealogie of Vertue* (1608). By looking at the details of the text itself—above all the specific choice of virtues and vices and the way in which these virtues and vices are depicted—we can start to see how this Christian imperative was married with several Stoic principles.

VIRTUES, CHRISTIAN AND NEO-STOIC

The kinds of virtues that Hall chooses for his collection are what made his approach neo-Stoic. In seventeenth-century London, Stoicism and Christianity would not have been seen to be at odds. The early modern perception of Stoicism derived primarily from the works of Cicero and Seneca, both of whom espoused doctrines that had long been thought to be in basic agreement with Christianity. As early as 4 CE, St. Ambrose had assimilated Cicero's notion of the four cardinal virtues of *honestas* (*prudentia, justitia, fortitudo, temperentia*) into Christian doctrine.[76] Until the mid-fifteenth century, a collection of forged letters between Seneca and St. Paul was thought to be genuine. And, across the Renaissance, humanists on both sides of the Protestant / Catholic divide thought that Seneca and Cicero "put Christians to shame."[77]

Hall wrote his *Characters* in this context, having already begun to outline the connections between Seneca and Christianity in his *Heaven upon Earth*. In reading Hall's *Characters,* we must therefore not only "try to see the world through his eyes, the eyes of a Calvinist minister," as McCabe says, but to do so while recognizing just how compatible many aspects of this tradition were with the contemporary perception of Stoicism.[78] As Phillip Smith puts it, "The great web of English Protestantism had been woven partly of Stoic threads."[79] These include the Stoic emphasis on virtue being the only good, its insistence on the values of constancy and tranquility (summarized in the motto "bear and forbear"), and the importance of moderating unruly passions and desires, which for Du Vair and Lipsius "stirred up storms within the soul."[80] A further thread is found in the idea of following the *recta ratio,* or right reason, which for the Stoics meant following nature but in its Christian adaptation could be understood as following God.

Hall's choice of virtues illuminates the balance he wishes to establish between Stoic and Christian frameworks. The characters of virtue that Hall chooses are wisdom, honesty, faith, humility, valor, patience, true-friendship, true-nobility, and the good magistrate. This set seems to be derived from a combination of the four cardinal virtues; the three major theological virtues (faith, hope, and charity); their four minor complements (chastity, fidelity, abstinence, and humility); and the numerous variants on the seven Christian virtues that these two lists combine to be, such as the "seaven glorious graces" of the soul, published by Nicholas Breton in 1605 ("1. Vertue. 2. Wisedome. 3. Love. 4. Constancie. 5. Patience. 6. Humilitie. 7. Infinitenes").[81] In Hall's list, "wisdom" seems to be the cardinal virtue *prudentia*; "honesty," translating Cicero's *honestas*; "faith," the first theological virtue; "humility," the fourth minor theological virtue; "valor" the cardinal virtue *fortitudo*; "patience," a version of the cardinal virtue *temperentia*; and "the good magistrate" the cardinal virtue *justitia.* Smith has also argued that "the good magistrate" is "heavily indebted" to Seneca's *De clementia* (and that Hall's later character of "happiness" is inspired by Seneca's *De vita beata*).[82] "True-nobility" and "true-friendship" not only share attributes with the theological virtue "charity" and the "glorious graces" of "constancie" and "love" but with Stoic notions. Hall's sketch "Of the Truly-Noble" emphasizes a nobility that is not hereditary but self-made.[83] In addition, Seneca's letter, at least in Boyce's account, is thought to stand behind the sketch of "True-Friendship."[84]

Hall's mix of Christian and Stoic virtues may perhaps be best seen in the character of a Valiant man, a type who

> undertakes without rashnesse, and performes without feare: he seeks not for dangers; but when they find him; he beares them over with courage, with successe. He hath oft times lookt death in the face, and passed by it with a smile (. . .).
>
> He is the maister of himself, and subdues his passions to reason; and by this inward victorie works his owne peace. He is afrayd of nothing but the displeasure of the highest, and runnes away from nothing but sinne (. . .). I know not whether [he] more detests cowardlinesse or crueltie. (. . .)
>
> He lies ever close within himself, armed with wise resolution (. . .). His power is limited by his will (. . .). Hee commands without tyrannie and imperiousnesse, obeies without servilitie, and changes not his minde with his estate. (. . .) He is so ballanced with wisdome, that he floats steddilie in the midst of all tempests.[85]

Three key qualities define this sketch. The first derives from the Stoic tenet of subjecting "passions to reason," of carrying out objectives without "feare," and of being directed by the "will." This approach results in the type possessing something akin to a Roman virtue of self-mastery. While incorporating these Stoic aspects, Hall is careful to note that this type remains "afrayd" of "the displeasure of the highest" and the problem of "sinne." As Henry Sams recounts, some early modern divines detected "pride" in Stoicism's praise of fearlessness.[86] Hall's comment seems directed toward rendering the Valiant Man compatible with Christianity and thus free from this kind of censure.

The second quality present in the sketch of the Valiant Man is the praise of constancy and tranquility. The Valiant Man "beares over" the dangers that find him—recalling the motto "bear and forbear." But this character can do so due to his capacity for meditation, achieving "inward victorie" through remaining "close within himself" and developing "wise resolution": performing the qualities that Hall desired his readers to obtain from his own devotional treatises. With both a Christian and Stoic inwardness, the Valiant Man can be likened to a ship that floats "steddilie" in the midst of "tempests": an image that combines the typical Stoic metaphor of the storms of our soul with an image of Noah's ark. Where, in Lipsius's comment, the perfect sage should be as "firm and immovable as a rock among the waves," for Hall, this image of steadfastness has been translated into a religious register. The third quality found in this sketch is the cardinal virtue of temperance, which holds not only a Stoic inheritance but an echo of the Aristotelian virtuous mean—which early modern English Protestants, as Joshua Scodel has argued, found compatible with Christian faith.[87] The Valiant Man stands between the extremes of "cowardlinesse" and "cruelite" and is able to carry out his actions without being either excessive or deficient: commanding "without tyrannie and imperiousnesse" and obeying "without servilitie" (another nod here to the neo-Roman idea of freedom).

Hall thus not only picks up on the formal connection that Casaubon already pointed to between character-writing and Seneca but is also inspired by the specific Senecan qualities these figures should embody, while working to adapt them to suit Christian ends.[88] These three neo-Stoic ideas—prioritizing reason, constancy, and temperance as a means to self-control and mastery—extend to other virtues. Where Hall's Wise Man wants to know "most and first himself," and his Patient Man is described as someone whom "no anguish" can master, both are also described as exemplary Christians.[89] The passions of the Wise Man are envisaged as servants "ready to be commanded by reason, by religion," and the Patient Man is described to be in possession of "Christian fortitude."[90] These Christian echoes resound all the more clearly in the sketch of the Faithfull Man, described as someone who "walkes every day with his Maker, and talkes with him familiarly," and the Humble Man, "a true Temple of God built with a low roofe."[91] The combination of these two traditions foregrounded a profound praise of the life of contemplation. As Markku Peltonen puts it, the "fullest account of the *vita contemplativa*" was offered by "the English Seneca" Joseph Hall.[92] For Hall, the Wise Man is he who indeed "seeks his quietnesse in secrecy, and is wont both to hide himselfe in retirednesse, and his tongue in himselfe," a man who "confineth himselfe in the circle of his own affaires, and lists not to thrust his finger into a needlesse fire."[93]

It is not only the particular lexicon and the virtues chosen that place these characters into a Christian framework but the way in which Hall structures his *Characters,* particularly how he places each character in time. His *Characters* are rarely specific: he seldom mentions places, details of external appearances, or concrete aspects of a character's life. The Humble Man, for example, is described as someone who "frequenteth not the stages of common resorts," without these "common resorts" being named.[94] The Honest Man is someone for whom "the mishap of following events may cause him to blame his providence," without any examples of the kinds of circumstances to which this refers.[95] And if the Wise Man is described as a "Logician," where "his working minde doth nothing all his time but make syllogismes," this does not describe his concrete occupation as much as his mental habits.[96] These descriptions are thus less indebted to Theophrastus's close and detailed observations of Athenian men than to the tone of the spurious, introductory definitions that preface his sketches. Hall's portraits indeed similarly begin with proverb-like summaries of the quality in question: "The honest man (. . .) looks not to what hee might doe, but what hee should."[97] If these characters of virtue are written in the present tense, this is a timeless present, describing qualities that seem unchangeably true and are not anchored to a specific setting: something that echoes religious writing more than Hall's ancient Greek forerunner.

CHOOSING NEW VICES

Hall's adaptation of Theophrastus's vices, in particular the new vices that Hall pens, also reflects the presence of a neo-Stoic framework.

Hall chose fifteen vices for his volume. The range of characters he includes suggests that he is working from Casaubon's 1592 edition, with its twenty-three sketches (as opposed to the fifteen sketches present in the earlier translations or Casaubon's 1599 text with its additional five characters).[98] At least half of Hall's characters are inspired by Theophrastus. Hall writes sketches of irony (hypocrisy), superstition, flattery, ambition, and mistrust.[99] He adapts Theophrastus's character of "Boasting" (*De ostentatione* in Casaubon's translation) into his figure of "Vainglory," with this sketch beginning "All his humour rises up into the froth of ostentation."[100] He makes a "presumptuous man" of Theophrastus's sketch of "Overzealousness": a type whose actions "are bolde, and venturous, and more full of hazard than use"—who, as Theophrastus put it, "stands up and promises more than he can deliver."[101] And both Hall's "Male-content" and "Busie-Bodie" have Theophrastan foundations: the former to Character 17, "Ingratitude" (with Hall describing how, when a present is sent to this type, "he asks *Is this all*? and *What no better*?"), and the latter, a man who "makes up a perfect tale," to Theophrastus's Rumormonger.[102] Of the remaining six vices, two are cardinal sins (sloth and envy), one uses the language of the tenth commandment (covetousness), and another is defined by godlessness: the Profane Man.[103] If "the Superstitious hath too manie Gods," writes Hall, "the Prophane man hath none at all."[104]

This leaves two sketches, of the Inconstant and the Unthrift. The former is someone whose shifting desires and attitudes means that "he is servile in imitation," "an ape of others," and "any thing rather than himself," contrary to the constant self-knowing figures of virtue.[105] Given the *topos* Hall cites in his *Meditations* that "the World is a stage: Every man an actor; and playes his part here, either in a Comedie or Tragedy," it does not seem, as McCabe thinks, that the direction of Hall's critique across the collection derives from unauthentic "theatricality," how "the vices have neither real values nor real identities—they merely act a part."[106] Rather, the issue is in a lack of "constancy," embodied by this sketch but present across the volume, an incapacity for a person to know themselves and act in conformity with this notion. While this sketch recalls Stoic ideas, the Unthrift is more indebted to Hall's Protestantism: a type who refuses the "ascetic compulsion to save" characteristic of Calvinism.[107] With these new vices, Hall thus further projects the *Characters* into a changed context. These are characters who do not only personally "torment and delude themselves" and socially cause "dissension and enmity," issues they share with the figures in Theophrastus's original, but characters who also "theologically" "oppose themselves to the saving grace of God."[108]

Where, in 1597, Hall wanted to be the first "English Satyrist," by the time he came to write his *Characters of Vertues and Vices,* he was firm in wishing this text *not* to be read in that way. In the Proem to the second volume of the *Characters* dedicated to characters of vice, Hall warns the reader against reading the *Characters* as part of a satirical tradition: "Perhaps in some of these (which thing

I do at once feare, and hate) my stile shall seeme to some lesse grave, more Satyricall."[109] Once an ambition, the possibility of a satirical style has now become a trap, and a trap into which Hall is concerned he might have fallen. Six years later, however, a different set of characters felt much less concerned with separating these two endeavors. By turning to them, we can start to trace the arc from explicit to implicit forms of Stoic moral instruction.

The Overburians

In the second 1614 edition of the Overburian characters, the reader is introduced to the set of sketches with the announcement that they are "witty descriptions of the properties of sundry persons."[110] This subtitle indicates a striking absence of a focus on "virtue" or "vice," in contrast to the title of Hall's volume. Instead, this title emphasizes the fact that these characters are written with "wit" and that they describe a range of people. Whatever moral instruction these characters may contain, it is no longer worn on the sleeve of the volume in which they are encased. Just as ideas of virtue and vice are not to be found in the title, the ordering of characters is not arranged by positive or negative characteristics but instead follows a more literary structure, where "A Countrey Gentleman" is followed by "A fine Gentleman"; "A good Woman" by a "Very Woman," and "An Host" is placed in between "A Servingman" and "An Ostler."

Equally, while Hall compares his *Characters* to Tablets of Laws and moral philosophy in his "Premonition," the Overburian characters diminish religious rhetoric and instead compare character-writing to the forms of painting or music. Here, a "Character" is described as

> a picture (reall or personall) quaintlie drawne in various collours, all of them heightened by one shadowing. It is a quicke and soft touch of many strings, all shutting up in one musicall close: It is wits descant on any plaine song.[111]

While the Overburian volume seems to have inherited from Pirckheimer, Casaubon, and Hall the view that character-writing is related to images, it newly adds the musical comparison and does not pair this genre of writing with any call to morality, either by mentioning moral philosophy or explaining the ethical purchase of pictures and song. Why then might there be a case to make that this volume contains any intention at moral instruction at all? Two pointers suggest the operation of a moral context at work. The first is the story behind "A Wife." The second are the patterns of moral and political judgment that emerge across the *Characters,* which follow Hall in having a Stoic quality. Unlike Hall, however, this collection uses Stoicism as a springboard for a politics that often seems more closely linked to republicanism—and on one occasion to its antimonarchical variant—rather than to a life of contemplation and retreat. To examine the presence of moral and political instruction in this collection, we first, however, need to observe the collection's claims to depicting the social world.

SOCIAL TYPES

Seventeenth-century London was a splintered patchwork of different social groups. West London was home to Westminster, the courts and the Houses of Parliament, and their gentlemen; East London to the port, the brothels, and the theaters (peopled by sailors, acrobats, actors, ballad-singers, bear-wards, clowns, fencers, puppet-showmen, unskilled workers, and immigrants); and the city center to servants and craftsmen working in luxury trades, as well as printers, booksellers, hawkers, and chapmen, as Peter Burke so masterfully describes.[112] With their own jargon, geography, and gestures, and occasionally their own traditions of religion, literature, and history, these London groupings were separate worlds.[113] This distinction of worlds, often based on profession, would become central in the series of urban riots that characterized the long century: by soldiers and sailors in 1629 and 1638 on Fleet Street and Charing Cross, by weavers in 1675, by apprentices and servants in 1710.[114] As Christopher Hill writes, the London of the 1630s and 1640s was further split politically. It was "a training school in radical politics, not unlike most universities today," made up, as universities are, of an array of political groups with different perspectives, all ready to proselytize.[115] London's division into established groups may also have influenced attitudes toward new arrivals whom people did not want to incorporate, with the early calendars, or almanacs, recording xenophobia toward Scots, Dutchmen, and Frenchmen.[116]

This was the world in which the Overburian *Characters* was first published and that gave rise to the many editions published year after year. It was a world in which groups based on rank, profession, geography, politics, and nation constituted neighboring social universes while serving as the lens through which individuals saw themselves and classified others. From the 1614 edition onward, the Overburians relished representing many aspects of this divided society: penning portraits of occupations ("A Courtier," "A Servingman," "An Host," "A Pedant," an "An Ostler"), national types ("A Welchman" and "An affected Traveller"—whose "attire speakes French or Italian" and who himself "speakes his owne language with shame and lisping"), and social status ("A Country Gentleman" and "A fine Gentleman").[117] These were paired with a set of sketches that lead on from Overbury's "A Wife" ("A good Woman," "A very very Woman") and a number of portraits that correspond to the figures of vice and virtue present in Hall ("A Dissembler," "A Flatterer," "An ignorant Glory hunter," "A Tymist," "A Wise-man").[118] Later additions include combinations across categories, such as "A drunken Dutch-man resident in England," "A French Cooke," and "A vaine-glorious Coward in Command."[119]

The titles of the Overburian figures show a further change in the direction of representing the society. Where the contents page of Hall's volume lists abstract virtues, which the book then goes on to exemplify, the Overburian volume instead runs through the ever-expanding set of types in turn: there is no sense, for example, that "Hosting" is a quality that will then be embodied by "An Host."[120] If both Theophrastus's and Hall's character sketches tread a careful balance between an exemplified quality and a recognizable figure, the Overburian volume shifts the weight to the latter: opening a vista for the representation of characters who seem like people you could bump into in the street. This is mirrored by the dropping of the definite article. In the Overburian characters, we do not find "The Wise Man," as in Hall's titles, but "A Wiseman." We even encounter figures prefixed by the deictic "this"—"This Yeoman," indicating a Yeoman that is really right here—as well as those prefaced by the personal possessive: "My Taylor."[121]

In addition to broadening character-writing to depict social attributes rather than moral dispositions and working to emphasize the recognizable more than the representative, the Overburian collection returns to the level of situated detail that was present in Theophrastus's original set of characters but lost in Hall. "A Country Gentleman," for example, "is a thing out of whose corruption, the generation of a Justice of peace is produced." Nothing "under a sub-poena can draw him to London, and when hee is there, hee stickes fast upon everie object, casts his eyes away upon gazing, and becomes the prey of every cut-purse." When he comes home, "those wonders serve him for his holliday talke." If he goes to court, he wears "yellow stockings," and in winter, he is found in "a sleight taffetie cloke, and pumpes and pantaffles."[122] Where Hall's characters lacked the color of circumstance, preferring a more general outline, in this character we gain knowledge of this type's usual profession, how he behaves on an adventure to London and back in the country, and the finest details of what can be found on his feet in all manner of situation. This difference holds true for the more obviously moralistic titles in the Overburian collection. Where Hall describes how "The Flatterer" has speeches "full of wondring interjections," where all the "titles are superlative," the Overburians get straight to the example that "A Flatterer" "praiseth his grace of making water."[123] When Hall epitomizes this type as "the eare-wig of the mightie, the bane of Courts," the Overburians tell us exactly which courts this type frequents instead: fitting the guests of "the court of wards and ordinaries" with "wives or whores."[124]

Often, across the Overburian *Characters* the concrete set of rituals that make up one figure are used as an analogy to describe another: a literary structure that not only helps establish the volume itself as a coherent world but also implies that seemingly different types hold some basic equivalences within society. The rituals of "A Saylor," for example, in the 1622 impression, are compared to those of a Divine: as "a fore-winde is the substance of his Creed; and fresh water the burden of his prayers."[125] The rituals of "A very woman" are analogous to those of a Scholar: "she reads over her face every morning, and sometimes blots out pale, and writes red."[126] And the quotidian activities of "A Prison" are akin to those of both a ship and a university. "The Masters side is the upper decke: They in the common Jayle lie under hatches and helpe to ballast it; Intricate cases are the tacklings, Executions the Anchors": it is "an University of poore Schollers, in which three Arts are chiefly studied: To pray, to curse, and to write letters."[127] If analogy, as George Boas thought, is the beginning of "all science"—where "the similarities that exist among things and events give the scientist a clue to possible identities which he will then use as a basis for classification"—these Overburian characters gain a social scientific quality in making each social and professional grouping seem like the mirror of another, thus exposing the means by which they can be brought together and separated.[128]

The "Newes from any Whence: or Old Truthes under a supposall of Noveltie" that follows the Overburian characters further emphasizes these qualities. This paratext is not drawn from ancient philosophy or rhetoric but rather is structured around understanding how people from certain places—and sometimes the places themselves—think and speak. Across the Overburian editions, we hear "Newes" from Germany and Venice, court and country, "my Lodging" and "the Bed." Just as a character foregrounds the way in which habits and daily rituals are shaped by a person's type, "Newes" indicates how these phenomena are determined by a particular place, "old truthes (. . .) under a supposall of Noveltie." The "Country Newes" is "that reputation is measured by the acre and (. . .) rost beefe is the best smell."[129] The "Newes from Venice" adopts both images and ideas from its location, proclaiming "that the most profitable bancke is the true use of a man's selfe." The news from "my Lodging" and "the Bed" is conceived through a similar structure, respectively revealing, through the extended metaphor of a bedroom, "that Flatterie is increased from a pillow under the elbow, to a bed under the whole bodie," "that love is a dream," and "that great sleepers were never dangerous in a state."[130] It is not that the meaning of any of these phrases is novel—that the highest value is man's right use of the self, that flattery tends to increase, that love stands outside of reality, and that the state need not fear those who are inattentive. Rather, the innovation here is how the place in question shapes the conceptual vocabulary through which each of these truths are enunciated. Like the *Characters,* "Newes" enters the perspective of a particular type, bringing to light alternative habits of mind that constitute a particular way of perceiving and that embrace particular jargon. Anne Southwell's "Certain Edicts from a Parliament in *Eutopia,*" present in later editions of the Overburian collection, also follows this model: it lists the kinds of gendered behaviors that would be present in a better world, like "Item, no Lady that silently simpereth for want of wit shall be call'd modest."[131]

One last stylistic innovation became a hallmark of this volume: its use of clear opening aphoristic definitions or conceits. Where Hall and Theophrastus focus on defining their *Characters* through the observed description of typical behavior, the Overburians often begin with a metaphorical opening formula, such as "A fine Gentleman is the Cynamon tree, whose barke is more worth then his body" or "An ignorant Glory hunter is an *insecta animalia*; for he is the maggot of opinion."[132] Character types, in this adaptation, are understood through comparison, where particular qualities of elements of the natural world (a tree or an insect) are deployed to highlight an attribute that the type in question shares. Compare Hall's sketch of "The Superstitious" as the man who is "fond in observation, servile in feare" and Theophrastus's prototype as "the sort who washes his hands, sprinkles himself with water from a shrine, puts a sprig of laurel in his mouth and walks around that way all day."[133] The Overburians, by contrast, begin their sketches with a simile.

If the Overburian character marked the beginning of a form of social documentation, rhetoric was clearly not excluded from this process. Neither was the idea that character-writing came with a moral purpose, a point that becomes clear in the immediate context of its composition.

"A WIFE," A PRISONER, A WIDOW

The volume was printed after Overbury's murder in the Tower of London in 1613, a murder to which his poem "A Wife"—a blazon of virtues that women should possess in order to become marriageable—is very much connected.

The rumor was that Overbury had written "A Wife" in order to dissuade his close friend Robert Carr, Viscount Rochester and later Earl of Somerset, from marrying Frances Howard, Countess of Essex.[134] Howard was already married and, in 1613, was in the process of petitioning the church courts to grant an annulment of her marriage to Robert Devereux, third Earl of Essex. Overbury had become significantly implicated in this affair after Carr had asked him to write his love letters to Howard.[135] Overbury's knowledge of their relationship would have been a problem at the nullity trial, and Howard took action to silence him. Carr wrangled him a diplomatic post abroad that he knew Overbury would refuse, leading to his imprisonment in the Tower. Howard then bribed an apothecary's assistant to poison the state prisoner.

The plot succeeded: Overbury was killed on September 15, 1613. Details of Overbury's murder only came out into the open two years later, when Carr and Howard were arrested and put on trial. Though they were convicted and sentenced to death, they managed to dodge execution and instead served a six-year sentence in the Tower. The Overbury scandal—which involved sexual license, suggested witchcraft through its association with poisoning, and had a whiff of Catholic conspiracy (could they next kill the royal family, provoke a Catholic insurrection, invite a Spanish invasion, and then crown Carr king?)—became "the talk of all England."[136] It was written about in ballads, libels, broadsides, and pamphlets and later came to be understood as a predictive sign of the future tribulations of the English monarchy.[137] The popularity of the scandal underwrote the publication success of the Overburian characters. Lisle, the publisher of Overbury's poem, decided to capitalize on the mystery surrounding his murder by adding elegies, in the seventh edition, "on his now known untimely death."[138]

Two months after Overbury's murder, thinking that they had got away with it, Carr and Howard got married. At the time, connections were made between Overbury's poem "A Wife" and Howard. Ben Jonson wrote a congratulatory poem to Carr, which read: "May she, whome thou for spouse, to day, dost take, / Out-bee that *Wife*, in worth, thy friend did make."[139] These events give Overbury's "A Wife" a particular kind of status. It is a poem embedded in a network of action, due to both its purpose and its consequences. It is also one with a moral intention: its author hoped that, by depicting an ideal wife, he could encourage one person to choose not to pursue another. Given that "A Wife" prefaces the Overburian sketches, the way in which it incorporates moral implications is particularly relevant, as this establishes the dynamic between the reader and the text. It is not only the context, however, but the form of "A Wife" that reveals a desire to provide moral instruction. This is because "A Wife" is not a poem that explicitly mentions Howard or Carr. It therefore functions not only on the level of targeted and individualized advice but also as generalized normative counsel, directed at two ends.

The first generalized advice to be taken from Overbury's poem is addressed to men. In one of the elegies to Overbury incorporated in the 1622 edition of the *Characters,* by W. S., we find the idea that Overbury explains "How Good, and Great men ought, and All, to chuse / A chast, fit, noble Wife."[140] This is a poem, in other words, for all men, not just Carr. The process of teaching in Overbury's poem works as follows:

So till now
We onely knew we must love; but not how
But here we have example, and so rare,
That if we hold but common sense and care,
And steere by this Card; he that goes awry,
Ile boldly say at his Nativitie,
That man was seal'd a foole (. . .).[141]

If male lovers knew beforehand that they needed to love, what Overbury's "A Wife" teaches them is *how*. This is a curious word, given that the poem is focused more on identifying the appropriate qualities of a wife than on the process of *how* men should love their wives. This makes the how of loving into a choice of whom to love. The idealized wife in this poem provides an "example" of the kind of wife a man could hope to find: she is a "card," in its obsolete sense of "compass" ("The circular piece of stiff paper on which the 32 points are marked in the mariner's compass") with which you should steer in order to find a real woman who is like her.[142] Overbury's own poem provides some indication as to the stakes of this marital choice: "My selfe I cannot chuse, my wife I may; / And in the choyce of Her, it much doth lie, / To mend my selfe in my posterity."[143] "A Wife," as seen in the response elegy and in the poem itself, is here perceived as a poem with an intention to instruct readers for a specific purpose. It provides men with an example of the kind of woman they should love, for the purpose of giving them a chance to become better—to "mend" themselves—in the future.

The way in which this poem is directed to a male audience points to another, more speculative political reading of it. A different rumor about the circumstances of Overbury's murder drew instead on how Robert Carr was a favorite of King James VI and I and on how Overbury's closeness to Carr had made him the "favorite's favorite."[144] In David M. Bergeron's account, Overbury was imprisoned because James wanted "to break up this cozy, potentially dangerous arrangement," derived from not one love triangle but two.[145] As John Chamberlain reports in a letter of April 29, 1613, "The King hath long had a desire to remove him from about the Lord of Rochester, as thinking yt a dishonor to him that the world shold have an opinion that Rochester ruled him and Overburie ruled Rochester."[146] In this version of events, Overbury was killed by Carr in order to prevent him from describing their own love affair. This context could ground a different reading of the poem. King James referred to a later favorite and lover, George Villiers, Duke of Buckingham, as his "wife"—writing, in a letter of December 1623, "And so God bless you, my sweet child and wife, and grant that ye may ever be a comfort to your dear dad and husband."[147] If this was language James had also used to Carr, Overbury's poem about the need for men to choose good wives could be read as a poem about the need for kings to choose good courtiers—which would cohere with the biting character sketch of "A Courtier" added later to the collection. James had himself made similar associations between the choice of a wife and good governance in his own 1599 *Basilicon Doron.* James used this text to teach his son "how to become a perfite King indeede," part of which involved advice on how to choose "a godlie and verteous Wife."[148]

A second aspect of normative counsel in Overbury's poem is directed toward women. This process is encouraged and outlined in a different elegy by R. C.: "A perfect Wife, a Worke nor Time can fade, (. . .) / This none can equal; Best, but imitate."[149] Any woman reading this poem should recognize that, as she will never be able to *be* the wife in the poem, she should accordingly settle for likeness through a process of copying. Overbury's "Wife" provides an example of virtue that is not only intended to indicate the kind of person a man should want for a partner but to show the kind of person a woman should become. "A Wife" thus sets up a dynamic between reader and text, where the reader either learns how to navigate the choice of a partner or how to best become an ideal partner themselves.

Both kinds of instruction rest on this interplay between an ideal wife and a real wife that the poem foregrounds. The axle on which these two different kinds of moral instruction turn is that the unmarried Overbury has written a "Wife" who can also be thought of as "his wife," in the same way we might refer to Sylvia Plath's "Daddy." This conceit is expressed across the response elegies. The elegy "Of Sir Thomas Overburie his Wife and Marriage" begins by imagining this wife as "an uncloath'd Soule, by potent Alchymie / Exraught from ragged Matter." It then turns to consider Overbury:

Thou hast made
A Wife more innocent then any Maid,
Eva'hs state, before the falls, decyphered here,
And Plato's naked vertu's not more cleare
Such an Idea as scarse wishes can
Arrive at.[150]

These verses position the wife in the poem as an unclothed soul, innocent, prelapsarian, naked, and clear, most like a Platonic virtue or Idea. She can be all of these things because Overbury has "made" her, because she is not a wife that is part of the world's "ragged Matter." This focus on the idealized woman links Overbury's poem with the exemplary tradition, comprised of portraits that the individual should strive to emulate. However, just as much as the elegies see the wife in the poem as an ideal woman, they play with the possibility that a real woman has led to this representation:

Pigmalions Image made of Marble stone,
Was lik'd of all; belov'd of him alone.
But heer's a Dame growne husbandlesse of late,
Which not a man but wisheth were his Mate.
(. . .)
Juno vouchsafe, and Hymen, when I wed,
I may behold this Widdow in my Bed.[151]

This elegy by D. T. instead imagines the wife in the poem as the real wife. She has a life in time and would now be a "Widdow" following Overbury's death and so could remarry the speaker.

Both the context in which "A Wife" was written and the responses to it, as incorporated within the Overburian volume, thus outline four different possibilities for its instructive aims. This is first a poem designed to attack a specific person (Frances Howard). It secondly carries out this attack by suggesting to another person (Robert Carr) that he should be choosing a different kind of woman as a wife. Third, in never explicitly addressing either individual, it also becomes a general piece of normative advice for men on what kind of wife should be chosen and a general piece of normative advice for women on how to make themselves this kind of woman through imitation. Fourth, it holds the potential to be read as a covert political poem, offering advice to the king on the kinds of courtiers he should choose and to courtiers on how to merit his affection. Together, these four possibilities create an interplay between the general type and the specific individual. This, in turn, establishes a reworked form of character-writing for moral instruction that prepares the reader to understand how the Overburian character sketches will operate. But what kind of moral instruction, exactly, do these sketches propose? Without an explicit religious framework—a clear sense of who is virtuous and who is vicious—and with its new characters who are more particular than they are archetypal, what moral lessons can we imagine the Overburian sketches to impart?

THE OVERBURIAN MORAL FRAMEWORK

As in the case of Hall, a morally didactic intention in Overbury's characters can be discerned by considering the kinds of virtues that are repeatedly praised and the kinds of vices repeatedly denigrated. These patterns reveal a clear moral framework, which incorporates an idealization of temperance, the importance of a fit between an individual's natural, reasonable self and their external appearance, and an ideal of self-knowledge and self-reliance. These patterns provide an implicit moral schema, which this set of characters intends to instruct. This schema shares several key values with the traces of Stoicism found in Hall and pertains to both the "moral" and "social" types in the collection.[152]

A first value visible across a number of Overburian sketches is the repetition of ideas of temperance, the fourth cardinal virtue. This can be found from the very first character: "A good Woman." She is defined as a woman who in her choice of clothes does not go to an extreme: "She weares good clothes, but never better; for she finds no degree beyond Decencie."[153] "A good woman," in other words, does not move away from the stable grounding of what is "good" and decent or fitting, never stretching to what is "beyond" or "better." Her clothes are never excellent or luxurious but remain at this "degree"—a word that, along with "beyond," indicates a scale on which she is situated and where she has chosen to remain. The relationship to clothes in "A good Woman" is similar to how the character "A Wiseman" relates to his body. He is described as a man who "maintains the strength of his body, not by delicacies, but temperance."[154] His body is strong in the same way that the "good Woman" has clothes that are good: it is maintained by self-restraint rather than by outside improvement. "A Wiseman" avoids "delicacies" in the same way that "A good Woman" is satisfied with "Decencie." Both are guided by ideals of moderation, or neo-Stoic "temperance": a virtue that Hall praises in his own collection.[155] To extend this to a more explicitly social figure, "A Noble and retired House-keeper" is likewise defined as "one whose bounty is limited by reason, not ostentation."[156]

A second moral quality present in the Overburian characters is that man's essential nature lies in his rationality, an idea that also bears a Stoic inheritance. It emerges across these characters in the way that certain attributes are repeatedly criticized or valorized. The same "Wiseman," for example, is praised for being "the truth of the true definition of man, that is, a reasonable creature," where "A Melancholy Man" is by contrast "a man onely in shew" who "comes short of the better part; a whole reasonable soule, which is mans chiefe preheminence."[157] The "Wiseman" is then a true man because he is reasonable, whereas the "Melancholy Man" is a man only in appearances because he is not. These exhortations come hand in hand with a praise of self-knowledge, gained when characters recognize their reasonable nature and match this with their actions in the world. This emphasis on self-knowledge can be seen perhaps most clearly in the critiques of characters who lack this quality. "The true Character of a Dunce," for example, is critiqued as someone who "very seldome understands himselfe" and "An ignorant Glory hunter" as someone who, "to make sure of admiration, he will not let himselfe understand himselfe."[158]

Part of self-knowledge, and of respecting the "reasonable soul," involves being true to nature in other ways by achieving a correspondence between body and soul. This is something that represents a departure from Stoic philosophy, which does not place a high value on anything external. It is part, however, of no less persistent a moral thread. Where the "Wiseman" "lookes according to nature, so goes his behaviour."[159] On the other side of the coin, "A fine Gentleman" is chastised for trying to make himself more than what he has *naturally* got.[160] The comparison with "the Cynamon tree" seen earlier is intended to show that his "barke is more worth then his body," that he is someone who "hath read the Booke of good manners (. . .) purchased legs, haire, beautie, and straightnesse, more then nature left him."[161] For both characters, staying close to "nature" is prioritized, and this can be done both in your "lookes" and in your "behaviour." The "fine Gentleman" is mocked not for his artifice but more for constructing an exterior—"the barke" of the tree, which metaphorically plays with both his appearance and his speech—that is more elaborate than his true self. The lack of a fit with nature further emerges in the number of Overburian characters who do not seem to have achieved quite the right balance between their internal and external qualities. "A Braggadochio Welshman" is described as "the Oyster that the Pearle is in, for a man may be pickt out of him" and "The true Character of a Dunce" as having "a Soule drownd in a lumpe of flesh (. . .) that Prometheus put not halfe his proportion of fire into."[162] Both of these characters are more exterior than interior, more oyster or flesh than man or soul. To become like "A Wiseman," both will need to find ways for their natures or souls to shine through their external casing.

The collection makes clear that this lack of self-knowledge is not a problem because it takes characters away from an idea of an authentic self but because it means that they are dependent on others and therefore subject to other people's opinions, whims, and wills: a third quality that reappears across the collection and that takes us back to Stoic sources. "The true Character of a Dunce" seldom "understands himselfe" because he "speakes just what his bookes or last company said unto him, without varying one whit."[163] "An ignorant Glory hunter" is similarly reliant, as he spends his time relating "battels and skirmishes, as from an eye witnesse, when his eyes theevishly beguiled a ballad of them":

telling stories that are not his but require someone else's narrative.[164] This critique of dependence extends through the volume. It can be found in the criticism of "A Flatterer," who is unable to exist without someone to copy (he is "the impression of the last terme, and will be so, untill the coming of a new term or termer"), as well as in the critique of "An ignorant Glory hunter" who lets "fashion" dictate the entirety of his actions to such an extent that "his behaviour is another thing from himselfe, and is glewed, but set on."[165] Just as the Overburians criticize those who are dependent, they praise those who master themselves and are therefore free. "A Noble Spirit" is free from pain and thus able to guide his own fate:

> He is the Steeres-man of his owne destinie. (. . .) Thus time goeth not from him, but with him: and he feeles age more by the strength of his soule, than the weaknesse of his bodie: thus feeles he no paine, but esteemes all such things as friends, that desire to file off his fetters and helpe him out of prison.[166]

Unlike "A Timist," this character controls his own destiny. This links him to "A Wiseman," who is celebrated for not relying on external help to generate peace of mind: "His peace commeth not from fortune, but himselfe."[167] He has also built such a strength of soul that he can reconsider pain as liberating rather than harmful—which aligns with the key Stoic virtue of controlling the passions by reason.

The problem of being dependent on someone else emerges not only in relation to attributes of a character's personality but their social position.[168] "A Servingman," for example, is criticized for being "a creature, which though hee be not drunke, yet is not his owne man." Similarly, "An Host" is "none of his owne: for hee neither eates, drinkes or thinkes, but at other mens charges and appointments."[169] The character of "A Timist," critiqued for moving with the times (in a clear and striking opposite to Theophrastus's *akairos*), unites a social position of dependence on others with a sense that this is a kind of servitude of the inner self. He is described as someone who "danceth to the tune of Fortune," reveres "a Courtiers Servants servant," and therefore becomes "first his owne Slave."[170] These are characters who are not what we might call self-possessing, who are not their "own men." The sketch of

"A Courtier" is similarly slavish, a type who "followes nothing but inconstancie" and "is to bee found onely about Princes."[171]

The idea of "being your own man" in contrast to being "someone else's man" (like the Servingman), present across these sketches, alludes to the Roman-law understanding of what it means to be free: a man not subject to the will of another, who is not in their "power," but who is able to act independently and according to their own will. For the Romans, this was the distinction between being a *liber* and a *servus,* between being a freeman and a slave. The political philosophy of classical republicanism begins from this premise, using it to argue that true liberty could therefore only be achieved within a free state. In one of the paratexts to the Overburian characters, we find a direct link between freedom as self-ownership and republicanism. This is "The Forraine Newes of the yeere 1622: From the Low Counties," which includes the statement that the "surest grounds of a mans liberty is, not to give another power over it."[172] If it is only in a free state that freedom can be achieved, it is clear why the Republic of the Low Countries has been chosen as the mouthpiece of this philosophy. Here was a state that had entirely rid itself of monarchy, having overthrown its dependence on Spanish rule in the previous century.[173] Though this statement emerges as a prosopopoeia, its link to the ethic that undergirds so many of the sketches seems worthy of note. In particular, as the Overbury affair had provoked a wave of "libellous commentary on Carr and Howard" that bolstered "an ongoing interrogation of authority in England, and provided occasion for more radical, even republican, comment," as historian Andrew McRae has written.[174]

A politics not only appears in the paratexts to the volume but in its approach to gender. True to its Stoicism (and more generally to republicanism), the Overburian collection not only repeatedly emphasizes the virtue of self-ownership but makes explicit that self-ownership is exclusively for men.[175] For the Overburians, to be a virtuous man is to control your own destiny, but to be a virtuous woman is to be dependent on another's. "A good Woman," for example, is not someone praised as her own person but rather as someone for whom her husband's "good becomes the businesse of her actions."[176] "A good Wife," likewise, is a "mans best moveable."[177] This is striking in the context of how these women's male mirrors—"A Wiseman" and "A Noble Spirit"—are described.

The presence of a coherent framework within the Overburian volume tells us that this collection should not simply be seen as social description but as an implicit approach to the moral instruction via character sketch begun in English by Hall. While it borrows this from Hall, it stakes out key differences. The Overburians' Stoicism, first, does not necessarily lead to the praise of a life spent in solitary contemplation. Rather, the volume is able to praise many different kinds of political officeholders.[178] "A Franklin," for example, someone who belongs to the class of landowners that ranked below the gentry, is valorized for participating in labor with his workers: "Though he be Master, he saies not to his servants, goe to field, but let us goe; and with his owne eye, doth both fatten his flocke, and set forward all manner of husbandrie."[179] These sketches also critique those who do not best serve the Commonwealth, such as the hoarding "Ingrosser of Corne," who "when his Barnes and Garners are ful (if it be a time of derth) he will buy halfe a bushell i'th'Market to serve his Household," and praise those who, in contrast, fulfill their social roles well.[180] Consider, for example, the character of "A Reverend Judge," who is admired for delivering his mind "plainly and freely; knowing for truth, there is no place wherein dissembling ought to have lesse credit, then in a Princes Councell."[181]

A further distinction with Hall can be found in how the Overburians put more of a premium on self-ownership than on constancy. Indeed, recognizing the importance of a *liber / servus* distinction in the Overburian volume helps make sense of some of its more surprising features. It clarifies how a character like "An excellent Actor" can be praised, in spite of how he takes on many different identities. Rather than worrying about the actor being too changeable, like Hall, the sketch argues that "all men have Beene of his occupation: and indeed, what hee doth fainedly, that doe others essentially."[182] The actor does not pose a problem for the moral schema in the Overburian characters because this schema does not depend on the maintenance of an unchanging self but on a self that is free by virtue of its self-ownership and self-possession.

These patterns of judgment thus reveal that the Overburian characters not only have a relationship with instruction but also encourage an ethics and politics that is consistent and particular. The Theophrastan character, in the Overburians' hands, has maintained the work of moral instruction for which Hall used it, while diminishing the religious framework and sharpening its political edge. Many of the qualities the Overburians praise indeed do not seem so different from the values that Hall celebrates, even if they refuse to Christianize this tradition and take a different political approach. The manner in which the Overburians do this has become, however, implicit: requiring the reader to do the work of discerning which characters are virtuous and which vicious and using this as a means to shape their own behavior.

In their balance of implicit instruction, and their provision of a kind of social knowledge, the Overburian sketches represent a major development in English character-writing. In this volume, the character combines the moral, the social, and the literary: becoming a form devoted to the concrete description of social types, newly organized in a collection structured not by axiological opposition but by aesthetic sense. Svetlana Alpers, looking at Dutch painting of the seventeenth century, discusses how painting moved from being narrative to being descriptive.[183] Observing the previous century's allegorical moral portraiture, she explains how seventeenth-century paintings were newly mimetic: changing their mode from the narration of a theological story to a description of the world. What is essential both in her story and in the one I have traced here, from Hall to Overbury, is that this shift did not mean a move away from morality but a move toward a kind of instruction that worked in a very different way. As the century progressed, however, this imperative would soon find itself replaced by a new and pressing need to use the character for a singular end: that of providing essential social discernment across England's turbulent decades. From "A Button Maker of Amsterdam," we now move to the character of "The Roundhead."

4

Civil War Characters

HOW TO WRITE POLITICAL TYPES

In the introduction to his 1651 *Leviathan,* written in the midst of the English Revolution (1640–1660), Thomas Hobbes uses a strange metaphor. Wisdom, he says, is acquired more readily by reading other people rather than reading books—even if the former often proves a trickier task. The best way to go about this task, he advises, is to read yourself, as the Delphic maxim *nosce teipsum* invites. If you delve into yourself, and learn to understand your own hopes, dreams, and fears, you will gain a sense of the hopes, dreams, and fears of other people. Yet this approach will only get you so far, as the objects of other people's passions are harder to discern. These, he says, "are so easy to be kept from our knowledge, that the characters of man's heart, blotted and confounded as they are with dissembling, lying, counterfeiting, and erroneous doctrines, are legible only to him that searcheth hearts."[1] What we are frightened of, what we truly wish for, whom we most deeply love, are secrets penned in bad handwriting, or "characters," on our hearts, which we have blotted out through our lying and pretending. While anyone can read *themselves,* it is only the searcher of hearts who can read the secret passions of *other people.* For Hobbes, the solution to this problem was to avoid presenting pictures of particular men and to furnish a demonstration of mankind in general. For a number of Civil War character writers, the solution was to write sketches of types of people. These two kinds of character—character as language and character as person—were elided again and again in the sketches of this period.

Thus far, we have seen the character sketch used to instruct virtuous political behavior in ancient Greece, in the tumult of 1527 Nuremberg, and in early seventeenth-century London. We have seen the sketch deployed as a tool to teach people how to behave, to encourage them to adopt specific behaviors, and even to nudge them into particular belief systems. In the buildup to the English Civil War, the character sketch started to do something different. The first argument of this chapter is that character writers in this period—faced with urgent demands of discerning who people really were in order to determine whether to trust them—began attempting to reveal the new kinds of people that had started to populate the country.

As a means to picture Royalists and Roundheads, Levellers and kings, the character sketch of this period fits less closely with moral philosophy and more neatly within the world of news exchange that populated the emerging public sphere.[2] Characters were no longer only written by philosophers like Theophrastus, humanists like Pirckheimer, or moralists like Hall but instead by a whole host of satirists, polemicists, political actors, and simply anonymous scribblers. The world in which they operated had become abuzz with publications like the *Informator Rusticus,* the *Kingdomes Weekly Intelligencer,* and the *Daily Intelligencer of Court, City and County,* with their promises of insight into different subcultures—a promise that the sketches themselves amply fulfilled.[3] It is in fact within a contemporaneous character sketch that we might best begin to imagine how this public sphere felt to its participants, how exactly it operated. This sketch is entitled "Pauls Walke," a familiar name for the central nave of St. Paul's Cathedral, a famed place for news exchange.[4] "Pauls Walke," its author John Earle (c. 1598–1665) writes, is "the Lands Epitome, or you may call it the lesser Ile of Great Brittaine. It is more then this, the whole worlds Map, which you may here discerne in it's perfect'st motion justling and turning."[5] It is within this bustling world, inside a cathedral, full of people telling each other the latest news, that we must imagine people reading the hundreds of characters of political types printed in the seventeenth century.

Earle's sketch is not only instructive, however, as a piece of social documentation. Rather, in its elaborate, figurative style, it also tells us about the kinds of details that Earle thought were necessary in order to convey the essence of this place in London. In these sentences, Earle repeatedly compares Paul's Walk to other things. The nave is "the Lands Epitome," "the lesser Ile of Great Brittaine," and the "whole worlds Map." Earle does not give us details of the nave's size or date of construction, he does not tell us about the number of people in the cathedral or the positioning of news sellers, and he does not provide an account of himself as an observer. Rather, in an attempt to communicate the nature of this nave, Earle uses metaphors. In this, he answers the unspoken question of what kind of information a character writer should provide in order to determine the essence of someone or something.

Earle's three choice comparisons for the nave—"the Lands Epitome," "the lesser Ile of Great Brittaine," and the "whole worlds Map"—are not, however, just ordinary metaphors. They are all, in fact, versions of a single literary figure, the microcosm, a figure in which a person, place, or thing can be shown to embody, in miniature, the qualities of something much bigger. This figure has a theological and political corollary: the idea that humankind represents a miniature version of the universe. In Earle's sketch, the nave is a condensed representation of Great Britain, exemplifying it to such an extent that we might think of it as a smaller island of the country itself. If the nave is an island in relation to Britain, it is equivalently a "map" in relation to the world—a word that once also meant "a representation in abridged form; a summary or condensed account of a state of things; an epitome."[6] The nave is a "map" in this sense because, in its hustle and bustle, it embodies the globe's unstoppable motion. It is in the nave that you can feel the globe in "it's perfect'st motion justling and turning." The microcosm binds these images together, as suggested by the title that Earle gives to his collection of characters: "Micro-cosmographie: Or, a Peece of the World Discovered."

Metaphor, and microcosm in particular, served as central methods in the thirty-four new characters printed between 1614, the year the Overburian volume came out, and around 1640. At this point, on the eve of the Civil War, the question of how to understand and represent the character of a person, place, or thing was turned inside out and upside down.[7] To rival the method of writing characters via resemblances, metaphors, and microcosms, a new, more empirical set of characters began to appear. These new sketches not only shifted the method of the character sketch but changed its physical form. Multiple sketches of different types were no longer bundled together in one collection, like Hall's *Characters of Vertues and Vices,* the Overburian collection, or Theophrastus's own *Characters*. Instead, singular sketches of an individual political type were often printed on their own, ready to be bought by a reader keen to gain an impression of a novel feature on their social horizon.

The character sketch is something of an empty vessel, a form people use to understand the essence of someone or something. For this reason, it is especially apt to show us what elements were considered necessary to discern this essence at a given moment. Prior to the Civil War, the dominant method was rhetorical, full of literary tropes, resemblances, metaphors, and microcosms. During the Civil War, an alternative method took root: one that relied on observed detail, foregrounded veracity, and often disavowed rhetoric. This is the second argument of this chapter: that the period of the Civil War catalyzed a discernable shift in the kinds of information perceived as necessary to determine the essence of someone or something.

In some ways, it is not surprising that character writers reconceived the methods needed to understand the true nature of someone or something in the mid-seventeenth century. In 1961, Wilbur Samuel Howell discerned two "revolts" that happened in the seventeenth century in which the disciplines of both logic and rhetoric were profoundly transformed by a new desire to bring in the concrete observation of nature.[8] The Aristotelian scholastic logic that accepted "as new truth only what could be proved to be consistent with the old" gave way to an inductive method that subjected "physical and human facts to observation and experiment."[9] This was embodied by the founding of the scientific academy of the Royal Society in London in 1660, with its commitments to Francis Bacon's methods of induction and empiricism. Within the Royal Society, the elaborate methods of Ciceronian rhetoric, full of tropes and figures, gave way to a plainer style designed to assist in the transfer of information.[10] As the first historian of the Royal Society, Thomas Sprat, wrote in 1667, "There is one thing more, about which the Society has been most sollicitious; and that is, the manner of their Discourse."[11] Their discourse was defined by mentions of observation in phrases like "I have seen" and by its "Mathematical plainness," its intention "to reject all the amplifications, digressions, and swellings of style: to return back to the primitive purity, and shortness, when men deliver'd so many *things,* almost in an equal number of *words.*"[12]

Five years later, Michel Foucault massively expanded Howell's argument. It was around 1650, Foucault claimed, that there was a momentous change in what he calls the Western *episteme*: the deep structures of thinking, rules, codes, or conditions of possibility that ground all discourses and disciplines at any given moment.[13] In Foucault's view, a Renaissance *episteme* (1500–1650) defined by relations of resemblance, in which "the universe was folded in upon itself" and in which new truths were those thought to be consistent with the old, started to give way to a classical equivalent (1650–1800), in which truth was to be found "in evident and distinct perception."[14] It was a move, Foucault says, from a space of knowledge dominated by *interpretation* to one dominated by *order.* This essential difference between these two *epistemes* can be best seen in two natural histories of animals, one written under each knowledge regime. In Ulisse Aldrovandi's 1640 *A History of Serpents and Dragons,* we find interwoven descriptions of resemblances, virtues, legends, and stories as a means to capture the essence of a given animal. In John Jonston's 1657 *Natural History of Quadrupeds,* written after the momentous shift, we find instead an account of a horse divided into headings concerning its "name, anatomical parts, habitat, ages, generation, voice, movements, sympathy and antipathy, uses, medicinal uses."[15] In Foucault's words, "The essential difference lies in what is missing in Jonston. The whole of animal semantics has disappeared, like a dead and useless limb."[16] Using a term that will prove central to shifts in the practice of character-writing, that of "anatomy," Foucault continues: "The words that had been interwoven in the very being of the beast have been unravelled and removed: and the living being, in its anatomy, its form, its habits, its birth and death, appears as though stripped naked."[17] The Renaissance interest in semantics, interpretation, and rhetoric had given way to a classical alternative, with its prioritization of order, empirical analysis, anatomy, and plain style.

Since Foucault, a number of historians—including Frances Yates and Ian Hacking—have narrated similar versions of this story.[18] Yet more recent scholarship has troubled its neat dichotomies. Courtney Weiss Smith, for example, has discovered a tradition of empirical writing, in the work of Robert Boyle and others, that remained profoundly rhetorical.[19] Ian Maclean has likewise asserted that the Renaissance world contained arguments for resemblance as well as tools to overcome them—in this way resisting the somewhat totalitarian nature of Foucault's *episteme,* which does not account for how people escape the prism of a preconceptual knowledge framework.[20]

My account in this chapter aligns with these more recent approaches, which recognize the presence of multiple modes of thinking at a given moment. When we turn to the sketches written during and after the Civil War, we indeed find two styles of writing characters coexisting simultaneously: one more rhetorical, the other more empirical. This is not to say, however, that this coexistence was a happy one. The authors of these two kinds of sketches were not only conscious of each other but defended their respective method of character-writing and mocked that of their detractors. My point here, however, is not only that paradigm shifts are messier than we think. Rather, it is to emphasize that the partisan squabbling about method visible in the sketches written during this period often maps onto the more deadly partisan and political struggles that were happening in the Civil War.

The break that Foucault and Hacking trace in the English Renaissance *episteme,* I argue, is anchored in the politics of the English Revolution. Royalist character writers largely used the old rhetorical method, but republican writers often shifted to the language of the new science.[21] There is a conceptual grounding for this split. The older rhetorical style was committed to a stable and hierarchal system of connections, with the king sitting at the very top. This is perhaps best expressed in the poet Wye Saltonstall's figurative sketch of "The World," written in 1631, which tellingly begins by comparing the world to "a Scale or Praedicament of Relation, wherin the King is the *summum genus,* under whom are many subordinate degrees of men."[22] With its system of resemblances, its reliance on preexisting commonplaces, and the elaborate nature of its style, the rhetorical method "was admirably suited to such a stable world," as Howell says.[23]

The new scientific mode, in contrast, "had to abandon the unusual pattern of speech that would delight the aristocrat, and to teach the everyday pattern that would convince the commoner."[24] As Sprat himself puts it, in 1667, the purveyors of the new science preferred "the language of Artizans, Countrymen, and Merchants, before that, of Wits, or Scholars."[25] While the royalist and the republican camps both intended to use character-writing to expose the nature of other people, they often stood divided on the question of style. This division influenced characters of political types, characters of places, and characters of nations, as well as the character sketches published after the death of Charles I and Cromwell. By excavating how epistemological changes correspond to the seventeenth century's high watermarks of politics, this chapter ultimately argues that the much-discussed transformation from rhetorical to empiricist style during this period happened far more in response and in relation to new political necessities than has previously been acknowledged. In this, it departs from literary histories of the character sketch that have framed its stylistic changes as independent of seventeenth-century Britain's own turbulent transformation.[26]

After the Restoration, these two opposite methods of character-writing—one rhetorical and one empirical—continued to jostle with each other. In the 1660s, some character writers attempted to fully restore the old rhetorical mode of writing sketches: collections of characters written in the prewar years were republished, reedited, and in one case "revived."[27] Their editors used the older style of listing resemblances to express how the Restoration justly equilibrated the microcosmic relationships between the person and king and the person and God. The genre of character-writing had, however, been indelibly changed by the uses to which republican writers put it during the Civil War. The approach that they inaugurated—determining someone's character through a more empirical observation—did not easily die off. Instead, it led to the character sketch becoming a vehicle for a documented account of a named person's life (which was often appended to biographies and histories) or of a phenomenon, treated via empirical analysis and observation. By the end of the century, the character sketch thus served as a name for two distinct kinds of writing. On the one hand, it referred to books of rhetorical, figurative, and literary sketches of types in the royalist, resemblance-based mode. On the other, it signaled an empirical, observed account of a given person or specific topic.

This chapter traces this story by focusing on three periods of character-writing. First are the prewar sketches (1614–1641), which overlap temporally with reeditions of Hall and with the Overburians. These sketches borrow some aspects of style from the latter set, even as they lessen their moral emphasis in preference for a focus on pleasurable, witty decoration. Second are the Civil War characters (1641–1660), in which we find a new emphasis on adapting the character sketch as a means to discern political types and in which there is struggle over what it takes to write them. It is in this moment that we see royalist writers often prioritizing rhetoric and republican writers instead searching for empirical information about these figures and describing them in a stripped-down style. Third are the sketches published after the Restoration (1660–1688), in which these two separate styles of character-writing ossify into two different kinds of text.

Prewar Characters: Rhetoric and Analogy

Between 1614 and 1641, thirteen books of characters were printed in Britain. Several of these were written in dialogue with the Overburian sketches, and all shared elements of the Overburian style, even though they departed from that collection's neo-Stoic interests and moralizing intent. Just as the Overburians had done, they treat social types rather than Hall's vices and virtues. Echoing the Overburians' style, they are structured around what we might call an extended definitional metaphor or conceit and become highly wrought, rhetorical portraits. In line with the promise of "many witty characters" that had been added to Overbury's initial poem, these characters are also imagined as a kind of gallery, grouping together a collection of miscellaneous figures.[28] I refer here to the collections of characters written by John Stephens, Nicholas Breton, John Heath, John Earle, Francis Lenton, Richard Braithwaite, Wye Saltonstall, Donald Lupton, Thomas Jordan, and Henry Parrot, along with the anonymous collection *The Rich Cabinet* and the initialized R. M.'s *Micrologia*. These character books were incorporated with other material when first published, including epigrams, epitaphs, and essays (although, as will become clear, titles promising essays and characters rarely provided both), as well as religious material.

Alongside the trend of writing collections of miscellaneous characters, in these years, writers started to publish characters of one type or of types grouped around one location, trait, or idea. These sketches were also inspired by the Overburian collection in terms of their style and subject matter, even if they focused on one kind of figure. They include the clergyman Thomas Tuke's page-long *The Picture of a Picture: or, The Character of a Painted Woman* (1616) and the debtor and author Geffray Mynshul's collection *Essayes and Characters of Prison and Prisoners* (1618). Often these individualized sketches were printed on their own, as these two texts were, but sometimes they emerged as part of other collections. They were, above all, found in religious appeals, sermons, "true relations," and "abstracts."[29] The "character of an Arminian," for example, first appeared in the anonymous *An Appeale of the Orthodox Ministers of the Church of England against Richard Mountague* (1629).

As these two trends of writing characters of people, places, and things were developing in the early seventeenth century, a different meaning of "character" was being popularized in discourse. This was the link, true to its etymology, between "character" and the practice of writing itself (whether as letters or handwriting)—a link that, while old, became of central interest in a moment where several new writing systems were being developed and the structure of other languages understood and systematized. "Character" was used to refer to secretary hand, as in David Browne's *The New Invention, Intituled, Calligraphia* (1622); to shorthand, following Timothy Bright's *Characterie; An Arte of Shorte, Swifte and Secrete Writing by Character* (1588); and to the attempts at establishing a phonetic alphabet, such as Robert Robinson's *The Art of Pronuntiation* [. . .] *Divers Characters, by which Every Part of the Voice May Be Aptly Known* (1617).[30] It was further used to describe the emerging analyses of non-Latin alphabets, as in the *Caracters and Diversitie of Letters used by Divers Nations* (1628). This was no scholarly discourse but one highly familiar to the character writers themselves, which provided a central source of their repeated and foundational puns and metaphors.[31] To understand the prewar character sketch, the metaphors that character writers used to understand their own craft, as well as the intricacies of its rhetorical style, prove essential.

THE RHETORICAL FORM

While the Overburian volume of 1614 had subtly continued Hall's moralizing project, the set of other character sketches that the Overburians inspired up until 1640 no longer aimed at this effect. Instead, these books of characters often focused more squarely on something that has always been essential to the genre: the display of wit and the cultivation of pleasure. Across the prewar collections, several rhetorical features emerge repeatedly, including the use of microcosm, the technique of *enargeia* (describing a scene with extreme vividness), the figure of *parison* (where a corresponding structure is used across a series of phrases), the rhetorical technique of *paradiastole,* which includes redescribing virtues as vices, and the definitional conceit.[32] As we will see, several of these features are not simply anodyne formal norms. Rather, they reflect both an epistemological commitment to believing in the value of resemblance as a route to knowledge and a political commitment to believing in a world structured by hierarchy.

We find this first in the anonymous 1616 compendium titled *The Rich Cabinet Furnished with Varieties of Excellent Descriptions, Exquisite Characters, Witty Discourses, and Delightfull Histories.* This is a volume arranged alphabetically, in which the reader is invited to approach a particular idea, type, or concept. When a reader flicks through to find a type like the "Cuckold," they will find a character sketch. When they get to topics like "benefits," "God," "Knowledge," or "Liberty," they will come across a discourse or history instead. Uniting the genres in the *Rich Cabinet* are the kind of adjectives that precede them, which reveal a relationship with writerly brilliance: descriptions are "excellent," characters "exquisite," and discourse "witty." The purpose that the printer Richard Jackson gives for publishing this text supports this language. He sees himself as providing passages "full both of honest revelation for Wit, and useful observation for Wisdome."[33] In the sixteenth century, and in the work of Hall and the Overburians, the emphasis fell more on wisdom, with wit as a means to encourage readers to get there. For the *Rich Cabinet*, however, wit held primacy.

The commitment to wit shapes how the *Rich Cabinet* describes typical figures. In the entry for "Man," for example, we find several rhetorical devices at play. The entry begins with a *prosopopoeia*, spoken by "Man," revealing the overarching vision of man as a microcosm: "A little world I am, and all controule / As Gods vicegerent, but the inward soule."[34] After the *prosopopoeia*, the sketch in the *Rich Cabinet* begins with a paragraph structured around the notion that "Man is the image of God." This extends through a series of parallelisms, united in form. The human being is described as "the choyce creature of his love, the commaunder of all creatures, the labourer of the earth, the observer of nature, the devicer of formes, and the student of grace."[35] These parallelisms expose how the idea of the microcosm is tied up with commitments to both equality and hierarchy. On the one hand, the rhetorical structure across this series of parallelisms is doing everything it can to create the impression of symmetry. The writer here deploys the figure of *parison*, the use of the same structure across a series of clauses. (Here the structure is that "man" is the X of Y, whether that is "the *choyce creature*" of "his love" or "the student" of "grace"). Each of the clauses within this structure is almost equal length: an isocolon matched by an anaphora, with every clause prefaced with the definite article. The clauses are further connected on the basis of their sound: the first two clauses ("the choyce creature of his love, the commaunder of all creatures") alliterate and are united by the reworked repetition of the word "creature."

This play of similarities, this making of things "even"—as George Puttenham might put it, having translated *parison* as the very "figure of even"—is, however, contrasted with the language of command and control (Man is "Gods viceregent," he is "the commaunder of all creatures") and the fact that these parallelisms are all about man's place in relation to a structure tightly ordered by hierarchy.[36] We can indeed rephrase the parallelisms to observe that in relation to God, man is the chosen creature; in relation to the creatures, man is in command; in relation to the earth, man is a worker; in relation to nature, an observer; to forms, a creator; and to grace, a student. Taken together, we find an essential balance between the microcosm as a figure that unites otherwise separated elements and one that does so while retaining a sense of everything having a proper relation and place. This is a dynamic that will recur again and again in the character sketches of this period.

The next set of characters, Geffray Mynshul's 1618 *Essayes and Characters of Prison and Prisoners,* seems at first to be uninterested in rhetorical play. Mynshul was himself a prisoner in the debtor's prison of King's Bench in Southwark. While imprisoned, he decided to use the character and the essay to expose his knowledge of what the prison is like. His title page bears the adage that "experience is the best teacher."[37] He further reveals, in his preface, that he has "gathered a handful of Essayes, and few Characters of such things as by owne experience, I could say *Probatum est*": it is proved. His departure from the *Rich Cabinet* becomes clear in the next sentence. In Mynshul's words, these sketches are *not* designed to "please the reader, or shew exquisitnes of invention, or curious style."[38] Rather, this collection should serve as a testimony to an experience of hardship. Mynshul hopes the reader does not find delight in his description but instead uses this testimony to modify their attitudes toward the punishment of debt. Indeed, he explains that he is only printing this, on the one hand, in the hope that "some obdurate creditors may reade it, and by reading mollifie their strong harts," and on the other, so that "it may be as a caveat to young gallants, to terrifie them how they run in debt, wherein they may know that imprisonment is of all miseries most lamentable."[39] Given that the transmission of his own suffering is his objective, Mynshul insists that invoking the Muses for rhetorical "invention" to help him write would be useless. "Since what I write is nothing but sorrow (. . .) therefore my phrase shalbe altogether unpollished, being the servant of my more dull apprehension."[40] So far, it seems, we should not expect many devices of rhetoric.

However, within the text, Mynshul in fact filters his own experience of prison precisely through a number of figures. His "Character of a Prison" begins with a definitional conceit: "A Prison is a grave to bury men alive," and is then structured by a list of comparisons, each beginning with "it is."[41] Within this list, the initial conceit is supplemented by the figure of the microcosm. He calls the prison a "*Microcosmos,* a little world of woe, it is a map of misery," using "map" in that same epitomizing sense we saw prior. The sketch then details how the prison literally embodies the worst parts of the world of the city, relying on the device of *enargeia,* or vivid description. The prison "is a place that hath more diseases perdominant in it, then the pest-house in the plague tyme"; "it is as Innes of Court" only that it is peopled with powerless lawyers; it is the "Chrurgions hall" where no one can be healed.[42] The prison is, as Mynshul puts it in a clever chiasmus, "a little common wealth, although little wealth be common there."[43] As was typical with the Overburian collection, Mynshul's character ends with a one-phrase paradiastolic summary: "In a word, it is the very Idea of all misery and torments, it converts joy into sorrow, riches into poverty, and ease into discontentments."[44] Where the *Rich Cabinet* uses *parison* to embody the relationships of equality and hierarchy present in the notion of the microcosm, "The Character of a Prison" brings in other figures to ground its idea of the prison as a world unto itself to help the reader see all the different worlds it encompasses and to show its capacity of converting virtues into vices, pleasures into miseries (Figure 4.1). These formal moves also made their way into the stylistic bloodstream of the Theophrastan sketch.

Given the nature of Mynshul's writing—which is not dissimilar to the style of the *Rich Cabinet*—it seems that his disavowal of rhetoric might best be simply read as a typical act of *sprezzatura,* of shrugging off his own writerly brilliance, in a gesture of false modesty.[45] I would indeed suggest that his stylistic choice reflects a belief in the power of rhetoric to carry out his objectives: Mynshul may have thought that by providing a set of extended metaphors to show what debtors' prison was *like,* he would be able to scare readers away from committing the kinds of crimes that would lead them to it. It is this belief in the power of metaphorical character-writing that would be upturned in the century's major political upheaval.

MICROCOSM AS STYLE AND METAPHOR

When Earle wrote his *Micro-cosmographie* ten years after Mynshul, he was adamant that his characters were created for the purpose of pleasure. The preface announced that they were "written especially for his private Recreation, to passe away the time in the Country."[46] In his hand, the character sketch thus dropped the *Rich Cabinet*'s interest in "useful observation for Wisdome" and avoided Mynshul's commitment to testimony. Yet while distinct from Myn-

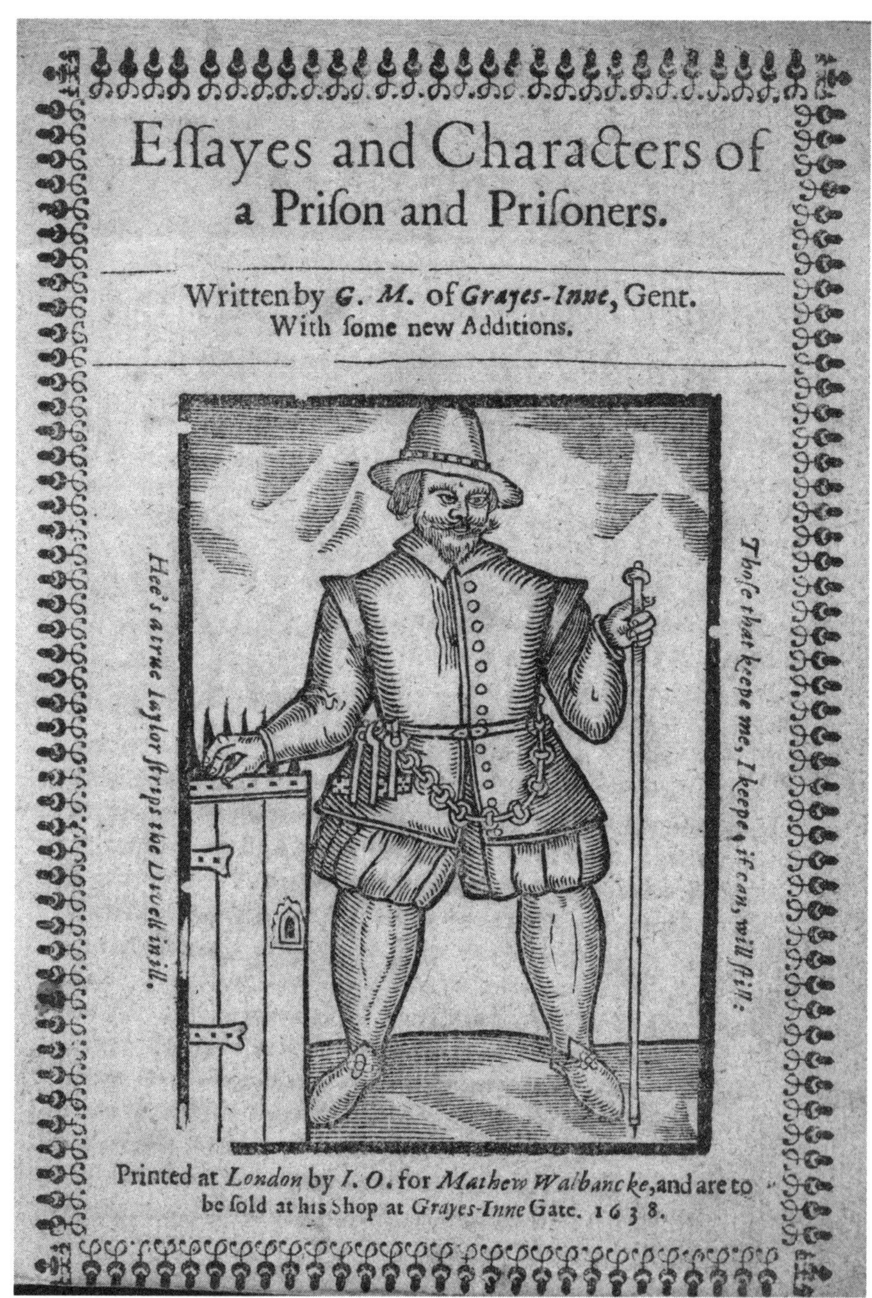

Eſſayes and Characters of a Priſon and Priſoners.

Written by *G. M.* of *Grayes-Inne*, Gent.
With ſome new Additions.

Hee's a true Iaylor ſtrips the Divell in ill.

Thoſe that keepe me, I keepe, if can, will ſtill:

Printed at *London* by *I. O.* for *Mathew Walbancke*, and are to be ſold at his Shop at *Grayes-Inne* Gate. 1638.

FIGURE 4.1. A later 1638 edition of Mynshul's *Characters of a Prison and Prisoners* embraces this rhetorical power even further by including an image of a jailor as its frontispiece. *Credit:* STC 18320, Houghton Library, Harvard University.

shul and the *Rich Cabinet* in this sense, Earle draws on similar rhetorical structures for his characters.

For Earle, it is not only that man, or prison, or Paul's Walk is a microcosm; rather, the microcosm is the guiding structure through which the world should be comprehended. "A Bowle Alley" should be understood as "the Embleme of the world" and "A Childe" as "a man in a small Letter."[47] The microcosm, in Earle's collection, is a figure that comes hand in hand with the other techniques used in the *Rich Cabinet* and by Mynshul. This becomes especially clear in the conclusion to Earle's character of "A Taverne":

> To give you the total reckoning of it. It is the busie mans recreation, the idle mans businesse, the melancholy mans Sanctuary, the strangers welcome, the Inns a Court mans entertainment, the Schollers kindnesse, and the Citizens courtesie.[48]

The Tavern is epitomized here through a list of parallelisms describing sets of relations. These parallelisms are united through *parison.* Here the skeleton structure is that the tavern is "the A man's B" or simply "the A's B": the "busie mans recreation," "the idle mans businesse," or "the Citizens courtesie." The repeated definite article at the beginning of each clause contributes to the sense that each clause is even or equal, as does the similar length of each clause and the simple fact that this list is brought together without conjunctions in asyndetic parataxis. Just as in the *Rich Cabinet,* certain words are repeated across clauses to draw each relation even closer together: "busie" becomes "businesse" and "Court" makes its way into "courtesie." Between each antithetical pair, we find further links through figures like chiasmus (between the first two clauses) and alliteration (between the third and fourth). All this works to render each kind of person's use of the Tavern symmetrical or structurally equivalent: no one use seems better than the other, but they are made equal. That said, for the Tavern to be of any use to any of these people at all, these positions must remain in place: if the Tavern becomes more business for the busy man, he will avoid it. In this, the sketch embodies the clear fixity of a set of appropriate relationships within a given structure—in this case, not a theological structure, but rather each person's individual sense of the value and meaning of a given location.

In the *Rich Cabinet,* for Mynshul, and for Earle, the character sketch was thus as an exercise of rhetoric or wit used to reveal the essence of someone or something, whether man, a prison, or a tavern. The use of rhetoric does not prejudice the sketches' claims to providing a description of these people and places but rather contributes to it. For these writers, describing a subject involves explaining what a person or thing is *like* through analogies, resemblances, and similitudes. To do so, they found especially attractive the specific figures of the microcosm, *parison,* vivid description, and the definitional conceit. When combined, these devices worked to support the deeper notion that everything had its proper relation and place, making the writing of these characters particularly adept to describe a world with clear and fixed hierarchies.

These stylistic norms continue beyond Earle's collection. They appear again in a book of sketches called *Micrologia: Characters, or Essayes, Of Persons, Trades and Places, offered to the City and Country,* by a certain R. M., published in 1629. Here, "A Player" is described as an "Epitome of Time, who by his representation and appearance makes things long past seeme present": a phrase that draws together both the microcosm and the definitional conceit.[49] Two years later, Richard Braithwaite's *Whimzies: Or, A New Cast of Characters* adopts a similar approach to defining types via conceits, with characters such as "A Sayler" who is "an Otter; an Amphibium that lives both on Land and Water."[50] The work of *parison,* seen in the *Rich Cabinet* and Earle, has a similar uptake. The character of "New-gate" prison in the *Micrologia,* for example, concludes with the phrase that the prison is "a Cage of uncleane Birds, a Coope of Conycatchers, and an Abisse of all Abominations."[51] *Parison* is also a favored rhetorical tool in a 1634 collection, by Donald Lupton, entitled *London and the Country Carbonadoed and Quartered into Severall Characters.* Here we find a "Character of London" described as "a glory to her Prince, a common gaine to her Inhabitants, a wonder to Strangers, an Head to the Kingdome, the nursery of Sciences."[52] Just as the uses of *parison* before, this list sets up a system of tightly structured relations, which cannot be substituted.

But what is it about the character as a form that particularly invites microcosmic thinking? What allows the character to move from discussing man or a prison or a tavern as a microcosm to using the microcosm as the overarching structure for a collection of

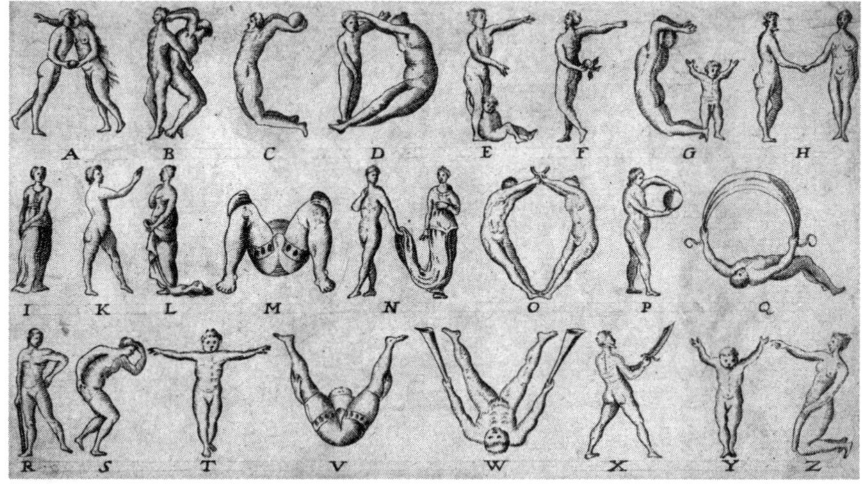

FIGURE 4.2. *Caracters and Diversitie of Letters Used by Divers Nations* [. . .] *with Exemplary Descriptions of Very Many Strang Alphabets* (Frankfurt, 1628). *Credit:* British Library Collection, G.7483, 2*4r © The British Library Board.

sketches? Earle's and R. M.'s microcosmic collections show us how the character sketch itself was considered as a brief form that could contain in it a "total reckoning" of its subject. This notion of the character is supported by the use of the word "character" within the separate domain of handwriting. Here it referred to brief written marks—such as shorthand—that contain within them several sounds, and sometimes even words. As Henry Dix puts it, in his 1633 *New Art of Brachygraphy* (ancient Greek for "short," *brachys,* and *graphein,* "to write"): "What are Characters? Short marks made with the pen, by which we expresse either letters or words."[53] Earle himself draws on this parallel, with that definitional conceit of a Childe as "a Man in a small Letter." This conceit betrays a conceptual link between the person and writing, a link that is soldered in the language of character. This very connection was also being made elsewhere in the year that Earle's collection was published when the 1628 *Caracters and Diversitie of Letters Used by Divers Nations* included an alphabet of human characters (Figure 4.2).

METAPHORS FOR CHARACTER-WRITING

Alongside the link between characters and handwriting, another metaphorical understanding of the character had taken root among these prewar writers. This was a link between the character sketch and the visual arts: from painting, to fashion, to interior furnishing. The vision of the prewar character sketch as a form interested in depicting resemblances becomes even clearer if we turn to how character writers considered their own practice.

"I shall not unfitly resemble the Painter," R. M. argues in his preface to the *Micrologia,* who, "being to figure forth the fury of a mad dogge, the better to expresse it, stood long curiously pidling about the froth or fome issuing from his mouth; but finding nothing frame fitly to his intention; rashly takes up his pencill, dashes it against the Picture, minding to spoyle it, howbeit this sudden Accident prevailed to make his worke more excellent."[54] Just as the painter's decision to depart from the accuracy of representing a dog's foaming mouth ended up making his painting more excellent, so with "these sudden touches" R. M. hopes to "pencill out these meane characters with a more lively tincture, than if I had been tediously curious in contriving, or vainly vainglorious to embellish them with the quaint eare-hony of finest elocution."[55] These characters are paintings because their author has found a balance between two pitfalls: the too-curious contriving of faithful representation and the too-vain excesses of authorial, and rhetorical, "invention."[56] This is not, however, the only work that the visual comparison does. By the end of the preface, R. M. adds a further argument: his sketches, like paintings, are concerned with appearances. "I only allege this," R. M. concludes. "I have not searched deeply into any mans matters, a little I confesse I have touched their manners, and perhaps started their humors."[57] The character sketch is a painting because of its focus on someone's or something's exterior.

Two years later, in 1631, Wye Saltonstall also used this metaphor, associating his collection of characters with pictures by choosing the title "speaking pictures," *Picturae Loquentes: Or Pictures Drawne forth in Characters.* He does so, however, with one caveat: that "these Pictures are not shadowed forth with those lively and exact Lineaments, which are required in a Character."[58] By pairing the qualities of vividness and precision—the qualities of being "lively" and "exact"—Saltonstall, like R. M., shows the character sketch to tread a middle path between authorial invention and faithful representation. The character sketch, in his view, is a form that *requires* this balance. As his prefatory material continues, Saltonstall develops this argument further by going on to "confesse" to the reader that "these Pictures are not drawne in colours, but in Characters." Punning on the idea of the "character" as a letter (the building blocks for his "Pictures"), Saltonstall also reiterates that his own sketches are not "lively," not colorful.[59] To express his false modesty, Saltonstall denigrates his painterly capacities as a character writer in a gesture of *sprezzatura,* encouraging his readers to imagine that these sketches will only be dull pictures.

Richard Braithwaite's *Whimzies,* published the same year as *Picturae Loquentes,* adds new possibilities to the comparison between character sketches and the visual arts. He first explains that he is not like those character writers who too closely respond to audience desires, who "strive in each particular, either for Style or Subject, to please the various palats of all men," and in doing so "prove an excellent Taylour to fashion the age."[60] Rather than trimming his characters to suit specific trends or fashions, Braithwaite seeks to avoid the recent fashion of "strong lines," which have come to be discredited because "they smelled too much of (. . .) opinionate singularitie."[61] He here refers to the kind of character writers who do not balance between the lively and the exact, who err too far toward "vainly vainglorious" embellishment. "Hee writes best," Braithwaite makes clear, "that *affects* least; and *effects* most."[62] Rather than fashioning himself as a tailor or a painter, Braithwaite sees himself as dealing with interior furnishings. "My provision," he says, explaining the method of his characters, "was how to furnish the maine building," while avoiding any unnecessary, affected "ornaments" or "imbellishments."[63] Braithwaite's sense of the best kind of character sketch is one that involves a diminishing of authorial flourish. "Selfe-opinion mak's a mans selfe his owne Minion," as he pithily puts it.[64]

In using visual metaphors to describe their own craft, these writers invite us to ask a series of important questions. If the character sketch is like a painting, should it faithfully represent reality or add details to reality to make it seem more attractive? Should sketches be realistic or fantastical, impartial or partial? Is this an art that prioritizes the author or the object? These questions took on additional pertinence in the early seventeenth century as another literary genre began to develop in Britain, following its widespread popularity over the Channel. A genre more comfortable with partiality, subjectivity, and flourishing the personality of the author: the essay.

Brathwaite's issue with "opinionate singularitie" indeed could have something to do with the gradual elision of the character and the essay over the opening decades of the seventeenth century. In 1618, Mynshul's *Characters and Essayes* had combined two very different kinds of forms, bringing together an essay "Of Jaylors, or the Maisters of prisons" followed by "The Character of Jaylor." In Mynshul's text, the essay and the character are distinguished in two clear ways. The essay retains a personal pronoun and betrays a consciousnesses of its own status as something experimental and tentative—true to its etymology, from the Latin *exigere,* to weigh.[65] Meanwhile, the character as a genre avoids authorial intrusion and speaks with definitional precision in order to make its description take on the status of fact. Mynshul's essay "Of Jaylours," for example, begins with the qualification that it is difficult to make a type of anyone, given human variety: "All Jaylors are not alike, some are more worthy then other, I onely touch the worst sort of them." "The Character of Jaylors," in contrast, starts stridently: "A Jaylor is as cruell to his prisoners, as a dogge-killer in the plague time to a diseased curre."[66]

This divide between the essay and the character continued to be upheld in the satirist and playwright John Stephens's 1615 volume.[67] Yet a little more than a decade later, Earle and R. M., although their titles indicated that they were writing "essayes and characters" or "Characters, or Essayes," included only one form that served synonymously the function of both. Salstonstall was also guilty of making this equivalence, referring to his *Picturae Loquentes* as "These meane Essayes."[68] This underhand association offers one explanation for why character writers were keen to distinguish their craft from that of the essayist by emphasizing their ability to balance representation and invention and their interest in reducing their "opinionate singularitie" as much as possible.

By 1641, the desire to see the character as a genre free from "opinionate singularity" becomes palpable in a set of sketches written by the royalist actor, poet, and playwright Thomas Jordan. His *Pictures of Passions, Fancies & Affections,* published twice that year, establishes upfront the need to picture "the proper praises of those men, / Whom Providence, by a decree of Fate, / Hath made the succours of our suffering State."[69] Jordan aims to accomplish this task by writing "The Character of the Parliament of England" before proceeding onto a standard series of characters: "A Drunkard," "A Valiant Man at Arms," "a Usurer," "A Mountebanck." The character of Parliament not only took up new subject matter but also relied on a new adjective to explain its approach to this subject: Jordan promises to "picture the proper praises of those men" with an "impartial pen."[70] The concept and valorization of impartiality, as Kathryn Murphy and Anita Traninger have argued, was "below the radar" at the beginning of the seventeenth century.[71] It was precisely in this mid-century moment that there was an upsurge in the use of the term. In their account, "There are no titles in English which contain the word 'impartial' before 1600; two before 1640; 114 before 1660; and 405 between 1660 and 1700."[72] Jordan, in hoping to write an "impartial" character of Parliament, betrays that the epistemological landscape was starting to move away from the "schooling in partiality" offered by the rhetorical practice of *in utramque partem disserere,* or taking sides. Instead, it was moving toward the emergence of the discourse of objectivity with which impartiality is "crucially bound up."[73] This new discourse, as Jordan's character already makes clear, affected the practice of character-writing.

Revolution: Writing Political Figures

Between 1640 and 1660, the genre of character-writing became a major form through which to engage in politics, an agile mode in which people could understand the fast-expanding set of political positions, identities, and roles that were appearing around them. As a quantitative indication, of the 117 characters of people, places, or things written between these dates, 82 are directly entangled with questions of politics. These were characters of Puritans; Roundheads; affectionate minds to king and Parliament; malignants; Jesuits; noble generals; cavaliers; antimalignants; new state reformers;

ranters; and independents and agitators. There were sketches of Charles I and II and Cromwell; of loyalty, tyranny, and monarchy; of Worcester's "late hurly-burly"; and of the covenant. Another change in this period pertains to material history: the character book came to be replaced by the individual sketch. Of the total number of character sketches written in the period, only 21 titles refer to character books, while 96 characters stand on their own. At a time when people on all sides were trying to make sense of new types and had become especially interested in the terrible behavior of a small range of characters, we accordingly find an increased tendency to move away from galleries of portraits to individual sketches.

Alongside this new deployment of the character as a form, "character" also quietly continued to be understood as one of the building blocks of language. In this period, however, this is not only as a word or sound's epitome, in the form of a mark of shorthand or phonetics, but as its true and perfect representation. Philosophies of language elaborated ideas of "true," "universal," or "real character," where signs could be construed that would visually represent their words faithfully, similar to a rebus. But what was it about the character form that opened itself up to this new political usage? How did this usage in turn change the form itself? And what relationship might this have had with the other major use of "character" in this period, as something approaching a true, perfect, and universal representation?

TRUTH, EXACTITUDE, DISCOVERY

The year 1641 marks not only the moment in which character-writing started to deal more fully with politics but also the year it started to be used to discern the truth behind appearances. We can begin to see this simply by taking a closer look at the titles of the Civil War character sketches, which start to become more and more obsessed with the idea of providing a "true" character of a range of social types. The language of truth emerges repeatedly in the titles of this period. There is the 1641 *The True Character of an Untrue Bishop* and *The True Character of a Dissembling Brownist.* In 1642, *A True Character of an Affectionate Minde to King and Parliament* and *A True Character of Worsters Late Hurly-Burly.* In 1643, *The True Character of Such as are Malignants in the Kingdome of Scot-*

land; in 1644, *The True Character of a Noble Gennerall*; in 1645, *The True Character of Mercurius Aulicus* and *A True Character of the Covenant*; and in 1647, the pseudonymous Tom Tel-Troth's *The True Character of an Ordinance of Parliament in Generall.*

The first text in this list, the anonymous *True Character of an Untrue Bishop,* already starts to play with the generic potentials of this idea. This sketch is concerned with the contradictions between the bishop's own proclamations and the actions he carries out, his "untruths": "If you demand of what Religion hee is; I know not. Hee doth protest hee is not a Papist, and I would willingly beleeve him; yet hee persecutes Protestants, and so I must necessarily doubt him."[74] The bishop is criticized for not being "true" on two related grounds: he is neither "loyal," "faithful," or "steadfast" to one conviction, which others can easily perceive, nor "truthful" or "veracious" in explaining who he is in a way that corresponds to the nature of his identity.[75] If one wants to believe him, one cannot; his appearances are deceiving. For the writer of this character, this means that the bishop is "like the Pictures, which by severall lights, hold forth a severall representation: on the one side you see a pleasant Angel, on the other side a grim Satyr."[76] While the character writers in the prewar period compared their own sketches to paintings, this writer is trying to reverse the way in which people themselves show different images according to the angle from which they are perceived. In this they are like anamorphic pictures, those popular distorted figures that change shape—like the skull in Hans Holbein's 1533 painting "The Ambassadors"—when you see them from a different angle.[77] Accordingly, this character writer does not represent the figure of the bishop by writing a sketch that might be likened to a picture. Rather, he produces a character that calls itself "true" instead and that works, as it were, to reveal the painting of the person as seen from all sides. The style of this character is not as much tied to conceit as to the revelation of contradictions between the bishop's words and deeds, a style in which the untruth of the bishop is made plain for all to consider.

A similar structure of exposing contradictions as a method of writing character appears in *The Character of a Right Malignant* (1645), likely written by the author and historian Thomas May. May had sided with Parliament in the political crisis of 1640–1642 and had become a parliamentary propagandist in both pamphlets and newsbooks.[78] Here he exposes the nature of the royalist Malignant by enumerating his beliefs, which are shown to be paradoxical, incoherent, and ridiculous. The Malignant

> is one that professes love to the Protestant Religion; but hatred to all that Party through Europe, which maintaine it. (. . .) The Spaniard hee loves better then Englishmen heretofore used to doe, by reason of some hopes that hee has of their doing good in Ireland, and is much reconciled to the French, because he thinks they will invade England.[79]

While May uses a structure of enumeration similar to those used in the characters of the prewar period, in their uses of *parison,* the overarching implied anaphora has shifted from what the Malignant *is*—as in "The Taverne *is* the . . ."—to what the Malignant "professes": love of the Protestants but hatred of the party in Europe who maintain them. This move from *being* to *doing* continues in the next clause, structured around identifying whom the Malignant "loves" and to whom he is "reconciled." The identity of this character is not to be found in a set of parallelisms about what he *is* in relation to other people but in what he himself says and feels.[80] This shift betrays a changed commitment to determining the nature of a person by listing what they profess, rather than by stating their position within other people's value systems. May is keen to differentiate himself from this earlier tradition, emphasizing that he is not building a character from his own rhetorical invention but from reporting on the tenets of the Malignant's own system of belief:

> That a Parliament would destroy the liberties and priviledges of it selfe, with other paradoxes of the same kinde, of which nothing can so well enforme you as his owne discourses: for unless you take them from himself, they are too strange for another man to beleeve, much more to invent.[81]

Here, May wants to make clear that he is not the creator of this character, as the Malignant's "discourse" is so strange that it could be invented by no man other than the Malignant himself. The character sketch is thus no longer an exercise of ornate rhetorical work by a writer as a singular, lively painter, nor even an act of interior decoration, but is positioned as a means of letting the character's own discourse speak. It is an *ethopoeia,* which, to claim its truth value, affirms it is wearing the clothes of *prosopopoeia* instead.

This attempt to make partisan characters seem true when they are obviously partial is perhaps best exemplified in the anonymous *A True Character of Worsters Late Hurly-Burly,* published in 1642. The opening asserts that this character provides "as exact an account of the present condition, and the passages of this distracted place, as I can afford you, without fearing the checks of truth, or the pen of any Animadversor." Yet despite this pronouncement, it proceeds to explain the battle from the perspective of a Roundhead.[82] This is not only betrayed by the use of the first-person plural to describe one of the battle's parties but by the inclusion at one point of a loaded threat: "Then the Malignants shall see, that wee whom they call *Roundheads,* will deale squarely with them and make them but *Rattels* for Children to play withall."[83] The notion of an "exact" representation, we see here, was not necessarily at odds with a representation that was partial. If this is testimony to how far, as Murphy and Traninger put it, the idea of impartiality was "a concept *in statu nascendi*" in the seventeenth century, one thing that had quite clearly emerged by the 1640s was the desire among character writers to treat the form of the character as a purveyor of precise knowledge nonetheless.[84]

The concern with determining the truth or exact nature of a person, event, or thing transforms the character into a means of "discovery," thereby firmly shifting the intention of this genre away from leisure and wit and toward political urgency.[85] Characters assumed new political urgency in this period precisely because they came to be seen as useful for the purpose of showing people whom they needed to fear, avoid, and keep at bay.

We find this approach to the character in the anonymous *Jesuits Character* (1642), which proclaims on its title page that it is

> a Discovery, on purpose made unto this end, that all men knowing him by this Description might beware of him, as of one which is the most Subtill, Obstinate, Cruell, Counterfeit, Ambitious, Vicious, Treacherous, and Rebellious Person in the World.[86]

The call for a discovery here is felt to be of particular urgency, as it is not self-evident who is to be trusted; the Jesuit, like the Untrue Bishop, is "counterfeit." This sketch provides a way to see through his misleading appearances and in doing so provides "all men" with the knowledge of his nature so that they can learn to "beware" of the Jesuits they encounter. The character's promise of serving as a "discovery" to this end established a new role for the form of the character that would gain much currency. The character was no longer confined to describing someone's external appearance, as a painter does. Rather, it could go beyond surface impressions, look beyond the mask, and pierce into someone's interior. The next year, an edition of anonymous characters was published in this vein, featuring "Bishops. Dumb dogs. Non-residenciaries. Men-pleasers. Unpreaching ministers." It proclaimed itself to be "Necessary to be knowne in these times of discovery," thereby setting a tone for the task that character writers increasingly believed it was necessary for characters to fulfill.[87] Seen as a means of exposure or revelation, the character sketch became an essential part of the political landscape. The word "discovery" itself was electric with political significations. In a pamphlet entitled *Englands Discoverer,* the Levellers Creed was exposed and reprimanded in 1649, and in a treatise that same year under the name of "The Discoverer," the Leveller John Lilburne's "reall plots and stratagems" were laid bare.[88]

This idea that characters were the appropriate form for a "discovery" of a person's true nature recurs in *The True Character of Such as are Malignants in the Kingdome of Scotland,* published in 1643. Written by the Commissioners of the General Assembly of the Kirke of Scotland, this text emerged from their decision to send "Directions to Ministers" concerning Malignants by way "of information and direction."[89] The genre in which they decided to carry out this task was, somewhat extraordinarily, a character. The Commissioners argue that Malignants, similar to the Jesuits and the Untrue Bishop, are dangerous because they can "deceive" the people, a verb with the double meaning of leading someone into sin and deluding them.[90] It therefore seems necessary to the Commissioners to find a means by which ministers can determine who within their congregations might be of this persuasion so that they can root them out: "because Enemies of this kinde may prove most dangerous if they be not discovered and avoyded."[91] This is, however, a very delicate task, for which there is "great need of wisdome, and the Spirit of discerning." It is as if the ministers, should they find the wrong congregants to be Malignants, are at risk of turning their friends into their enemies "and by that mistake" multiplying "enemies against our selves."[92]

This character also works by describing the Malignants through an account of their discourse and actions. They can be "known" by seven "practises," seven kinds of actions they habitually carry out, including "censuring and calumniating" about the civil and ecclesiastical meetings held between the Kirke and the kingdom; "dispising or misregarding" public resolutions; and "attributing to his Majesty whatsoever is plotted by bad Counsellors, or acted by the Popish and Praelaticall party."[93]

The Malignants' character is described not through conceit, resemblance, or figures of rhetoric but through perceptible actions, listed in a series of present participles. The degree to which this character sketch lacks ornamentation indeed shines a light on how far the prewar character writers' claims to not using figures of invention were a form of *sprezzatura*. Where Mynshul and Saltonstall expressed false modesty that their sketches were only dim pictures, free from eloquence, in order to prevent a reader's harsh criticism, this character sketch is actually written without recourse to elaborate literary devices. There is a real, qualitative difference here between previous character books that claimed to be nonrhetorical but actually were and *The True Character of Such as are Malignants,* which instead positions itself as a work of discovery, carried out in a plain prose style, unencumbered by metaphor.

This sketch thus reveals how far the character has come to focus on what someone can be found *doing,* rather than to what their essence can be compared. When the Presbyterian ministers encounter people who carry out these actions, the Commissioners of the General Assembly instruct them to "discern and try these Malignants and to reclaime or censure them according to the Acts of the Assembly, and to make report of their dilligence."[94] The character sketch here takes on targeted administrative effects: not only, as in *The Jesuits Character,* to broadly reveal to "all men" the kind of people they should avoid, but to inform an organized body how to spot, trial, and censure people who fulfill a particular description. The character as a vehicle of discernment and discovery, for showing something clearly that is not evident at first sight, had become full-fledged.

A NEW METAPHOR: ANATOMY

This association between the characters and veracity—the characters as discovery, as exact, as true, as anatomies, or as a looking glass—corresponds to the ways in which the word "character," when used in the context of its associations with language, was starting to be reconsidered in the 1650s. During this time, new ideas about the relationship between language and things were being articulated in precisely the same terms of a "true character," "real character," or "universal character." This can be seen as early as 1641 in theologian and natural philosopher John Wilkins's treatise *Mercury, or the Secret and Swift Messenger.* Wilkins devotes a chapter of this text to the idea of writing an artificial language, or "universal character," "to expresse things and notions, as might be legible to all people and countries."[95] He proposes imagining an artificial language to be equivalent to numbers, music, and chemical or astronomical notations: as a set of symbols with no relationship to phonetics but that rather provide mimetic images of what they are to represent. In this way, "characters," as the historian Lia Formigari describes, would be able to "refer immediately to things and notions," and bypass sound.[96] These ideas were picked up on and developed in different ways by the linguistic scholar Francis Lodwick (1647, 1652) and the clergyman and linguist Cave Beck (1657), who were concerned with creating characters to be "understood by all alike," in Lodwick's expression, and by the author and translator Thomas Urquhart (1653), who wished to propose a means for finding a better "proportion betwixt the sign and the thing signified."[97] In the prewar period, the popular understanding of "character" as shorthand, or phonetic markings, influenced how character writers approached their work. Now, this new mid-century understanding of linguistic character began to influence the character sketches of the Civil War.

In particular, the act of character-writing—now seen as mode of revealing an unseen truth about a person or thing—came to be commonly described with a new metaphor: anatomy. Although this metaphor had appeared in relation to character in Thomas Heywood's earlier *Philocothonista, or, The Drunkard, Opened,*

Dissected, and Anatomized (1635), it became commonplace in the unstable decades of the Civil War. Authors could mobilize anatomy to claim their sketch revealed the true nature of people or things misperceived by others. Consider Richard Ward's *The Character of Warre: or the Miseries Thereof Dissected and Laid Open from Scripture and Experience* (1643), which mobilizes an implicit idea of the character as an anatomy through the language of "dissecting" and "laying open" the miseries of war. This metaphor proves congenial to Ward's purposes of showing "the true nature of this heavy plague of Warre, which now threatens our desolation, and the downfall of our Church and State," providing him with a conceptual framework to justify the "truth" about war that he claims to possess.[98]

This language also appears in the anonymous *A New Anatomie, or Character of a Christian, or Round-head. Expressing his Description, Excellencie, Happiness, and Innocencie* (1645), a character written to revise the world's misjudgment of this type.[99] Like Ward's *The Character of Warre,* this was a character type designed to correct erroneous appearances by providing a view from the interior. The world's misjudgment of the Round-head does not come from the Round-head's purposefully deceiving appearance—unlike the cases of the Untrue Bishop, the Jesuit, or the Malignants. Rather, it stems from how others have erred in their approach to understanding him. The reader will find, in this sketch, "how far this blind world is mistaken in their unjust censures of him," as the title continues. Writing a character as an anatomy is an effort to amend this perspective, not by working from the vantage point of sight or appearances but by starting from the inside. The character writer here recognizes that the Round-head's problem lies in how he looks—a problem that makes him like "the Kings daughter, all glorious within, though hee weare his worst side outmost."[100] This explains why the Round-head is so reproved: "And the true cause why the world loves him not, Is, because they know him not, and are so blind as they cannot discerne into his excellencies, they being veiled in the world as Christs sometimes were."[101] Just as the Presbyterian ministers were instructed to use a character to "discern" Malignants whose appearances might be deceiving, this character's readers are entreated to use it to "discerne" the Round-head's excellencies that do not meet the eye at first sight.

Where Donald Lupton's earlier character of London "Carbonadoed and Quartered" had imagined the character sketch as hacking its subject apart and quartering it, the language of anatomy here positions the character as more interested in looking at its subject's dead body from its interior. While the metaphorical use of "anatomy" in the period could refer to both dividing a subject and examining its interior (an example of the former can be found in the *Anatomy of Melancholy*), the sketch of the Round-head shows one character writer less interested in "anatomy" as a figure of division than as a means to vindicate this figure from a different perspective.[102]

PLAIN-SPEAKING PARLIAMENTARIANS AND ROYALIST RESISTANCE

Writers of characters, then, attempted to claim the truth of their characters through comparisons to anatomy, by associating them with discovery and discernment, and by basing their descriptions on perceptible qualities such as actions or beliefs (or on highlighting the incoherencies between what someone does and what they profess). Yet character writers also took advantage of another strategy during this period as they increasingly became aware that certain kinds of style were more or less compatible with the truth they wished their characters to embody.

Consider the anonymous *The True Character of Mercurius Aulicus* (1645), which criticizes this royalist newsbook for its art, gloss, artifice, and rhetoric, suggesting that these are ways to disguise its lies in truth and thus deceive readers: "For, their fained lives, and miracles are described with so much Art, so fine a glosse is set upon them, they are so artificially disguised, and so much Rhetorique is used, that men who see a lye revested with the garments of truth, are easily mistaken."[103] Aulicus, this character argues, is like a magician who "artificially" makes people think that they are seeing the truth, even if they are seeing only the resemblance of it: "Aulicus can, and doth play the Magician very artificially; for, he casteth a mist afore the eyes of them that read his book: which maketh them to thinke that they see things really as they are; when they see but the meere shadow, and resemblance."[104] Together, these claims present not only a sustained critique of linguistic "artifice," and of trusting appearances—the idea of a mist here recalls the blindness or veil under which the character of the Round-head had been erroneously seen—but a critique of the idea that resemblance is an adequate means of accessing verity.

In response, this character suggests that it is not sufficient just to reveal how far *Aulicus*'s methods are stylistic tricks of conjuration. Certainly, the reader should use this character to be able to discern those tricks—just as they should become aware of the hypocrisies of bishops, Jesuits, and malignants who seem harmless but are not. Yet as a character it must also advocate developing a counter-style that does not traffic in these trades: "For, wisemen know that Art is more Prodigall then nature, and that truth needs not many words."[105] Truth here becomes associated with the natural and the brief, in contrast to "art," "artifice," verbosity, and rhetoric. "I never suspect a cause so much, but when I heare a Lawyer very Rhetoricall in defending of it," the character concludes.[106] The conflict of the moment is here played out at the level of form and style: the royalists, through the character of their newsbook, are associated with gloss, magic, rhetoric, and "artifice." In this context, it does not seem surprising that a few years later, the link between "artifice" and the royalist cause would be clinched by the "purely *artificial* person of the state" in Hobbes's *Leviathan*.[107]

The various formal changes traced here were not felt consistently across all the characters printed in this period. Rather, certain changes often came with factional associations. We have seen the move away from rhetoric in sketches of Jesuits, malignants, bishops, and royalist newspaper books such as *Mercurius Aulicus,* as well as in a laudatory character of a Roundhead. Characters with explicitly royalist commitments, however, do not exhibit these innovations. Rather, in these cases, we see the persistence of the older approaches to thinking about character.

This is exemplified in the anonymous *The King no Tyrant or the Character of Them Both. Being the True Mirrour of a Commonwealth* (1643). This text uses the character form initially to discuss, in classical fashion, the difference between four systems of government: democracy, aristocracy, oligarchy, and monarchy. It structures its progress through these systems on a hierarchical basis: "Before, I dare ascend unto the supremacy of Monarchs, who are in this world the Vice-gerents and the seconds to God," it explains, it will expose "the dangers of subordinate governments in which many Nations have delighted and practised, of these there are two sorts Democracy and Aristocracy, to which peradventure some will adde a third which is Oligarchy."[108] Figuring the monarch as vicegerent to God adapts the commonplace of man as a microcosm that we saw in the *Rich Cabinet,* with man as a little world who does "all controule / As Gods vicegerent, but the inward soule."[109] Placing the monarch in this position is a way of ensuring the monarch's place within a metaphysics structured in part by principles of microcosm and hierarchy. This becomes particularly clear in the images used to describe both democracy and monarchy.

The problem with democracy, in the eyes of this character writer, is the problem of too much liberty, a problem that will eventually undermine the kingdom itself: "There is no Commonwealth more loose then that wherein the Common people enjoy the greatest liberty, which procureth immoderate lightnesse, sedition, and destruction of the Kingdome."[110] In this state of anarchy that results from democracy, the common people, it continues, are

> termed to be those, the Alphabet of whose government begins in a crosse and retrograde order, resembling much the Hebrew, Chaldean, and Syriack Language, that are written from the right hand to the left, with points instead of vowells, so this popular government begins topsey-turvey, from the meanest to the highest, and as wanting vowells, that is, Royall government; it endeth without a point or period, with flat Destruction, which is, Let detraction overtake it.[111]

Democracy is figured here (in a sentence structure as anarchic as it claims this system of government to be) through a comparison with an alphabet. Democratic government is likened to Semitic alphabets written from right to left, where vowels are optional diacritic markings to be added to the principal letters and—at least in this character writer's view—punctuation is inessential. In this way, it figures a kind of political rule that reverses the natural order of things, beginning "topsey-turvey," "from the meanest to the highest," and ridding itself of essential elements, the "vowels" and punctuation, that give it direction, "a point," and purpose. Its sentences do not rise and fall, with breaks between them, but are instead a chaos of "flat destruction."

If this is the political system to be avoided, this character tells us what is to be praised: the natural order of things, untouched and unshaken; straight and continual rather than "crosse and retrograde"; appropriately separating the "meanest from the highest" and in doing so refusing all ideas of horizontality. This is equivalent to Saltonstall's hierarchical image of "The World" as "a Scale or Praedicament of Relation, wherin the King is the *summum genus*, under whom are many subordinate degrees of men."[112] Here, however, the character of the monarch adds the importance of resemblance or imitation. In this sketch's argument:

> That Art is the most perfect which doth most imitate Nature, but a Monarchick Common wealth in which as in a naturall body we may see an head and many members, doth most imitate Nature, therefore a Monarchick Common wealth must be the most perfect Commonwealth.[113]

If the body politic is to be an image of the body itself—just as man's own body is an image of the world—what is required, as the standard argument goes, is "as in a naturall body," one head ruling "many members."

The use of the character as a form to discuss and maintain ideas of monarchical supremacy and structures of hierarchy, in the moment when the Protectorate was being established and these ideas severely challenged, appears not only in the content of characters but in their form and style. This emerges clearly in the royalist John Cleveland's *A Character of A Diurnal-Maker* (1653), a character directed in name against newsbook writers but in its content aiming at a much broader critique. It begins,

> A Diurnal Maker is the Sub-Almoner of History; Queen Mab's Register: one, whom by the same Figure that a North Country Pedler is a Merchant, you may stile him an Author; It is the like over-reach of language, when every thin-tender-cloak'd-Quack must be termed a Doctor; when a clumsie Cobler usurps the Attribute of our English Peers, and is a vampt Translator: List him a Writer, and you smother Jeffrey in Swabbers Slops; the very name of Dabler over-sets him.[114]

The starting concern here, as in the character books of the prewar period, is to determine what the Diurnal Maker *is* by a process of comparison. It begins by investigating what he is in relation to History, and what he is in relation to an Author, both of which are carried out through analogy. What unites each of these analogies is an underlying structure of hierarchy, animated by the notion that the Diurnal Maker is someone naturally on a low rung who is attempting to pretend he is somewhere higher and whom the world is accepting as such. He is a North Country Pedler pretending to be a Merchant; a Quack who "must be termed" a Doctor; a Cobler who has "usurped" a lordship. As this last verb and the two compounds "over-reach" and "over-set" betray, he is currently surpassing his rightful place and status. This is a problem that perhaps reaches its clearest expression later in the text, where Cleveland notes that "to call him an Historian, is to Knight a Man-drake."[115]

An earlier pamphlet, written by Cleveland in 1644, critiquing diurnal writers, has been credited with registering Cleveland's embitterment with Cromwell. In Claire Labarbe's account, Cleveland was not only attacking lowbrow newsbook writers in his *The Character of a London-Diurnall* but was rather metaphorically voicing "a conservative opposition to the passing of time which diurnals recorded."[116] Cleveland, as Labarbe puts it, was using this character to write against the forces of modernity, "forces of change which he strongly opposed."[117] Indeed, as she continues, Cleveland here rants at Cromwell, alluding to him as a "Barbarous Rebell" and critiquing his recent military exploits.[118] Details from Cleveland's biography support her reading: by 1645, after voicing his opposition to Cromwell's election as member for Cambridge in the Long Parliament of 1640, Cleveland lost his fellowship at St. John's College, Cambridge.

Cleveland's later 1653 sketch, written in the first year of Cromwell's Protectorate, might also be mined for its political implications. In Labarbe's phrasing, "Cleveland's judgment on the diurnal format was in fact entirely political."[119] It should not then be surprising that the structure of this later character is, in its form and its content, not too dissimilar from the "Character of a Protector" that Cleveland would publish in 1654. This reads:

What's a Protector; he's a
stately thing
That Apes it, in the
nonage of a King.
A Tragick actor,
Ceasar in a Clowne,
Hee's a brasse farthing
Stamped with a Crown.
Aesops proud Asse
Mask't in a Lyons skin;
An outside Saint lyn'd with
the Devill within[120]

Both of these characters—not only in their content but in their style and above all in their use of analogy—betray a royalist approach to the writing of a character. The royalism of both texts lies in their assumption of a hierarchical system, where each node stands in its proper place so coherently and cohesively that analogies can be drawn from different domains that deal with structures of relations—where a Cobler's relation to a Merchant is equivalent to an Ape's relation to a King.

CHARLES I AND CROMWELL CHARACTERED

After Charles I was killed in 1649, character sketches of him were decisively split between the royalist form and what we might call a more republican style—one focused on highlighting a person's actions, words, and practices and concerned with proclaiming and accounting for its veracity.

An example of a royalist character, designed to pronounce Charles I's virtue and thereby reprimand the regicide, can be found in the anonymous *The Martyr of the People, or the Murdered King* [. . .] *with a Character of his Life and Vertues* (1649). This account is structured by listing Charles's virtues and by elaborating a set of resemblances. The introduction to the character begins, "I shall give you a brief Character or Epitome of the personal vertues and graces of this pious Prince, which made him both glorious in life and death."[121] It then proceeds to describe each of Charles's six graces (four cardinal virtues, plus two Christianized qualities): "his

Pietie and Religion," "his Wisdom and Prudence," "his Justice," "his Christian fortitude and magnanimitie," "his Temperance," and "his Mercie and Clemencie."[122] In exemplifying these qualities, the author makes choice comparisons between Charles and other figures. Charles showed himself to be "a second David, a man after Gods owne heart, whose conversation was in Heaven."[123] Charles is also seen in the superlative, as "the wisest King in Christendome."[124] Compared to a future King David, to God's own heart, and understood as the "wisest King," it is no surprise that he is positioned as a singular ruler, impossible to copy.[125] "This Age," the author writes, "shewes not a man of abilitie to take up his Princely Pen, whose stile and eloquence may be the object of their wishes, but never of their imitation."[126] If Charles is a pen, we may wish to be able to write in his style, but we will never be fully able to imitate it. He is further seen as a Christlike "firme Rock against the popular rage" and "the Temple of the holy Ghost" (comparisons compounded by the report that Charles answered, during his trial, "with our Saviours words, *God forgive them, for they know not what they say*").[127] The character concludes with an elaborate list of what, after Charles's death, England has become, a list that offers a kind of *paradiastole,* that rhetorical technique that can be used to redescribe virtues as vices. "Now our glory is departed from our Israel," it says,

> England is become a Widow, our Churches turned into Stables, and Temples become Court of Guards; the royall Palaces of our late King, made Garison; the patrimony of the Church, the Souldiers salary.[128]

With an aphoristic rhyming couplet, the character then affirms Charles's position at the top of a hierarchy: "We have lost the chiefest of all Earthly things: / The highest, lowest, and the best of Kings."[129] This royalist character's commitments to hierarchy are thus mirrored in its use and choice of metaphor. Like other royalist characters, it deploys elaborate figures and takes up the approach, seen earlier in the century, of writing characters of virtue.

In contrast, we find *The None-such Charles his Character,* published anonymously but written by the architect, diplomat, and agent Sir Balthazar Gerbier in 1651 (Figure 4.3). This sketch operates in a different mode. It is highly interested in proving its claims about Charles to be *true,* just as many of the Civil War characters before it. It frames itself, similar to an anatomy, as needing to carry out a "serious inspection" of the state of the nation in order to understand why God has brought down "so signall a wrath (. . .) upon that Family."[130] This takes the form of a long narrative, which comes with empirical documentation. Gerbier explains how his character has been "Extracted out of divers Originall Transactions, Dispatches and the Notes of Severall Publick Ministers and Councellours of State as wel at home as abroad," several of which are extracted as evidence within the text itself.[131] The character pairs this insistence on veracity and evidence with the description of actions, promising to show "the late Kings proceedings."[132] This leads to more of a historical focus, requiring this character, unlike the previous, to begin "with a succinct description of the originall Causes of those dismall Fates, which proceeded from his owne, and from his Conforts Progenitors": a genealogical account that explains Charles's murder by describing the reigns of James VI and I and Henry IV.[133] Instead of enumerating Charles I's qualities and framing them through comparisons, this character extends into an account of his family history, his political actions, and his documents of state. It offers the revelation of the occasional political "stratagem," it appeals to "impartiall Readers," and it affirms at several points how its account "is proved to be true" by recourse to sources.[134] "Who can reject its truth?" the author asks in relation to the claim that Charles is a tyrant.[135] "Is it not manifestly true" it questions, that the armies do public good?[136] The scope of this treatise, it promises, is to show "the true and originall causes of such disasters."[137]

Given the significance of these political obituary characters, the character took on a new relationship to death: from quartering, to anatomizing, to being a final funerary oration.[138] When Cromwell died in 1658, a number of character sketches were again written in this style. Cromwell is memorialized in characters that ally themselves with narrative, that recount the story of his life, and that position themselves as a kind of history, similar to Gerbier's character of Charles. *An Exact Character or, Narrative of the Late Right Noble, and Magnificent Lord, Oliver Cromwell* (1658), for example, begins with his birth—Cromwell "was born at Huntington

FIGURE 4.3. Frontispiece to *The None-Such Charles His Character.* The caption under his portrait refers to an old prophecy about the succession of monarchs in England, where Mars, the god of war, is Henry VIII; Puer, a boy, is Edward VI; Alecto, a fury, is Mary; Virgo, a maiden,

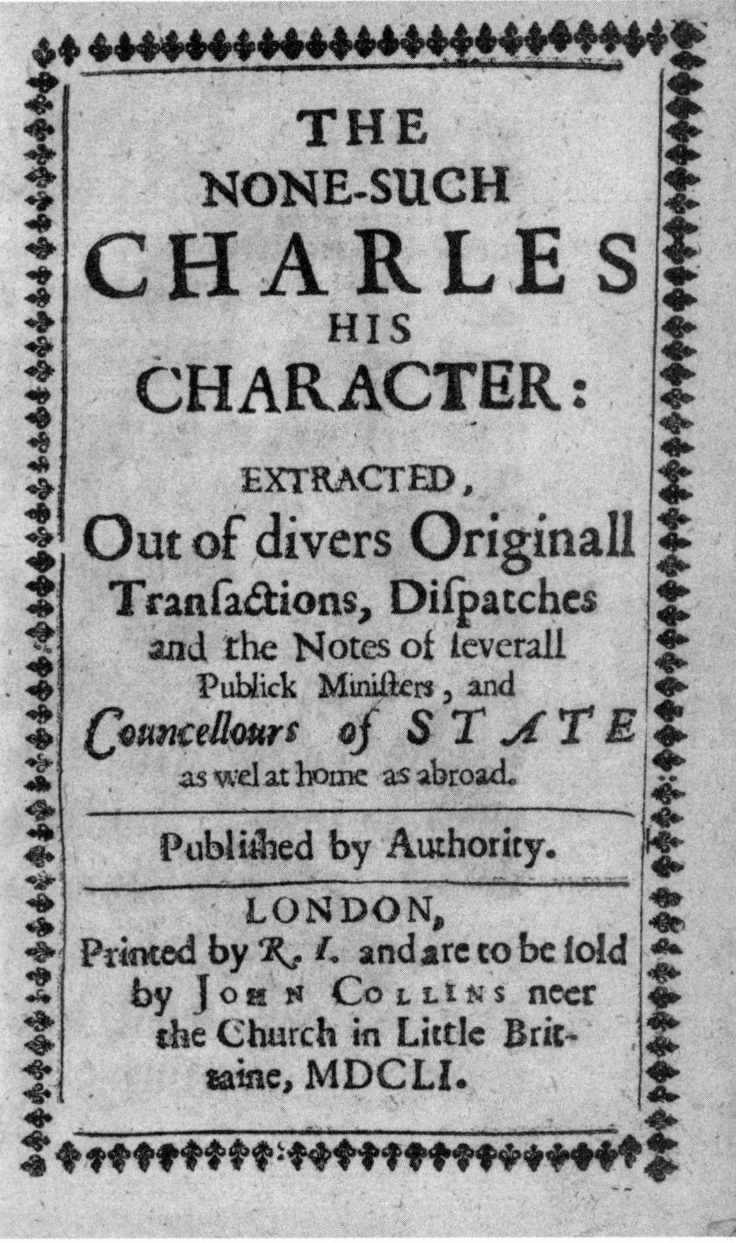

THE
NONE-SUCH
CHARLES
HIS
CHARACTER:

EXTRACTED,
Out of divers Originall
Tranſactions, Diſpatches
and the Notes of ſeverall
Publick Miniſters, and
Councellours of STATE
as wel at home as abroad.

Publiſhed by Authority.

LONDON,
Printed by *R. I.* and are to be ſold
by JOHN COLLINS neer
the Church in Little Brittaine, MDCLI.

is Elizabeth I; Vulpes, a fox, is James VI and I; Leo, a lion, is Charles; followed by Nullus, no one. *Credit:* GEN *EC65 G3133 A651na, Houghton Library, Harvard University.

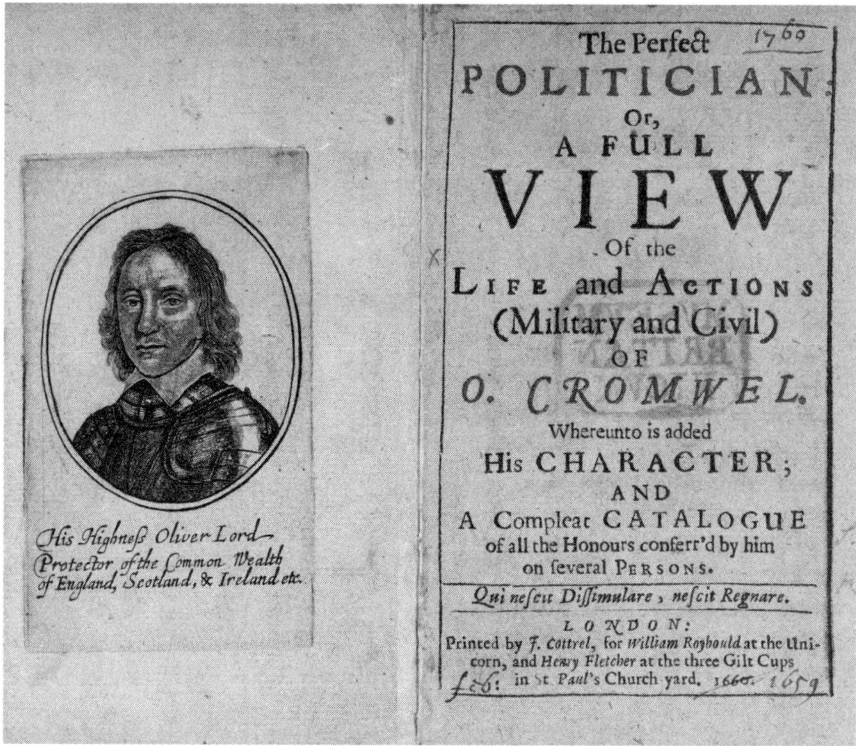

His Highneſs Oliver Lord Protector of the Common Wealth of England, Scotland, & Ireland etc.

The Perfect
POLITICIAN:
Or,
A FULL
VIEW
Of the
LIFE and ACTIONS
(Military and Civil)
OF
O. CROMWEL.
Whereunto is added
His CHARACTER;
AND
A Compleat CATALOGUE
of all the Honours conferr'd by him
on ſeveral PERSONS.

Qui neſcit Diſſimulare, neſcit Regnare.

LONDON:
Printed by *J. Cottrel*, for *William Roybould* at the Unicorn, and *Henry Fletcher* at the three Gilt Cups in St *Paul's* Church-yard. 1660.

FIGURE 4.4. Frontispiece to *The Perfect Politician,* 1660. *Credit:* British Library Collection, E. 1869 (1). © The British Library Board.

of Honourable Parents"—and extends through his education to his marriage before describing his qualities.[139] We find this style too in *The Perfect Politician: or a Full View of the Life and Actions (Military and Civil) of O. Cromwel,* a history "whereunto is added his character" (Figure 4.4).

Its author begins by emphasizing veracity: "I indeavor to keep pace with Truth, so near as possibly it may be traced."[140] It seeks to do so in the form of a history that presents "the Epitome of great Cromwels Actions, from his home near Huntington, to his Tomb in Westminster."[141] When the text describes "his character," on page 346 of its long account, it does not give an overarching structure of his general vices or virtues, which it then goes on to exemplify, as we saw in the royalist character of Charles. Rather, before discussing any virtues, it describes Cromwell's precise actions: his choice of privy council, his rise to power, his speeches, and his approach to secrecy.

CHARACTERS OF NATIONS CAUGHT IN BETWEEN

As the decade ended, this tussle over how to use the form of the character played out not only over explicitly political subjects but also in the burgeoning trend of using the character to write about nations. In 1659, the English diarist John Evelyn wrote and anonymously published *A Character of England, as it was lately presented in a Letter, to a Noble Man of France.*[142] Evelyn had spent time in France and had previously translated several French texts, one of which detailed his personal observations of French customs. When he decided to deploy his knowledge of this country in a character, Evelyn did not, however, write a character of France. Rather, he himself adopted the character of a Frenchman, writing as if he were a foreigner observing English customs and prefacing this with the statement that he was only this text's translator.

The speaker, commissioned to write a character of this nation, begins by exposing the directions he has received from his patron: "My Lord, You command me to give you a minute account of what I observed, and how I passed that little time which I lately spent in England."[143] The form requested for this "minute account," derived from observation and lived experience, is not a genre with which the speaker is familiar, and he spends time justifying the request only to focus on "the little Remarkes of my hasty, and desultory Peregrination."[144] Despite this, the speaker cannot help but begin with a more abstract idea about the nature of a national character—a sense of a nation beyond one's own journey though it:

> It must be avowed that England is a sweet, and fertill Country. *Terra potens armis, atque ubere gleba*[145]: That the Fields, the Hills, and the Vallies are perpetually clad with a glorious, and agreeable verdure; that her provisions are plentifull; her staples important; and her interest very considerable.[146]

Before, however, he goes too far, he stops himself with a reproach: "But these, my Lord, are not the *Memoires* which you demand."[147]

Instead, he returns to his post and starts to recount his travel narrative: "After a short passage from Calais, we came on shore at Dover . . ."[148]

Evelyn's approach to writing the character of a nation was not to everyone's liking. That same year, an anonymous *Character of France* was published as "an answer to a late slanderous pamphlet, called The Character of England."[149] This text is split into two parts: a character of France and a rebuttal to the claims of *A Character of England,* housed under the title *Gallus Castratus.* The critique of Evelyn begins by parodying his narrative style: "My Lord, you command me to give you a minute account, as I understood your meaning, I have discoursed as little of truth as I could, and endeavoured to render my self as ridiculous as my fanatick Genius could permit me."[150] It is the "minute account" and the free play of Evelyn's "fanatick Genius" that are most cause for concern and lead this writer to conclude that Evelyn's account is "so unfit to bear the name of a Character, that it may well be stiled the Leprosie of France cast upon England."[151]

In writing *A Character of France,* Evelyn's detractor instead borrowed an older interpretative method, relying on rhetorical style as a means to truth. This character contains a clear structure of vices and virtues, even if it is cleverly adapted to show the vices of France and the virtues of England. It is also full of rhetorical figures, bringing together, for example, France's social and geographical characteristics with extended conceits. In relation to French fashion, the writer proclaims, "As for their Cloathing the Camelion is not more colourable, the Aire not more changeable, the Wind not more unconstant."[152] The character writer further emphasizes how attributes of the nation's land are directly mirrored in its inhabitants: France's "soile (like their faces) cannot much boast of its charms every where."[153]

A year later, in July 1660, two new characters of nations were published, written along similar lines: *The Character of Italy* and *The Character of Spain.* These characters are framed not as narrative accounts but as catalogues of vices followed by virtues, written with a plethora of rhetorical techniques.[154] Both were also published anonymously, and printed, as *A Character of France* was, by Nathaniel Brook, suggesting a possible shared authorship. Both begin with a summation of the nation in question through an extended conceit, based on one geographical characteristic. For Spain, this is the notion of a baking desert: "Tis Nature's Sweating-tub, a Nest of Wolves, the very Seat of Hunger and Famine (. . .) the Soyl barren, and but a desart."[155] For Italy, it is the idea of a lumpy, swollen territory, plagued by disease: "Tis a Cisalpine Clod, a Gowty Leg of that Huge Monster the World, a rotten Charnel (. . .) the Merdaille of Nations, and the Excrement of the Earth."[156] This connection leads both texts to assert links between natural and man-made features of the nation and inhabitants' personal characteristics: the Spanish are so ambitious and proud "that it is hard to judge whether the Countrey, or the mindes of the Inhabitants are most aspiring and mountainous"; the Neapolitans, "according to the quality of the Soyl, of a fiery boyling temper"; and the Genoan "is as lofty as his Building, so proud and gallant in his garb."[157]

Jacques Bos, Paola Gambarota, and Jean Robertson have all grouped these characters of France, Spain, and Italy with Evelyn's *Character of England.*[158] Yet because these three characters reassert the old method of character-writing in response to the proposition of a new approach, it does not seem right to group them together. Rather, what we see here is two rival methods of discerning the essence of a nation. The presence of this rivalry indicates a messiness in the transition between paradigms of thought in the mid-seventeenth century. These individual character writers were not as much passive agents of changing epistemes. Rather, they were active participants in a live debate over how to represent the essence of someone or something.

Restoration: Two Styles

This tension between two modes of writing character—one rhetorical and literary, one more empirical—was to play out from the end of the Commonwealth in 1660 until 1688. This date marks not only the arrival of William of Orange but also the first French printing of Jean de La Bruyère's *The Characters or the Manners of the Age*, which would reshape the genre once again. The stylistic and political debate that began in the Civil War, between the painterly mode of character-writing, associated with hierarchy and royalism, and the anatomical equivalent, associated with republicanism, continued into this period. Within these decades, the former style was often used to describe types, such as "A Religious Prince" and "The Flatterer," collected in character books. The latter style, on the other hand, was more often used within works dedicated to single subjects, whether named individuals or things such as coffee, poetry, and nations. The coexistence of these two styles is attested in a striking "character of a character," which combines the associations of both modes together and therefore epitomizes the range of things that the genre had become in late seventeenth-century England.

THE AFTERLIFE OF RHETORIC

Immediately following the restoration of the monarchy, with the coronation of Charles II in 1661, an adaptation of the Overburian *Characters* was likely written by Lewis Griffin, entitled *Overbury Revived; or A Satyricall Description of the Vices of our Present Times in Essayes and Characters.* This volume was the first of a wave of new rhetorical character books—republished or newly written—reviving not only the analogical method but also the practice of writing galleries of sketches, as opposed to individual types. This volume further reasserted the association between the character and the essay, as its title makes clear. These commitments came with explicit preferences for a renewed royalism, a royalism that can be found in the adoption of the figures of microcosm and analogy.

The politics of this collection emerge most clearly in the characters "Of Man in General," "A Religious Prince," and "The Rump Parliament." In the first of these, Griffin uses the figure of the book of nature to explain the character of a man as a picture of God. "This visible world is a great Book written by the hand of God for his own glory and mans use; Every Creature is a leaf or page of this Volume, but man is the picture of the Author set in the Frontispiece."[159] Griffin reasserts an ordered world, in which God is the author of the book of nature and man is his image and acts as the earthly steward of other creatures. This framework of belief is also present in the sketch of "A Religious Prince," who is defined as "a representative of God, in a threefold respect; as a Man, as a King, and as a Christian."[160] The Prince is here especially close to God:

not only because, as a person, the Prince is created in God's image, but because, like God, the Prince is a King and (though it seems strange to assert this) a Christian.

This, Griffin is careful to indicate, is not an empty abstraction but a reassertion of a fundamental truth that had been denied before the Restoration. "England in those late bloody times," the sketch continues, was "tormented with an evil spirit, which could not be driven away, till we had sent for David the anointed of the Lord, our lawful King."[161] In this reading, Charles II—a new David, just as his father was also called—had come to deliver England from its essential sin of breaking the system of hierarchy. Griffin's objection to "The Rump Parliament" indeed lies in how "they had destroyed Gods Image in their own souls and Mans Image in the Kings Body."[162] We saw this kind of destruction mirrored stylistically in a move away from chains of analogies within the character form. Here, Griffin contributes to the restoration by bringing back this mode of thinking.

Griffin's volume also re-sutures the link between the character and the essay. His title promises both genres, but his volume shows only one. If the individual characters of the Civil War were too concerned with asserting their own veracity to call themselves attempts or "essays," Griffin's 1661 volume asserted that this connection was possible again. His double title corresponds with the way in which his volume works as a miscellany, putting these political and metaphysical characters next to characters familiar from the prewar period: "A Player," "a bad Wife," "An happy Rustick," "A Whore." This miscellaneous quality, following Bacon and Montaigne, was typical of the essay but had stopped being associated with the individual characters printed during the revolution.

Published that same year, the pseudonymous *Confused Characters of Conceited Coxcombs* by Verax Philobasileus, or "a true lover of the King," forged similar bridges between the character and the essay, apologizing for what he calls his "Essayes" before his volume begins.[163] Like Griffin, the author not only connected essays, miscellaneous characters, and royalism but also reasserted the style of analogy. Definitional conceits reappear: "A Flatterer," for example, is someone "with the legs and feet of Nebucadnezers immagined Image." A sketch of "The Good Old Cause," nominally referring to Cromwell's New Model Army, is similarly structured through a definitional conceit. Presented in the form of an Aristotelian pun, the conceit riffs on the meaning of "cause" to ask in what sense it can be considered a "cause" at all: "A cause then is either. Efficiens, materialis, formalis Principalis, minus principalis, finialis. (. . .) This now may be called an old Cause, because it hath its product from self seeking that branch of Original Corruption, but how it may be called Good I know not."[164]

THE AFTERLIFE OF EMPIRICISM

At the same time, another kind of character was fast emerging in the later part of the century. Following all the associations with death and character, this form of character writing established a link between character, biography, and history.[165]

Characters, and Historical Memorials (1662), a set of brief biographies by the Church of England clergyman Clement Barksdale, provides a central example. Barksdale's volume foregrounds an association between character and history that had antecedents in Plutarch's *Parallel Lives* and was being significantly developed by Izak Walton's series of lives written between 1640 and 1678.[166] Barksdale's sketches often begin at the genealogical beginning, just as the obituaries of Cromwell had done. He introduces the character of John Donne, for example, by noting that "he was born in London, of good and virtuous Parents."[167] This link between character and biography was aided by the continuing trend of including character sketches as part of an obituary. In these obituaries, details of a person's birth provide the standard starting point. The obituary of "the cheating sollicter" Richard Farr, for example, similarly begins, "Richard Farr was born in Warwickshire, near Killingworth, his Father a Tanner of honest fame and reputation."[168]

The joining of the character with origin appears not only in characters of people but also in characters of things, both concrete and abstract. The first of many *Characters of Coffee and Coffee-Houses,* printed in 1661, opened with these lines: "A Coffee-house is free to all Comers, so they have Humane shape, where a Liquor made of an Arabian Berry called Coffee is drunk. Six or seven years ago was it first brought into England, when the Palats of the English were as Fanatical, as their Brains."[169] This sense that the knowledge of something was tied up with the knowledge of its origin also can be found in *The Character of Poetry,* which opens with the argument, "That which gave Birth to Poetry, and hath supported its Reputation among the most Ingenious of every Age, is the desire of Imitation which is interwoven with every Man's Essence."[170] As this approach to writing character is concerned with the depiction of beginnings and endings, it became formally tied up with writing in narrative, as we saw in the death sketches of Cromwell.

In the 1660s, one character writer foregrounded the personal narrative, gained from experience, as a route to knowledge. The indentured servant George Alsop, who wrote *A Character of the Province of Mary-land* (1666) in order to convince other laborers to join him in the colonies, is careful to assert that all he knows to be true comes from experience. "What I present I know to be true, *Experientia docet*; It being an infallible Maxim, That there is no Globe like the occular and experimental view of a Countrey."[171] With this statement, Alsop not only justifies the *experiential* method of writing a character but renders all other methods suspect: it is an "infallible" truth that the best way to gain knowledge of the world is through "the ocular and experimental view," a phrase he repeats across the treatise.[172] The difference between his statement here and that of Mynshul, earlier in the century, is that his style coheres with his stated intention. Asserting that this is a character he "knows" to be "true," Alsop is careful to preempt the critique of writing an imaginative fancy. "I protest," Alsop's preface affirms, "what I have writ is from an experimental knowledge of the Country, and not from any imaginary supposition."[173]

The role of the personal narrative also informs one of the few characters written by women in this period, the anonymous *The Young Maids Character of an Ungrateful Batchellor* (1677). This text is structured as several stories told by different women about bad men, all instigated by one narrator, who is trying to make sense of her "woeful experience," in the company of others who have suffered similar fates.[174] It is written, the title page affirms, as a warning, being a "full discovery of all those Tricks, Cheats, and Delusions, whereby young men do often deceive, and many times ruine their too credulous sweethearts."[175] When each new story begins, this narrator foregrounds that these lamentable misadventures have been really experienced by her "she-Confidents."[176] "The next whose misfortunes urg'd her to declare her Story," she writes, "was a Countrey-Farmers Daughter, who thus bemoan'd her disasters."[177]

Where experience and personal testimony provided one route that character writers used to justify how they came to an understanding of their subject matter, documentary evidence provided another. This is visible in numerous cases, from the inclusion of state papers in Gerbier's character of Charles all the way to obituaries, which began to publish personal documents such as diaries and letters alongside a funerary character of a person's life.[178]

Thus, alongside the resurgence in figurative sketches that used a more rhetorical mode to describe typical figures, a different set of character sketches continued to assert how and why their character sketches were true. Dealing with topics from the lives of individuals, to coffee, to poetry, to Maryland, to an ungrateful bachelor, these character writers did not spend time detailing what these phenomena were *like*. They did not, for example, begin by comparing the coffee bean to another aspect of the natural world, by punning on John Donne's name, or by explaining, in an elaborate comparison, how poetry is to painting as words are to images. Instead, these authors relied on details of history, referenced their own status as firsthand observers, and offered documentary evidence to shore up their claims. The republican mode of character-writing, begun during the Civil War, had thus left its mark. Character sketches published after the Restoration continued to have a documentarian impulse, committed to evidence and empirical analysis.

SAMUELL PERSON'S COMPILATION

The coexistence of both modes of writing in this period is perhaps most visible in Samuell Person's 1664 extraordinary character of a character, which brings together almost all the associations and ideas about character-writing that the form had accrued over the century, from royalist and republicans, from people interested in analogies and those keen on empiricism, from authors who aligned themselves with visual artists to those who saw themselves as practicing anatomical science. Person's character appears in his *An Anatomical Lecture of Man. Or a Map of the Little World, Delineated in Essayes and Characters*. The title alone reflects a combination of ideas of character: anatomy, geography (recall the "map"), the figure of the microcosm, and the framing of essay and character as synonymous. The prefatory material adds several familiar elements to this amalgam, claiming that the characters that follow are free from wit and rhetoric, written instead in "plain Essayes" and "meaner language."[179]

In Person's character of a character, we first find the conceit of associating the character with the book of the world: "a little Enchiridion that Enspheares much, like *Homers Iliads* in a nut shell." He then provides a pun of the character as a letter or mark, "a stigmatizing Iron to those that are bad, branding them with a black *Theta,* the worst characteristical letter."[180] This leads Person to describe the character as being simultaneously a picture (a representation) and a true sign through which an individual can be recognized, "the Picture or Draught of each person, it has not only the *signatura rerum,* but also, *Personarum* stamped upon it."[181]

Yet Person also does not ignore character-writing's associations with history, time, origin, and narrative, explaining that characters "may be termed petty Chronologies or Chronicles."[182] Furthermore, the character is geographic, microcosmic, and anatomic: "a Microcosmography or a Map of man" as much as "the Anatomy of the Soul, which rips up mens Qualities (. . .) and there sees within them; a kind of Legitimate augury that looks into the intestines of things." Characters are related, as we saw, to shorthand—they "agree with those other Characters, called Brachigraphy." They are also related to the idea, seen in Earle, of being "every mans Physicks Epitomized."[183] Yet while it brings all these associations together, Person's collection also adds a new feature: images of many of the types he describes, from "A Gyant" to "A Fool," that serve as a frontispiece (Figure 4.5).

+ + +

By the end of the century, there were two methods of writing characters in seventeenth-century England: one more rhetorical, and one more empirical. The Civil War played a central role in cultivating the latter, as authors were keen to affirm the truthful nature of the polemic types they depicted. The necessity to quickly communicate the true nature of maligned figures in the midst of the English Revolution thus left a profound mark on the form, generating a kind of character-writing that was interested in proving its claims by

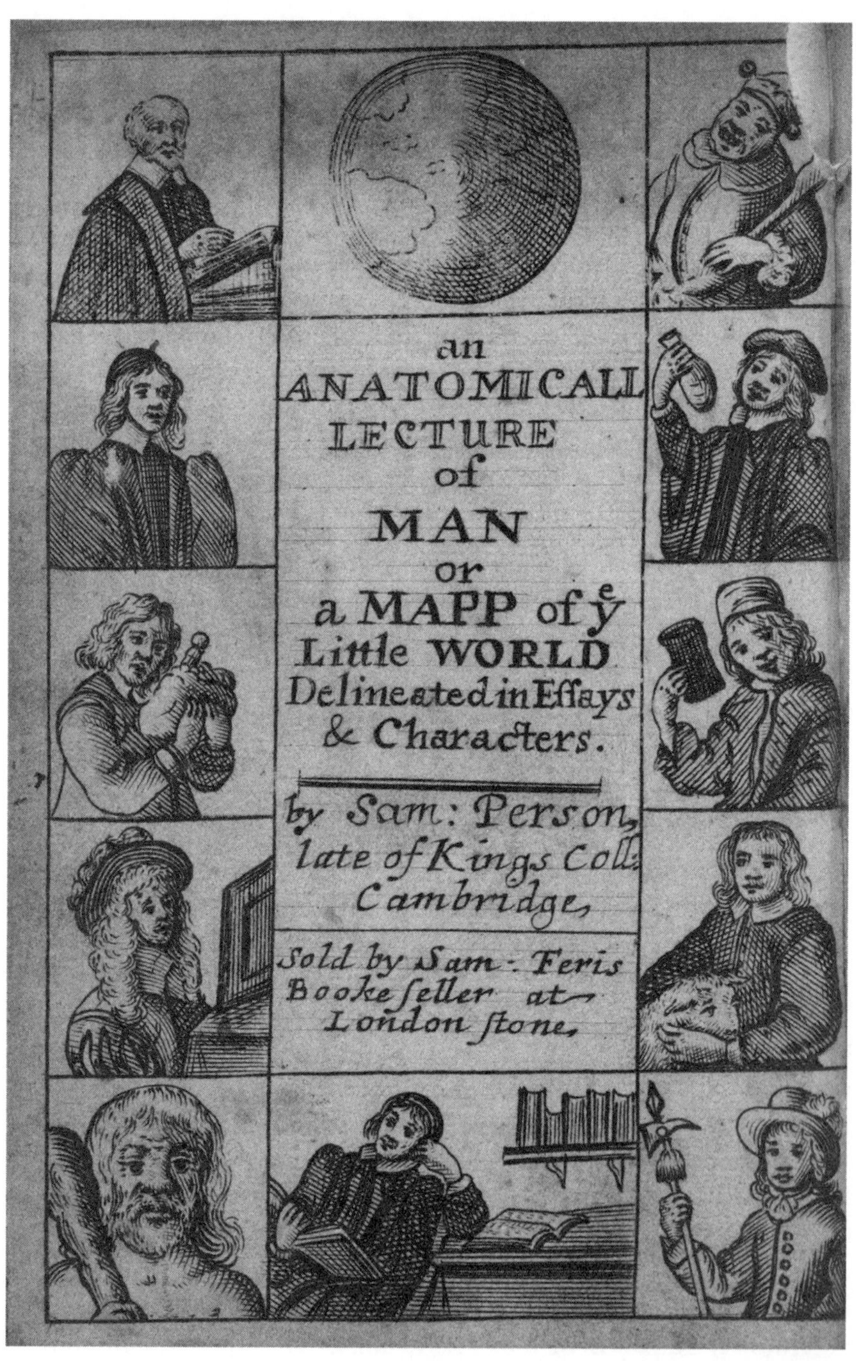

FIGURE 4.5. Samuell Person, *An Anatomical Lecture of Man. Or a Map of the Little World, Delineated in Essayes and Characters* (1664), A1v. *Credit:* GEN *EC65 P4318 664a, Houghton Library, Harvard University.

recourse to the language of truth, discovery, exactitude, and experience and sometimes by furnishing documentary evidence.

Yet across the Channel, although the conflict of the Fronde was unfolding at the same time as the English Revolution, these developments in character-writing did not take place. In France, the Theophrastan character sketch was not thrown into the drama of politics. Instead, character writers deepened the form's links with moral philosophy, adapting it to suit a different intellectual, political, and religious climate.

5

Developing Moral Satire

THE CHARACTER IN FRANCE

"To characterize," the 1694 dictionary of the Académie française explains, is "to mark the character of a person, a passion, a vice or a virtue."[1] The character, in seventeenth-century France, as these examples of vice, virtue, and the passions make clear, was not a genre most immediately defined in relation to political types. Rather, it remained moral: a form associated with the presentation of good and bad qualities and the depiction of feelings. This is striking when we consider it alongside the major developments in English character-writing in the same period. Socially and politically, both countries experienced major upheavals around the 1650s—the English Revolution, on the one hand, and the intermittent civil war that has come to be known as the French Fronde (1648–1653), on the other, led by the French nobility in an attempt to curb the power of the king.[2] On a textual level, meanwhile, the major English adaptations of Theophrastus's *Characters* were freely available in France. Hall, Overbury, and Earle were all translated into French before 1671, and the French translation of Hall's *Characters of Vertues and Vices* even holds the honor of being "the first English book made available to French readers in their own language."[3] However, unlike English character-writing, with its interest in designating new political factions, schisms, and groups in order to provide social knowledge, French character-writing remained wedded to the old moral ambition to reform readers.

This chapter is concerned with the most significant and famous French character writer: Jean de La Bruyère, an erstwhile treasurer of France, counselor to the king, private tutor, and gentleman. In 1688, La Bruyère wrote a bestselling duplex edition of Theophras-

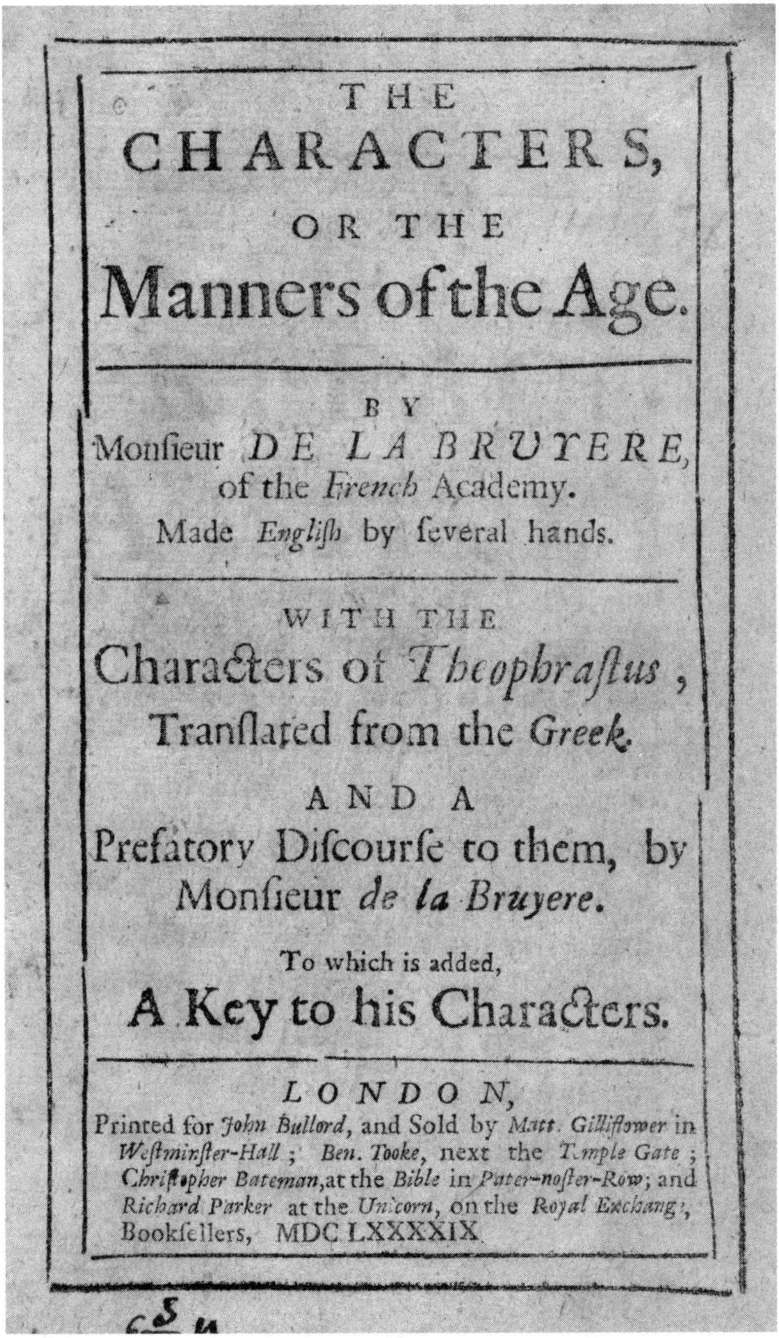

THE

CHARACTERS,

OR THE

Manners of the Age.

BY

Monſieur *DE LA BRUYERE*,

of the *French* Academy.

Made *Engliſh* by ſeveral hands.

WITH THE

Characters of *Theophraſtus*,

Tranſlated from the *Greek*.

AND A

Prefatory Diſcourſe to them, by

Monſieur *de la Bruyere*.

To which is added,

A Key to his Characters.

LONDON,

Printed for *John Bullord*, and Sold by *Matt. Gilliflower* in *Weſtminſter-Hall*; *Ben. Tooke*, next the *Temple Gate*; *Chriſtopher Bateman*, at the *Bible* in *Pater-noſter-Row*; and *Richard Parker* at the *Unicorn*, on the *Royal Exchange*, Bookſellers, MDC LXXXXIX.

FIGURE 5.1. The first English translation was published just over a decade later, in 1699. *Credit:* *FC6 L1157 Eg699c, Houghton Library, Harvard University.

tus's *Characters,* which combined his own translation of the original Greek text with a modern adaptation (Figure 5.1). The latter, presented under the title *The Characters or the Manners of the Age,* painted the mores of seventeenth-century France in a sixteen-chapter compendium of maxims, sketches, aphorisms, reflections, and essays, collectively described as "remarks."[4] The work was such a hit that it ran into eight editions in five years, in an effort of publishing and republishing that has recently been described as a modern "media enterprise."[5]

Within this media enterprise, La Bruyère developed a new path to moral reform through character-writing: one that paired satirical portraits with theological reflections, exposing human corruption in order to justify the truth of Christianity and to Christianize social practices. We can call this new path *moral satire.* In developing moral satire, La Bruyère departed from the tactics of negative imitation, present in the sixteenth-century translations, and the neo-Stoic implicit instruction found in Hall and Overbury. For La Bruyère, character sketches could no longer carry out reform on their own, as these earlier translators and adapters thought, but would need to be paired with a reflective discourse.

La Bruyère has typically been read as one of the seventeenth-century French *moralistes,* alongside François duc de La Rochefoucauld and Blaise Pascal. The term is usually used to designate a group of authors, from Montaigne to the eighteenth-century Vauvenargues, who were more concerned "with moral psychology rather than with morality as such" and who provided acute descriptions of human nature free from "moral lessons."[6] As one scholar has put it, "What the *moralistes* meant by *morale* had less to do with moral principles than with mores and manners, less with ethics than with *ethos.* (. . .) Moralists observed without being concerned with commandments or ethical doctrines."[7] It is their presumed rejection of normative pronouncements that made the *moralistes* so appealing to Nietzsche, who describes them as "French masters of soul searching" whose incisive remarks "are like accurately aimed arrows, which hit the mark again and again, the black mark of man's nature."[8] La Bruyère, viewed in this light, has often been placed among the "detached analysts of human passions," not someone interested in trying to shape a reader's actions.[9] Indeed, he presents a world so static, so fixed, so impossible to reform, that

Roland Barthes—in a dated expression—described the experience of reading him as akin to hearing a new profession of "the Hindu law which prescribes the immobility of things and of castes."[10]

Since the 1990s, however, this interpretation has been substantially challenged, above all by the scholarship of François-Xavier Cuche, who has definitively contextualized La Bruyère as both a significant Catholic religious thinker and a social reformist: two impulses that in La Bruyère's work are deeply intertwined.[11] Cuche has shown that from 1673, La Bruyère was part of a group called the Petit Concile, an organization that included the French bishop Jacques-Bénigne Bossuet, the archbishop François Fénelon, the playwright Jean Racine, the satirist Nicolas Boileau, and the church historian Claude Fleury. This organization began as a Bible reading group but extended into one of the "major intellectual poles of French Catholicism in the second half of the seventeenth century."[12] Its aim was to uphold two fundamental projects: providing Christian apology, the theological genre designed to justify the truth of Christian belief, and attempting to "Christianize customs and social practices, in the framework of a modern state."[13] The works of its members—from Fleury's 1681 *Manners of the Hebrews,* to Fénelon's 1699 *Adventures of Telemachus,* to La Bruyère's own *Characters or Manners of the Age*—were designed, as Cuche concludes, to "lead man and society to their profound vocations, that is to say vocations that are divine."[14] The group tasked themselves with critiquing misery and excessive inequality (in part because they are an obstacle to believing in a just God), promoting more primitive, ancient ways of life (such as those of the Athenians and the Hebrews), sketching precise social interventions (including civic physical education and a more widespread study of languages), and believing in the importance of a prosperous monarchical state, characterized by open commerce.

The Petit Concile was optimistic. They believed in progress and in the possibility of social change. This distinguished them from the other major intellectual pole of French Catholicism in the seventeenth-century: Jansenism. Jansenism offered an approach to Catholicism that began from a close study of Augustine, taking its name from Cornelius Jansenius, the Bishop of Ypres, who published a three-volume interpretation of Augustine's system in 1640. His interpretation emphasized the importance of the doctrine of original sin and underlined the rarity of God giving a person the grace needed to cure it, as well as the precariousness of grace once received.[15] The Jansenists, who maintained that only God's predestined grace could permit someone to lead a moral life, were not optimistic social reformers as much as ascetics interested in retreat.[16] The Petit Concile did not share this sensibility, even if they were influenced by other aspects of neo-Augustinian philosophy: theirs was a form of "Catholic social thought that defied all pessimism," Cuche writes.[17] Cuche was able to develop this contrasting view of La Bruyère, not only because of the context of the Petit Concile but also because he—unlike "the majority of critics"—took seriously the final, sixteenth chapter of La Bruyère's *Characters or Manners of the Age,* which was dedicated to theology.[18] Cuche heeds La Bruyère's own admission that though the fifteen previous chapters were concerned with "discovering the falsehood and the ridiculousness" of man, they did so in order to prepare for the last chapter, in which "atheism is attacked, and perhaps confounded."[19]

I too see La Bruyère as someone fundamentally interested in moral and social change, who thought that he could get there by pairing character-writing with theological reflection. Since Cuche, the meaning of the term *moraliste* itself has shifted, away from a kind of writing defined by the absence of normative pronouncements to one characterized by certain aspects of form: *moraliste* writing is "generally in prose, non-fictional, fragmentary."[20] Now the *moralistes* are seen as writers for whom the act of description and the work of social, political, and religious critique were often very much entangled. For Larry Norman, the "praise of ancient moral simplicity" in La Bruyère's comments on Theophrastus is a form of "biting criticism" against Louis XIV's contemporary regime.[21] For Damien Tricoire, La Bruyère's interest in practical reform means that he should be read as a precursor to Enlightenment *philosophes* like Voltaire and Diderot.[22] For Christophe Schuwey, La Bruyère's "media enterprise" was in fact all part of this project, a means for him to "act in the world" repeatedly, in multiple editions of the same text.[23] Where Cuche is interested in how La Bruyère, in his optimism, founded "a new apologetic," I argue that *The Characters or Manners of the Age* founded a new defense of character-writing.[24] This defense is moral satire, where satirical sketches combine with moralizing theology in the service of Christianizing both the reader and their society.

La Bruyère's moral satire represents a departure not only from the English approach to character-writing but from the way in which character-writing had developed in France. His *Characters or Manners of the Age* moves beyond an earlier French neo-Stoic revival, associated with translations of Hall. It also moves beyond empiricist character sketches of the passions, which aimed to show how to understand people's feelings from their external manifestations. La Bruyère could not trust that a reader would be reformed by browsing exemplary portraits of a virtuous sage. He was equally unconvinced that one could understand someone's interior from sketches of their actions. Just like the Civil War in England, the upheaval of the Fronde, paired with a pessimistic neo-Augustinian philosophy, significantly disturbed the notion that a person's actions were a good guide to their motives.

Instead of taking inspiration from earlier French character writers of a neo-Stoic or empiricist bent, La Bruyère set himself alongside La Rochefoucauld and Pascal. Where La Bruyère departs from previous character writers, he thus joins these *moralistes*—understood, in light of this new scholarship, as fragmentary writers who balance acute psychological description with an attempt at reform. La Bruyère's character-writing, as I argue, is most closely linked to the argumentative structure present in both La Rochefoucauld's *Maxims* and Pascal's *Pensées*. Like *The Characters or Manners of the Age,* both texts make two key gestures: an initial move of laying out corrupted human nature, followed by the deployment of a set of sophisticated arguments, which uses this portrait of corruption as a means "to make a Man a Christian."[25] These authors' procedure of first diagnosing individual and social pathologies before proceeding to offer cures or therapies might even be considered a version of the process that the Frankfurt School later made famous under the banner of critical theory.[26]

In the form of moral satire, La Bruyère introduces a new connection between character-writing and moral philosophy, one that is distinct from the native tradition of character-writing in France, as well as earlier moral readings of character sketches. In his *Characters or Manners of the Age,* La Bruyère wanted to find a moral form that did not rely on the work of exemplarity and that acknowledged his reigning mistrust of appearances. To do so, he developed moral satire: a form characterized by skepticism about the capacity of sketches to reform readers on their own. La Bruyère's duplex edition has other noteworthy qualities, which break with a number of assumptions that undergirded the humanist translations. In choosing to translate Theophrastus *and* write his own adaptation, La Bruyère betrays a refusal to imagine that the original depictions of Athenian men could still shape contemporary readers. In promising that his adaptation would represent "the Vices of the mind," unlike Theophrastus, La Bruyère further departs from the belief that someone's nature could be discerned from their behavior alone. For La Bruyère, the pedagogical nature of Theophrastus's *Characters* could no longer be taken for granted, due both to how long ago it was written and to its focus on people's actions rather than motives. In his careful questioning of how this ancient text could do new moral work, his promise to represent the interior, and his incorporation of theological reflection alongside sketches, La Bruyère thus outlines a new approach to Theophrastan character-writing as a strategy to change the world around him. To understand La Bruyère's decisive break with the tradition of character-writing, however, first requires a sense of what it meant to write a character sketch under the reigns of Louis XIII (1601–1643) and Louis XIV (1638–1715), what it meant to depict social mores in the French *grand siècle*.

French Character-Writing

One major trend of character-writing in seventeenth-century France involved theorizing the emotions, or the passions.[27] The notion of the passions was a subject of deep debate in the period, in which defenders of the value of the passions set themselves against neo-Stoics, who wanted to control the passions through reason. The passions were also a subject that combined many emerging fields of study, from the more biological physiology to moral philosophy as well as physiognomy, the art of determining someone's character from their facial traits.

In 1635, the twelve-year-old Henry de Boyvin du Varoüy decided to translate Adamantius's *Physiognomy*: a text by a fifth-century CE

Jewish Alexandrian philosopher. In his preface, du Varoüy claimed that this work would provide readers with "the clues that nature has placed in the human body by which one can discover the morals, and inclinations of a person."[28] This, he maintains, is "a science" of interpreting "mute things" and discerning from these "unmistakable signs" the nature of people's mores and inclinations.[29] Flicking through the *Physiognomy,* the reader would learn, for example, that "small eyes which shine or throb think only of deceiving and doing harm."[30] One major work of character-writing that emerged in France in the 1640s was written in precisely this vein and well represents an approach to the genre as a means to discern an individual's animating passion from a study of their behavior. It is this assumption that La Rochefoucauld and Pascal would challenge after the Fronde, providing La Bruyère with a new model to adopt in his own writing.

This work is *The Characters of the Passions,* a five-volume study written by Louis XIV's personal doctor, Marin Cureau de La Chambre, from 1640 to 1662. La Chambre writes characters out of an underlying desire to determine man's interior from his external appearance. In his approach, he only substitutes Adamantius's focus on interpreting unchanging physical attributes, like small eyes, for an investigation of the range of external manifestations of internal passions. His precise approach to providing something like a human science, a key for interpreting other people's natures, is to show how the passions make individuals act so that their animating passions can be recognized and their behavior made foreseeable. This project of better comprehending the connection between external appearances, or actions, and their internal causes, or passions, was also taken up by René Descartes in his 1649 *The Passions of the Soul.* Alongside La Chambre's *Characters of the Passions,* Descartes's treatise presents an important context against which La Bruyère reacted in his character-writing.

La Chambre was interested in carrying out an extensive study of the passions in order to benefit the fields of "medicine, moral philosophy and politics."[31] The reader who assiduously studies his volumes would gain, he claims, "the art of knowing men."[32] This is an art that uses people's actions to discern the nature of their overriding passion, which can then be used to explain their future behavior. It works through two main mechanisms: indicating which actions are tagged to specific passions (being bilious, for example, expresses an inclination to anger) and then explaining how one set of passions helps to predict another.[33] This second approach will help the reader determine, for example, that a man who acts as if he is timid is in fact inclined to avarice, which in itself reveals that he is suspicious, incredulous, and a bad friend. "Although one does not notice any particular signs of all these last qualities," La Chambre continues, "one does not fail to judge that they are to be found there, because one has connected the principle from which they take their origin."[34] The assumption here is that what we see of another human being is useful data for discerning who they really are, as long as we are furnished with the right method of interpretation. "Nature, having destined man for civil life," La Chambre's first treatise on the passions begins, "was not content to have given him a tongue in order to reveal his intentions; she also wished to imprint on his forehead and eyes the images of his thoughts, so that if his word should contradict his heart, his face might contradict his word."[35] Where, for Hobbes, man's character was an unknowable question of the heart, for La Chambre, the face is its window.

The line that La Chambre started to trace reached a high point with Descartes's *The Passions of the Soul.* More than ten years earlier, Descartes had written his *Dioptrique,* accounting for the physical processes that lead to sight. But in *The Passions of the Soul,* he wanted to determine whether, assuming a series of causal processes can explain how we see, what the processes would be to explain how we feel and where they would be located. He first clarifies that the "passions of the soul" refers to all the kinds of perception or knowledge that are found inside us that our soul did not create. These are opposed to the actions of the soul, which the soul produces directly.[36] Building on this distinction, Descartes proposes an explanation for the origin of the passions of the soul and for their effects.

In Descartes's argument, we begin by perceiving something in the world—for example, seeing a flame or hearing a bell—through our sense organs. These organs then excite the nerves in the brain, which in turn produce a feeling in the soul. "Thus when we see the light of a torch and hear the sound of a bell," Descartes explains, "this sound and this light are two different actions which, by that very fact that they excite two different movements in some of our nerves, and by their means in the brain, give the soul two different feelings."[37] The feelings they provoke do not end in the soul but incite and dispose the soul "to want the things for which they prepare their bodies."[38] The feeling of fear, for example, incites the soul to want to flee, an action that requires the participation of the body. Pairing the two examples together, we move, that is, from the perception of an object in the world (seeing the torch), to a physical effect (the eyes excite the nerves in the brain), to a feeling (fear), to its concomitant desire (to flee), to a physical behavior (the body's motion).

Through emphasizing the central role of the body, and focusing on this empirical process, Descartes hopes to fulfill his desire not to "explain the passions as an orator or moral philosopher, but only as a physician."[39] Though his methodology certainly distinguishes him from these other roles, his intention to point to the relationship between the passions and the actions seems to continue the project of moral philosophers like La Chambre.[40] While La Chambre underlines which behaviors are signs of which passions, Descartes examines which passions cause which behaviors.[41] Both approaches, however, rely on the idea of a correspondence between interior passions and exterior actions.[42] If we understand this correspondence, the theory goes, we will be able to see into other people's hearts. As the century wore on, however, confidence waned that people's behavior would be so easy to interpret.

The Effect of the Fronde

In the major accounts of the writings provoked by the Fronde, the literary genre of the character is not mentioned as a political vehicle. Although satire became "one of the great literary genres of the Fronde," the desire for satirical expression did not take the form of writing sketches of factions.[43] This device was not used to help readers make judgments in a moment of mistrust and disharmony. The Fronde, unlike the English Revolution, did not therefore directly transform the practice of character-writing. But this is not to say that it did not leave a significant mark on the thinking behind that genre. Its effects are not found in the kinds of characters that this genre represents as much as in the way that they are represented. The crisis of the Fronde, paired with the rise in neo-Augustinian philosophy, contributed to a changed understanding of the correspondence between passions and actions. This is especially apparent in the work of La Rochefoucauld and Pascal. Where La Chambre and Descartes saw a correspondence between interior passions and exterior appearances, post-Fronde writers like La Rochefoucauld and Pascal were not so confident. Having been through a civil war, in which people who once seemed virtuous proved themselves otherwise, these writers focused instead on unmasking "the black mark of human nature" behind seemingly positive human qualities.

ABSENT POLITICAL CHARACTERS

In Hubert Carrier's many lists of the eclectic forms of writing that emerged over the course of the Fronde, character-writing does not appear. There were "letters, tales, narratives, dialogues, multi-character playlets, farces, ballets, even tragi-comedies, portraits, predictions and visions, consolations and regrets, paraphrases of psalms or hymns, sermons, panegyrics, satires, songs and triplets, not forgetting speeches, epitaphs, epigrams and other Latin pieces"—but never characters.[44] Nor does Joël Cornette mention character in his discussion of the "great diversity of format" in the Fronde literature, a body of work so large and so wide ranging that he dubs it "an Estates General of words."[45] If the Fronde literature is an Estates General, the third and most populous estate is by far the Mazarinades: a genre of personal invective against the eponymous chief minister that runs to about 6,000 works.[46]

Within the more restricted set of Mazarinades, there are no character sketches of Mazarin, nor any of the *frondeurs,* the regent, or Mazarin's supporters. The closest we get to a character sketch are two anonymous portraits of Mazarin, neither of which is at all Theophrastan: *The Ambitious Man, or the Portrait of Aelius Sejanus in the Person of Cardinal Mazarin,* written in 1649, and *The True Character of a Tyrant, or All of Mazarin's Maxims,* published in 1650. The former portrait is structured as a parallel between the two figures, continuing a tradition of Plutarchan parallel lives, which paired famous Greeks with famous Romans, and was much imitated by early modern authors.[47] It uses the history of Sejanus to help explain and predict Mazarin's moves, rather than detailing Mazarin's typical actions or appearance and using this to access his motivating passions. The character writer of this sketch is most intent on illustrating how "the final disloyalties of Sejanus" mirror those of Mazarin: "Sejanus removed the Emperor Tiberius from the city of Rome: and Mazarin in a moment of popular rejoicing removed the King from *Palais Royal*."[48] The latter portrait also has little interest in descriptions of Mazarin's habits. It instead describes Mazarin's character by ironically outlining eleven of his "maxims," from "1. Never forgive" to "11. Never out of sincerity, always out of intrigue."[49] In France, unlike in England, the Theophrastan character seems not to have been used to illuminate the schisms that political crisis uncovered or provoked.[50]

A number of circumstances might explain this difference. Perhaps the terms of the Fronde favored literary genres that dealt with the individual, Mazarin, as opposed to types or groups.[51] This could explain why, while character-writing was in abeyance, the genre of portraits and parallels had astronomical success, alongside the *romans à clef*, such as Madeline de Scudéry's *Le Grand Cyrus* (1648–1653), with its clear correspondence to particular individuals.[52] One might also underline how the Fronde both produced and relied on fewer social schisms, as compared to the English Revolution. It was free from the scourge of additional religious conflict—and therefore from the further subcategories of political orientations this could generate—and there was "no French parallel to the Leveller movement," as Richard Bonney has claimed.[53] With fewer new types created by the conflict, there may have been less of a need to characterize their unfamiliar natures. Finally, there is the fact that the Fronde emerged in a society distinctly less socially mobile than England. (Debate still rages about whether it failed because the bourgeoisie was too underdeveloped to play its historical role in leading the first stage of the revolution.) This could have meant that the equivalent urge to classify people more generally, in order to make sense of a dynamic and moveable world of new, undefined combinations of social, economic, professional, and political types, simply did not present itself.[54]

While there is probably some truth in all these explanations, a simpler answer might lie in the fact that the characters of social and professional types written by the Overburians and Earle were not translated until the conflict had long subsided, when James Dymocke, an English Catholic living in France, published a translation that combined aspects of the two in 1671. To put this counterfactually, if this set of characters had been translated sooner, there would have been a precedent for seeing character-writing as a sociological rather than a purely moral form. In this case, French writers would have been presented with the possibility of a literary tool with which to make sense of any new social types that presented themselves during the Fronde. Without this initial groundwork, the character in France had no foundation to move away from its familiar function as a genre for describing individuals, passions, vice, and virtue.

Dymocke's translation did not, however, have a major impact on the development of character-writing in France, with only one edition printed and very few epigone imitators.[55] Even if the Overburians and Earle had been translated earlier, that is, it is certainly possible that this more social method of character-writing might not have caught on in France. Resistance to the character sketch taking on a more social function of representing trades and other equivalent categories may have been heightened in France as compared to England as a result of *honnêteté*: the ruling ideal of social desirability for the noble class, which involved eschewing the world of professions and specialization.[56] Just as the law of *dérogeance* meant that in France, noble status would be lost by participating in a trade, the choice to write about these professions by a member of the noble class would not be taken lightly.[57] For Erich Auerbach, it is in part the valorization of *honnêteté* that explains why the popular and professional classes were only represented in the literature of the period as grotesque bit parts.[58] In the years after the Fronde, we instead find major works by two *moralistes,* La Rochefoucauld and Pascal, grappling with the question of whether it was still possible to associate people's actions with their internal motives.

FALSE VIRTUES: LA ROCHEFOUCAULD

La Rochefoucauld participated in the Fronde after having carried out several attempts to block Mazarin's power across the 1640s.[59] After the conflict was over, he began writing a series of maxims and essays that would eventually be gathered under the title *Reflections or Sentences and Moral Maxims,* first printed in 1664.[60] La Rochefoucauld's desire in this work, as he put in a letter of December 5 of 1659 or 1660, was to disabuse those who believed in the "truth of virtues."[61] This intention is intimately connected with the conflict through which La Rochefoucauld had just lived. He was a man who had staked his whole life on obeying the value system of the aristocracy—who, up to the age of thirty, spent his time benefitting from a "militant and optimistic age"—only to experience "the ruin of his class, his ideology and his life."[62] His work, demystifying seeming truths and virtues, is a testament to this disenchantment.

As Jean Rohou intimates, because the Fronde marked the end of the value system of heroism, aristocrats like La Rochefoucauld were left without a means to satisfy their drive to recognition.[63] What came to fill this lacuna was the value of *honnêteté,* developing the means to please polite society not through martial honor but through a high degree of complaisance and refined social graces. This was a much less violent social ideal than heroism, but it was also much harder to secure. Where martial competence could be proved by deed, *honnêteté* relied on impressions: leaving it to individuals to try to see behind other people's veneer of politeness. Both La Rochefoucauld and Pascal questioned this new ideal for the ease with which it could lapse into falsity. This perspective set the stage for La Bruyère's *Characters,* which evinced a similar skepticism about the difficulty of discerning someone's "morals and inclinations" from the "clues" given to us by nature, as Adamantius and his seventeenth-century imitators had promised.

Rather than providing a way to decipher or explain someone's appearances, La Rochefoucauld wanted to outline how far appearances were deceiving, particularly the appearance of virtue. "Our virtues, more often than not, are only vices in disguise," announces the epigraph to his maxims, a work he later summarizes as "having spoken about the falsity of so many apparent virtues."[64] Instead of trusting the presentation of virtue, and determining which passion might be its cause, La Rochefoucauld questions the nature of the initial impression. Behind apparent virtue, he claims, there will often be a vicious motivation: "What we take to be virtues," his first maxim reads, "are often nothing more than a combination of various actions derived from various interests."[65] In Jon Elster's expression, this makes La Rochefoucauld "one of the main originators of what has been called the hermeneutics of suspicion."[66]

For this reason, La Rochefoucauld's work calls to mind the rhetorical technique of *paradiastole,* which involves redescribing vices as virtues and virtues as vices.[67] As we saw in the previous chapter, *paradiastole* held a major place in early modern moral and political thought, often because it was seen as a moral danger: *paradiastole* exposed how language alone could change the moral character of a person in a given situation. With the use of this figure, "even Satan himself can be transformed into an angel of light," worries the rhetorician Johannes Susenbrotus. With the help of *paradiastole,* writes Hall, "the Curtizan is *bona femina,* the Sorcerer a wise man, the oppressor a good husband."[68] Quentin Skinner recounts how, in the English Renaissance, the power ascribed to the art of eloquence, and to *paradiastole* in particular, led to a series of metaethical problems involving how to agree on whom to admire and why.[69] In seventeenth-century France, La Rochefoucauld's adoption of this figure introduced similar issues: in particular, the way in which a new disjuncture between virtuous behavior and vicious motives starts to make the description of appearances on their own redundant and a new search for moral reform paramount.

For La Rochefoucauld, the greatest of these vicious motives is *amour-propre*: the old Augustinian notion concerning the practice of self-idolatry rather than the love of God. This notion had been revived in 1640 with the publication of *Augustinus* by Jansenius.[70] In its new meaning, a Jansenized notion of *amour-propre* came to indicate something closer to "interested egocentrism, as opposed to altruism."[71] The presence of a psychological foundation of interests and egoism put significant pressure on the notion of a possible correspondence between behavior and motives. Where La Chambre traced a straight line from the body to the heart—with a man's bilious behavior pointing to his irascible disposition—La Rochefoucauld's insistence on the human being's corrupt nature would sever, or at least kink, its direction.

AGAINST NEO-STOICISM

With this moral philosophy, few of the methods promising moral improvement that were circulating seemed possible for La Rochefoucauld to uphold—especially those offered by neo-Stoicism. Alongside characters of the passions, seventeenth-century France saw many works of neo-Stoicism published, which provided the reader with character sketches of virtuous sages to imitate. This wave of exemplary writing found a central inspiration in the translations and adaptations of Joseph Hall. Two years after Hall's *Characters* appeared in London in 1608, it was translated by the Parisian Huguenot Jean Loiseau de Tourval.[72] Though Tourval's translation of Hall was highly popular, it was a different adaptation of Hall that was to have the most impact.[73] This was the Catholic Urbain Chevreau's 1659 *The School of the Sage*.[74] Chevreau's volume ran to eleven editions in twenty-one years, and an Italian translation of it was also published in 1666.[75] In Chevreau's text, the life of the Stoic sage, to which Hall had gestured, is elaborated in a set of chapters dedicated to his different qualities: his charity, indifference, force, constancy, prudence, conversation, and mental tranquility. Chevreau's stated aim is to use this description of the sage as a paragon for imitation, a sage who "is so much his own master, that nothing is capable of subjecting him, apart from virtue."[76]

Chevreau explains his choice of title to his reader thus: "I wanted this book to have *The School of the Sage* as its title, in order to show you the path that you have taken."[77] This offers a version of the kind of exemplarity present in Hall's *Characters of Vertues and Vices,* in which the reader is entreated to "fall in love" with portraits of virtue and then embody them. Both Hall and Chevreau are not content with depicting vice alone but want to depict positive types that their readers can imitate. This logic of imitation is also present within Chevreau's sketches of exemplary figures. "The True Christian," for example, "fortifies himself by examples, serving himself of past things as infallible demonstrations."[78] The importance of exemplarity was part of a wave of French neo-Stoicism that extended beyond Chevreau, embodied in works such as Sébastien de Senlis's *The Maxims of the Sage* (1648); Puget de La Serre's *The Spirit of Seneca* (1657); P. Jean Marie de Bordeaux's *Christian Epictetus* (1658); and Jean Testu du Mauroy's *The Honesty of Customs according to Seneca's Maxims* (1666).[79] Positive exemplarity can also be found elsewhere, in earlier works such as Pierre Boitel's depiction of illustrious men (1617).[80]

La Rochefoucauld, however, found both neo-Stoicism and moral exemplarity unconvincing. "Whatever difference that there is between good and bad examples," he comments in a remark on "Des Exemples" in his later *Miscellaneous Reflections,* "one will find that both have produced almost equally negative effects."[81] Given that virtues are neighbors to vice and that we are so full of falsehood, we use examples, he concludes, just as much "to lead us away from the path of virtue, as to follow it."[82] Rather than sketching virtuous character types, the genre that most appealed to La Rochefoucauld, and others close to him with a similar philosophy, was the portrait.[83] After having emerged in Mlle de Scudéry's novels, the portrait became a salon genre, highly popular in the salons of Mlle de Montpensier and the Marquise de Sablé. Both were frequented by La Rochefoucauld, who penned a portrait of himself for one of the collections that emerged from these *jeux.*[84] The rules of this genre were very different from those of the Theophrastan character: the aim was to fix a person, not a type, and to even allude to them by classical pseudonym, initials, or simply their real name.[85] In its profound aim to see through appearances and cut through doubt, it is a genre deeply anchored in a suspicious moment.

If moral exemplarity was not a possible remedy for human vice and falsity, neither was the strategy of self-control offered by the neo-Stoics. For La Rochefoucauld, it was an absurd fiction to imagine that the patient training of tranquility or *ataraxia* would shift people from their base of *amour-propre.* The first four editions of his *Maxims* were accordingly prefaced with a frontispiece showing a small cherub labeled "Love of the truth." The cherub holds a mask of serenity that he has ripped off a bust of Seneca to reveal a face weathered by time and riven with worry that had been hiding beneath it.[86] This does not mean that La Rochefoucauld abandoned the search for a cure, however, and in the essayistic reflections that follow his maxims, he offers normative remedies. These include, for example, the notion that to make society livable, "each person must retain his or her freedom: we must see each other, or not see each other, without subjection."[87]

This double move of revealing human corruption and proposing means of remedying it introduces a philosophical structure into La Rochefoucauld's text that is close to the structure of Christian apology. La Rochefoucauld exposes this most clearly in his representation of his *Maxims* after its publication. In a letter of February 6, 1664, to Thomas Esprit, the brother of Jacques Esprit (a *moraliste* with whom La Rochefoucauld initially collaborated on the *Maxims,* along with de Sablé), La Rochefoucauld defends his *Maxims* from the attacks of criminality that they had provoked by arguing that his target was to criticize pride, "which, as far I've heard, is not necessary for salvation."[88] It seemed to him that "the miseries and contradictions of the human heart cannot be exaggerated enough to humiliate the shameful pride with which we are filled" in order to make us see our need for Christianity to support and restore us.[89] This opens up a path to moral instruction in La Rochefoucauld's collection, which would involve placing the human being in the context of their vices in the hope to eventually make them realize their need for improvement. The question of how far this path is indebted to neo-Augustinian or Jansenist currents remains an issue of debate.[90] What is crucial for our purpose—understanding how La Rochefoucauld informed the method of La Bruyère—is the presence of this double move: of breaking the human being down and, in doing so, indicating how to build them back up again. How exactly this works is not made clear in the text, but the letter suggests that the more we read about "the miseries and contradictions of the human heart," the more we will realize our need for Christianity to be able to reform them.[91]

PASCAL'S CHRISTIAN APOLOGY

Pascal's *Pensées,* published posthumously in 1670, embraces a similar structure in a more explicitly apologetic work.[92] In one of his early *pensées,* he writes that the first part of his envisaged apology for Christianity will show the "wretchedness of man without God" and will highlight that "nature is corrupt, proved by nature itself" (§4).[93] The second part will show the "happiness of man with God" and reveal that "there is a Redeemer, proved by Scripture" (§4).[94]

The *pensées* in the first part show Pascal surprised that "the vanity of the world should be so little recognized" (§14), as he considers this a dominant social passion and "the cause and effect of love" (§42).[95] The vanity that animates love is part of a broader idea of the human being as subject to pride and presumption

(§333). Here we see a version of the *amour-propre* central to La Rochefoucauld's anthropology and a similar act of substituting a seeming virtue for a vice. This connection between La Rochefoucauld and Pascal continues in how the *Pensées* emphasizes the broader problem of deceptive appearances. For Pascal, we are constantly deceived by our two means of truth, reason and the senses, which are "not only both not genuine, but are engaged in mutual deception" (§41).[96] Explicitly referencing the Cartesian model, Pascal explains that the process by which sensory perception is converted into the passions of the soul (*les passions de l'âme*) is full of error. He writes, "The senses deceive reason through false appearances, and, just as they trick the soul, they are tricked by it in their turn: it takes its revenge. The senses are disturbed by passions [of the soul], which produce false impressions. They both compete in lies and deception" (§41).[97] Like La Rochefoucauld, Pascal was also at odds with neo-Stoicism's approach to moral instruction, thinking that Epictetus overstretched his notion of human capacities, ignoring our corrupt nature.[98] The simple act of imitating a sage would not be sufficient for Pascal, as natural human error "cannot be eradicated except through grace" (§41).[99]

More so than La Rochefoucauld, Pascal makes explicit the religious argument that undergirds the *Pensées* and explains how its two parts fit together. "For a religion to be true," Pascal says, "it must have known our nature; it must have known its greatness and smallness, and the reason for both. What other religion but Christianity has known this?" (§201).[100] By exposing our nature's smallness—the falsity of our reason and senses—alongside our imagined greatness—our vanity, pride, and presumption—Pascal offers an argument for the truth of Christianity through its unique understanding of the human status as being "both." The two parts of Pascal's unfinished work—a first part revealing the contradictions of our nature and a second showing the remedy—are interlaced in precisely this way. The very fact of this human contradiction reveals the truth of Christianity and the cure it presents for human iniquity.

Pascal thereby proposes a more elaborate version of the rhetorical and theological move found in La Rochefoucauld: aiming, through his remarks, to lead his reader "to the verge" of faith.[101] This move represents a particular strategy for how to carry out moral instruction, markedly different from those that we have considered so far. It is this two-part process, of revealing the human being's limitations in order to pave the way for religious reform, that provides a precedent for La Bruyère's *Characters or Manners of the Age*.

La Bruyère's Moral Satire

La Bruyère was forty-three by the time he published his duplex edition in 1688.[102] He had been educated by the Oratorian order—where he would have picked up Augustinianism—had taken a degree in law, and had benefitted from a substantial inheritance, which he had used when he was twenty-eight to buy the position of "Treasurer of France, General of Finances at the Caen Office."[103] This post came with a number of responsibilities, most of which he ignored: for the thirteen years that he held it, he did not go to one meeting at the Bureau of Caen. Instead, he became a counselor to the king at twenty-nine, a position that conferred nobility. This gave him a set of connections that offered him the opportunity to become a governor. Over a period of fifteen years, he tutored the children of the marquis of Soyecourt-Belleforière and the grandson of one of the most major *frondeurs*: Louis II de Bourbon-Condé. When Condé died in 1686, La Bruyère was liberated from his teaching responsibilities but continued to benefit from the ability to live in any one of the three residences of the Condé in Chantilly, Versailles, and Paris. He received a generous pension, maintained the title of "Monsieur le Duc," and was employed as a gentleman in the court of the Duke of Enghien.[104]

Two years later, he published his translation of Theophrastus's *Characters,* followed by his own *Characters or Manners of the Age*—a collection that brought together maxims, aphorisms, and sketches. Each of these works has a separate preface. The first print run of this duplex edition sold out in two weeks, an indication of the immense popularity that it would garner: La Bruyère produced at least eight new editions, perhaps nine, before he died in 1696.[105] Each of these editions expanded in size, and by the eighth edition of 1694, the number of "remarks" had increased threefold.[106]

In this work, La Bruyère developed a new means for carrying out moral instruction through character-writing, distinct from both the native French tradition and the earlier moral interpretations across Europe. He made three major changes. First, La Bruyère decided to add his own adaptation of contemporary mores (*The Manners of the Age*) to Theophrastus's ancient portraits. Second, he decided not to depict external actions but internal motives. And third, he developed a technique of moral satire by pairing an account of man's interior viciousness with a theological argument, with the aim of Christianizing both individuals and the social customs of their societies.

ATHENS AND PARIS

In the preface to his translation of Theophrastus, La Bruyère indicates, following Casaubon and Hall, that there are three ways to teach morality, with Theophrastus representing the third option. "What probability is there to please all the so different tastes of Men, by one single Tract of Morality?" he asks, given the diversity of human desire and taste.[107] Some people, he continues, "search for Definitions, Divisions, Tables and Method (. . .) desirous to have explain'd what Vertue is in general, and then every Vertue in particular, what difference there is between Valour, Fortitude and Magnanimity; the extreme Vices, either in defect or excess, betwixt whom each vertue is placed."[108] Others are satisfied "to have Manners reduced to the Passions, and to demonstrate them by the motion of the Blood, by the Fibres and Arteries," and still others, that the "whole Doctrine of Manners ought to tend to their Reformation; to distinguish the good from the bad, and to discover what is vain, weak and ridiculous, from what is good, solid and commendable."[109]

Where both Casaubon and Hall divided moral philosophy into dogmatic, paraenetic, and Theophrastan methods, La Bruyère proposed a different threefold classification: a first group of Aristotelian moral philosophers, with their tables and their interest in excess, deficiency, and means; a second group of moral philosophers interested in the physiology of the passions; and finally a group not interested in the explanation as much as the reformation of mores and the concrete discovery of the vices and virtues held by individuals.[110] Just as La Bruyère's own *Characters or Manners of the Age* sparked a wave of interpreters interested in guessing the particular individuals who inspired his vicious personae, this comment has led editors to speculate about the referents for these categories in seventeenth-century France.[111] The most likely trio might be a contemporary Aristotelian like Nicolas Coëffeteau, who wrote a *Table of Human Passions* in 1620; a physiologist like La Chambre (or perhaps Descartes); and then La Bruyère himself.[112] With this, La Bruyère distances Theophrastus's *Characters,* as well as his own, both from Aristotelian approaches to virtue as well as empiricist explanations of the passions.

Once hooked onto the third approach, La Bruyère makes one important clarification. The only issue with people who take this third approach to moral philosophy, he writes, is the way in which they reconcile "the Antients and Moderns."[113] In distinguishing the good from the bad in people, and discovering what is vain, weak, and ridiculous, they "infinitely solace themselves in the reading of Books." Presuming that "the Principles of Natural and Moral Philosophy" are simply repeated [*rebattus*] "by the Antients and Moderns," they then erroneously apply them "to the Manners of the times," just as we saw the humanist translators do in chapter 2.[114] From these principles they have read about, from these ancient "Images" that have become familiar to them, this third kind of moral philosopher starts to "correct men": a process, however, "from whence nevertheless they are not capable of deducing instructive inferences."[115] Theophrastus is then classified within this third school of moral philosophy—integrating "principles" with "Images" of men. But at the same time, La Bruyère preemptively critiques reading him in order to make fallacious deductions from the ancient to the contemporary—an error derived from the contentious supposition that between these periods, time has been suspended.[116]

This does not mean that we should only read the ancients *or* the moderns. La Bruyère had earlier said that people who read old texts live in ignorance, "not at all toucht with the Men that are about them, and with whom they live." Those concerned only with the moderns, on the other hand, are criticized for having "a great deal of Wit without Learning."[117] As both of these approaches present their own problems, the reader is left with a number of unsatisfactory options. If they use the ancients to judge the moderns, they will fall into the error of imagining that everything is commensurable. If they read only the ancients, they risk ignoring the world around them. And if they read only the moderns, they forsake learning.[118] The answer that La Bruyère proposes, in a canny bit of marketing, is a balance that involves publishing an ancient text with a modern adaptation appended to it. La Bruyère's edition of Theophrastus not only shows off that he can read ancient Greek, "legitimizing himself as learned," but also presents his text as a means of resolving the pressing quarrel between the ancients and the moderns.[119] This balance, however, requires him to develop an anthropology that links together the ancient and the modern, without relying on the notion of time's suspense that he has just critiqued.

La Bruyère outlines a particular vision of human nature in order to deal with this problem. When we read Theophrastus's *Characters,* despite "the diversity of Place and Climate [and] the long interval of time" between when it was written and when it is being read, "we may admire to know our selves there, our Friends, our Enemies, those whom we live with."[120] This tells us that "Mens Souls and Passions change not, they are yet still the same they were, and as they are described by *Theophrastus,* Vain, Dissemblers, Flatterers, Selfish, Impudent, Importunate, Distrustful, Backbiters, Quarrelsome, and Superstitions."[121] If human souls and passions remain the same, what does change are our customs, which "vary with the times."[122]

This perpetual variance in customs means that "we who are now Modern shall be ancient in a short time," as La Bruyère puts it.[123] Just as we regard the customs of the ancients as obsolete, he continues, so too will future generations see the customs of seventeenth-century France, when they hear of "the capital city of a great kingdom, which hath neither publick places, baths, fountains, amphitheaters, galleries, porticues, nor publick walks, which was notwithstanding a prodigious city." They will see our lives as historic, he says, when they are informed

> that some pass up and down the street only to seem to be in haste; that there is no familiarity or conversation there, but all is confusion, and as it were an alarm by the noise of coaches: which to avoid one must often run into the middle of the street, as fast as if he were on

> a race (. . .) that the inhabitants go to church, visit ladies and their friends, with offensive weapons, and that there is no person but carries at his side, where with at one push to murder another.[124]

If we would judge future generations for refusing themselves the pleasure of delighting in our cultural artifacts, on the basis of our strange customs, so too must we refuse our bad instinct of avoiding the works of the ancients for their barbarous mores. We must also, as La Bruyère's anthropological description of his own society makes clear, avoid taking our own customs too seriously. In this, La Bruyère offers a kind of "cultural pluralism."[125] "With a Language so pure, such nicety of Habit, Manners so cultivated, such good Laws, and white complections, we are Barbarians to some sort of people," he later quips.[126]

According to La Bruyère, the customs depicted in Theophrastus's *Characters* were just as anchored in their moment as contemporary French customs are in their own. This makes it difficult to agree with Gloria Vivenza that the "main difference between Theophrastus and La Bruyère" is that "Theophrastus's characters are abstract and universal, while La Bruyère portrays characters belonging to seventeenth-century French society."[127] La Bruyère is not providing a contemporary version of an abstract text but is instead recognizing the interplay of the universal and particular in both his and Theophrastus's *Characters*. This double sense is what led him to combine the ancient and the modern in one volume. It is a choice that he hopes will allow him to maneuver between the pitfalls of being "too remote" from the customs of the past and "too near those now in vogue" to be able "to make a just Observation of either."[128]

Thus La Bruyère offers a new way of theorizing the character sketch: as something that must at once be respected for its universality and rendered modern in its accoutrements. This represents a significant shift from the sixteenth-century Latin translators, who imagined it possible to simply use the Theophrastan sketch as a means of instructing contemporary mores. It is also a departure from those who only provide adaptations: either by expanding Theophrastus to include abstract virtues in the manner of Hall or adapting the form, like the Overburians and their successors, to provide new portraits rich in sociological detail.

La Bruyère's interest in balancing the belief that "Mans Souls and Passions change not" with a sensitivity to the transience of manners also affects the structure, content, and form of his own *Characters or Manners of the Age*. Structurally, this text combines reflections on the unchangeable corruption of human nature and targeted critiques of seventeenth-century French society. It is organized as a miscellany, around subject headings that range from the universal ("Of Man," "Of Women") to the more temporally specific ("Of the City," "Of the Court," "Of the Libertines or Wits of the Age"). In terms of content, the collection includes just as many statements dedicated to human self-interest as comments about the particularly nefarious quality of specific social and political conditions. Though careful in his prologue to deny that he is an "infallible" writer of maxims, La Bruyère makes many remarks about human corruption that carry this universalizable force.[129] Consider, for example, one of his epigrams: "The shortest and best way to make your Fortune, is to convince People tis their Interest to serve you." This advice is presented as relevant to the past, present, and future, given its insight into a fundamental fact about human nature. La Bruyère also lays out a thought experiment, imagining a situation in which there are two people left in the world. In this scenario, he says, no matter when it took place, a race to land possession would occur:

> Suppose there were but two men on the whole earth who possest it entirely to themselves, and parted it between them, I am perswaded there would be quickly some cause of rupture created, tho it were only for the limits of their divisions.[130]

These comments are, however, balanced with other remarks that frame particular social and political structures as especially blameworthy. Indeed, it is this aspect of La Bruyère's collection that allows a historical sociologist like Johan Heilbron to place La Bruyère among the thinkers who helped to develop the modern "idea that human beings can be understood from the social arrangements they form."[131] We can find this orientation in a number of places. It is evident in La Bruyère's comment that "under an arbitrary Government, Interest, Honour, and the service of the Prince, supply the place of a natural affection to our Country": a statement that suggests that self-interest can be bounded when a government is legitimate.[132] An interest in pinpointing particularly bad contemporary customs also emerges in the chapter "Of the Goods of Fortune," which contains many entries dedicated to critiquing the "partisan," a social type of the *nouveau riche* tax collector that had begun to appear in seventeenth-century France. It can further be found in La Bruyère's critique of the dominance of newspapers and his disdain for the social sphere. To this end, he writes character sketches like that of the figure of Boevius, who "lies down at night in tranquility relying upon some false news, which dies before morning, and he is oblig'd to abandon it as soon as he awakes," and of Narcissus, who

> rises in the Morning to lye down at Night, is six hours in his Dressing-Room (. . .). He reads exactly the *Dutch Gazzette*, *Barbin's News*, and the *Mercure Gallant*. (. . .) He walks with the Ladies in the Park or Meadows. He is religiously punctual in his Visits: He will do the same to Morrow, which he has done to day, and did yesterday. Thus he lives, and in this manner he will die.[133]

Rather than contenting themselves with truths, *Boevius* and *Narcissus* go in for "false news." Rather than structuring their lives to the service of improvement, of themselves or others, they are "religiously punctual" in their social visits. La Bruyère's description makes their lives seem pointless and repetitious. His choice of classical names for both, meanwhile, reflects the balance between the universal and the historic in the collection: their names place these characters outside of time, while the description places them firmly in a specific historical context.

VICES OF THE MIND

La Bruyère affirmed that, in writing his own characters, he had surpassed an essential aspect of Theophrastus's method. In the preface to his translation of Theophrastus, he writes, "I have mostly applied my self to the Vices of the mind, the secrets of the heart, and to all the interiour part of Man, which *Theophrastus* has not done."[134] Rather than focusing on "a thousand exterior things, which are observed in Man, by his Actions, his Words, his Gate," in imitation of Theophrastus; La Bruyère's new characters are "imploy'd about the thoughts, sentiments and inclinations of Men," in order to "discover the principle of their Villany and Folly."[135] From this principle, we will be able to "easily foresee all that they are capable to say or do; and abate our wonder at a Thousand Vicious and Frivolous actions, of which their Life is full."[136] La Bruyère's innovation is the promise to discover all that is beneath what is on show; that he himself can, as Moriarty puts it, "see through to the interior of other people."[137]

After almost a century of writing on the passions and other aspects of humanity's interior, La Bruyère could leave this arena untouched. All the more so since external appearances—someone's actions, words, and gait—could no longer be thought trustworthy sources to determine someone's nature after the Fronde. As La Bruyère's stated wish to discover "the principle" underlying villainy betrays, he is interested instead in what lies beneath what we see. La Chambre had used this language to the same effect in looking for "the principle from which [qualities] originate."[138] Only by discerning the principle, La Bruyère intimates, will we be able to stop our incredulity at how people behave. It is this separation between inwardness and outwardness, highlighted by the *moralistes,* that forces La Bruyère to write satirical portraits that open up people's motivations and interests. The catalyzing role of the Fronde and the English Civil War in cultivating this desire, at least in the realm of character-writing, might render more specific Jacques Bos's claim that seventeenth-century character sketches exhibited a "rise of the sense of inwardness," which "created a gap between character and personality," between how people act and what they think.[139]

The style of La Bruyère's own portraits reflects this new interest in representing interiority.[140] La Bruyère often accesses an individual's "inclinations" or "secrets" through authorial intervention: a technique that has so far stood at a remove from character-writing. Consider, for example, this portrait of a man called Alsippus:

> Whence comes it that Alsippus salutes me today, smiles, and throws himself almost out of the Coach to take notice of me. I am not rich, and am afoot; according to the rules now in vogue, he should not have seen me. Oh now I have hit on't, 'twas that I might see him in the same seat with a person of the first quality.[141]

In addition to portraying Alsippus's obsequiousness actions toward the narrator, the sketch reveals his motive: "Oh now I have hit on't, 'twas that I might see him in the same seat with a person of the first quality." The secret behind this type's unusual fawning, so out of custom with "the rules now in vogue," is that he wants to show off to the narrator.

While, in the case of Alsippus, the "vice of the mind" is a particular breed of self-interest, in the case of other characters, folly and villainy can have a different "principle," one of a more social or economic nature. The last remark in "Of the Goods of Fortune" compares two characters on this basis, one named Giton and one named Phedon:

> Giton has a fresh Complexion, a smooth Face, a steady and resolute Look, large Shoulders, a full Crest, a firm and deliberate Step; he speaks boldly, and must have every word repeated that is spoken to him, and is but indifferently pleas'd with any thing:
>
> He extends his Handkerchief, he puts it to his Nose, he blows hard enough for all to hear him, he spits about the Room, and sneezes aloud; he sleeps by Day, he sleeps by Night soundly, he snores in Company, he takes up more room than any one else in walking, or at Table; he takes the Wall of his Equals, he stops, they stop; he goes forward, they go forward: all are govern'd by his motions, he interrupts, he informs.
>
> Let him talk as long as he thinks fit, he is never interrupted, the Company is of his Opinion, and his News is constantly the truest: if he sits down you see him in an Elbow-Chair, he crosses his Legs, wrinkles his Brows, pulls his Hat over his Eyes, and will be seen by no body; he raises himself afterwards, and discovers a proud and confident Forehead: He is merry, very laughable, impatient, cholerick, a Libertine and a Politician; he believes himself a great Wit, and a great Genius, but 'tis certain he is Rich.

> Phedon has hollow Eyes, a red Face, a lean Body, and a meagre Look, his Sleep is little, and his Slumbers light; he is a thinking Man, but with the Sense he has the air of a Blockhead, he forgets speaking what he knows, or talking of those accidents with which he is acquainted; when he sometimes speaks he is foolish and concise in his Relations; he is never harken'd to, or taken notice of.
>
> He praises, he laughs at others Jests, he is of their Opinions; he runs, he flies to do 'em little Services; he is a flatterer, complaisant, busie, mysterious in his Affairs, superstitious, scrupulous, a Coward, and sometimes a Lyar; he steps lightly and softly, he seems afraid to

> tread the ground, he walks with his Eyes downward, he dares not raise 'em on those who pass by him;
>
> he never makes one of a Company for discoursing on Affairs of general Concern; he puts himself behind him who speaks, he steals away with what he has heard without being observ'd; he uses no place, he takes up no room, he pulls his Hat over his Eyes, that he may not be seen, he folds and shuts himself up in his Cloak; there is no Street or Gallery so crouded or throng'd but he finds a way to sneak through without jostling, and creeps along, and no one perceives him;
>
> if he is desir'd to sit, he puts himself on the brink of the Seat, he talks low in Conversation, and has a bad accent; however, he is free with the Publick, angry with the Age, and but indifferently pleas'd with the Ministers and Ministry; he seldom opens his Mouth but to reply, he blows his Nose under his Hat, he spits in his Handkerchief, he gets into a corner to sneeze, and the Company must never know it, he costs no body a Complement or a Salutation. In short, he is very poor.[142]

As with Alsippus, the principle animating both of these characters' behavior is announced last, rather than at its beginning.[143] These figures are not billed as sketches of "The Rich Man" and "The Poor Man" but as journeys through the manifold social behaviors, beliefs, and thoughts of two people. Finally, a principle arrives explaining *why* it is that they treat themselves, and are treated by others, in such distinct manners. This structure encourages the reader to first ask themselves what might unite this set of descriptions before the author reveals it to them. Not a humor, a vice, a political belief, or a passion: it is simply their social station. Indeed, the fact that Giton is "merry, very laughable, impatient, cholerick, a libertine and a politician," or that Phedon is "a flatterer, complaisant, buise, mysterious in his Affairs, superstitious, scrupulous, a coward, and sometimes a lyar," does not prove to be what is most essential. Everything, as the progress of the sketch makes clear, comes down to money.

La Bruyère's sense that a degree of wealth changes numerous aspects of an individual—from their complexion to their manner of speaking, their effect on others, their ability to sleep, their inhabiting of space, and even their manner of sneezing and blowing their nose—is a pioneering work of social critique. Most importantly, though, wealth also shapes how these two figures consider themselves. Thus La Bruyère shows himself not only able to see into man's interior and reveal his secret motivations, as in the case of Alsippus, but to show the reader secret principles underlying things about these characters that they themselves cannot see. Giton "believes himself a great Wit, and a great Genius, but tis certain he is Rich." Phedon, on the other hand, is a "thinking man" but considers himself to have "the air of a Blockhead." This is a distinct break from Theophrastus and his seventeenth-century English adapters.

A first-person, authorial voice intervenes not only to reveal the social and psychological motivations behind a character's actions but also to make judgments about that character's future.[144] This aligns with La Bruyère's earlier promise to write sketches in order to easily "foresee" all that someone is and will be capable of saying or doing. This posture of authorial omniscience coheres with the normative statements that La Bruyère scatters across the collection—such as the notion that "an Author should be fond of reading his Works to those who know how to correct and esteem 'em."[145] La Bruyère's move into the future is something that Theophrastus's snapshot method—more or less capturing a day in the life of a type—does not permit, beyond its implication that a person's character will always render them predictable. In the portrait of *Arsène*, for example, La Bruyère underlines how this man "fancies he has as much Wit as he Wants, and more than he will ever have"—tacking on a remark about this person's future from an omniscient author.[146]

Just as the *moralistes* influenced La Bruyère's desire to take an authorial standpoint that would allow him to peer into people's interiors, other aspects of seventeenth-century philosophy influenced his interest in developing a much stronger authorial presence than previous character writers. Harald Wentzlaff-Eggebert has argued that La Rochefoucauld's choice of the word "Reflections" for the title of his work reveals his engagement with a Cartesian distinction between immediate evidence and the discovery of truths through critical examination.[147] In a moment of doubt and the mistrust of appearances, and in a courtly world that involved "an elaborate system of veils and masks," the question of personal judgment—of how to digest, interpret, and distill immediate evidence via examination—was essential.[148] More than that, as

Auerbach remarks, it was socially necessary, with a class having developed in the court of cultivated individuals, "equipped with the fund of knowledge required to make judgments in matters of taste," who were denied other uses for their learning in the professions due to the ideal of *honnêteté*.[149]

La Bruyère was profoundly aware of this pull toward critical examination. Near the end of his *Characters,* he cites Descartes's *Discourse on Method* on this issue: "Descartes rule, never to decide on the least truth, before it's clearly and distinctly known, is convenient and just, and ought to extend to the judgment we give of persons."[150] With this, La Bruyère provokes us to think that his portraits might represent a way of achieving Cartesian clear and distinct truths about people. Just as Descartes begins in the first person, from the clear and distinct truth of the subject, La Bruyère uses his first-person perspective to help us correctly judge other people.

ADDING APOLOGY: CHRISTIANIZING MAN

The moral purchase of La Bruyère's *Characters or Manners of the Age* does not only lie in its capacity to explore the pernicious nature of contemporary conditions and reveal people's base motivations. The text also nudges readers to find an external framework, in accepting the truth of Christianity, as a means to change themselves. Through this framework, La Bruyère manages to reconcile two seemingly contradictory impulses: believing in the continuity of human vice over time and attempting to reform it. This is the bind of a despairing neo-Augustinian satirist and a hopeful moralist, one who sees writing at once as a means to highlight the incorrigible faults of human nature and as a means to change them. The solution that La Bruyère develops, in the form of moral satire, is his attempt to release himself from this tension.

La Bruyère opens the preface to his own *Characters or Manners of the Age* by laying out the work's moral intention, explaining that "the World may view here the Picture I have drawn of it from Nature, and if I have hit on any defects, which it agrees with me to be such, it may at leisure correct them."[151] The goal of moral correction is indeed "what a Man ought chiefly to propose to himself in Writing," a point extended when he proclaims that "we should neither write nor speak but for Instruction."[152] This is La Bruyère the moralist, a man keen to use his literary production as a means to act in the world. At the same time, he also adopts another persona: that of a neo-Augustinian satirist. His own adaptation, La Bruyère says, is an imitation of Theophrastus's "ingenious Satyrizing" of the Greeks.[153] But even more than the satirist, who typically "despair[s] of man and society," to borrow the words of one critic, La Bruyère often expresses—as we have seen in his preface to Theophrastus—the unchangeable badness of human nature, something he borrows from Augustine.[154] This is perhaps nowhere more apparent than in the opening to "Of Man":

> Let us not be angry with Men, when we see them stubborn, ungrateful, unjust, proud, Lovers of themselves and forgetful of others; they are made so, 'tis their Nature, they can no more prevent it than a Stone from falling to the Ground, or Fire from flying upwards.[155]

From the eighth edition onward, La Bruyère includes a claim in the preface to his *Characters or Manners of the Age* that reiterates that man's corrupt nature persists across time and space. Although, he says, his title is "the Characters, or Manners of the Age," and although he frequently takes inspiration "from the Court of France, and Men of my own Nation," his remarks "cannot be confin'd to any one Court or Country, without losing a great deal of the compass and usefulness of my Book, and destroying the general design of the Work, which is to paint Mankind in general."[156] As Bernard Roukhomovsky comments, La Bruyère's vision of human nature grew darker over time, leaving us with a bleak vision of ourselves "with a strong Augustinian tinge."[157]

The problem emerges when we take these two claims together: La Bruyère asserts that human nature is unchangingly vicious, while his collection seems desperate to improve it. Within his *Characters*, La Bruyère often in fact appears highly skeptical of the power of satire to correct. Not only is it as difficult to change a person as it is to stop a stone from falling, but also "we strive in vain to correct a Blockhead by Satyr." Ultimately, a figure like *Arsène* in "Of Polite Learning" "is incapable of being corrected by this Picture."[158]

Like La Rochefoucauld and Pascal, La Bruyère is also highly skeptical of Stoic moral solutions, thinking them ridiculous in their blithe optimism. "Stoicism is a sport of the Mind, an Idea," he says, "something like Plato's Republick" in its utopian nature.[159] Stoics "feign" that we can achieve self-control and are pleased to call the "phantom of virtue, and imaginary constancy" that they construct, a "wise man."[160] The Stoics, La Bruyère concludes,

> have left Mankind full of the same defects they found them, and not cur'd them of the least weakness. Instead of painting Vice in its most frightful and ridiculous forms, to correct their Minds, they have form'd an idea of perfection and heroicism, of which they are not capable, and exhorted them to what is impossible.[161]

While the Stoic wise man would "stand firm on the Ruins of the universe," a real person "cries, despairs, looks fiery, and is out of breath, for a Dog lost, or a China dish broke in pieces."[162] All this encourages us to think that the right solution is not describing an exemplary and implausible life of virtue but instead "painting vice." But, as soon as we do so, we confront the problem that La Bruyère does not believe that he can reform people through satire.

La Bruyère's skepticism about the moral effects of the satire he is writing, a problem in large part linked to his determined view of human nature, finds little precedent in the Roman tradition, with which he was familiar.[163] Horace's satire is designed to imitate a habit his father taught him of showing him bad examples of men in order "to enable [him] to steer clear of follies."[164] Juvenal, likewise, is trying to shine a light on a particularly vicious moment, in order to restore the shared norms that were once in place but are currently being violated.[165] Horace and Juvenal do not enter into La Bruyère's contradiction because, to put it most simply, they do not hold as fixed a view of human nature being bad and therefore leave space for us to get better. This can happen either through readers avoiding the behavior they have seen in satirized figure or by using the negative portrait of a socially disrupted world in order to rebuild it.[166]

One reason why La Bruyère does not seem to offer us as clear and uncomplicated a means of reform through satire as someone like Horace or Juvenal might be because of the Christianized reading that he would have had of the Roman satirists.[167] With the satiric discourse of someone like Persius having been long subsumed into "an agenda of instruction" within the "Christian moral and political landscape," the means of reform through satire had become as much external as internal to the text: with the Roman imperatives of how to instruct sitting within an exterior Christianized framework that promised a clear strategy of redemption to rid oneself of vice.[168] La Bruyère, in making satire an unreliable means of moral instruction, is not then be simply opting to become "an amused observer of society," as Russell Goulbourne claims.[169] Rather, he is relying on a religious framework to pick up the work of moral instruction where satire falls short.[170]

The two inheritances to which La Bruyère points for his work suggest as much. In the preface to his translation of Theophrastus's *Characters,* he explains that he does not feel discouraged by "two Works of Morality which are in every ones Hands" and that "some may think these remarks are imitations."[171] These seem most likely to be Pascal's *Pensées* and La Rochefoucauld's *Maxims,* as La Bruyère notes that one "explains the nature of the Soul, its Passions, its Vices, discusses the most serious motives that lead to Vertue, and will make a Man a Christian" and the other observes "that self-love in Man is the cause of all his errors" and "attacks every part where he finds it without intermission."[172] La Bruyère asserts that his work is "less sublime than the first, and less delicate than the second," with the "sole design" being "to render man reasonable."[173] These two admired authors, however, remain key reference points for La Bruyère, and he engages with aspects of their work directly on several occasions.[174] This connection encourages us to read La Bruyère as he would have considered himself, a *moraliste* interested in both psychological description and the reforming of mores.[175]

This proximity becomes all the more apparent when we consider the remarks in his final chapter, "Des Esprits Forts," rendered in the 1700 English translation as "Of the Libertines, or Wits of the Age."[176] Here, just as Pascal and La Rochefoucauld have done, La Bruyère offers a glimpse of theological redemption for the corruption of human nature, in a chapter that Emmanuel Bury calls the "climax of an explicitly apologetic and moral work."[177] This chapter critiques those who do not have knowledge of God, provides a series of proofs for God from the logical to the instinctive ("a secret Instinct whispers me that there is a God, and it never does that there is none. I need no further proof"), and outlines the joy to be had in choosing to believe.[178] It then proceeds to argue that "those who dare deny the Being of a God hardly deserve that one should strive to demonstrate it to them, or at least that one should argue with them with more seriousness than I have done hitherto."[179] As these people are "so ignorant," they should not be reasoned with but should instead be treated in unserious forms—such as, we might think, satire, character, and ridicule. In reading his own text, he hopes that the unfaithful man "will yield himself convinc'd thro the multitude of proofs which religion lays before him": finding in it "the greatness of his Priviledges, the certainty of his refuge, the reasonableness of hopes."[180]

In the preface to his 1693 discourse on being received at the Académie française, La Bruyère makes this point even more forcefully. The people who appreciated his *Characters* without problem, La Bruyère defends, were "pious and enlightened men," who recognized "the plan and economy" of his whole book.[181] They were able to observe

> that of the sixteen chapters of which it is composed, there are fifteen which, being concerned with discovering the falsehood and the ridiculousness which are found in the objects of human passions and attachments, tend only to ruin all the obstacles which first weaken, and then extinguish in all men the knowledge of God; that thus they are only preparations for the sixteenth and last chapter, where atheism is attacked, and perhaps confounded.[182]

It is only, he continues, overly sensitive romantic poets who do not comprehend his work due to their "delicacy of conscience."[183] To appease even these readers, La Bruyère states again, more calmly, "I try, in my book on manners, to decry, if it is possible, all the vices of the heart and mind, to make man reasonable and closer to becoming a Christian."[184]

Indeed, as Cuche has masterfully shown, when the final chapter of *The Characters or Manners of the Age* enumerates the obstacles to faith, in order to challenge them, it "treats exactly the same points" that La Bruyère has covered in the previous fifteen entries.[185] These are obstacles like "our passions being directed to false objects" (here we might think of Narcissus and his religiously kept social visits), our subjection to "illusion" (the idea that we are committing to the truth, for example, in reading the news, as Boevius does), and our vice of self-interest (embodied so well by the snobbish Alsippus).[186] The thinking here is that *The Characters or Manners of the Age* can reform people like these by encouraging them to rid themselves of the obstacles preventing their "knowledge of God." This opens up the possibility that if there is redress for human wrongs, it cannot only come from the satirist but from God, with the satirist, as La Rochefoucauld does, encouraging this process by forcing readers to see how much they need it. In this La Bruyère finds a means to uphold a fidelity to the Augustinian idea of original sin, and corrupt human nature, without becoming pessimistic. In this way, he avoids the paradox of combining his "programmatic declarations" of reform with his "admissions of powerlessness."[187]

ADDING APOLOGY: CHRISTIANIZING CUSTOMS

Simply reforming the individual, however, was not sufficient for La Bruyère. True to his association with the Petit Concile, he wanted to change pernicious social conditions as well. The last remark in the whole collection in fact concerns economic inequality, differentiating between the kind of inequality that is man-made (and therefore subject to critique) and the kind of inequality that would be acceptable in the eyes of God (and is therefore justifiable):

> Some inequality in the conditions of men, for order and subordinations sake, is the work of God, and demonstrates a providence: too great a disproportion, and such as is generally seen amongst them, is their own work, and an incroachment of theirs upon one another. All extreams are vicious, and proceed from Men, compensation is just, and proceeds from God.[188]

This final remark offers an aspect of La Bruyère's Christian apology that exonerates God from the problem of extreme economic inequality, something that could have led a libertine or wit of the age into a profound atheism. Where "some inequality" between people is both natural ("the work of God") and prudential to maintain social stability, La Bruyère sees the "too great" "disproportion" that characterizes his society as wrong. In contemporary society, La Bruyère suggests, we have been led to "extreams," away from the "just" society imagined by God.

The problem of "extream" disproportion appears again and again in *The Characters or Manners of the Age*. La Bruyère complains that "the strange Disproportion" that "many Pieces of Money set between Men" would be roundly critiqued if we had not become so habituated to it as something "we experience every day."[189] He tells stories about how advantage is gained unfairly, how merchants of the same trade find different fortunes, leaving the children of some in "extream misery" and those of others some of "the first at Court."[190] He contrasts an account of a healthy, young "Lord of an Abby" with an account of "one hundred and twenty Indigent Families, who have no Fire to warm 'em in the Winter, no Cloaths to cover their Nakedness, nor Bread to eat; their Poverty is extream and shameful."[191] Extreme poverty not only is "shameful" but can work to dehumanize people entirely. La Bruyère expresses this point most forcefully in his depiction of peasants. Here, a narrator observes the peasants as if from another historical moment, in order to make their subjection seem all the more unnecessary, cruel, and strange:

> We meet with certain wild Animals, male and female, spread over the country. They are black and tann'd, united to the Earth, which they are always digging and turning up and down with an unweary'd resolution. They have something like an articulate voice, when they stand on their feet they discover a manlike face, and indeed are men, at night they retire into their Burrows, where they live on brown Bread, Water, Roots and Herbs. They spare other men, the trouble of sowing, labouring, and reaping for their maintenance, and deserve, one would think, that they should not want the Bread they themselves sow.[192]

La Bruyère is conscious here that the peasants have been dealt an unfair hand of terrible fortune, reduced to an existence comparable to that of "wild Animals."

In his last remarks in *The Characters or Manners of the Age,* La Bruyère implies that there is an alternative. Just as this text intends to rid people of their personal vices in order to make them Christian, it aims to rid society of its vices by advocating for a less unequal distribution of wealth—one free from the "vicious" man-made "extreams" of poverty described over the course of the collection. It is in reverting to a less unequal society, La Bruyère suggests, that we will be able to achieve a more Christian way of living together.[193] Though we cannot change our nature, we can become Christians and use this religious framework to assist us in transforming our customs. But what should we change our customs to? "Posterity," La Bruyère says, will find it strange that we celebrate people who live in "gawdy splendour (. . .) a sort of men, treated with the last contempt amongst the Hebrews and greeks."[194] "Our state and magnificence," he continues, do not "afford us more advantage over the Athenians plain way of living" nor "against that of the first men, great by themselves, and independent on a thousand exteriour things, which afterwards were invented perhaps to supply the defect of that true grandeur, which is now no more."[195] La Bruyère imagines drawing on the social customs in the early communities of the early Christians, Hebrews, and ancient Greeks, continuing the "idealization of primitive community" that was typical to the Petit Concile.[196]

While La Bruyère's satire, like Hall's, is directed toward religious ends, unlike Hall, La Bruyère did not feel that portraits alone could accomplish the moral task he set himself.[197] Rather, his satirical remarks needed to be complemented by theological reflections designed to lead the reader to abandon their freethinking and take up religion in order to fully mend themselves and their society. Following La Rochefoucauld and Pascal, La Bruyère thus constructed a work that showed man's misery in order to bring him to redemption. By doing so in the form of characters, La Bruyère sketched a new possibility for the genre: that portraits of human corruption can inspire a reader to search for a moral framework able to redress these issues. With the notion of moral satire, La Bruyère resolves the problem inherent in attempting to reform a human nature that is unchangingly corrupt. While nudging specific kinds of personal and social reforms, *Characters or Manners of the Age* ultimately makes an overarching call to faith.

+ + +

Since the time of the first Latin translations, the entanglement of Theophrastan *Characters* with moral and political objectives had rested on several key assumptions: that Theophrastus's character types could be found in contemporary society and were not distant, historical portraits but universal and accurately described; that there was a close relationship between reading about the actions of other people and shaping one's own actions; that the way we behave is who we are; and that there is no intrinsic opposition between comedy and instruction.

A closer look at seventeenth-century France has shown several of these assumptions start to give way. To La Bruyère, Theophrastus's *Characters* no longer seemed able to accurately represent a person—rather, in displaying behavior but not motives, they seemed to him simplistic and shallow. Convinced that the imitation of good behavior was not enough to achieve actually *being* good, he did not see the Athenian portrait of mores as an obvious key to reforming the contemporary world. Instead, La Bruyère's adaptation—which argued for circumscribed continuities between past and present, opened up the interior, and took a new approach to moral reform—forged a delicate alternative means for character-writing to retain its moral status.

But when David Hume came to read La Bruyère some years later, he was not so convinced of the validity of this revised method. In 1748, he wrote a number of texts treating different aspects of "character" that interpret the Theophrastan tradition in ways that problematize its very status as philosophy.

6

Turning Away from Theophrastus

DAVID HUME IN 1748

The Enlightenment Scottish philosopher David Hume was an avid reader of La Bruyère, a Francophile, and someone who was very much aware of the Theophrastan tradition. Hume, however, was no longer convinced that character sketches could be used for moral or political objectives. Sixty years after La Bruyère positioned the character sketch as a device to discover "the principle" of people's "Villany and Folly," Hume—also surrounded by a public culture full of character sketches—developed similar concerns about the capacities of this form.[1] Specifically, he sought to work out whether sketches could hold philosophical potential on their own and whether philosophy should be more concerned with representing appearances or uncovering guiding principles. In 1748, Hume decided to state his view on the matter. In a series of essays, he effectively rejected Theophrastan character-writing as a method of practicing moral philosophy. Moral philosophy needed to move away from character-writing, he claimed, and it would do so by turning toward metaphysics. With this, Hume heralds the waning of the Theophrastan tradition: the trend of interpreting these sketches as philosophy.[2]

To the extent that scholars have addressed Hume's relationship with the character sketch, they have suggested—as Annette Baier does, for example—that Hume was inspired by Theophrastus.[3] A closer look at a number of Hume's writings tells a more nuanced story. This story emerges from a set of polemic comments at the beginning of Hume's 1748 *Enquiry concerning Human Understanding* (commonly known as the *First Enquiry*)[4] about the presence of two manners of writing "Moral Philosophy or the Science of human Nature": the easy and obvious manner and the accurate and abstract manner.[5] The easy and obvious philosophy represents vice and virtue, as well as instances from common life; places "opposite Characters in a proper contrast"; and is associated with poetry and rhetoric.[6] Hume compares this kind of philosophy to *painting*. The accurate and abstract philosophy, on the other hand, aims to examine human nature in order "to find those Principles, which regulate our Understandings," and is compared by Hume to *anatomy*.[7] As I argue in this chapter, we should understand the easy and obvious manner of writing philosophy to encompass character-writing. When Hume calls for philosophers to move away from the easy and obvious philosophy, we should therefore understand him to be calling for philosophy to move away from character sketches.

In *Essays, Moral and Political,* also published in 1748, Hume embodied his argument in practice. Though these essays abound with questions about character—famously asking, for instance, whether there can be a "national character"—they are not themselves character sketches. Instead, these essays embrace a version of the accurate and abstract manner of reasoning. In his "Of National Character," Hume does not, for example, sketch a set of national types but rather attempts to determine how a character of nation is formed in the first place: whether the explanatory principle behind the character of a nation is more likely to be its climate or its institutions. Hume invokes the Theophrastan tradition in order to show precisely how and why he must move away from this mode of writing philosophy. To attend closely to these maneuvers is to see more clearly the role that character plays in his early writing. Hume does not embrace Theophrastus but rather rejects the manner of philosophy that Theophrastus inspired.

Studies of the methodological discussion in Hume's *First Enquiry* have not discussed this inheritance of the Theophrastan tradition.[8] Though Kate Abramson's 2007 essay clarifies the distinction Hume draws between "philosophical anatomy and painting," it does not uncover the tradition of philosophical painting that had developed in the genre of character-writing. As Abramson clarifies in an earlier piece, her focus is less on "the content of Hume's 'two species of philosophy'" than on the question of whether Hume intended to combine them.[9] This chapter tackles the former problem instead. It proposes that, once we see the Theophrastan tradition behind the easy and obvious mode, we can better understand Hume's departure from significant aspects of this method.[10] Once we recognize that Hume is describing character-writing in the *First Enquiry*, it becomes harder to keep his own essayistic approach to characters isolated from this methodological discussion about his philosophy. Any decision to separate Hume's philosophical *Enquiries* and his *Essays* is indeed problematic, given Hume's purported desire that his *Enquiries* and his *Essays* should both "be regarded as containing his philosophical sentiments and principles."[11] By placing Hume's 1748 texts—his *First Enquiry* and his *Essays*—in relation to each other, we can start to see how they are united by a shared methodology. The status of characters and principles, however, can be traced back even further to his first major work: his 1739–1740 *Treatise of Human Nature*. It is with this text that we will begin, in order to ground the role of these concepts in his later writing.

This rereading of Hume has two implications. It first supplements our understanding of Hume's role in the development of political thought. Hume is typically seen as embodying a shift from premodern to modern political thought in his preference for structuring the political sphere through laws as opposed to virtues. As James Moore argues, Hume's political science represents a shift away from shaping virtue toward "the discovery of general truths, or generalizations substantiated by observation and experiment."[12] A central observation Hume held here was that people are generally "knaves," that "all citizens fundamentally follow their own private passionate interests."[13] Where premodern political thought, to put this most simply, is characterized by a consensus that the health of a political system was maintained by the character and spirit of citizens or subjects, represented by the notion of virtue, because Hume believed human beings to be driven by passion, he argued that the health of a political society would need to be guaranteed by its institutions instead.[14] His arguments thus mark the end of the virtue politics with which this book started.

Uncovering the importance of Hume's reworking of the methods of philosophy thus encourages us to see another facet to this shift:

one that encompasses Hume's rejection of one typical *means* of virtue politics, the character sketch. If all we need to do is avoid vices in our political life, it makes sense to prioritize written paintings of them. If, on the other hand, we need to anatomize the political sphere in order to understand its principles, we will need a different kind of writing entirely. Hume's "Of National Characters," I argue, reflects his fidelity to a method of uncovering the "principles" behind national characters, as opposed to sketching them: a method that left a troubling precedent for Immanuel Kant, who used Hume's essay in his later development of scientistic racism. Hume's essay is often understood in response to the climatic determinism developed by Enlightenment philosophers. By setting it in dialogue with the Theophrastan tradition of rhetorically sketching national characters, we can better see the break that Hume's move to principles represented in the development of the human sciences. While La Bruyère evinced a skepticism about character sketches carrying out social and political work on their own—and therefore decided to supplement his depictions of social misery with theological pronouncements about the need to create a more egalitarian society—Hume saw this combination as no longer tenable. Instead of pairing literary description of typical figures with a few concluding normative maxims, Hume made a search for political maxims his principal focus. His aim was to answer foundational political questions, like what made the best constitution for a new commercial society.

Understanding Hume's turn away from the Theophrastan tradition has a further, related implication for our understanding of the historical separation between philosophy and literature. In his 1979 *Philosophy and the Mirror of Nature,* philosopher Richard Rorty argues that the eighteenth century was a turning point in the direction of Western thought, from which it has not diverged. Rorty explains that in order to distinguish philosophy from the natural sciences, Kant set out to veer philosophy toward epistemology. By framing philosophy as a discipline concerned with questions about *what we can know,* Kant hoped to carve out a unique place for philosophy, separate from the one newly occupied by the natural sciences but erected on just as rigorous a foundation. Where natural scientists would concern themselves with observing the world, philosophers would ask questions about what makes these observations count as knowledge in the first place. When we consider the history of the character sketch and center Hume rather than Kant, we find a different history. Eighteenth-century philosophy did not only wish to distinguish itself from the natural sciences but also from a kind of writing we now call literature. The earliest sense of "literature" in English as we understand it today indeed dates to the year after Hume's pieces.[15] As Jacob Sider Jost puts it, "Hume's binary opposition of the anatomist and the painter takes place at a transitional moment in the history of the concept of literature itself."[16]

This new classification—literature—came to be used to designate all that the easy and obvious kind of moral philosophy had once encompassed: portrayals of virtue and vice, consideration of observations and details from common life, and representations of typical characters.

Character and Principle in the *Treatise*

Hume repeatedly returns to the problem of philosophical method across his work. Indeed, it serves, in slightly different guises, as the introduction to each of his three major philosophical treatises: *A Treatise of Human Nature* (1739–1740), the *First Enquiry,* and the *Second Enquiry*: *An Enquiry concerning the Principles of Morals* (1751).[17] Although it is in the *First Enquiry* that Hume makes clear his rejection of the Theophrastan tradition of writing moral philosophy through character sketches, he lays out an important conception of the ideas of both "character" and "principle" in the *Treatise*. This grounds the use of both concepts in his later writing.

In January 1739, when Hume was twenty-eight, the first volume of *A Treatise of Human Nature* fell, as Hume puts it in his autobiography, "dead-born from the press."[18] It was a work largely written during Hume's three-year stay in France, which involved time in Paris, in the university town of Rheims, and in the village of La Flèche, where René Descartes was educated.[19] "Rather naïvely," as Dennis C. Rasmussen writes, "expecting that a long, dense, difficult philosophical tome would produce an immediate revolution in thought," Hume was inevitably disappointed in the work's reception.[20] It would be ten years before Hume attempted to revivify this work in writing the *First Enquiry,* a text that attempted to express the arguments of the *Treatise* in "a more accessible form."[21]

The *Treatise* is subtitled "an attempt to introduce the experimental method of reasoning into moral subjects," which clarifies this text's aim and project.[22] Hume traces the "experimental method" back to Francis Bacon's inductive reasoning, which worked to transform natural philosophy: the branch of philosophy concerned with physical and natural sciences.[23] Hume explains this method most succinctly in the anonymous defense of the *Treatise* he published in 1740, *An Abstract of a Book Lately Published; Entituled A Treatise of Human Nature*. It involves "examining several phaenomena," determining whether "they resolve themselves into one common principle," tracing "this principle into another," and then arriving "at those few simple principles on which all the rest depend."[24] Given that this method starts from experience, its practitioners can "draw no conclusions" separate from observed phenomena, and indeed, they talk "with contempt of hypotheses."[25]

The area in which Hume desires to apply the experimental method, following Locke, Shaftesbury, Mandeville, Hutcheson, and Butler, is that of the "moral subjects": defined as "Logic, Morals, Criticism and Politics"—maintaining the typical distinction of philosophy into natural and moral domains.[26] Underlying each of these sciences, Hume argues, is an idea of "human nature": the topic that the *Treatise* aims to confront directly.[27] "In pretending therefore to explain the principles of human nature," Hume declares, "we in effect propose a compleat system of the sciences, built on a foundation almost entirely new, and the only one upon which they can stand with any security."[28] This new foundation is designed to overturn the ancient approach to human nature, which relied on eloquence, sentiment, and figuration rather than "regular science."[29] "Most of the philosophers of antiquity, who treated of human nature," Hume argues, show more "of a delicacy of sentiment" "than a depth of reasoning and reflection."[30] They have contented themselves "with representing the common sense of mankind in the strongest lights, and with the best turn of thought and expression," rather than "following out steadily a chain of propositions, or forming the several truths into a regular science."[31] Contrary to this bad example, Hume wishes to determine if "the science of man will not admit of the same accuracy, which several parts of natural philosophy are found susceptible."[32] Instead of "representing" "mankind in the strongest lights," Hume instead proposes "to anatomize human nature in a regular manner, and promises to draw no conclusions but where he is authorized by experience."[33] As we will see, the key terms used in these descriptions of two kinds of philosophy will reappear again in Hume's *First Enquiry*.

Hume's call for a more anatomical style of philosophy was the culmination of developments that had been gradually evolving since the beginning of the early modern period.[34] Descartes, Spinoza, and Hobbes had all also wanted their philosophical enquiries to proceed scientifically. For Descartes, this was expressed as a desire to work from clear and distinct first principles; for Spinoza, this meant elaborately extending the geometrical method into moral philosophy; and for Hobbes, this involved putting his "inquiry" on "the tracks of science" in order to correct the errors of previous "moral Philosophers."[35] In the *First Enquiry*, Hume has his own version of framing this historic split. He chooses to principally align himself with anatomy, not geometry, and he contrasts this method with an approach to philosophy that is redolent of character-writing. What is special in this instance of the long-standing struggle between speculative science and civic rhetoric is that character-writing had historically been understood as an innovative, third method of philosophy rather than one of two standard approaches to be combined in a new synthesis.

The "few simple principles" that Hume discerns from this method of anatomy are as follows. First, that all ideas are derived from impressions, that "we can never think of anything which we have not seen without us, or felt in our own minds."[36] In this Hume continues Locke's line of thought that "no ideas are innate," correcting only Locke's terminology.[37] Second, that "we are determined by custom alone to suppose the future conformable to the past": that our experience of perceiving causation in the world is simply derived from experience.[38] The example Hume gives here is of two billiard balls. In his words, "When I see a billiard ball moving toward another, my mind is immediately carried by habit to the usual effect, and anticipates my sight by conceiving the second ball in motion," even if "there is nothing in these objects, abstractly considered, and independent of experience, which leads me to form any such conclusion."[39]

Third, that the soul "is nothing but a system or train of different perceptions, those of heat and cold, love and anger, thoughts and sensations, all united together, but without any perfect simplicity or identity."[40] In this Hume rejects Descartes's approach to considering thought as the essence of the mind. "Since every thing, that exists, is particular," Hume argues, "it must be our several particular perceptions, that compose the mind": a perspective that vanquishes the idea of "substance" and replaces it with "particular perceptions."[41] Here Hume turns to the example of a peach:

> As our idea of any body, a peach, for instance, is only that of a particular taste, colour, figure, size, consistence, etc. So our idea of any mind is only that of particular perceptions, without the notion of anything we call substance, either simple or compound.[42]

Fourth, the principle of the association of ideas—the one aspect of the *Treatise* that Hume says could "intitle the author to so glorious a name as that of an *inventor.*"[43] This is the notion that "there is a secret tie or union among particular ideas, which causes the mind to conjoin them more frequently together, and makes the one, upon its appearance, introduce the other."[44] This secret tie can be broken down into the categories of resemblance, contiguity, and causation. Hume writes that it will "be easy to conceive of what vast consequence these principles must be in the science of human nature, if we consider that, so far as regards the mind, these are the only links that bind the parts of the universe together, or connect us with any person or object exterior to ourselves."[45] The significance of "the inherent principles and passions of human nature" is further emphasized by how, as Hume makes clear later in the *Treatise,* they are "inalterable."[46] This means that while Hume does leave open some opportunity for his philosophy to reform, he had no sense, as David Fate Norton puts it, "of reforming the fundamental dispositions of human nature itself."[47]

The role that character plays within this framework is coherent with the nature of the principles.[48] Given that the mind is only a "system of different perceptions"—where one thought "chaces another, and draws after it a third, by which it is expell'd in its turn"—it would seem that Hume would not be able to maintain a sense of human character.[49] This, however, is not the case. Hume uses an analogy to explain why. "I cannot compare the soul more properly to any thing than to a republic or commonwealth," he argues, "in which the several members are united by the reciprocal ties of government and subordination, and give rise to other persons, who propagate the same republic in the incessant changes of its parts."[50] Within the binding structure of the soul or mind (here used interchangeably), our thoughts therefore come and go like generations of citizens.

As the republic does not only "change its members, but also its laws and constitutions," so the human mind or soul does not only change "impressions and ideas, but "the same person may vary" their "character and disposition."[51] This does not dissolve an idea of character because of the link that remains between one version of the republic—or the person—and another, which Hume understands to be tied together "by the relation of causation."[52] "Whatever changes" that the person endures, Hume outlines, their "several parts are still connected by the relation of causation."[53] In order for the republic or the person to imagine itself, and to be imagined, as a fixed unit, there needs therefore to be memory, of "that chain of causes and effects, which constitute our self or person."[54] While this is not entirely sufficient, given that we imagine ourselves to have the same identity despite having forgotten our actions on certain days, Hume is content to dismiss this as a "grammatical" rather than philosophical difficulty.[55] What is important is that "an object, whose different co-existent parts are bound together by a close relation, operates upon the imagination after much the same manner as one perfectly simple and indivisible."[56] The similarity in these two processes allows us to *imagine* a "principle of union" binding a structure, even when one is not there.[57] This leaves people in a position to perceive other people's characters, as if they were something "perfectly simple and indivisible."

This imagined stability of human character proves essential in the moral philosophy Hume elaborates in the second and third volumes of the *Treatise*. For Hume, our judgment of other people can only be correct if it is based on an action that derives from their perceived character, which "shews certain qualities, which remaining after the action is perform'd, connect it with the person, and facilitate the transition of ideas from one to the other."[58] We are not encouraged, that is, to judge people for actions that are outside their character but for those that cohere with our perception of the individual as if they were a body "simple and indivisible." This provokes the crucial questions of how to recognize character traits in other people and how to judge them.[59] Hume suggests that, as the judgment of character is derived from perceptions, our sense of which qualities are to be approved and which critiqued is not a question of "reason" but one that concerns how particular qualities create "particular pains and pleasures."[60] The work of the moral philosopher, Hume argues, in "all enquiries concerning these moral distinctions," is to show "the principles, which make us feel a satisfaction or uneasiness from the survey of any character, in order to satisfy us why the character is laudable or blameable."[61] To explain a vice or virtue becomes a task of "giving a reason," or principle, for "the pleasure or uneasiness" it provokes.[62]

The *Treatise,* in this way, attempts to establish a science of human nature by inductively finding a number of animating principles in which character is at once only a suite of perceptions as well as an imagined unity. This unity holds particular significance in moral philosophy: it is the only agent that can be judged, and it is a site for the discovery of further principles designed to unlock why particular traits create particular impressions. From this new empirical foundation, we can start to see how Hume aimed to build "a compleat system of the sciences."

Painting and Anatomy in the *Enquiry*

The *First Enquiry* opens with an essay on the "two different Manners" of writing "Moral Philosophy, or the Science of human Nature."[63] This essay picks up several threads present in the introduction to the *Treatise* and the *Abstract* but frames them in a different way, going beyond the two different philosophical styles that operated in antiquity and in Hume's contemporary moment.

The first species of moral philosophy Hume calls the "easy and obvious Manner."[64] The moral philosophers who write in this manner work from a particular sense of the human being as a creature characterized by action and guided by the drivers of taste and sentiment.[65] These drivers lead human beings to pursue or avoid objects according to the value they seem to possess and "the Light, in which they present themselves."[66] This gives the representation of these objects an essential role. The species of philosophers that write in this manner are accordingly careful to "paint" virtue in "the most aimable Colours," borrowing from "Poetry and Eloquence" in order to do so.[67] The result is a treatment of virtue designed to "please the Imagination and engage the Affections": a rhetorical method of writing about ethics designed to achieve vividness and pleasure.[68] The work of these philosophers involves selecting "the most striking Observations and Instances from common Life" and placing "opposite Characters in a proper contrast."[69] Philosophers do this in order to allure the reader to virtue "by the views of Glory and Happiness," directing their steps by sound "Precepts and most illustrious Examples."[70]

Many of the qualities Hume lists as central to the easy and obvious philosophy recall the way in which several writers we have encountered have described character sketches, from the associations Hume draws with painting to the connections with poetry, the depiction of quotidian life, and the presence of contrasting types. The visual comparison to "painting" and "colour" appeared in numerous editions of Theophrastan character sketches, including La Bruyère's expression of his desire to "paint Mankind in general."[71] The relationship Hume invokes between the easy and obvious philosophy and "poetry" has a similar inheritance. In particular, it recalls Casaubon's striking idea that character-writing balances both philosophy and poetry, being an "intermediate genre" between these two fields.[72] Hume's representation of the quotidian likewise resonates with Casaubon, who likened Theophrastus's *Characters* not only to "images of mores" and "ethical icons" but *imagines vitae quotidianae*: "images of daily life," a phrase he borrows from Cicero.[73] It is, however, Hume's last phrase that perhaps makes this connection most obvious: the easy and obvious philosophy places "opposite Characters in a proper contrast." While Theophrastus only depicts one kind of character, as we know, there had been a long-standing tradition of depicting contrasting qualities, exemplified in Joseph Hall's 1608 promise to show "Vertue and Vice strip't naked to the open view."[74]

The easy and obvious philosophy then seems to hold several connections to character-writing. The chance that this is a direct reference is made all the more probable due to a series of contextual

FIGURE 6.1. David Hume's bookplate in his 1612 copy of Isaac Casaubon's edition of Theophrastus. *Credit:* Rare Books and Special Collections, McGill University Library, Montreal.

factors. Character, as Thomas Ahnert and Susan Manning have discussed, permeated the Greek and Roman classical authors who were the basis of Hume's eighteenth-century education.[75] Cicero, in particular, was a favorite reference of Hume's: an "authority," as Hume puts it, "from which there can be no appeal."[76] Greek and Latin editions of the *Characters* were newly published in Glasgow in 1743 and 1748. And Hume even owned a copy of Casaubon's edition of Theophrastus (Figure 6.1).[77] David Hume, we might say, found character-writing all around him. By the mid-eighteenth century, there were not only translations and adaptations of Theophrastus but lengthy theorizations of the genre, as Henry Gally's 1725 *The Moral Characters of Theophrastus* attests, with its "Critical Essay on Characteristic-Writings."[78] Character-writing was a form of writing with which Hume was familiar and from which he was keen to diverge.

This link between the easy and obvious philosophy and character-writing becomes most clear, however, when Hume lists the names of philosophers who are representative of both manners, the easy and obvious and the accurate and abstract:

> The Fame of *Cicero* flourishes at present; but that of *Aristotle* is utterly decay'd. *La Bruyere* passes the Seas, and still encreases in Renown: But the glory of *Malebranche* is confin'd to his own Nation, and to his own Age. And *Addison*, perhaps, will be read with pleasure, when *Locke* shall be entirely forgotten.[79]

Here, Hume counterposes a trio of Cicero, La Bruyère, and Joseph Addison, the English playwright and essayist who had co-founded the newspaper *The Spectator*, with Richard Steele, in 1711. This trio represents the easy philosophy. They stand against Aristotle, the French rationalist philosopher Nicholas Malebranche, and John Locke—who together represent the accurate and abstract philosophy in contrast. What, we must ask, unites the former group? One answer is an affinity for character types. Cicero was accredited with developing the technique of *notatio*, or character delineation; La Bruyère, as we know, had just written a best-selling adaptation of Theophrastus; and Addison's *Spectator* often incorporated many descriptions of character types, including that of Mr. Spectator himself and his coterie.[80] In Theresa Schön's words, "Addison and

Steele's method of choice was the Theophrastan character sketch."[81] As Margaret Turner writes, "There is nothing new in the suggestion that the *Tatler* and the *Spectator* show signs of the influence of La Bruyère."[82] Addison describes figures like Tom Folio, the book collector, allegorically named in the style of La Bruyère, and sketches highly Theophrastan types like the political Upholsterer, "who seemed a Man of more than ordinary Application to Business."[83] This latter sketch is particularly reminiscent of Theophrastus's original set. The political Upholsterer

> was a very early Riser (. . .). He had a particular Carefulness in the knitting of his Brows, and a kind of Impatience on all his Motions, that plainly discovered he was always intent on Matters of Importance. (. . .) He had a Wife and several Children; but was much more inquisitive to know what passed in *Poland* than in his own Family.[84]

In the style of the spurious epilogues later added to the ancient Greek collection, Addison even ends his account of the political Upholsterer with a warning. He has sketched him, he explains, "for the particular Benefit of those worthy Citizens who live more in a Coffee-house than in their Shops, and whose Thoughts are so taken up with the Affairs of the Allies, that they forget their Customers."[85]

Given the range of qualities that Hume associates with the easy and obvious philosophy, one might rightly caution that Hume could be referring to nonsystematic moral philosophy as a whole, in which character sketches are simply included. Yet the choice of writers on Hume's list of easy and obvious philosophers challenges this, as they all clearly share a commitment to delineating typical figures. Regardless, however, of whether character-writing is meant exclusively or more inclusively, alongside other ways of approaching nonsystematic moral philosophy, Hume clearly calls for a turn away from Theophrastus and the genre he had inspired.

The contrast Hume draws between the easy and obvious trio and that of Aristotle, Malebranche, and Locke serves to introduce the other species of philosophy: the accurate and abstract, which sees the human being as a "reasonable rather than an active Being."[86] It endeavors accordingly to form the "Understanding" more than cultivate "Manners": taking human nature as "a Subject of Speculation" and examining it in order "to find those Principles, which regulate our Understandings, excite our Sentiments, and make us approve or blame any particular Object, Action, or Behaviour."[87] These philosophers are frustrated by how philosophy has not yet "fixt, beyond Controversy, the Foundation of Morals, Reasoning and Criticism" and instead incessantly speaks about "Truth and Falsehood, Vice and Virtue, Beauty and Deformity," without ever determining "the Source of these Distinctions."[88]

The method of these philosophers is instead to proceed from "particular Instances to general Principles," always pushing their "Enquiries to Principles more general" and remaining dissatisfied until "they arrive at those original Principles, by which, in every Science, all human Curiosity must be bounded."[89] While their speculations might seem "abstract, and even unintelligible to common Readers," this does not matter to them, as they "aim at the Approbation of the Learned and the Wise" and find satisfaction enough in the discovery of "some hidden Truths, which may contribute to the Instruction of Posterity."[90]

With this description, Hume breaks from the tradition of framing character-writing as a third approach to moral philosophy. For Casaubon, character-writing was the ancients' third and "most elegant" way of instructing mores, beyond dogmatic philosophy and exhortatory paraenesis.[91] For Hall, the character-writer was similarly a "third sort" of philosopher, beyond those who spend time in "deepe discourses of humane felicitie, and the way to it in common," as well as those who think it "best to applie the generall precepts of goodnesse or decencie, to particular conditions and persons."[92] For La Bruyère, finally, Theophrastus offered a path to moral philosophy beyond those who, on the one hand, "search for Definitions, Divisions, Tables and Method," and those who, on the other, are satisfied "to have Manners reduced to the Passions, and to demonstrate them by the motion of the Blood, by the Fibres and Arteries."[93] But for Hume, character sketches were no longer a third alternative path to moral philosophy. Rather, they were one of two doxas to be superseded by the style of his *First Enquiry*.

The *First Enquiry*, Hume continues, would go beyond both the easy and obvious and the accurate and abstract. On the one hand, Hume felt himself to be similar to the philosophers in the accurate and abstract school. In August 1737, Hume advised his friend

Michael Ramsay that, in order to best prepare to read the *Treatise*, Ramsay should familiarize himself with "*La Recherche de la Verité* of Pere Malebranche," a reference that followed Hume's recommendation of Locke's *Essay concerning Human Understanding* in a previous letter.[94] On the other, Hume admired the stylistic qualities of the other set: La Bruyère, as *The Oxford Dictionary of Philosophy* puts it, "was a particular favourite of David Hume."[95] As his argument proceeds, Hume lays out how one could unite the two manners of philosophy and therefore surpass this distinction.[96]

Hume begins by praising the easy and obvious manner for offering a combination of two types: the "Character" of "the mere Philosopher," who is remote from the world, and "the mere Ignorant."[97] If "the most perfect Character is suppos'd to lie betwixt those Extremes," this easy philosophy helps someone find their way there.[98] This instinct toward an Aristotelian virtuous mean is present across Hume's earlier writing. His 1742 *Essays, Moral and Political* include several pieces that similarly praise a union between two "Extremes." "Of Essay-Writing," for example, recommends a "League betwixt the learned and conversible Worlds," and "Of the Middle Station of Life" offers a panegyric to being between the "Extremes" of wealth and poverty.[99] The easy philosophy is to be praised further for corresponding to the natural balance present in human nature by respecting man as a reasonable, sociable, and active being, one for whom "Nature has pointed out a mixt kind of Life."[100] Simply carrying out the easy philosophy cannot, however, solve the question of how to write philosophy in the present. (Something that perhaps underlay Hume's decision to withdraw "Of Essay-Writing" and "Of the Middle Station of Life," from future editions—essays that were described by one biographer as too "Addisonian.")[101] Due to the reigning general opinion that the "abstract and profound" philosophy is to be rejected and despised—a kind of philosophy that Hume now names as "metaphysics"—he wishes to at least consider "what can reasonably be pleaded in their Behalf."[102]

This lays the groundwork for a second solution to the problem of the two styles, which works to balance between extremes in a different way. The "easy and humane" philosophy requires "the accurate and abstract" model as its foundation: the underlying "science of man" that the *Treatise* was so keen to establish.[103] The easy and obvious philosophy, Hume argues, cannot attain sufficient "Exactness" without the accurate and abstract, on which it relies to provide "accurate Knowledge of the internal Fabric."[104] The "inward Search or Enquiry" of the latter method is as necessary to the easy and obvious philosopher as anatomy is necessary to the painter.[105] As Hume puts it, recalling the presence of these terms in the *Abstract* and the *Treatise*, "The Anatomist presents to the Eye the most hideous and disagreeable Objects; but his Science is highly useful to the Painter in delineating even a *Venus* or an *Helen*."[106] Here we move from a combination of forms of life to a sense that the second manner of philosophy—as hideous and disagreeable a practice as it might be—is the required basis for the first. If the painter is concerned with appearances, using "the richest Colours" to depict "Figures" with "engaging Airs," they must also direct their attention to all that lies beneath: the "inward Structure of the human Body," its muscles, bones, and organs.[107] The accurate philosophy should not be despised for this: even if "Obscurity" is painful to the mind and eye, the ability to "bring Light from Obscurity" is "delightful and rejoicing."[108]

All this does not, however, simply clinch the argument for the accurate and abstract method of philosophy. The "Obscurity" of this method, Hume says, has led it into "uncertainty and error." "A considerable part of Metaphysics," he explains, is "not properly a Science" but penetrates "into Subjects utterly inaccessible to the Understanding" and becomes entangled with superstition.[109] Rather than praising this bad kind of anatomy for its ability to lay the groundwork for painting, Hume sets out to propose a different kind of combination. We must first begin, he argues, by cultivating a "true Metaphysics" to replace and destroy "the false and adulterate": the kind of metaphysics that does not confine itself to experiment and experience.[110] "The only Method of freeing Learning, at once, from these abstruse Questions," he argues, "is to enquire seriously into the Nature of human Understanding"—giving us the later title of his work—"and show, from an exact Analysis of its Powers and Capacity," that it is not fitted for this kind of speculation.[111]

This enquiry will furnish a knowledge of the operations of the mind, which it will separate and classify, and thus build a kind of "mental Geography."[112] Through proposing "Distinctions" between parts of the mind such as reflection and perception, it will be able to construct a true system of the mind, like Kepler's "true System" of the planets.[113] It will thus hope to "discover" the "secret Springs and Principles, by which the human mind is actuated in its Operations," akin to Newton's discovery of the laws and forces of nature.[114] It is probable, Hume outlines, that in this search we will find "one Operation and Principle of the mind" to depend on another, which may ultimately lead to finding "one more general and universal" animating principle.[115] In this, the new method becomes aligned with the practices of geography, astronomy, and mechanics, rather than eloquence and poetry.[116] Hume's philosophical method here distinguishes itself from the connections between character and anatomy we have seen before. Indeed, this method is not about sketching at all but writing a systematic account of cognitive principles.

Hume proposes that this enquiry—which necessarily will be abstract and difficult by virtue of never having been done before—should then be rendered as clear, easy, and obvious as possible: an approach that combines the best aspects of both manners of moral philosophy. "Happy, if we can unite the Boundaries of the different Species of Philosophy," Hume concludes, "by reconciling Profound Enquiry, with Clearness, and Truth with Novelty!"[117] With this proposed synthesis, Hume moves moral philosophy, the "science of man," away from both the representation of characters of virtue and vice and speculative metaphysics. Moral philosophy, in Hume's hands, instead becomes a search for the underlying general and universal principles of diverse phenomena, which acknowledges its boundaries at the limits of experience.[118] By taking from the first species of philosophy a commitment to aspects of style—clarity and novelty—and from the second a revised approach to method, based on finding "principles," Hume gives us a sense of the form of his philosophy.[119] As Hume had put it in a 1739 letter to Francis Hutcheson, he intends "to make a new Tryal, if it be possible to make the Moralist and the Metaphysician agree a little better."[120] If Hume is going to deal with characters, he will do so in this fashion.

"Of National Characters"

Along with the *First Enquiry,* in 1748, Hume published *Three Essays: Moral and Political,* which contained the essay "Of National

Characters," and a further volume of essays under the heading *Essays, Moral and Political.*[121] Hume's comments on philosophical methodology in the *First Enquiry,* which amount to a rejection of character-writing, encourage us to reconsider how he described character in his own essays—above all, in "Of National Characters."[122] The writing of national character, which had flourished in London in the previous century, remained a popular genre in 1748: one that incorporated a kind of writing that we might associate with "painting," on the one hand, and "anatomy," on the other. When he chose to write "Of National Characters," Hume gave himself an arena in which to avoid both of these models and practice the synthesis of styles he described in the *Enquiry*. This essay accordingly becomes an exposition of an alternative way of incorporating questions of character into moral philosophy.

Hume's essay is typically read in dialogue with the Enlightenment philosophers of climatic determinism—Montesquieu, Abbé du Bos, and Thomas Jefferson—and their precedents in Hippocrates and Strabo and later in Albertus Magnus and Jean Bodin.[123] There is, however, a formal precedent of equal importance for Hume: the Theophrastan model of rhetorically sketching the character of a nation and the developments in this model toward the end of the seventeenth century. Consider Owen Felltham's pioneering *Character of the Low-Countreyes* published in 1648, the first full-length character of a nation.[124] This sketch consists of highly wrought, figurative "observations" of the vices and virtues of this nation and its people; opening with a comparison of the Low Countries to "a universall Quagmire, Epitomiz'd, A green cheese in pickle."[125] Felltham's sketch would fit into Hume's understanding of the "easy and obvious" manner of writing philosophy. It uses conceits, microcosms, and parallelisms; aims to be both "pleasant and profitable"; and sets characters of virtues and vices in opposition to one another.[126] The figurative style present in this sketch continued in the following decades, appearing in the anonymous 1692 *A Brief Character of Ireland* and in Edward Ward's two treatises, respectively published in 1698 and 1699: *A Trip to Jamaica: With a True Character of the People and Island* and *A Trip to New-England with a Character of the Country and People.*

If it seems clear why Hume's essay would reject this method of writing national character, it is important to underline his decision to move away from another popular paradigm that had come to complement the rhetorical mode by the end of the century. This was the attempt to discern national character by means of statistics, as in William Petty's posthumous *The Political Anatomy of Ireland* (1691). In his treatise, billed as "the first Essay of Political Anatomy," Petty, an MP for the Parliament of Ireland, provides tabulated statistics about numerous topics: the kinds of land in Ireland; population size, fluctuation, and quantities of people by age, health, religion, nationality, and wealth; housing; employment; domestic produce and trade; the quantity of animals; the composition of the government and other institutions; and changes in the value of debt, currency, land, goods, and people.[127] While Petty is an important forerunner to several of Hume's arguments—with Hume citing him in a later essay, "On the Populousness of Ancient Nations" (1752)—Hume's national character is not carried out in a statistical mode.[128] Neither this political anatomy, nor the earlier anatomies of the 1650s and 1660s, which were still associated with rhetoric (promising "The Dutchman Anatomized" or "The Italian Anatomiz'd by an English Chyrurgion" in their subtitles, before describing them in figures), would do.

If Hume's essay takes anything from Petty, it is his sense that manners cannot be so easily tabulated, and instead require a different kind of analysis.[129] Petty treated the manners of national types largely by questioning their origin, proposing to "deduce" Irish manners from a number of sources, geographical, social, historical and political: "from their Original Constitutions of Body, and from the Air; next from their ordinary Food; next from their Condition of Estate and Liberty, and from the Influence of their Governours and Teachers; and lastly, from their Ancient Customs."[130] But Petty does not attempt to get to the "general and universal" principle, to divide these factors into different categories, and determine which of them is most significant. His medley of causes, therefore, was not sufficient for Hume. In "Of National Characters," Hume works to extend Petty's political anatomy by going further into the "internal fabric" to determine the principle by which groups of people can have a national character at all.

"Of National Characters" begins with a principle. This is not a principle, however, that has been discovered by the patient work of the abstruse philosopher but one "established" by "the Vulgar." "The Vulgar," Hume writes, "are very apt to carry all *national Characters* to Extremes; and having once establish'd it as a Principle, that any People are knavish, or cowardly, or ignorant, they will admit of no Exception, but comprehend every Individual under the same Character."[131] As we might predict, Hume finds this kind of judgment deeply problematic. First, Hume does not trust "The Vulgar." "The vulgar," as he puts it in the *Treatise,* are apt to take "things according to their first appearance," as opposed to "philosophers," who attempt to find the "vast variety of springs and principles, which are hid."[132] This leads us to the second issue: "the vulgar," in the case of national characters, accordingly do not search for a general, secret, and hidden principle but give a prejudice about a particular people the status of a "Principle" instead, which they do not correct even where they meet with exceptions. This is the prime kind of reasoning that Hume more generally wished to reject, a reasoning that would fall foul of the Newtonian maxim *Hypotheses non fingo,* I contrive no hypotheses.[133] Third, the vulgar take their thinking "to Extremes," a posture we have seen Hume reject in his search for balance elsewhere. Hume's essay is designed to correct all three errors, thinking about "national character" by a different means entirely.

Hume's first means of correction is to replace the opinion of the vulgar with the opinion expressed by people "of Sense." These people, while condemning the "undistinguish'd Judgments" of the vulgar, are nonetheless happy to believe that some qualities are more prominent in some nations than others. They do so, however, while acknowledging that this is a probability that can admit of exceptions—such as that of the Spaniard Cervantes's "Wit and Gaiety," characteristics usually understood to be the province of the French.[134] Yet this more concessive statement, while less extreme, cannot conclude the discussion. For it leaves unanswered the question that most interests Hume: how and why do national characters emerge, both in particular and in general? To answer it, Hume will need to move away from the representation of particular attributes and their exceptions. Instead, he must consider causes: he must make writing about character a case of writing about how characters can emerge. Where La Bruyère attempted to "discover the principle" of an individual character type's "Villany and Folly,"

Hume sets out in his essay to understand the principle that forms national characters in the first place.

Hume suggests two possible causes for national characters—moral and physical—which he then proceeds to define.[135] Moral causes are thought to be the circumstances that "work on the Mind as Motives or Reasons" and render "a peculiar Set of Manners habitual to us."[136] These causes include the type of government, economic situation, and geopolitical standing of a particular nation. Physical causes, on the other hand, are "Qualities of the Air and Climate," which do not work on the mind, but "insensibly" affect "the Temper, by altering the Tone and Habit of the Body"[137] For both kinds of causes, Hume leaves room for exceptions: these are causes that render either mental or physical behavior "habitual," that prevail "among the Generality." While Hume says it will seem "evident to the most superficial Observer" that "the Character of a Nation will very much depend on *moral* Causes," he proceeds to justify this argument in any case. He does so via one definition, that "a Nation is nothing but a Collection of Individuals," and one affirmation, that the "Manners of Individuals are frequently determined" by moral causes.[138] From here, Hume can argue that, just as moral causes affect individuals (poverty, for example, debases "the Minds of the common People"), they will also affect national collectives. Seeing this as a truism, Hume goes on to describe how "the same Principle of moral Causes fixes the Character of different Professions."[139] The case in point here is the difference between a soldier and a priest, who "are different Characters, in all Nations, and all Ages" due to a difference "founded on Circumstances, whose Operation is eternal and unalterable," coming from aspects of the ways of life of these two professions.[140] Although countless character sketches of soldiers and priests were composed across seventeenth-century Europe, Hume's approach is not solely to depict them. Rather, it is to ask how it is that these two different character types continually occur.

Having laid out the case for moral causes, Hume needs to dismiss the possibility that physical causes may be equally relevant. He confesses that it might indeed, "at first sight, seem very probable" that physical circumstances have a great influence over our behavior, "since we find, that these Circumstances have an Influence over every other Animal."[141] As the "human Mind is of a very imitative

Nature," Hume continues, it is therefore impossible for a group of people to convene without them "acquiring a Similitude of Manners."[142] And as the "Propensity to Company and Society is strong in all rational Creatures," a propensity that "makes us enter deeply into each other's Sentiments," passions, and inclinations, all these qualities also spread, "as it were by Contagion, thro' the whole Club or Knot of Companions."[143]

National character in human beings—unlike animals and plants—is not produced by physical causes because human beings have a particular "Nature" as "rational Creatures." That nature is to imitate and adopt each other's manners by "Contagion." Hume had already highlighted the significance of this term in his 1742 essay "Of the Rise and Progress of the Arts and Sciences." There, he had argued that we are able to determine "those Principles or Causes, which are fitted to operate on a Multitude" with much more ease than "those which operate on a few only."[144] He notes that

> when any *Causes* beget a particular Inclination or Passion, at a certain Time, and among a certain People; tho' many Individuals may escape the Contagion, and be rul'd by Passions peculiar to themselves; yet the Multitude will certainly be infected with the common Passion, and be govern'd by it in all their Actions.[145]

The sources for this argument go even further back. "No quality of human nature is more remarkable," Hume had written earlier in the *Treatise,* "than that propensity we have to sympathize with others, and to receive by communication their inclinations and sentiments, however different from, or even contrary to our own."[146] We find this, Hume says, "conspicuous in children, who implicitly embrace every opinion propos'd to them," and in people "of the greatest judgment and understanding, who find it very difficult to follow their own reason or inclination, in opposition to that of their friends and daily companions." But it is also to "this principle" that we "ought to ascribe the great uniformity we may observe in the humours and turn of thinking of those of the same nation."[147] The question of the genesis of national character is therefore the fundamental question of moral philosophy because it is the question of human nature: the issue of determining the fundamental principles by which human beings differ from plants and animals. It is also a causal question that Hume's philosophy permits us to attempt to answer, as it concerns a multitude. This exposes why national character must then be treated in a similar way to "the science of man": via a patient enquiry into its "secret springs and principles."

The essay then details this process of contagion, attempting to answer the question of how different nations develop different manners initially. Hume argues here that Nature originally distributed temperaments unevenly: "Tho' Nature produces all Kinds of Temper and Understanding in great Abundance, it follows not that she always produces them in like Proportions."[148] If any of these dispositions "be found in greater Abundance" in a given place, it will "naturally prevail" and "give a Tincture to the national Character."[149] Failing this, in cases where "no Species of Temper can reasonably be presum'd to predominate," Hume argues that "Persons in Credit and Authority" will surely have different characters and "their Influence, on the Manners of the People, must, at all Times, be very considerable."[150] Having initially been formed from either one of these sources, national character will get stronger with each generation. This allows Hume to "assert" that when national characters do not depend on fixed moral causes, they "proceed from such Accidents as these, and that physical Causes have no discernible Operation on the human Mind."[151] The essay provides nine examples of national character being shaped by moral causes or contagion: examples of Jews, who live in different climates but have the same manners; of towns on either side of a border, with different customs despite their shared geography; and of empires that span a variety of geographies, such as that of China, but retain a national uniformity of manners. At the end of this list, Hume notes one important exception, which reveals how important a science of human nature is to this essay's project and why it therefore cannot limit itself to the work of a simple character sketch.

"If the Characters of Men depended on the Air and Climate," Hume writes, "the Degrees of Heat and Cold should naturally be expected to have a mighty Influence, since nothing has a greater Effect on all Plants and irrational Animals."[152] If physical causes, that is, *are* important, the one place we would see them is at the extremes of the world. Despite previously affirming that physical causes do not affect the human mind, characterized by its capacity for sympathy, in one rushed sentence Hume claims, "And indeed there is some Reason to think, that all the Nations, which live beyond the polar Circles or betwixt the Tropics, are inferior to the rest of the Species, and are utterly incapable of all the higher Attainments of the human Mind."[153] An explanation of this "Reason" does not appear in this edition of the essay, only being added in a footnote to the edition of 1753 before a major revision in 1777. In this note, Hume exposes that he is thinking about "negroes" and "whites."[154] Hume's claim here is as follows: since none of the "Negroe slaves dispersed all over Europe" have distinguished themselves by showing "symptoms of ingenuity" in developing "ingenious manufactures" and arts and sciences—as compared to the "the most rude and barbarous of the whites"—they must therefore be "naturally inferior to the whites."[155] In the face of evidence that explicitly disproved this claim—for example, the fact that in Jamaica, "they talk of one negroe as a man of parts and learning"—Hume is intransigent. "It is likely," he belittles, "he is admired for slender accomplishments, like a parrot, who speaks a few words plainly."[156]

This claim rests on Hume's notion of contagion. Hume believes that if black people have not adopted what he thinks are European manners—the "ingenious manufactures" and arts and sciences—through a process of sympathetic contagion, they must lack the capacity for sympathy. And, as sympathy, for Hume, is the fundamental quality of the human mind, they must therefore be "naturally inferior" to other human beings who possess this capacity. If we return to the original essay, it is telling that Hume uses the conjunction "and indeed" to link the idea that climate affects plants and irrational animals with the idea that people who live in intemperate climates are inferior. It suggests that Hume thinks that people who live in intemperate climates, like "Plants and irrational Animals," could then be affected by *physical* causes, the causes that he dismissed earlier by relying on an account of human sympathy.[157] But as this would not explain the differences between "negroes" and "whites" that Hume perceives, despite their living in the same climate of Europe, he must postulate an original difference—prior to either physical or moral explanations—instead. This final rejection of climate as a factor is consistent with the way in which the rest of Hume's essay dismisses possible cases of the influence of physical causes between northern and southern populations.

Hume's decision to combine the question of the character of the human being with the question of the character of the nation, and to attempt to answer both by searching for underlying principles that shape behavior, thus leads him to assert "an original distinction" between "breeds of men" and their respective capacities to access "the higher Attainments of the human Mind."[158] With this, Hume enters a developing conversation about race that had begun in early modern philosophy. Though Renaissance climate theory had posited a division of human beings into environmentally informed types, a different concept of race began to emerge in the mid-eighteenth century.[159] An insight into changes in medical experimentation helps clarify this shift. In the seventeenth and early eighteenth centuries, naturalists rarely worried about whether a drug would be effective on peoples of different races, and when they did, "they were concerned that differences in climate, not racial constitutions, might render a drug ineffective."[160] In the later eighteenth century, this changed: a difference in race was thought to be a difference in person. Hume embraced this latter way of thinking.

Aaron Garrett argues that Hume had comparatively little impact on the politics of race in the eighteenth century, finding Hume's legacy to lie more in the "disturbing precedent" it set the human sciences, whereby "when a phenomenon proves stubborn and counter to theoretical aims," you should "push it from the class of those phenomena to be legitimately considered with whatever means are at your disposal."[161] Though Garrett's account of Hume's manipulation of method seems spot on, Hume's legacy is in fact more extensive. Consider its role in Edward Long's infamous 1774 *History of Jamaica,* "the classic text of 18th-century European pseudo-scientific racism."[162] When Long wants to discredit the learning of an educated Jamaican boy, he directly quotes Hume's argument from "Of National Characters" as his crutch, deriding him as "a parrot who speaks a few words plainly."[163]

Hume's particular argument and methodology also made their way into Kant's early theorization of race in 1764—the philosopher who has been called "the first to propose a rigorous scientific concept of race."[164] Decades before the three *Critiques,* and the effort at total systematization that scholars have linked to Kant's theory of race, Kant picks up both Hume's method of prioritizing moral causes as the motors for national character and his sense that, when this explanation does not apply, an "original distinction" between people's respective capacities to access "the higher Attainments of the human Mind" must be at play.[165] It seems then that Hume's shift to attempting to find the principles behind the phenomenon of national character, rather than to depict these characters themselves, was sufficiently systematic for Kant to adopt it in his own racial theory. In addition, Hume's affirmation of the natural status of racial difference is thought to have informed Voltaire's distinction between *nature* and *mœurs*—traits respectively derived from race or from education and government—as well as Jefferson's similar distinction between the racial and cultural influences on both black slaves and Native Americans.[166]

Hume's new approach to the "science of man" not only helped inaugurate the human sciences by applying the question of the animating principles of reality to a series of different phenomena but also exemplifies how easily this method could be turned to justify theories of racial difference—a legacy that would extend far beyond Kant into the nineteenth century.[167] There were, however, more benign effects of Hume's new method. When we turn to the many diverse essays he wrote in the same period as the *First Enquiry*, we can start to observe a coherent approach to character: one that refuses to stray into Theophrastan character-writing.

Character in Hume's Essays

Hume's interest in collective habits, as aspects of reality whose causes we can determine by virtue of their operation "on a Multitude," explains the ubiquitous presence of "characters" across his early essays. The essays frequently split people into two species or categories, introduce typologies, and reduce political positions to character traits. Hume also writes texts entitled "characters." But, as they are more akin to other genres, such as impersonated dramatic monologues (as in Hume's essays "The Epicurean," "The Platonist," "The Sceptic," and "The Stoic") or historical portraits of existing individuals (such as Hume's character of himself, of Robert Walpole, or of the heads of state and political figures that animate his histories), they seem too far from the Theophrastan model of depicting collective habits to be an evolution of it.[168] To see the full transformation of this Theophrastan model from representative sketches of observed behavior to generalized analysis, we need to consider Hume's other essays. A closer look at them further exposes how he did not trust the literary sketch as a means of moral transformation or a source of knowledge. Before turning to these essays, however, it is worth pausing to elaborate on why the texts Hume decides to entitle "characters" do not fit the Theophrastan model.

Although close attention to the standard form of character-writing easily distinguishes it from both "personated" dramatic monologues and written portraits of named individuals, one could claim that, with these characters, Hume was attempting to revolutionize the Theophrastan model.[169] We could find a basis for this in the argument of Donald T. Siebert, who proposes that there is a transformation of the Theophrastan character into "a kind of psychograph of an historical individual" in historical writing in the eighteenth century.[170] Yet the English character as "psychograph" had already developed a century earlier, as detailed in chapter 4. Moreover, it did not replace the Theophrastan character, as character writers continued to embody collective habits in one figure. We should not then classify Hume's historical characters or dramatic monologues as part of the Theophrastan tradition.

Baier points to a different set of characters to show the influence of Theophrastus on Hume: the representation of virtues and vices in book 3, part 3 of the *Treatise*. Working from Hume's declaration to Frances Hutcheson that he wanted to take his "Catalogue of Virtues from Cicero's *Offices*," Baier claims that "it is not so much Cicero's rather pompous *Offices* as Theophrastus's *Characters* that Hume seems at times to be emulating in this list."[171] Hume is interested, she writes, in listing the kinds of virtues that make someone a good fellow citizen, qualities like meekness, dexterity, friendship, self-assertiveness, cleanliness, and good humor: a mirror image of the "moral nastiness" we find in Theophrastus.[172] While, at the level of content, this seems exactly right, at the level of form, it would be harder to justify.

A closer look at the sections of the *Treatise* that are concerned with vices and virtues indeed reflects Hume's unwavering preference for principles over characters. Whenever Hume describes character, he is concerned to find its animating principles, origins, and effects—which appears distinctly un-Theophrastan once we place him in dialogue with the existing tradition of character-writing. The first section of book 3, part 3 of the *Treatise,* for example, concerning "the origin of the natural virtues and vices," begins with an account of how "the chief spring or actuating principle of the human mind" is that of pleasure or pain: an account that allows for a particular understanding of vice and virtue.[173] This section of the *Treatise* details how the virtuousness or viciousness of an action must depend on character because these are "durable principles of the mind" rather than aleatory actions.[174] It then forewarns that to "discover the true origin of morals (. . .) we must take the matter pretty deep, and compare some principles."[175] Hume's descriptions of particular attributes are thus to be understood in a framework designed to look for principles—a move away from a tradition in which the description of attributes was sufficient moral philosophy in itself. It is this innovation in the representation of collective dispositions with which Hume should be credited, rather than with a continuation of the previous Theophrastan method.

Character, in the Theophrastan sense of a collective disposition, newly reworked to reveal principles, appears across Hume's essays in four guises. First, some essays attempt to find the universal laws underlying phenomena that had previously been depicted in character sketches, such as superstition and enthusiasm. The seventeenth century had seen countless characters of "The Superstitious," after Hall's initial sketch (which itself directly follows Theophrastus's character 16), as well as figures of "Enthusiasts" paired with those of "Anabaptists, Independents, Brownists (. . .) Levellers, Quakers, Seekers, Fift-Monarchy-Men, & Dippers." Yet Hume's approach to these dispositions is not to sketch them but to understand "the true Sources" of these "two Species of false Religion" and trace their "Influence on Government and Society," "the natural consequences of each."[176] His essay "Of Superstition and Enthusiasm" thus proceeds to detail how both positions are derived from the state of "the Mind of Man."[177] Superstition emerges from "Weakness, Fear, Melancholy, along with Ignorance"; enthusiasm, from "Hope, Pride, Presumption, warm Imagination along with Ignorance"—qualities that Hume further qualifies as "a presumptuous Boldness of Character."[178] If Bacon animates Hume's experimental method,

Hume takes the kind of analysis that Bacon used in his own essay "Of Superstition" much further. Where, for Bacon, "the Causes of Superstition" were to be found in external factors, such as the presence of too many "sensuall Rites and Ceremonies," for Hume, they are internal instead.[179]

In Hume's view, people with superstitious or enthusiastic temperaments are led to hold different kinds of religious and political outlooks. Because superstition derives from "Sorrow, and a Depression of Spirits," the person suffering from it does not believe themselves worthy to approach the divine. They therefore have recourse to someone else to carry out this task, making it "an infallible Rule, that Superstition is favourable to Priestly Power."[180] Enthusiasm, on the other hand, is contrary to authority: the presumptuousness that founds it makes the enthusiast believe themselves "sufficiently qualified to approach the Divinity, without any human Mediator," a belief that creates furious and violent outbursts, extreme resolutions, and a general "Contempt of Forms, Traditions and Authorities."[181] Superstition is accordingly "an Enemy to Civil Liberty, and Enthusiasm a Friend to it."[182] Hume points to the Quakers, the Independents, the Anabaptists, and the Levellers as examples of the consequences of enthusiasm (citing four of the eight categories paired with Enthusiasts in the earlier sketch), an "Observation" that is said to be "founded on the most certain Experience," as well as "on Reason."[183]

We have previously seen political and religious positions reduced to attributes of character, as with Theophrastus's sketch of the Oligarch or the anonymous Civil War writer's sketch of a Jesuit, and we have seen character sketches that work to expose motives for action, as in La Bruyère. Hume's approach, however, is to compose an analytical essay in search of behavioral rules and consequences. This follows the understanding of character that he outlined in the *Treatise*: as a unit that creates impressions on other people, provoking a series of effects that can be explained by a number of principles. By drawing this aspect of the *Treatise* together with the methodological statement of the *First Enquiry*, we have a means of understanding one of Hume's approaches to character in his essays: an approach that does not involve painting but provides an anatomy of causes and consequences, rendered clear and easy in its manner.

A second species of character-writing that can be found in Hume's essays is an invocation of character types in the service of broader arguments. This makes it seem that Hume perceives the world as already separated into character types, part of a social landscape that he must acknowledge in order to advance new ideas. We have already glimpsed this method in "Of Essay-Writing," which begins with the division of "The elegant Part of Mankind" into "the *learned* and *conversible*."[184] The purpose of this essay is not to depict either species but to make a case for the necessity of their reunion, given that "the Separation of the Learned from the conversible World seems to have been the great Defect of the last Age."[185] By doing so, Hume hopes to establish a "Commerce" between the two domains, where "Materials" of "Conversation and common Life" are manufactured by "Learning," reaching a similar argument for synthesis as in the *First Enquiry*.[186]

It should not come as a surprise, then, that when Hume wrote "Of Commerce" in 1752, he continued to elide the language of "commerce" with the arguments in "Of Essay-Writing" and the opening of the *Enquiry*. The essay similarly begins by dividing mankind into "two classes," that of "*shallow* thinkers" and that of "*abstruse* thinkers." Hume then spends a number of pages justifying why we should praise a version of the latter.[187] He argues that when we discuss "general subjects," we will need to find "general principles" and will therefore need to borrow from the tools of abstruse thinkers.[188] For Hume, a comprehension of "general subjects" is not only the "chief business of philosophers" but that of politicians concerned with "the domestic government of the state."[189] Hume explains that he opens an essay on "commerce, luxury, money, interest, etc." in this unusual way in order to justify an approach to these topics that will involve a search for "principles, which are uncommon, and which may seem too refin'd and subtile for such vulgar subjects."[190] The characters of the *shallow* and the *abstruse* are thus once again not sketched but used in the service of another argument.[191] Rather than simply saying that an understanding of commerce will demand a search for general principles, Hume frames this whole debate through an invocation of types of character.

The third approach to character found in Hume's essays is one that refuses to see character itself as the ultimate end point. While

Hume already clarified in "Of Commerce" that the general principles of this art are not based in character, this approach is rendered most explicit in the essay "That Politics May be Reduced to a Science." Hume here moves an analysis of politics away from character in order to get to the most general axioms from which one can deduce consequences. He begins by noting that he should "be sorry to think, that human Affairs admit of no greater Stability, than what they receive from the casual Humours and Characters of particular Men," and proceeds to mount an argument that more stable causes are found in laws and government.[192] These causes, he argues, are so great, "that Consequences as general and as certain may be deduced from them, on most Occasions, as any which the Mathematical Sciences can afford us."[193] From this basis, he can therefore pronounce, for example, "as a universal Axiom in Politics," that the best forms of monarchy, aristocracy, and democracy are respectively "an hereditary Prince, a Nobility without Vassals, and a People voting by their Representatives."[194] This provides one of the first "Principles of this Science"—an idea Hume then elaborates further in the essay "Of the first Principles of Government," which immediately follows this essay in the 1741 collection.[195] To truly understand the domain of politics, one cannot simply rely on character sketches of particular monarchs. Nor can one rely on analysis of the principles that underlie these characters, such as—if they are superstitious—the basis of their superstition. Instead, he argues for going beyond this level of analysis into axioms about political structures, untouched by the character of a person.

Finally, there are essays by Hume that intend to cultivate in the reader a better judgment of character. They continue the initial purpose that the spurious Proem gives to Theophrastus's *Characters*—that, through this text, readers will learn to associate with the finest of men—but do so through essayistic analysis rather than imagistic representation. In "Of the Delicacy of Taste and Passion," for example, Hume proposes that the cure for the latter is to refine the former. "I am persuaded," he argues, "that nothing is so proper to cure us of this Delicacy of Passion, as the cultivating of that higher and more refined Taste."[196] Taste is what "enables us to judge of the Characters of Men," and it is developed in part through the liberal arts.[197] Curing the delicacy of passion is a case of convincing the reader to cultivate "a Relish in the Liberal Arts," through which they will better learn to judge other people.[198] Yet Hume is not advocating for the power of the literary sketch to change our social behavior. Significantly, he does not embody this principle by writing character types but by writing an essay to convince people to profit from the liberal arts.[199] Character, in terms of the representation of collective dispositions, is for Hume everything but the character sketch: a crucial part of his philosophical armory, not the means of his expression.

Philosophy and Literature

In the dialogue affixed to Hume's 1751 second *Enquiry concerning the Principles of Morals,* we find a speaker so concerned about the "Uncertainty of all these Judgments concerning Characters" that they are encouraged to try to find "a Standard for Judgments of this Nature" by "tracing Matters (. . .) a little higher, and examining the first Principles."[200] Hume uses an image to express the nature of this problem:

> The Rhine flows North, the Rhone South; yet both spring from the same Mountain, and are also actuated, in their opposite Directions, by the same Principle of Gravity: The different Inclinations of the Ground, on which they run, cause all the Difference of their Courses.[201]

This image might serve well to illustrate two methods of writing that would follow two different courses in the decades after Hume's separation of moral philosophers into learned, abstruse anatomists who search for the secret springs and principles of reality and easy, conversational, shallow painters who represent characters. While both have their source in the mountain of moral philosophy, and both, in their own ways, are actuated by an attempt to grasp reality, they follow two very different courses, eventually discharging in seas that we now respectively call "philosophy" and "literature." While, from the perspective of the sea, we cannot see the single spring of these two rivers, by training our eyes on Hume, we get somewhere close to the source.

The separation between these two domains of thinking—which we might also describe in terms of knowledge and wisdom or science and art—had significant effects.[202] The first of these is a sense, visible in Hume's aesthetic works, that if a philosopher is to discuss matters artistic, they must do so by finding animating principles. It does not seem surprising that it is in the 1750s that works of aesthetics start to emerge, inspired by the precise task of understanding the principles behind the experience of works of art and literature. Alexander Baumgarten's *Aesthetica* (1750), coining the name of this genre, indeed embraces with the "failed hope," as Kant puts it, of bringing "the critical estimation of the beautiful under principles of reason, and elevating its rules to a science."[203] The second effect consists of an increasing pressure on character writers, writers of literature more broadly, and novelists in particular, to justify their work's worth and utility, often by eliding it with history. As Guido Mazzoni highlights, in eighteenth-century England, France, and Germany, the well-worn "phobia for poetic falsehood" widely spread.[204] To take one example, in 1751, the English cleric and novelist "Francis Coventry felt the need to explain why wise men, metaphysicians, men of science and learning, and politicians involved in the affairs of state should consider that the reading of novels is worthy of a serious man."[205]

Rorty likewise claims that this eighteenth-century paradigm shift continues to shape our conceptions of the disciplines of philosophy and literature to this day. He argues that Kant is the key philosopher who effectuates this shift. Rorty explains that Kant develops a new conception of philosophy, one that makes "epistemology-and-metaphysics" central and positions metaphysics as having emerged from epistemology, rather than vice versa.[206] To do so, Kant borrows from Descartes the "invention of mind" as a category for philosophical speculation, from Locke the idea that "mind" was the subject matter for a "science of man," and from both Hume and Descartes the sense that philosophy must be kept within the "limits of human knowledge."[207] This shift, Rorty explains, was a way of keeping philosophy alive at a moment where metaphysics "had been displaced by physics."[208] In order to ensure that philosophy would not sound out of date, in comparison to physics, and eventually become a discarded model, Kant positioned philosophy as *prior* to the sciences, as something "underlying."[209]

Rorty's lack of detail on the way in which Hume attempts something similar before Kant—in his desire to establish "a compleat system of the sciences" built on a science of human nature, which itself centrally concerns principles of cognition—is not what is most relevant here. Rather, it is the way in which Rorty's account, due to his focus on Kant rather than Hume, only attends to one side of the equation. Hume, as we saw, is keen to reject not only the current state of *metaphysics,* as a kind of "abstruse" and speculative reasoning, but also that other kind of moral philosophy akin to poetry, painting, and eloquence. By working from Hume, we can start to see how the Enlightenment shift in the history of philosophy was a means of distinguishing philosophy not only from metaphysics but also from literature.

The conclusion of Rorty's account is that when philosophy became "epistemology-and-metaphysics," it severed its relationship with poets, novelists, and psychologists and shifted the task of the philosopher from shaping a reader's actions to providing a truthful account of a given phenomenon. With this in mind, Hume's break with the "easy and obvious" philosophy sits all the more comfortably as something of an original sin. If we use this framing, we can catch a glimpse of an alternative mode of philosophy: one that existed before Hume's fall. The "easy and obvious" philosophy corresponds in many ways to the alternative Rorty proposes in "Philosophy without Mirrors"—a philosophy that combines Wittgenstein's "flair for deconstructing captivating pictures," Heidegger's way of distancing us from tradition, Dewey's sense that culture should be dominated not "by the ideal of objective cognition but by that of aesthetic enhancement," and Rorty's own pragmatic hope of eliminating "the Greek contrast between contemplation and action."[210]

The character sketches of ordinary vices and types that constitute the "easy and obvious" manner of moral philosophy present a version of knowledge that is social and contextual and one in which the aesthetic and the cognitive are inseparably linked.[211] They fit closely with a sense of philosophy as a practice of *phronesis* rather than *episteme*: akin to getting into a conversation with strangers, providing practical wisdom, Rorty says, or "acquiring a new virtue or skill by imitating models."[212] They were designed and imagined to play an essential role in Hans-Georg Gadamer's notion of *Bildung*—the process of education and self-formation, of making yourself into a projected *Bild,* or image—that Rorty praises as an alternative posture for the philosopher.[213] They are written in precisely the genres Rorty gives to these "great edifying philosophers," as opposed to the tidy, constructive arguments of the great systematizers: the forms of "satires, parodies, aphorisms."[214] And, in providing a description of an individual's type, they might just "perform the social function which Dewey called 'breaking the crust of convention,' preventing man from deluding himself with the notion that he knows himself, or anything else, except under optional descriptions."[215] Unlike Rorty's "philosophy without mirrors," however, this is a genre that is repeatedly likened to a mirror, a genre still interested in representation but one that shifts its lens from the depiction of the operations of the mind to sketching the body in the social world. This leaves open a sense of philosophy as a task for grasping some kind of truth: a task that Rorty might resist but one that seems more necessary in our current "stage" of philosophical conversation than it perhaps did when he developed these ideas in 1979.

Epilogue

A THEOPHRASTAN AESTHETIC

Hume's bold declaration that character-writing was one of two modes of philosophy to be superseded did not stop new character sketches from being translated or written. In 1772, Theophrastus's *Characters* was translated into Russian, in 1787 into Spanish, and in the eighteenth century, as J. W. Smeed has shown, there was a "wholesale imitation of the *Tatler* and the *Spectator*" into German.[1] These German-language "moral weeklies" (*moralische Wochenschriften*) flourished in Switzerland, Germany, and eventually Austria and contained all the same qualities as the English coffeehouse papers. Though character sketches often served "to sugar the moral pill," they were generally not, as the Swiss *Der Neue Eidsgenosse* clarifies in 1750, "written for philosophers."[2] In the Austrian sketches of the nineteenth century, the shift away from philosophy is even more acute. The indigenous Viennese sketch—a catchy pamphlet that lay about coffeehouses like "magazines in a hairdresser's today"—was "a form of writing designed not to change the world or improve the reader, but to entertain."[3]

Collections of sketches were published in England throughout the nineteenth century: from William Makepeace Thackeray's *The Snobs of England* (1846–7), to Henry Mayhew's 1851 *London Labour and the London Poor,* to George Eliot's 1879 *Impressions of Theophrastus Such,* her "last and strangest work."[4] They also continued in France, most popularly in the form of a multiauthor publication of *The French Painted by Themselves: A Moral Encyclopedia of the 19th Century* (1840–1842), which uniquely includes images of typical figures (Figure E.1). There were character

L'HORTICULTEUR.

C'EST surtout quand on voit certains goûts qui remplissent et rendent heureuse la vie d'un homme, que l'on comprend bien que chacun a besoin d'avoir sa madone de plâtre ou de bois qu'il puisse parer à sa fantaisie.

C'est ce qui explique comment des hommes souvent très-supérieurs consacrent toute leur vie à quelques fleurs, à quelques insectes, quelquefois à un seul insecte, à une seule fleur; tant un instinct admirable, ou quelquefois peut-être une sage philosophie leur enseigne à présenter le moins de surface possible à la fortune, à vivre tout bas, et à se contenter d'un bonheur facile à cacher aux yeux du monde.

Il ne faut pas croire que l'intensité et la violence d'une passion puisse se mesurer à la petitesse de son objet. Les horticulteurs, qui vivent dans les fleurs comme les abeilles, ont comme elles un aiguillon dangereux. Les passions douces s'entourent de férocité comme on entoure une plante précieuse de ronces et d'épines pour la préserver de la dent des troupeaux.

Cela me rappelle comment me fut un jour dévoilé l'atroce caractère des moutons, que j'avais toujours regardés comme l'emblème de la mansuétude et de la bienveillance. — Monsieur, me disait un berger avec lequel je venais de voyager sur la route d'Épernay, il n'y a rien de si méchant que les moutons; ils n'aiment pas plus l'herbe de ce champ qui est ensemencé, que celle de celui d'à côté qui ne l'est pas; eh bien! ils sont tous dans le champ ensemencé... Brrrr... brrr... Mords là, Médor, brrr... C'est donc pour me faire prendre par le garde et me faire mettre à l'amende. Tenez, en voilà un là-bas... un noir... qui agace mon chien. Ici, Médor...

FIGURE E.1. Illustration of the horticulturist, in *Les français peints par eux mêmes: Encyclopédie morale du dix-neuvième siècle* (Paris: L. Curmer, 1840). *Credit:* Typ 815.40.4053, Houghton Library, Harvard University.

volumes published in the twentieth century, including Elias Canetti's absurdist *Earwitness: Fifty Characters* (1974) and Roger Hargreaves's Mr. Men and Little Miss series (1971–), which stretches all the way from Mr. Tickle to Mr. Daydream, Mr. Nobody, and Little Miss Late—a woman who, like her Theophrastan predecessor, the Man with Bad Timing, is so late that if "you ask her round for dinner, she probably won't arrive until next week."[5] Along with the continued popularity of this latter work well into our own moment, new character collections have begun to appear. In 2017, Wulf Rehder, a retired professor of mathematics, sketched *Corporate Characters: 52 Shades of Business,* and in 2022, Frédéric Spinhirny, a director of a hospital in Tours, penned a collection of *Characters Today* in an effort to help managers understand the characters of people in their workforces.[6] Just as much as this tradition of collecting character types is alive and well, individual sketches of new political and social types continue to emerge in popular culture, whether those are descriptions of "the expert," "the hoarder," or "the Trumpist."[7]

However, if we turn back to Hume's comparison of philosophers who are painters (Cicero, La Bruyère, and Addison) and philosophers who are anatomists (Aristotle, Malebranche, and Locke), we can see that Hume's preference for the latter still holds. Today, in a department concerned with teaching works of moral or political philosophy, in Europe or the United States, you are not going to be reading La Bruyère or Addison. Rather, you will be studying Aristotle and Locke. In this, the contemporary moment seems Humean in spirit: it is the work of anatomy that counts as philosophy, not the work of painting.

Instead of character-writing continuing to be seen as part of philosophy, it came instead to be classified as literature. Though many of the major French nineteenth-century novelists, for example, saw themselves as direct inheritors of a lineage of character-writing made famous by moralists like La Bruyère, we now read them as literary writers, not sociologists or historians. Though Stendhal explains that the intention of his novel *The Red and the Black* (1830) was to provide a "portrait of society in 1829," though Honoré de Balzac began his *La Comédie humaine* (1829–48) with "studies of manners," and though Gustave Flaubert subtitled his *Madame Bovary* (1857) "provincial customs," today we read each work as high literature, as opposed to moral philosophy or social science.[8] Nonetheless, all these authors are in fact continuing a version of La Bruyère's project to "paint Mankind in general," even more accurately circumscribing this ambition by deciding to paint the manners of a particular year or given location.[9]

For a similar case, in our moment, we might turn to the American short-story writer Lydia Davis: a contemporary portraitist of mores with a talent for describing types. Across her writing—a writing itself unclassifiable, like much previous character-writing ("should we simply concur with the official title and dub them *stories*? Or perhaps miniatures? Anecdotes? Essays? Jokes? Parables? Fables? Texts, or in the Beckett idiom, *textes*?" asks Christopher Ricks)—we find a gaze that distances, that typifies, that seems as sociological as it is literary.[10] Like the original character writers, Davis frequently refuses to name her protagonists, instead settling for a role prefaced by a definite article.[11] Her stories have titles like "The Brother-in-Law," "The Mother," "The Housemaid," "The Great-Grandmothers," "The Patient," "Old Mother and the Grouch," "The Thirteenth Woman," and "The Professor." Sometimes they are even called things like "Two Types." Within her stories, there are definitions of typical categories, as well as people resisting the category that has been foisted upon them. Indeed, much of Davis's comedy comes from describing people who trouble the norms and expectations of their character types—as in "The Race of the Patient Motorcyclists." But even if character sketches abound in her fiction, Lydia Davis is typically seen as a literary writer, not a philosopher. Her character-writing is not considered as a legitimate method of moral philosophy or a self-evident route to social knowledge.

When character types do emerge in works that are classified as philosophy, they are most often used in the service of broader arguments (in a way we saw Hume himself do), rather than as providing a science of human nature in their own right.[12] To choose one example here, we might turn again to Richard Rorty, whose *Contingency, Irony, and Solidarity* (1989) "sketches a figure" of the "liberal ironist."[13] This is a type who combines the figure of "the ironist," defined as "the sort of person who faces up to the contingency of his or her own most central beliefs and desires," and "the liberal," characterized, following Judith Shklar, as "people who think that cruelty is the worst thing we can do."[14] Rorty uses this type in order to make an argument about how we might balance two competing claims of modernity: the desire to ground political concepts in some universal shared foundations and the recognition that we all live historically contingent lives. Pairing the two concepts together, he defines "liberal ironists" as "people who include among these ungroundable desires their own hope that suffering will be diminished, that the humiliation of human beings by other human beings may cease."[15] The character type of the "liberal ironist" helps us understand this, in a way that the concept of "liberal irony" might not, because it is easier to envisage someone concretely embodying and living out this complex idea as opposed to picturing the abstract notion in its own right.[16] In this, "liberal irony" seems to be like other categories that we process as character types, categories like "zaniness," for example, which, as Sianne Ngai observes, "always seems to revolve around our experience of a zany character."[17]

The work of this epilogue is to suggest that by turning back to a period when sketches were once seen as offering a route to a science of human nature, we can find new ways to grapple with several new Theophrastan types that proliferate at present. This involves making use of both the *genealogical* and the *anthropological* functions of intellectual history. That is, tracing a history to illuminate points at which our concepts may have become "confused or misunderstood"; or using alien descriptions from the past to help us see that "some of what we currently believe about, say, our moral or political arrangements is actually false." Looking at the Theophrastan tradition through these lenses, I would like to make two claims: that Hume's dismissal of sketches in 1748 has restricted our field of vision about what counts as philosophy and that a prior understanding of philosophy might more successfully attune us to the range of texts that hold moral and political potential in the public sphere. Rather than excavating the practice of making character sketches, I hope to use Theophrastan tools to better explain the sketches that thrive today.

To pursue these claims, I examine three Theophrastan types: "the mansplainer," "the antisemite," and "the host." The character sketch is always a curious mix between the hyperspecific and the universal, giving some types real longevity and others only a brief window of relevance. (The Absentminded Man, for example, is still visible to us, whereas the Button Maker from Amsterdam is hard to imagine.) My choice of these three examples should be taken in this spirit, in full consciousness of the fact that their pertinence is somewhat hostage to fortune. By using the range of arguments that we have encountered over the course of this book about how to read character sketches, I aim to exemplify the moral and political potential of these three figures. As I explained in the introduction, to best focus on the impact of individual characters, free from other narrative devices, I restricted my analysis throughout this book to free-floating character descriptions and collections of character sketches. In my discussion of "the host," however, I have taken the liberty to conclude with something different, instead exploring how a Theophrastan figure might be read when embedded in more elaborate literary architecture—in this case, two novels by Tolstoy. By indicating how we might read Theophrastan figures as they appear in a range of media, I here hope to open up new possibilities for this method of interpretation. Taken together, my analysis of these three figures is intended as a reflection on what a Theophrastan mode of interpretation would look like in action.

The philosophy of literature, as Barbara Carnevali has noted, has historically spotlighted different genres at different moments.[18] For the ancient Greeks, it was the theater. For the Romantic and post-Romantic philosophers—from the German Romanticists to Martin Heidegger—it was poetry.[19] For contemporary philosophers of literature, such as Alasdair MacIntyre, Martha Nussbaum, Richard Rorty, Cora Diamond, Jacques Bouveresse, and Vincent Descombes, it is often the novel.[20] (To borrow Nussbaum's explanation: the novel is "the central morally serious yet popularly engaging fictional form of our culture.")[21] In a similar fashion, my aim here is to expose the ethical and political interest of the basic element of the character sketch. In particular, to ask whether previous arguments about these moral and social types can help clarify the impact of similar types that emerge today.

One of the unique features of character sketches is that they are at once imagistic, moral, and cognitive figures. Isaac Casaubon captures this point especially well when we pair his phrase "ethical icons" with his arguments about how these sketches provide knowledge of virtue and vice via mimesis. Yet to the extent that the Theophrastan tradition has emerged in contemporary philosophy of literature, scholars have restricted their analyses to its possible cognitive status: to how the *ethopoeia* it embodies offers knowledge of a moral or practical nature.[22] This situates character-writing within literary cognitivism, a branch of the philosophy of literature interested in how literature offers different kinds of knowledge, ranging from "propositional knowledge, that is to say a general statement that a reader recognizes to be true or false; truths about the world, or about possible worlds, whether referential, modal, or counterfactual; the discovery of mental states of other individuals; or knowledge about language and the beliefs that are expressed in it."[23] Theophrastan characters here would sit alongside other literary characters who have carried diagnostic functions: characters like Herman Melville's Bartleby the Scrivener, who is now, as Amit Pinchevski has traced, commonly used by medical researchers "as a marker for the Autistic Syndrome Disorder in general, and Asperger's syndrome in particular."[24]

The reception of the *Characters,* however, as we have seen, includes not only arguments about this epistemic aspect of character-writing but arguments about its moral and political effects, questions about how these sketches make us behave. In analyzing the effects of three contemporary characters, I ask questions about these more performative aspects of sketches while also continuing to investigate what they might help us know.

To enter the territory of how literary description shapes behavior is to put a revived Theophrastan aesthetic into dialogue with alternative revivals of Platonic and Aristotelian equivalents. These two models have had a more illustrious and successful history than these forgotten Hellenistic sketches and continue to inform some of the major approaches to the ethics of fiction that persist into our moment.[25] The revival of Platonic arguments emerges, for example, in contemporary concerns about the representation of suicide on television, as well as in the bad effects of violent video games or pornography. It is also behind recent decisions made by state governors and companies about the ethics of fiction: from Penguin's decision to rewrite the misogynistic and racist parts of Roald Dahl stories to the "Don't Say Gay" bill in Florida, in which queer children's books were subjected to removal from school libraries.[26] In both cases, the worry is that characters that are seen as morally bad will lead their readers into bad behavior. A revival of the arguments in Aristotle's *Poetics,* on the other hand, alternatively drives analyses about the public role of fiction, which maintain that feeling compassion for suffering literary characters, who experience bad luck over the course of a narrative, can help train readers into good citizens.

Historically, Theophrastus's *Characters* has been read to offer something different. The question for us is whether it might still. To recap: over the centuries, readers and adapters of the *Characters* thought that bad characters could shape good behavior, either explicitly via a process of negative imitation or implicitly by instilling ideas about the right way to be through praising and blaming specific qualities possessed by social figures. Like Theophrastus himself, they saw how the character sketch could be used to delegitimize particular political views, suggesting that they are not rational opinions but an outgrowth of someone's personality and situation: something predictable and behavioral, rather than deliberate and reflective. Interpreters of character-writing further thought that by writing sketches of contemporary vices, people might be encouraged to adopt wide-ranging reforms—of both a social and religious nature—to get rid of them.

To be clear, I am not proposing that this alternative set of aesthetic arguments should cause us to move beyond the powerful proposals put forward by Theophrastus's teachers and predecessors. Far from neglecting the importance of the Platonic and Aristotelian modes, my claim here is simply that the Theophrastan tradition might nudge us to better examine a range of texts that these two schools of interpretation have not fully theorized. Though a Theophrastan aesthetic will necessarily have its own limitations, it may avoid some of the particular pitfalls present within these other models. In the Platonic approach, these include the problem of possible censoriousness and the problem of relying on a cohesive public sense of "the bad" to be avoided, which is often lacking.[27] Those who support the "Don't Say Gay" bill, to put it one way, are not in the same camp as those keen to revise Dahl's fiction—even if both believe that fiction has an important role in shaping a reader's behavior. In the Aristotelian approach, problems include the risk of an overreliance on compassion: an emotional effect that might lead a reader to develop condescending or romanticizing attitudes toward a real person who recalls a fictional character they have once encountered.[28]

Before considering what the Theophrastan method of interpretation offers us that the Platonic and Aristotelian models may not, however, it is worth pausing on an important question about the mobility of history. What might it mean to investigate whether these earlier arguments may be useful in understanding the impact of contemporary figures? Why does this move not slip into nostalgia, or anachronism, in its attempt to project ancient and early modern arguments into an overwhelmingly changed modernity? Over the course of this book, I have shown that the Theophrastan character sketch lost its status as moral and political philosophy for three reasons: growing doubts about the epistemic status of a genre that is not concerned with detecting the underlying inner principles of phenomena; a shift away from the political language of civic virtue; and suspicions about the relevance of ancient Greek figures. This last concern is the most easily answered of the three, as we are speaking now of new types, not claiming the continued relevance of those written in circa 319 BCE. Yet the other two—the worries that knowledge of a character requires knowledge of their interior and that social and political life cannot only be run by curbing ordinary vices—require more reflection.

My proposal is that, in our present moment, the foundations of these concerns seem to have given way. The proliferation of visual media, from television to film, platforms characters with a hidden interiority, which an audience usually cannot see. These mediums introduce us to flat characters: to types like Larry David, astutely characterized as a "social assassin" in one episode of *Curb Your Enthusiasm,* and the conductor Lydia Tár, the "textbook female narcissist" who is the subject of Todd Field's 2022 film of the same name.[29] These are not figures whose inner workings and thought processes are revealed to us in soliloquies, first-person narration, or free indirect discourse, but we nonetheless get to *know* them in some clear ways. Even contemporary novels—a medium historically feted for the privileged access it has to subjectivity—often end up depicting worlds in which "there exists no outside to type," as Merve Emre has argued.[30] Given that we are surrounded by characters like these, the Enlightenment worry that the sketch would need to show us people's internal motivations, not just their behavior, in order to provide genuine knowledge no longer seems so pressing.

In addition, a contemporary version of an older virtue politics is on the rise: ours is a moment increasingly interested in the ethics of ordinary civic behaviors, one in which our everyday use of language, our purchases of shopping bags, and even our methods of waste disposal have gained ethical and political connotations.[31] Reconsidering older humanist arguments about the effects of Theophrastan flat characters on ordinary behaviors might not therefore be a historical move that is too far out of joint with the present. Making claims about how the description of a figure like "the hoarder" might shape a person's ordinary behaviors, in a way that has something to do with ethics and politics, does not necessarily seem like an arcane throwback to an ancient virtue politics, or its early modern neo-republican equivalent, but rather chimes with existing aspects of social life today. Indeed, my interest in determining the impact of these particular literary devices seems to easily sit alongside many recent arguments about the moral and political effects of books, television, and films.[32] I refer here to the trend that has now come to be known as an "ethical turn": a movement that began in the United States in the late 1980s; has since spread to countries including France, Italy, and China; and, as we have seen, is at once scholarly and public.[33] (One might even say that the contemporary resurgence of virtue politics alongside the ethical turn—reviving a combination present in early modern Europe—suggests something of an interrelation between these phenomena.)[34]

If this goes some way to assuage historical concerns, one might further legitimately ask whether an interest in representation relies on a fanciful assumption that minor sketches can generate major effects. To this point, I can only underline that I focus on one kind of literary text, within a world of representations, and only on representation, in a world of other means of shaping moral, social, and political behavior. (Indeed, at some points in my discussions of the three types that follow, broader drivers are explicitly referenced.) There is no premium here on the character type as an exclusive device for providing knowledge and shaping action. Rather, I only claim this is one device that we have not yet fully understood, despite its ubiquity. My aim here is strictly descriptive, posing questions about what happens when we make types and how they inform and affect our social relations. What, I ask, are the uses and limitations of this practice of writing and speaking?

I would, nonetheless, resist the idea that this situates my arguments within a "post-political" ethical turn in political theory.[35]

Rather, I would say that I focus here on the effects of representations on the interpersonal aspect of public political life. In this, I have learned much from thinkers like Bernard Williams and Charles Taylor, who take psychology and community seriously, who believe, as Katrina Forrester summarizes, that "institutions and relations of power" are misunderstood if only viewed "through contracts rather than as interpersonal relations."[36]

With this in mind, we can now turn to the three types—beginning with the one perhaps most suitable to thinking about interpersonal relations and power.

The Mansplainer

"As a lady who covers politics," Marin Cogan wrote in 2012, "I'm intimately familiar with the mansplainer. You know who I'm talking about: he's the supremely self-impressed dude who feels the need to explain to you—with the overly simplistic, patient tone of an elementary school teacher—really obvious shit you already knew."[37] To understand a set of behaviors that have been observed in the social sphere, Cogan resorts to several Theophrastan devices. She provides the name of a type preceded by a definite article, she introduces this type with the proviso that he will be recognizable (implicit in most character sketches but made explicit here), she moves from the abstract type to the third-person "he," and she proceeds to recount his behavioral habits in conversation. In doing so, she provides a cognitive resource that can move from the abstract type to the particular case, introducing "the mansplainer" in order to expose "The Mittsplainer," revealing how Mitt Romney fits this particular model.

Seen from a Theophrastan lens, this sketch is doing a number of things simultaneously. First, it offers a means for individuals to comprehend the world around them—for Cogan, in this case, to be able to best understand Mitt Romney. This is its cognitive function: a function that gives rise to several questions and issues I will address shortly. For now, I summarize this aspect as a means by which an individual is comprehended, via recourse to a category that the reader is presumed to recognize: "You know who I'm talking about," Cogan underlines. Second, Cogan's sketch of "the mansplainer," as a type of vicious character, contains within it an ethical injunction that this is not the way to behave. It works, like Theophrastus's own sketches of idle chatterers and absentminded men, as a nudge for the reader to avoid these actions if they want to be free of similar ridicule themselves.[38] In this, just like the ancient collection, the sketch implies a kind of virtue politics: telling the reader that this is a trait that is not conducive to social harmony once it is seen for what it is. Third, given that this particular sketch highlights the fact of a gender-based power differential, it finds itself situated within broader debates about how to address these power imbalances, which move beyond sketches alone. The importance of gender is made explicit from the opening gambit: Cogan's "you know who I'm talking about" is patently addressed to other women, as she has been careful to identify herself as a "lady who covers politics" in the first line. Rebecca Solnit, whose 2008 essay "Men Explain Things to Me," made the concept famous (even though she herself did not mention the term), is careful to include a postscript in her book publication of the same title to this effect: "For the record, I do believe that women have explained things in patronizing ways, to men among others. But that's not indicative of the massive power differential that takes far more sinister forms as well or of the broad pattern of how gender works in our society."[39]

EPISTEMIC INJUSTICE

It is on the basis of a linkage between ethics and epistemology that I want to return to the cognitive claim by pointing to a central concept recently developed at "the border" between ethics and epistemology: Miranda Fricker's notion of "hermeneutical injustice."[40] This is one of two kinds of "epistemic injustice" that Fricker names, the other being "testimonial injustice," an injustice that "occurs when prejudice causes a hearer to give a deflated level of credibility to a speaker's word."[41] Hermeneutical injustice is defined as "the injustice of having some significant area of one's social experience obscured from collective understanding owing to a structural identity prejudice in the collective hermeneutical resource."[42] Marginalized groups, in this analysis, have aspects of their experience deliberately masked, "obscured," in ways that serve the interests of the dominant power. Central examples that Fricker gives of this include women suffering "sexual harassment in a culture that still lacks that critical concept" or enduring interpretations of their collective social experience that are "unduly influenced by more hermeneutically powerful groups (thus, for instance, sexual harassment as flirting, rape in marriage as non-rape, post-natal depression as hysteria, reluctance to work family-unfriendly hours as unprofessionalism, and so on)."[43] Hermeneutical power is here defined as the capacity to participate in the practices through which social meanings are generated. "Most obvious among such practices," Fricker writes, "are those sustained by professions such as journalism, politics, academia, and law."[44] Hermeneutical injustice is therefore the injustice of either not having appropriate concepts to classify one's own social experience, due to systemic hermeneutical marginalization, or having these concepts dismissed, despite their being in operation. Rectifying this injustice involves a marginalized group being able to collectively develop these conceptual resources, which they can then use as a means to mobilize against oppression. Once "sexual harassment" is named as a concept, for example, organizers can begin campaigns to outlaw it in the workplace.

It is essential to underline the central role of power in Fricker's argument, the operation of a "structural identity prejudice" *obscuring* an individual's proper comprehension of their social experience. This aspect of her argument distinguishes it from claims that sit in more familiar Sapir-Whorf territory, where individual experience is limited by linguistic resources: claims like La Rochefoucauld's maxim that "some people would never have fallen in love if they had never heard of love," which maintain the belief that language shapes thought, that our available concepts dictate our possible experience.[45] Fricker is advancing a very different case: one that suggests there *is* a shared reality of oppression, which needs to be described by a set of appropriate concepts and eventually will. Note the teleology present in her notion of women suffering "sexual harassment in a culture that *still* lacks that critical concept" (my emphasis).

As is also clear from this final phrase, the philosophical unit on which Fricker concentrates is the concept. It is worth asking, however, whether there are certain concepts that take the form of characters, with there being an equivalent hermeneutic gap if someone is deprived of a particular concept that works to group together a series of behaviors that they perceive in others. As we saw in Rorty's use of "the liberal ironist," and in Ngai's understanding that "zaniness" is almost always understood through the character of "the zany," there are some concepts that seem most easily embodied in types. We might additionally turn here to the sociologist Pierre Bourdieu, who understands the practical effects that character-concepts provide in a way that presents a mirror image to Fricker's argument: "The fate of groups is bound up with the words that designate them: the power to impose recognition depends on the capacity to mobilize around a name, 'proletariat,' 'working class' etc."[46] In contrast to Bourdieu, on the few occasions when Fricker considers the hermeneutical effects of character types, they are never liberating, in this way, but rather repressive—for example, the "powerful bogeymen constructions of The Homosexual."[47]

It is important to clarify that naming a character need not impede the development of related terms that take different forms in order to avoid issues of essentialism. These include, in the case of "the mansplainer," a derived verb of "mansplaining," or the action of "being a mansplainer."[48] Bourdieu's own concept of *habitus* offers a similar option to avoid this issue, a concept defined as "the system of structured, structuring dispositions (. . .) which is constituted in practice and is always oriented toward practical functions," which was designed to overcome dichotomies between the conscious and the unconscious, the phenomenological and the structural, by suggesting that a person finds themselves in a field in which they make a set of coherent practical choices.[49] No one is *essentially* a mansplainer seen through this lens. Rather, mansplaining can happen in a given social situation, one that requires two adults, in conversation, in a relation of gender domination.[50]

With this framing in mind, we might sketch a role for the Theophrastan character, alongside the philosophical concept, in the pursuit of epistemic justice: a role that positions the character sketch again at the border of epistemology and ethics.

MORAL AND PRACTICAL KNOWLEDGE

This approach to the cognitive status of the character, as a tool to be used to achieve hermeneutical justice, goes beyond arguments made by Carnevali and Engel about character-writing as moral knowledge or character-writing as practical knowledge.

The former argument, expressed by Carnevali, is that we are much "indebted to Casaubon" for his sixteenth-century reading of Theophrastus's *Characters,* as he provides us with a "profound meditation on the nature and moral function of mimesis," showing us how the faithful description of mores is able to produce a kind of "moral knowledge" about the nature of a habit, custom, or affect.[51] The character writer, in this view, helps us understand the customs that exist all around us, naming and grouping disparate phenomena and offering them to the reader as moral knowledge, knowledge of mores.

A good example of how the character sketch can be used as a tool to interpret the world can be found in Thackeray's 1848 *Book of Snobs: By One of Themselves.*[52] His volume, Carnevali writes, gave the term "snob" "a univocal meaning," both defining this vice ("He who meanly admires mean things is a snob") and expressing this definition through a range of characters, from military snobs to great city snobs to clerical snobs, university snobs, and literary snobs.[53] In his "Concluding Observations on Snobs," Thackeray includes a striking anecdote that evidences this process. "The word Snob has taken a place in our honest English vocabulary," he writes, so that although we "can't say what it is, any more than we can define wit, or humour, or humbug," we know it when we see it.[54] As Thackeray himself experienced,

> Some weeks since, happening to have the felicity to sit next to a young lady at a hospitable table, where poor old Jawkins was holding forth in a very absurd pompous manner, I wrote upon the spotless damask "S—B," and called my neighbour's attention to the little remark. That young lady smiled. She knew it at once.[55]

The character, in this context, serves as a tool to comprehend aspects of social life: to make sense of the way in which two people had experienced a person's behavior in their company. The interpretation is made valid at the moment of shared recognition.[56]

Unlike a move between the literary text and the world outside of it, which selectively chooses a fictional figure and then applies it to a given person (in the way we saw Blakey Vermuele do, in the introduction, where she names "a frustrating and intrusive boss" a "Mr. Collins"), the figure of the snob is taken from the world, given a name, and then returned back to it, rendering literature itself able to "record, document, or bear witness to something about cognitive relation to reality."[57] In this the Theophrastan character seems to overcome one typical objection to literary cognitivism: that, if a text's value lies in a reader applying aspects of a fictional world onto the real world, "presumably that truth is not given in the work itself."[58] Rather than the application of the fictional to the real, Carnevali sees the sketch as providing knowledge itself. Character-writing, she claims, should therefore be seen as part of the shared basis of literature and the human sciences: the moral knowledge that we would gain from a novelistic portrait of mores is not "very far removed" from that provided by a historian or sociologist.[59] And, just like the historian and the sociologist, Carnevali thinks that the moral knowledge offered by character-writing is knowledge that is situated in a particular context: characters show us given habits at given moments in time.

For Engel, the *Characters* instead serves as an example of how literature furnishes a propositional "practical knowledge" of "what it is like" to experience a particular emotion or live a particular "kind of life."[60] It is essential for Engel's argument that he is describing literature's links with *knowledge,* rather than making the claim that literature provides a particular *account* of a particular kind of life. He imagines that literature is capable of accessing something more general and universal. In his view, "the rich tradition of *ethopoeia*" rests "upon the description of stable and well-known features of human nature": where a particular example of a specific behavior described in a literary work expresses a way in which one of these stable features can be deployed.[61] Maupassant shows us what fear "looks like"; Proust's *Albertine* "a way of being jealous"; Goncharov's *Oblomov* a "way of being slothful."[62] The character, in Engel's reading, therefore does not provide contextual knowledge as much as it offers the chance for us "to recognize cases of general truths," truths associated to the "laws of human psychology."[63]

An approach to character as a tool to be used to right the wrong of hermeneutic injustice, a tool at the border between knowledge and ethics, which encourages a reader to move from a written description of a general type to the act of classifying an individual person in this way, goes beyond both these arguments. Thackeray had not been deprived of conceptual tools due to "a structural identity prejudice in the collective hermeneutical resource." Rather, he was writing this collection with the affirmation that this was a book of snobs "by one of themselves."[64] Equally (or at least we must hope), the mansplainer is not a case of a "general truth" but a contextually bound, historical reality that the character sketch itself aims to obliterate.

REPRESSIVE OR LIBERATORY?

In moving into the territory of ethics, however, my argument encounters two problems that Carnevali's and Engel's accounts avoid. This is not the problem of whether the mores represented are universal or contextual. Rather, the first problem is how to identify whether a given appellation is correct: whether it can be justified to call Mitt Romney a mansplainer and on what basis we can judge the truth of this claim. One answer we have found in the previous examples points to a kind of knowledge in part derived from the conformity of an individual to the description of the general type and in part from consensus within a particular setting—an appellation finding justification if the reader knows who Cogan means, which comes from the lady smiling, knowing "at once" to whom Thackeray refers. This process of justification would accord with how a character type gets anchored in the imagination in the first place: living or dying by virtue of how accurately it is thought to describe a collective experience ("the mansplainer" would fall flat as a concept if the audience did not in fact know "who I'm talking about").

While this presents some resolution to the question of how to determine when character types describe and when they misdescribe, a second larger ethical and political issue looms: the way in which—true to that Greek etymology of "to categorize," *kategorein*—to classify can be "to accuse."[65] How do we determine, to put this in Fricker's terms, when characters are useful tools to help fill hermeneutical lacunae, unjustly created by structural prejudice, and when they are accusations, or "character assassinations," that work to deny an individual the liberty to be seen as complex and changeable, to be seen as they might consider themselves in their own terms?[66]

How to adjudicate between the potentially liberating type of "the mansplainer" and the more repressive type of "The Homosexual"?

Both Cogan's piece and Fricker's argument offer responses to these concerns. In Cogan's view, a label in fact works to humanize, rather than to blame, exonerating an individual from having chosen this behavior deliberately and instead placing them at the mercy of an unthinking habit they are forced into by society. "In a weird way," she writes, "if you see Mitt Romney's gaffes as merely mansplaining, they're somehow more tolerable, because it implies that they come from a lack of self-awareness rather than malice."[67] The character type of "the mansplainer," in this view, helps provide an offending man with the "self-awareness" that he had been lacking: revealing to him that he is not simply explaining but being condescending to a female interlocutor. Implied here is the idea that the character type has this clarificatory capacity because it emerges from a marginalized social position. From a marginalized standpoint, the male behavior is viewed in a new light. When expressed as such, this new term can provide the man with a changed awareness of how his actions are experienced.[68]

Power, as Fricker would say, is key. The woman classifying "the mansplainer" is finally able to process an experience she shares with others who are marginalized in a similar way, gaining a term to describe a behavior that she, and others like her, perceive differently to men but that had been obscured from her view due to a "structural identity prejudice." With this character sketch, she is offered a tool that can be used to disrupt a particular kind of "social script," in which linguistic male dominance is expected to be met with listening, or tacit approval.[69] In face of the costs present in disrupting social scripts, this character sketch gives a reluctant listener a possible strategy.[70] To give a contrasting example to clarify this point, one of the major ways in which we are currently classified is by digital platforms.[71] Corporations practice personalization of their users: they determine what type of person a user is and give them content according to that type, which means that users are denied the possibility of seeing certain material. If Spotify classifies you as a "glow gal," you will be suggested different music, for example, than the music you could have heard if you had been typified as a "last train sprinter."[72] Compared to the woman who classifies the man as the mansplainer, *from below,* as a means to register an aspect of her experience to which she has been blinded, this is a classification *from above,* where users are profiled in ways they are not aware of and cannot change by those who possess what Fricker calls "social power," defined as "a socially situated capacity to control others' actions."[73]

Needless to say, this epistemic account is necessarily cursory: the question of fully adjudicating when labels describe and misdescribe is too complex to be answered here, as is a proper evaluation of standpoint theory or social power.[74] What matters most is that the Theophrastan tradition has trained our gaze on a figure like the mansplainer, encouraging us to ask questions about how this sketch contributes to social and political life and to attempt to evaluate whether, like previous sketches in a similar vein, the mansplainer might be useful in teaching people how not to behave.

This character does so in two ways: offering a redescription of a particular behavior from a different perspective and encapsulating an implicit threat of ridicule to future offenders. In this, the mansplainer is a peculiar kind of category, one that does not encourage people to "spontaneously come to fit it"—as sometimes happens in social classification (where, as Ian Hacking argues, the classification of kinds of mill laborers in England and Wales led to changing work practices)—but rather entreats them to shake it off, as quickly as possible.[75] Like a spell, we call people mansplainers in the hope that eventually mansplainers will not exist at all. This offers another riposte to people who worry about the essentializing potential of a type. In fact, calling someone a mansplainer would not even be a thinkable linguistic strategy unless we believed that by using this description, we could encourage someone to change their behavior.

Unlike a Platonic approach to this type, which would worry about it generating more mansplainers in imitation, or an Aristotelian approach, which simply may not consider it as having ethical and political potential (because it exists outside of a narrative structure), a Theophrastan approach forces us to attempt to take it seriously.[76]

The Antisemite

A further link between character sketches and knowledge to which this book has pointed relates to their capacity to make propositions about the relationship between politics and psychology. The sketch, seen in this light, becomes a means of transforming what seems to be a rational political position into a behavioral habit. Isolating this function of the character sketch places it at a different juncture—not as much that between ethics and epistemology as that between politics and psychology—and puts it in dialogue with a different kind of literature. This is a literature that has often been most concerned with understanding particularly violent political positions as outcomes of certain personal or collective characteristics. It is a literature that has a number of important historical precedents and that has extended into contemporary debate—exposing a political function for the Theophrastan character that extends long after the glimpse we caught of it with Theophrastus's Oligarch. Two striking examples in which the form of the sketch is used to this effect—both of which emerge during or close after the Second World War as a means of grasping the nature of antisemitism—will help clarify this aspect of the character sketch's power and capacity.

"If a person attributes all or part of their own misfortunes and those of his country to the presence of Jewish elements in the community," writes Jean-Paul Sartre in 1944, "we say that they have antisemitic opinions."[77] But "this word opinion makes us stop and think": "It gives an inoffensive appearance to ideas by reducing them to the level of tastes. All tastes are natural; all opinions are permitted."[78] If antisemitism is a taste, or an opinion, "a person may be a good parent and a good spouse, a conscientious citizen, highly cultivated, philanthropic, *and* in addition an antisemite": a position that Sartre describes as both "dangerous and false."[79] Antisemitism, Sartre writes, is not a rational opinion but a "passion"; it is "a comprehensive attitude that one adopts not only toward Jews but toward people in general, toward history and society," "a conception of the world" and a "syncretic totality."[80] Rather than examining antisemitism as an opinion, one must therefore instead describe the antisemite's "entire personality" and write their "portrait."[81] This portrait is Theophrastan in its ascription of antisemitism to an ordinary vice, in its third-person "he," in its quality of examining the deployment of this vice across a number of contexts, in its maxim-like definitional introduction and conclusion, and in its figurative list of comparisons:

> We are now in a position to understand the antisemite. He is a man who is afraid. Not of the Jews, to be sure, but of himself, of his own consciousness, of his liberty, of his instincts, of his responsibilities, of solitariness, of change, of society, and of the world—of everything except the Jews. He is a coward who does not want to admit his cowardice to himself; a murderer who represses and censures his tendency to murder without being able to hold it back, yet who dares to kill only in effigy or protected by the anonymity of the mob (. . .). The Jew only serves him as a pretext; elsewhere his counterpart will make use of the Negro or the man of yellow skin. (. . .) Antisemitism, in short, is fear of the human condition. The antisemite is a man who wishes to be pitiless stone, a furious torrent, a devastating thunderbolt—anything except a man.[82]

Sartre's use of the form of the sketch to render the antisemite a character, rather than an ordinary person with antisemitic opinions, has three significant political implications. It first promotes the idea that a person's political opinions should be seen in dialogue with their other behaviors: a form of analysis that pushes people in particular directions on difficult questions about the separability of someone's political life and their apparent social virtues. It secondly encourages a search for the personal factors that have produced this trait—rather than allowing antisemitism to be accepted as a subjective taste or suggesting that it can be combatted by arguments that treat it as a rational opinion produced by external factors (by, for example, citing "the percentage of Jews who are bankers, industrialists, doctors, and lawyers," as Sartre details).[83] For Sartre, the relevant factors animating antisemitism are both psychological—extending his argument beyond cowardice into the avowedly psychoanalytic language of "sadism," "hysteria," and "paranoia"—and socioeconomic, with Sartre describing antisemitism as "a poor man's snobbery," a means for the white-collar proletariat to affirm that they belong to the elite.[84] It thirdly presents a particular orientation to the issue of how antisemitism can be combatted.

This third consequence will become most evident if we take a sideways glance to Theodor Adorno and his colleagues' 1950 study of "the rise of an 'anthropological' species we call the authoritarian type of man."[85] Adorno and his colleagues note the "marked similarity between the syndrome which we have labelled the authoritarian personality and 'the portrait of the anti-Semite' by Jean-Paul Sartre," registering that while "Sartre's brilliant paper became available" only after their data had been collected, the fact that his "phenomenological 'portrait' should resemble so closely" the syndrome they derived from their alternative methods of empirical observations and quantitative analysis is "remarkable."[86]

Like Sartre, Adorno and his colleagues find "the authoritarian type," or "potentially fascistic individual," to be a "total personality."[87] This type is a person whose ethnocentric convictions are derived from traits of conventionality, rigidity, weakness, fear, and dependency, traits that emerge in the ensemble of their beliefs and practices, "ranging from the most intimate features of family and sex adjustment through relationships to other people in general, to religion and to social and political philosophy."[88] This understanding of authoritarianism as being a character more than an opinion significantly influences the countermeasures recommended by Adorno and his colleagues. "The major emphasis," they argue, in facing the authoritarian type, should not be placed on "rational arguments" or on "appeals to sympathy" or "closer association with members of minority groups."[89] It should instead involve addressing "such phenomena as stereotypy, emotional coldness, identification with power, and general destructiveness."[90] This can happen in part by involving the voices of psychologists in the consideration of the problem: a panacea that will not, however, be sufficient, with Adorno and his colleagues recognizing that as these phenomena are part of "the total organization of society," they will only find full transformation when society itself is transformed.[91] With this, the social scientific study comes close to Sartre's conclusion, which similarly calls for a classless society as the only means to stamp out antisemitism for good.[92] As Sartre puts it, offering a response to the possible problem of essentializing this figure, "Since he, like all men, exists as a free agent within a situation, it is his situation that must be modified from top to bottom."[93]

The character sketch of the political type thus gains a further kind of cognitive status. It offers a vision of the world in which certain political orientations are treated as derivative of long-standing traits of personality and social position, as opposed to rational opinions with which to be argued on reasonable terms. This has the capacity to present dramatic changes to how these political perspectives are handled in the social sphere, both at the scale of a small group and at the scale of society as a whole. If fascism is an opinion that can be derived from someone's class position and their cowardice, we gain different ways to handle it than if we think of it as a response, for example, to patterns of migration. A focus may shift away from measures designed to address the latter group and toward dealing with the psychological and social issues motivating fascist individuals. If authoritarianism is not restricted to throwaway comments but is thought part of a total personality, we may be less willing to have these character types in our circles. And, if antisemitism is derived from a shared social position and a set of traits, we may be less susceptible to treat it as a political opinion and more inclined to discern the psychological, social, and historical details of these personality types. These literary descriptions, with their borrowings of many devices we have seen across the history of the Theophrastan character sketch, are thus given important political power.

The Theophrastan aesthetic might then be framed both as a recognition of this power and as an encouragement for readers to stay alert and alive to the question of which political ideas are being characterized at any given point. While, in the 1940s and 1950s, the focus was on the far right, by 1968, Joan Didion was writing a character of "the popular image of a professional revolutionary": a character by the name of Comrade Laski, from the headquarters of the Communist Party USA (Marxist-Leninist), whose political convictions she analyses, in a similar way to Sartre, as being derived from "dread":

> As it happens I am comfortable with the Michael Laskis of this world, with those who live outside rather than in, those in whom the sense of dread is so acute that they turn to extreme and doomed commitments; I know something about dread myself, and appreciate the elaborate systems with which some people manage to fill the void, appreciate all the opiates of the people, whether they are as accessible as alcohol and heroin and promiscuity or as hard to come by as faith in God or History. But of course I did not mention dread to Michael Laski, whose particular opiate is History.[94]

Where, we might begin to ask, does the typification of political positions happen most today: on the left, on the right, for the extremes, or for the center? The argument here is that the Theophrastan tradition both encourages us to be on the lookout for these figures and provides us with a set of tools to parse their possible performative effects: to look closer at new types like "Corbynistas," "conspiracy theorists," "liberal elites," and "experts," investigating how they make us see other people (and perhaps ourselves) and how they change the way we understand beliefs, political parties, and ideas.[95] It encourages us to recognize that these types can be used as a "weapon" in "the war of interpretation" of social and political life.[96] In doing so, it shows off the moral and political significance of this literary creation in a way that revivals of Platonic and Aristotelian arguments ignore.

The Host

Thus far, we have seen how the Theophrastan tradition encourages us to notice new types and examine their use in vocalizing aspects of social life that have previously been obscured. We have also seen how it shows us the power of making a political opinion into a personality trait, inviting us to be alert to the use of this strategy within political contexts. These claims have concerned free-floating characters, which appear in journalism, circulate online, and slip off the tongue in quotidian conversation. There are, however, Theophrastan characters tucked away in novels that also hold moral and political potential in their own right. A Theophrastan aesthetic would also encourage us to be sensitive to these characters as and when they appear within literary fictions. Though an analysis of this kind of figure departs from the character sketches I have considered across the book, which are isolated characters or collections of sketches, I carry it out in the hope that it may prove generative for literary scholars who are interested in how a Theophrastan aesthetic might come to bear when examining the novel.

To explore this, we might turn to the character type of "the host." We first encountered this figure in the Overburian volume, which emphasized the servile and dependent qualities of this type and thus helped build a picture of the volume's neo-Stoicism. Tolstoy's two major novels, *Anna Karenina* and *War and Peace,* offer rich descriptions of this character in two different guises, in which this moral valence undergoes a radical transformation. My claim here is that, just as in the Overburian volume, if we approach Tolstoy through a Theophrastan lens, we can perceive a network of moral judgment in his depiction of this figure, which signals broader commitments in these two works. Though Tolstoy is a preferred author by many philosophers of literature—Williams, for one, borrows Anna Karenina to illustrate his own concept of "moral luck"—focusing on the typical Theophrastan characters in his novels, as an illustration of his own philosophy, offers something different.[97]

György Lukács recounts how Tolstoy, in the preface to the Russian translation of Maupassant's works, established three postulates of an artistic attitude to reality: "first, a correct, i.e. a moral attitude of the author to his theme; secondly, clarity of expression or beauty of form—these two are identical; and thirdly, sincerity, i.e. a sincere love or hate of the thing the artist is presenting."[98] If we perform a Theophrastan analysis on Tolstoy's own novels, with this in mind, it is not hard to find an implicit ethical framework, a "correct moral attitude" standing behind the description of typical characters. An examination of one character type, respectively embodied by Anna Pavlovna in *War and Peace* and Stepan Arkadyevitch in *Anna Karenina,* will need here to suffice. This is the character of the host (or the hostess): a character type that the Overburians earlier chastised as a man who "neither eates, drinkes, or thinks, but at other mens charges and appointments."[99]

Tolstoy's presentation of this character type, in contrast, does not see this position as a vice as much as a virtue. At the party that opens *War and Peace,* the qualities that make Anna Pavlovna an excellent host are described with resolute admiration in the form of an extended conceit:

> As the owner of a spinning mill, having put his workers in their places, strolls about the establishment, watching out for an idle spindle or the odd one squealing much too loudly, and hasten to go and slow it down or start it up at the proper speed—so Anna Pavlovna strolled about her drawing room, going up to a circle that had fallen silent or was too talkative, and with one word or rearrangement set the conversation machine running evenly and properly again.[100]

Using the same kinds of literary devices as the character writers we have examined, Tolstoy transforms what might be a compromised social position—involving forms of dependence on others—into an esteemed quality. Anna Pavlovna is not the slave but the master, the "owner of a spinning mill," who controls the social world around her with deft and accomplished skill. It is not only the choice of the metaphor, and the inclusion of the immediate success of Anna Pavlovna's conversational interjections—setting the machine running again with "one word"—that betrays a Tolstoian ethic that values this quality, but its refraction in other characters that appear across Tolstoy's work.

Just as the Overburians' neo-Stoicism was gleaned from the repeated references across a range of character types to dependence as a vice and independence as a virtue; Tolstoy's praise of this particular kind of social deftness appears again and again in his fiction. The most obvious comparison point to Anna Pavlovna is the character of Stepan Arkadyevitch in *Anna Karenina,* a man who "liked dining, but still better he liked to give a dinner, small, but very choice, both as regards the food and drink and as regards the selection of guests."[101] Accordingly, the conceit that Tolstoy uses to describe Stepan Arkadyevitch's skill as a host is not that of the owner of a spinning mill but that of a cook. Stepan Arkadyevitch imagines the guests he has invited for dinner that evening (themselves a range of character types, from the "Moscow man" to the "practical politician" and the "well known eccentric enthusiast") as items on the menu.[102] The "pièce de resistance among the guests" are Sergey Koznishev and Alexey Alexandrovitch, and the "sauce or garnish" for Koznishev and Karenin is the eccentric Pestsov, who will "provoke them and set them off."[103] After the dinner unexpectedly starts in Stepan Arkadyevitch's absence, Tolstoy uses a very similar characterization as he used for Anna Pavlovna—only with a shift in metaphorical field—to describe the host's effortless work of getting the conversational machine running evenly again:

> On entering the drawing room Stepan Arkadyevitch apologized, explaining that he had been detained by that prince, who was always the scapegoat for all his absences and unpunctualities, and in one moment he had made all the guests acquainted with each other, and, bringing together Alexey Alexandrovitch and Sergey Koznishev,

> started them on a discussion of the Russification of Poland, into which they immediately plunged with Pestsov. Slapping Turovtsin on the shoulder, he whispered something comic in his ear, and set him down by his wife and the old prince. Then he told Kitty she was looking very pretty that evening, and presented Shtcherbatsky to Karenin. In a moment he had so kneaded together the social dough that the drawing room became very lively, and there was a merry buzz of voices.[104]

With Anna Pavlovna as the masterful overseer of a conversational spinning mill and Stepan Arkadyevitch as the deft kneader of social dough, Tolstoy implicitly presents us with a set of behaviors that he considers to be a social virtue: presentations in which we can clearly see the "moral attitude of the author to his theme."

This represents a different approach to the ethical and political role of the character type to that elaborated by Lukács, in part in reference to Tolstoy.[105] Though Lukács maintains that the "central category and criterion of realist literature is the type," what he means by this is not a reflection on the type as a means of displaying a set of qualities to be praised or blamed, which then work to instill a particular social ethic.[106] Rather, he refers to "a peculiar synthesis which organically binds together the general and the particular," which, when intensified, works to "illuminate the complex dialectic of the major contradictions, motive forces and tendencies of an era."[107] What is valued in the Theophrastan model is not so much the type as a source of an epoch's contradictions but as a site in which an author's moral evaluation is expressed and offered to a reader.

This moral evaluation can be extended outward from the depiction of these two figures. We can see this in how well Tolstoy's valorization of the particular skill of hosting coheres with Isaiah Berlin's view of Tolstoy's broader orientation to history and politics: one in which practical wisdom, social judgment, and instinct combine.[108] In Berlin's view, Tolstoy's tragedy is that he is a quintessential fox, with a wily instinct for the many, masquerading as a hedgehog, who wishes to know "one big thing."[109] Tolstoy's fox-like nature, Berlin writes, informs his approach to history, his recognition that "the actual stuff of history consists of ordinary men and women": "the specific relation of individuals to one another, the colours, smells, tastes, sounds and movements, the jealousies, loves, hatreds, passions, the rare flashes of insight, the transforming moments, the ordinary day-to-day of private data which constitute all there is."[110] History, in Tolstoy's view, was not "scientific knowledge" as much as "a special sensitiveness to the contours of the circumstances in which we happen to be placed."[111] I would argue, however, that we need not only turn to Tolstoy's own reflections on history to find this approach. Rather, we can already observe Tolstoy's valorization of "a special sensitiveness" to context in his laudatory descriptions of how Stepan Arkadyevitch and Anna Pavlovna perform a particular social role. Both figures are valorized for their ability to recognize the needs of the moment: to notice the too silent and the too talkative, to perceive Kitty's need to be told she looked pretty as much as Sergey Koznishev's need to be set off on a political discussion or Turovtsin's desire to be told a good joke.

This approach, as Berlin makes clear in a later essay on "Political Judgment," is not only a means of understanding history but a way of seeing politics. In order to make the claim that politics requires "a sense of direct acquaintance with the texture of life, a sense for what is qualitative rather than quantitative, for what is specific rather than general (. . .) what is variously called natural wisdom, imaginative understanding, insight, perceptiveness," Berlin here turns again to Tolstoy. The virtues we need in politics, Berlin says, are those possessed by novelists such as "Tolstoy or Proust."[112] Though the science of botany will help the gardener, and the laws of nutrition will help the cook, excellence in both does not require rule following as much as the "capacity to improvise"—a capacity the two figures of Stepan Arkadyevitch and Anna Pavlovna perfectly embody.[113]

In contrast, once again, to a Platonic or Aristotelian reading of these texts, a Theophrastan aesthetic, hooked on to the depiction of a character type alone, can work to reveal a myriad of rich detail about the philosophical and political commitments a text (or an author) may hold. This not only offers something for the scholar, however, but nudges the reader that they might want to adopt some of these highly prized qualities in their own behavior.

+ + +

Taken together, these three figures offer a glimpse of a Theophrastan aesthetic: a means of interpretation, derived from a Hellenistic philosopher, that teaches us to see the character sketch as a possible tool within the fight for epistemic justice, as a means of psychologizing political positions, and as a form that shows us the kinds of behavior that are to be praised or blamed. In a moment concerned with the effects of literature on its readers, we may indeed wish to turn to a Theophrastan way of parsing some of the representations that populate our social world. It is my hope that this book inspires new sensitivities to how we might interpret the effects of character types upon readers and listeners, effects often political and moral in nature. While the struggle cannot be fought "on the terrain of sensibility alone," it seems that in our moment, we might want to recognize not only the moral and political work of anatomy but that of painting.[114]

Abbreviations

Notes

Acknowledgments

Index

Abbreviations

Journal titles are abbreviated according to the style of Marouzeau's *L'année philologique*. The following additional abbreviations are used in the notes:

APSR	*American Political Science Review*
EEBO	Early English Books Online
FHS&G	William W. Fortenbaugh, Pamela M. Huby, Robert W. Sharples, and Dimitri Gutas, eds., *Theophrastus of Eresus: Sources for His Life, Writings, Thought and Influence,* 2 vols. (Leiden, Netherlands: Brill, 1992).
HLQ	*Huntington Library Quarterly*
MLQ	*Modern Language Quarterly*
MRFH	Marburger Repertorium zur Übersetzungsliteratur im deutschen Frühhumanismus
ODNB	*Oxford Dictionary of National Biography* (Oxford: Oxford University Press, 2004), online edition, all entries accessed April 22, 2022.
OED	*Oxford English Dictionary*
PMLA	*Publications of the Modern Language Association*
RHS	*Transactions of the Royal Historical Society*
TS	William W. Fortenbaugh and Robert W. Sharples, eds., *Theophrastean Studies: On Natural Science, Physics and Metaphysics, Ethics, Religion, and Rhetoric* (New Brunswick, NJ: Rutgers University Press, 1988).

Notes

Introduction

1. For recent biographies see J.-P. Schneider, "Théophraste d'Erèse," in *Dictionnaire des philosophes antiques,* vol. 6, ed. Richard Goulet (Paris: CNRS, 2016), 1033–1123; Laura Beatty, *Looking for Theophrastus: Travels in Search of a Lost Philosopher* (London: Atlantic Books, 2022). Throughout the book, I refer to the character as both a form and a genre, an ambiguity derived from its evolving status.

2. Diog. Laert. 5.36–38, trans. R. D. Hicks (Cambridge, MA: Harvard University Press, 1925).

3. Diog. Laert. 5.42–50.

4. Theophr. *Char.* 12.1–14, trans. Jeffrey Rusten (Cambridge, MA: Harvard University Press, 2003). Across the book, my lineation of the *Characters* is derived from Rusten's edition.

5. Theophr. *Char.* 8.1, 8.10. The abstract definitions and moralizing epilogues are spurious additions to the text.

6. Theophr. *Char.* 0.3.

7. Chapters 2–5 trace the extensive Latin, English, and French reception over the sixteenth and seventeenth centuries. The *Characters* was translated into German in 1606, Italian in 1620, Russian in 1772, and Spanish in 1787. For the philological reception of the work, and of Theophrastus's oeuvre more broadly, see Charles B. Schmitt, "Theophrastus," in *"Catalogus translationum et commentariorum": Mediaeval and Renaissance Latin Translations and Commentaries,* ed. Paul Oskar Kristeller and F. Edward Cranz (Washington, DC: Catholic University of America Press, 1971), 2:239–322.

8. For these intersections see Barbara Carnevali, "Literary Mimesis and Moral Knowledge: The Tradition of *ethopoeia,*" *Annales (HSS)* 65 (2010): 291–322. Where Carnevali uses the terms "moral sciences" and "moral knowledge" to recall the beginnings of the human sciences in this tradition, I have kept "human sciences" for ease of comprehension.

9. Beatty, *Looking for Theophrastus.*

10. David Hume, *Philosophical Essays concerning Human Understanding* (London, 1748), A1r.

11. Hume, *Philosophical Essays,* A2v–A3r.

12. Hume, *Philosophical Essays,* A1r.

13. As Socrates concludes (*Rep.* 607a), on the basis of this logic, "we can admit no poetry into our city save only hymns to the gods and the praises of good men." In Edith Hamilton and Huntington Cairns's translation (Princeton, NJ: Princeton University Press, 1961), 575–844, at 832.

14. *Poet.* 1450a23–5.

15. For arguments about how Aristotle's understanding of tragic spectatorship provides ethical learning through this process, see Martha Nussbaum, *The Fragility of Goodness: Luck and Ethics in Greek Tragedy and Philosophy* (Cambridge: Cambridge University Press, 1986), and "Tragedy and Self-Sufficiency: Plato and Aristotle on Fear and Pity," *OSAPh* 10 (1992): 107–159.

16. For ethics, see Karl Gottlieb Sonntag, *Dissertatio in prooemium characterum Theophrasti* (Leipzig, 1787); Theodor Gomperz, *Über die "Charaktere" Theophrast's* (Vienna, 1889). For rhetoric: Otto Immisch, "Über Theophrasts *Charaktere,*" *Philologus* 57 (1898): 193–212; David John Furley, "The Purpose of Theophrastus' *Characters,*" *SO* 30, no. 1 (1953): 56–60; Sophie Trenkner, *The Greek Novella in the Classical Period* (Cambridge: Cambridge University Press, 1958), 147–154. For comedy or poetics: Augusto Rostagni, "Sui *Caratteri* di Teofrasto," *RFIC* 48 (1920): 417–443; R. G. Ussher, ed., *The "Characters" of Theophrastus* (London: Macmillan, 1960), 5; R. G. Ussher, "Old Comedy and Character," *G&R* 24, no. 1 (1977): 71–79; Graziano Ranocchia, "Natura e fine dei *Caratteri* di Teofrasto: Storia di un enigma," *Philologus* 155 (2011): 69–91.

17. See Joanne Paul, "The Use of *Kairos* in Renaissance Political Philosophy," *Renaissance Quarterly* 67 (2014): 43–78, at 45; J. R. Wilson, "*Kairos* as 'due measure'," *Glotta* 58 (1980): 177–204.

18. See Pl. *Plt.* 307b1–9; *Ep.* 7 326a; Arist. *Eth. Nic.* 1104a8–9. Note too that Theophrastus's student Demetrius of Phalerum wrote a work entitled *Peri kairou* (Diog. Laert. 5.81). For Theophrastus's own treatise, see FHS&G 589 4a.

19. For a full etymological history, see Monique Trédé-Boulmer, "*Kairos:*" *L'à-propos et l'occasion* (Paris: Belles Lettres, 1992); Bernard Gallet, *Recherches sur "kairos" et l'ambiguïté dans la poésie de Pindare* (Bordeaux: Presses universitaires de Bordeaux, 1990).

20. Paul, "The Use of *Kairos,*" 45.

21. For Plato and *kairos*, see Melissa Lane, *Methods and Politics in Plato's* Statesman (Cambridge: Cambridge University Press, 1995); Dimitri El Murr, *Savoir et gouverner: Essai sur la science politique platonicienne* (Paris: Vrin, 2014). For Aristotle on *phronesis* and *kairos,* see Hendrik Lorenz, "Virtue of Character in Aristotle's *Nicomachean Ethics,*" *OSAPh* 37 (2009): 177–212.

22. Jacques Derrida, *The Politics of Friendship,* trans. George Collins (London: Verso, 2005), 30.

23. Ryan K. Balot, "The Virtue Politics of Democratic Athens," in *The Cambridge Companion to Ancient Greek Political Thought,* ed. Stephen G. Salkever (Cambridge: Cambridge University Press, 2009), 271–300.

24. Benjamin Boyce, *The Theophrastan Character in England to 1642* (Cambridge, MA: Harvard University Press, 1947); J. W. Smeed, *The Theophrastan "Character": The History of a Literary Genre* (Oxford: Clarendon Press, 1985); Michael Mangan, "The Issue of the Theophrastan Character" (PhD diss., Cambridge University, 1985). See also David Nichol Smith's comment, "The great lesson that the Theophrastan type of character could teach was the value of balance and unity," in his *Characters from the Histories and Memoirs of the Seventeenth Century* (Oxford: Clarendon Press, 1918), 30.

25. See, for example, Louis van Delft, *Littérature et anthropologie: Nature humaine et caractère à l'âge classique* (Paris: Presses universitaires de France, 1993).

26. Jensen's dissertation, by contrast, focuses instead on how the form of the Theophrastan character sketch can be used to observe shifts over time in what constitutes a moral vice. See Kristin Hay Jensen, "Building Character: Ethics, Habit and the Work of Theophrastan Characters," (PhD diss., University of Virginia, 2010).

27. See Quentin Skinner, "Meaning and Understanding in the History of Ideas," *History and Theory* 8, no. 1 (1969): 3–53, and *Visions of Politics: Regarding Method,* vol. 1 (Cambridge: Cambridge University Press, 2002).

28. See Ludwig Wittgenstein, *Philosophical Investigations,* 4th ed., trans. G. E. M. Anscombe, P. M. S. Hacker, and Joachin Schulte (Malden, MA: Wiley-Blackwell, 1953), §11, §546; Quentin Skinner, "A Reply to My Critics," in *Meaning and Context: Quentin Skinner and His Critics,* ed. James Tully (Cambridge: Polity Press, 1988), 260.

29. Skinner's pioneering work on rhetoric in the early modern period has highlighted countless instances in which Renaissance writers used rhetorical figures. See, for example, Quentin Skinner, *Reason and Rhetoric in the Philosophy of Hobbes* (Cambridge: Cambridge University Press, 1996), *Visions of Politics,* 3 vols. (Cambridge: Cambridge University Press, 2002), and *From Humanism to Hobbes: Studies in Rhetoric and Politics* (Cambridge: Cambridge University Press, 2018). Yet in his study of how Shakespeare deployed different kinds of rhetorical models in many plays, Skinner's formal analysis focuses on the level of individual texts rather than on the level of the genre. He thus leaves aside the question of what Shakespeare's choice to deal with certain questions in drama—rather than, say, sonnets—might have meant in his context. Here see Freddy C. Domínguez, "Book Review: Quentin Skinner, *Forensic Shakespeare,*" *Renaissance and Reformation* 39, no. 1 (2016): 200–202.

30. In this double focus on a series of immediate bracketed contexts, and the work of tracing a longer history over time, my method is somewhat similar to David Armitage's notion of "serial contextualism." See David Armitage, "What's the Big Idea? Intellectual History and the *Longue Durée,*" *History of European Ideas* 38, no. 4 (2012): 493–507.

31. Colin Burrow, *Imitating Authors: Plato to Futurity* (Oxford: Oxford University Press, 2019), 32.

32. On the Theophrastan characters that end up in Jonathan Swift's sermons, Alexander Pope's poems, and Tom Fielding's novels, see Smeed, *The Theophrastan "Character,"* chap. 3.

33. Boyce, *The Theophrastan Character,* chap. 3.

34. This also means I do not cover, in any great detail, how the history of the character sketch feeds into histories of related genres, like the biography, the novel, the essay, or the sermon. These are areas in which previous scholarship has already made inroads and would require studies in their own right to be dealt with in full. Likewise, I do not stray into linking up the history of character-writing with the history of psychology, or physiognomy, even if there are several shared aspects between these practices. See, respectively, Boyce, *The Theophrastan Character,* chap. 7; Smeed, *The Theophrastan "Character,"* chaps. 9 and 10; Martin Porter, *Windows of the Soul: Physiognomy in European Culture 1470–1780* (Oxford: Clarendon Press, 2005).

35. Here see Wittgenstein, *Philosophical Investigations,* §67.

36. Even though there was an early modern visual tradition of depicting society figures in places that ranged from costume compendia to playing cards, rarely were these images affixed to written Theophrastan sketches. See Marika Takanishi Knowles, *Realism and Role-Play: The Human Figure in French Art from Callot to the Brothers Le Nain* (Newark: University of Delaware Press, 2020); Kirsten J. Burke, "Print and the Early Modern Playing Card," *Oxford Art Journal* 44, no. 2 (2021): 183–205. There is a related trend of depicting national types that became popular in the seventeenth century. This includes Antonine de Fer's *Le Jeu de nations principals* (1662)—a game board with forty-three compartments, each showing a man and woman of a different country—and the later *Völkertafel,* made in Austria in the early eighteenth century.

37. A parallel can be drawn here with Alexander Nehamas's sense that it is hard to paint friendship: a kind of relationship that takes place in time, through repeated interactions, just like the manifestation of a behavioral trait. See Alexander Nehamas, *On Friendship* (New York: Basic Books, 2016), chap. 3. My thanks go to Joshua Landy for pointing me to this source.

38. To use M. H. Abrams's terms, the character sketch became less like a "mirror," in which reality could be truthfully reflected, and more like a "lamp": an inventive form used to creatively illuminate reality, "a radiant projector which makes a contribution to the objects it perceives." See M. H. Abrams, *The Mirror and the Lamp: Romantic Theory and the Critical Tradition* (Oxford: Oxford University Press, 1953), viii.

39. David Hume, "A Dialogue," in *An Enquiry Concerning the Principles of Morals* (London, 1751), L4r–M7r, at L11r–v.

40. The earliest sense of "literature" as we understand it today seems to date to the year after Hume's pieces, with Henry Fielding's *Tom Jones* describing "a very competent Judge in most Kinds of Literature." See *OED*, s.v. "literature," n., 3a.

41. Richard Rorty, *Philosophy and the Mirror of Nature* (Princeton, NJ: Princeton University Press, 2018), chap. 3.

42. Smeed, *The Theophrastan "Character,"* 81, 111, 120, 122. The way in which this stands in contrast to the many moral justifications that prefaced the nineteenth-century novel would be fertile ground for further analysis.

43. Smeed, *The Theophrastan "Character,"* 126.

44. Smeed, *The Theophrastan "Character,"* 118, 127.

45. Smeed, *The Theophrastan "Character,"* 120.

46. Alexis de Tocqueville, *Democracy in America,* trans. Harvey C. Mansfield and Delba Winthrop (Chicago: University of Chicago Press, 2000), 244, 62. On Tocqueville and the founding of the social sciences, see Jon Elster, *Alexis de Tocqueville, the First Social Scientist* (Cambridge: Cambridge University Press, 2009). On Tocqueville and La Bruyère, see Giulia Oskian, "La notion de caractère entre littérature et sciences sociales au 19ème siècle: Tocqueville et Stendhal," in *En deçà du bien et du mal: Morales de la littérature de la Renaissance à l'âge contemporain,* ed. Barbara Carnevali, Emiliano Cavaliere, and Katie Ebner-Landy (Paris: Hermann, 2024), chap. 8.

47. Here see Sebastian J. Moser and Tobias Schlechtriemen, "Sozialfiguren–zwischen gesellschaftlicher Erfahrung und soziologischer Diagnose," *Zeitschrift für Soziologie* 47, no. 3 (2018): 164–180; Tobias Schlechtriemen, "Social Figures as Elements of Sociological Theorizing," *Distinktion: Journal of Social Theory* 25, no. 2 (2024): 208–227.

48. I am indebted here to Phil Gershuny, a source of oral intellectual history, who many years ago told me that he had heard this explanation in a seminar given by Peter Burke.

49. On early modern virtue politics, see James Hankins, *Virtue Politics: Soulcraft and Statecraft in Renaissance Italy* (Cambridge, MA: Harvard University Press, 2019); Rachel Hammersley, *Republicanism: An Introduction* (Cambridge: Polity Press, 2020), chap. 2; Blair Worden, *The Sound of Virtue: Philip Sidney's "Arcadia" and Elizabethan Politics* (New Haven, CT: Yale University Press, 1996). The book extends these histories by showing the pan-European nature of virtue politics, by describing how it was directed toward all echelons of the population—not just rulers and the political elite—and by homing in on an important literary strategy that authors held at their disposal: the writing of typical characters.

50. Hume, *Philosophical Essays,* A1r.

51. Cora Diamond, *The Realistic Spirit: Wittgenstein, Philosophy, and the Mind* (Cambridge, MA: MIT Press, 1995), 375, 374.

52. Diamond, *The Realistic Spirit,* 370.

53. Deidre Shauna Lynch, *The Economy of Character: Novels, Market Culture, and the Business of Inner Meaning* (Chicago: University of Chicago Press, 1998), 4, 14.

54. When Lynch does talk about Theophrastus (see *The Economy of Character,* 27–29), she focuses on formal developments present in the late 1740s and 1750s revivals of the genre, not writers' sense of what this form was *for.*

55. Hélène Cixous, "The Character of 'Character,'" trans. Keith Cohen, *New Literary History* 5, no. 2 (1974): 383–402, at 389. The popularity of character also holds outside the academy, attested to by the fictitious trials of literary characters that have recently been staged. Here see Caroline Juillot, "Le Procès de Monte-Cristo: Essai de critique judiciare, ou comment peut-on juger un héros de roman populaire?," in "Débattre d'une fiction," ed. Marc Escola, Françoise Lavocat, and Aurélien Maignant, special issue, *Fabula-LhT* 25 (2021), §3 n. 11.

56. Evan Kindley, "The People We Know Best," *New York Review of Books,* March 25, 2021, 12–14, at 12.

57. See also Aaron Kunin, "Characters Lounge," *MLQ* 70, no. 3 (2009): 291–317; Aaron Kunin, *Character as Form* (London: Bloomsbury, 2019); Marjorie

Garber, *Character: The History of a Cultural Obsession* (New York: Farrar, Straus and Giroux, 2020). Kunin's work is most interested in what literary character *is,* rather than what people think character sketches can *do.* Garber similarly is more concerned with showing the connotative breadth and capacity of the concept of character than getting down to the forgotten practices of reading through which sketches were understood.

58. Rita Felski, *Hooked: Art and Attachment* (Chicago: Chicago University Press, 2020), 85. See also Rita Felski, "Identifying with Characters," in *Character: Three Inquiries in Literary Studies,* ed. Amanda Anderson, Rita Felski, and Toril Moi (Chicago: Chicago University Press, 2019), 77–126.

59. Blakey Vermuele, *Why Do We Care about Literary Characters?* (Baltimore: Johns Hopkins University Press, 2010), 244.

60. The role of the social figure in sociological theorizing has, as Tobias Schlechtriemen writes, "gone largely unnoticed until now." See his "Social Figures as Elements of Sociological Theorizing," 209.

61. Judith Shklar, *Ordinary Vices* (Cambridge, MA: Harvard University Press, 1984), 246.

62. Shklar, *Ordinary Vices,* 2.

63. Martha Nussbaum has developed the most extensive set of arguments here. See *Love's Knowledge: Essays on Philosophy and Literature* (Oxford: Oxford University Press, 1992), *Poetic Justice: The Literary Imagination and Public Life* (Boston: Beacon Press, 1996), *Not for Profit: Why Democracy Needs the Humanities* (Princeton, NJ: Princeton University Press, 2010), and *Political Emotions: Why Love Matters for Justice* (Cambridge, MA: Harvard University Press, 2013). While the later works encompass a wide range of cultural practices, they do not extend to character sketches. For other important work at this juncture, see Davide Panagia, *The Political Life of Sensation* (Durham, NC: Duke University Press, 2009); Jason Frank, *The Democratic Sublime: On Aesthetics and Popular Assembly* (Oxford: Oxford University Press, 2021).

64. Documents with "character" (and variant spellings) in their title as listed on EEBO for this date range, discounting duplicates and translations as well as titles that use "character" but are not characters themselves.

65. Thomas Hobbes, *Leviathan,* ed. Richard Tuck (Cambridge: Cambridge University Press, 1996), 10.

66. Jean de La Bruyère, *The Moral Characters of Theophrastus* (London, 1700), 2A8v.

67. This is, of course, not to say that caricaturing cannot have a racist dimension, which it does have beyond the periods this study considers. In the early modern period, Theophrastan racial characters were scant. On the depiction of race in Theophrastus's original text (one of only a handful of "extant references to black people in Greek literature" from the Hellenistic period), see Sarah F. Derbew, *Untangling Blackness in Greek Antiquity* (Cambridge: Cambridge University Press, 2022), 129n1.

68. On E. M. Forster's distinction between flat characters "constructed round a single idea or quality"—such as those penned by Theophrastus—as compared to their more well-rounded equivalents, see E. M. Forster, *Aspects of the Novel* (New York: Harcourt, Brace & World, 1927), 67.

69. Literary texts respectively favored by Bernard Williams, Martha Nussbaum, G. W. F. Hegel, and Hannah Arendt. See Williams, *Moral Luck: Philosophical Papers 1973–1980* (Cambridge: Cambridge University Press, 1982), 26–27; Nussbaum, *Love's Knowledge,* chap. 4; Hegel, *Phenomenology of Spirit,* trans. A. V. Miller (Oxford: Oxford University Press, 1977), 266–293; Arendt, "The Social Question," in *Reflections on Literature and Culture,* ed. Susannah Young-ah Gottlieb (Stanford, CA: Stanford University Press, 2007).

70. On the latter, see Alexander Nehamas, *Virtues of Authenticity: Essays on Plato and Socrates* (Princeton, NJ: Princeton University Press, 1999), chap. 13.

71. This is Nussbaum's claim in *Poetic Justice.*

72. In the latter case, it builds on arguments made by Barbara Carnevali and Pascal Engel for the ways in which the sketching of character provides moral or practical knowledge. Neither Carnevali or Engel position this as an alternative ancient aesthetic, however, separate to Aristotelian or Platonic models. See Carnevali, "'Literary Mimesis"; Pascal Engel, "Literature and Practical Knowledge," *Argumenta* 2 (2016): 55–76.

73. Looking at this shift through the lens of character-writing presents this slight difference with J. G. A. Pocock's narrative of the transformation away from virtues and toward manners. See his *Virtue, Commerce, and History: Essays on Political Thought and History, Chiefly in the Eighteenth Century* (Cambridge: Cambridge University Press, 1985), chap. 2.

74. In this I follow Richard Bourke's instinct that all revivals must provide grounds for establishing a continuity between the past and the present. See his *Hegel's World Revolutions* (Princeton, NJ: Princeton University Press, 2023), 279.

75. Gianluca Garelli described this turn to immediacy as "the sacrifice of discourse" in a conference paper given at the École des Hautes Études en Sciences Sociales in Paris, March 6, 2020. See also Anna Kornbluh's *Immediacy, or The Style of Too Late Capitalism* (London: Verso, 2023). On the moralization of everyday life, consider phenomena like language politics, microaggressions, the politics of ethical eating habits, and consumer habits more broadly.

76. Guido Mazzoni, *Teoria del romanzo* (Bologna, Italy: Il Mulino, 2011), 204. This quote is also present in the later English translation, *Theory of the Novel,* trans. Zakiya Hanafi (Cambridge, MA: Harvard University Press, 2017), 189, which I use here.

1. The *Characters* as Virtue Politics

1. Jeffrey Rusten, preface to *Characters*, in *Theophrastus Characters, Herodas Mimes, Sophron and Other Mime Fragments*, ed. and trans. Jeffrey Rusten and I. C. Cunningham, (Cambridge MA: Harvard University Press, 2002), 3–4, at 3.

2. Rusten, preface, 3. For the much-debated date, see Alan L. Boegehold, "The Date of Theophrastus's *Characters,*" *TAPhA* 90 (1959): 15–19; Robin Lane Fox, "Theophrastus's *Characters* and the Historian," *PCPhS* 42 (1993): 127–170, at 134–138.

3. Graziano Ranocchia, "Natura e fine dei *Caratteri* di Teofrasto: Storia di un enigma," *Philologus* 155 (2011): 69–91.

4. *Rh.* 2.12; 1.8; *Eth. Nic.* 1115a6–1128b33. See also *Eud. Eth.* 1220b21–1221b3, 1228a23–1234b11.

5. On Theophrastus's authorship, see Heinz-Günther Nesselrath, *Die attische mittlere Komödie: Ihre Stellung in der antiken Literaturkritik und Literaturgeschichte* (Berlin: Walter de Gruyter, 1990).

6. Diog. Laert. 5.50.

7. I refer here to FHS&G.

8. On his reclusiveness, see Jørgen Mejer, "A Life in Fragments: The *Vita Theophrasti,*" in *Theophrastus: Reappraising the Sources,* ed. Johannes Max van Ophuijsen and Marlein van Raalte (New Brunswick, NJ: Transaction, 1998), 1–28, at 11. On his oligarchic or monarchic political orientation, respectively see W. S. Ferguson, "The Laws of Demetrius of Phalerum and their Guardians," *Klio* 11 (1911): 265–276; Christian Habicht, *Untersuchungen zur politischen Geschichte Athens im 3. Jahrhundert v. Chr.* (Munich: Beck, 1979), 27.

9. Lane Fox, "Theophrastus," 133

10. For an evaluation of this hypothesis as probable, see Katie Ebner-Landy, "Did Theophrastus Deliver Eresus from Tyrants?," *CQ* 72, no. 1 (2022): 1–10.

11. Here see A. Podlecki, "Theophrastus on History and Politics," in *Theophrastus of Eresus: On His Life and Work,* ed. William W. Fortenbaugh, Pamela M. Huby, and Anthony A. Long (New Brunswick, NJ: Transaction, 1985), 2:231–250.

12. This aspect of the chapter builds on arguments in Katie Ebner-Landy and René de Nicolay, "Theophrastus's Oligarch and the Political Intention of the *Characters,*" *Cambridge Classical Journal* 69 (2023): 1–21.

13. Ryan K. Balot, "The Virtue Politics of Democratic Athens," in *The Cambridge Companion to Ancient Greek Political Thought,* ed. Stephen G. Salkever (Cambridge: Cambridge University Press, 2009), 271–300, at 292–293.

14. Rusten in fact translates *oligarchias* as the "Authoritarianism" in his *Characters,* 124.

15. Pl. *Resp.* 401b, 607a. For a rereading of this typical approach to Platonic aesthetics, which takes into consideration Socrates's earlier acknowledgment (605a) that the better sort might be attracted to characters "unlike them," see Jill Frank, *Poetic Justice: Rereading Plato's "Republic"* (Chicago: University of Chicago Press, 2018), 35. Frank's reading of Plato makes him closer to the interpretation I give here of Theophrastus.

16. Arist. *Poet.* 1450a23–25.

17. On the League, see Jack Cargill, *The Second Athenian League: Empire or Free Alliance?* (Berkeley: University of California Press, 1981). For Eresus's membership, see *IG* XII2 43B.21. Before joining the League around 377, Eresus was passed between Athens and Sparta during the Peloponnesian War (431–404), was under military rule by Sparta for sixteen years, and was then retaken by Athens in 389. See Thuc. 3.18–35; 8.23–103, and Xen. *Hell.* 1.6, 2.2, 4.8.

18. On the causes of the Social War (356–355), see Philip Harding, ed., *Translated Documents of Greece and Rome: From the End of the Peloponnesian War to the Battle of Ipsus* (Cambridge: Cambridge University Press, 1985). For the date of the Persian conquest, see P. J. Rhodes and Robin Osborne, *Greek Historical Inscriptions, 404–323 BC* (Oxford: Oxford University Press, 2004), 417.

19. For evidence of the tyrannies at Eresus, see *IG* XII2 526; *OGIS* 8; M. N. Tod, *Greek Historical Inscriptions* (Oxford: Clarendon Press, 1948), 253–263, no. 191; Charles Michel, *Recueil d'Inscriptions Grecques* (Brussels: H. Lamertin, 1900), no. 358; A. J. Heisserer, *Alexander the Great and the Greeks: The Epigraphic Evidence* (Norman: University of Oklahoma Press, 1980), 27–78; Alice Bencivenni, *Progetti di riforme costituzionali nelle epigrafi greche dei secoli IV–II a.C.* (Bologna: Lo scarabeo, 2003), 55–77; Aneurin Ellis-Evans, "The Tyrants Dossier from Eresos," *Chiron* 42 (2012): 183–212.

20. C. A. Brandis, "Theophrastus," in *Dictionary of Greek and Roman Biography and Mythology*, ed. William Smith (Boston: Little Brown, 1867), 3:1087–1091, at 1087.

21. Diog. Laert. 5.36. For skepticism about Theophrastus studying with Plato, see Werner Jaeger, *Aristotle: Fundamentals of the History of His Development*, 2nd ed., trans. Richard Robinson (Oxford: Clarendon Press, 1948), 115–116n1; W. K. C. Guthrie, *A History of Greek Philosophy* (Cambridge: Cambridge University Press, 1981), 6:35n1.

22. On the causes of Aristotle's departure, see Jonathan Barnes, *The Cambridge Companion to Aristotle* (Cambridge: Cambridge University Press, 1995), 4–5; Strabo 8.57.

23. Tiziano Dorandi, ed., *Filodemo: Stori dei filosofi* (Naples: Bibliopolis, 1991), 129.

24. Terence Irwin and Gail Fine, eds., *Aristotle: Selections* (Cambridge: Cambridge University Press, 1995), xiii. Marilyn Bailey Ogilvie and Joy Dorothy Harvey suggest this journey to Mytilene was part of a honeymoon, in their *The Biographical Dictionary of Women in Science: L–Z* (New York and London: Routledge, 2000), 1062. See here for Pythias's research collaboration with Aristotle.

25. This is maintained by Barnes, *The Cambridge Companion to Aristotle,* 14. For Theophrastus's presence in Assos, see Konrad Gaiser, *Theophrast in Assos: Zur Entwicklung der Naturwissenschaft zwischen Akademie und Peripatos* (Heidelberg: Carl Winter Universitätsverlag, 1985).

26. Barnes, *The Cambridge Companion to Aristotle,* 5.

27. Barnes, *The Cambridge Companion to Aristotle,* 5. For an alternative account, maintaining that Aristotle was summoned while still in Lesbos, see Robin Lane Fox, *Alexander the Great* (London: Penguin, 2006), 53.

28. Brandis, "Theophrastus," 1088; O. Regenbogen, "Theophrastos von Eresos," *RE* Suppl. 7 (1940), cols. 1354–1562, at 1357; W. Pötscher, "Theophrastos," in *Der kleine Pauly: Lexicon der Antike,* ed. Konrat Ziegler and Walter Sontheimer (Stuttgart: Alfred Druckenmüller Verlag, 1975), 5:720–725; Gaiser, *Theophrast in Assos,* 26; Mejer, "A Life in Fragments," 19; William W. Fortenbaugh and Roger Harmon, "Theophrastus," in *Brill's New Pauly* (Leiden, Netherlands: Brill, 2008); Katerina Ierodiakonou, "Theophrastus," in *The Stanford Encyclopedia of Philosophy*, ed. Edward N. Zalta (Winter 2020 Edition). These claims are in part based on Ael. *VH* 4.19, which describes Theophrastus's friendship with Philip. For Regenbogen, Theophrastus's "stay in Macedonia with Aristotle is certain, even if Ael. *VH* 4.19 is uncertain."

29. See Sonia Pertsinidis, *Theophrastus's "Characters": A New Introduction* (London: Routledge, 2018), 11; M. G. Sollenberger, "The Lives of the Peripatetics:

An Analysis of the Contents and Structure of Diogenes Laertius' *Vitae Philosophorum* Book 5," *ANRW* 36 (1992): 3793–3879, at 3843; James Diggle, introduction to *Theophrastus: "Characters,"* ed. James Diggle (Cambridge: Cambridge University Press, 2004), 1–57, at 2. For "after 334," see Rusten, introduction to *Characters,* in *Theophrastus "Characters," Herodas "Mimes," Sophron and Other Mime Fragments*, ed. and trans. Jeffrey Rusten and I. C. Cunningham, (Cambridge MA: Harvard University Press, 2002), 5–39, at 6.

30. Plut. *Mor.* 1126F. See also 1097B. The dates of this section (not mentioned by Plutarch) are informed by the account in Ebner-Landy, "Did Theophrastus Deliver Eresus from Tyrants?"

31. This detail is absent, for example, in the biographies by Brandis, Pötscher, Fortenbaugh and Harmon, and Ierodiakonou cited prior.

32. Plut. *Mor.* 1126E.

33. See F. W. Mitchel, *Lykourgan Athens: 338–322. Lectures in Memory of Louise Taft Semple* (Cincinnati: University of Cincinnati, 1970).

34. See Claude Mossé, *Athens in Decline* (London: Routledge, 1973), chap. 4.

35. *Vit. Marc.* 41.

36. I am very grateful to Mor Segev for helping me on the wild goose chase of figuring out what is going on in this image and, in particular, for pointing me to Edith Hall's blog post on the matter, "The Lyceum Goose Mystery," *The Edithorial,* March 4, 2017, https://edithorial.blogspot.com/2017/03/the-lyceum-goose-mystery.html?m=1.

37. Diog. Laert. 5.36–37.

38. For an account of the politics of the period, see Christian Habicht, *Athens from Alexander to Antony* (Cambridge, MA: Harvard University Press, 1997); A. J. Bayliss, *After Demosthenes: The Politics of Early Hellenistic Athens* (London: Continuum, 2011).

39. On the view of the former as oligarchy, see Plut. *Phoc.* 34.3; Diod. 18.65–66.

40. For the details of oligarchy under Demetrius, see Philoch. *FGrHist.* 328 F66; Strabo 9.1.20; Lara O'Sullivan, *The Regime of Demetrius of Phalerum in Athens, 317–307 BCE: A Philosopher in Politics* (Leiden: Brill, 2009), chap. 3.

41. Diog. Laert. 5.38; Mattias Haake, "Das 'Gesetz des Sophokles' und die Schließung der Philosophenschulen in Athen unter Demetrios Poliorketes," in *L'enseignement supérieur dans les mondes antiques et médiévaux,* ed. Henri Hugonnard-Roche (Paris: Vrin, 2008), 89–112.

42. Diog. Laert. 5.37.

43. Diog. Laert. 5.37.

44. On Demetrius and Theophrastus, see Diog. Laert. 5.47; O'Sullivan, *The Regime of Demetrius,* 197–198, 205. For the report that Cassander received from Theophrastus, see Diog. Laert. 5.37.

45. Diog. Laert. 5.37–39.

46. *Suda* 2804 = FHS&G 609; Plut. *Them* 25.1 = FHS&G 612; Ath. 435E = FHS&G 548.

47. Diog. Laert. 5.41.

48. Them. *Or.* 23.285c; Ath. 144e–f = FHS&G 603.

49. *Pol.* 1297b.

50. FHS&G 612.

51. Luisa Fizzarotti, "Per una nuova edizione del cosiddetto *De eligendis magistratibus*" (PhD diss., University of Bologna, 2019). See Andrew Szegedy-Maszak, *The "Nomoi" of Theophrastus* (New York: Arno Press, 1981), 102, commenting on ll. 18–28 of the text. See also J. J. Keaney and Andrew Szegedy-Maszak, "Theophrastus's *De eligendis magistratibus*: Vat. Gr. 2306, Fragment B," *TAPhA* 106 (1976): 227–240, at 231.

52. Lane Fox, "Theophrastus," 133.

53. Lane Fox, "Theophrastus," 133.

54. Diog. Laert. 5.47; Theophrastus, *Characters*, ed. Rusten, 46n1.

55. Alfred Körte, "ΧΑΡΑΚΤΗΡ," *Hermes* 64 (1928): 69–86; Arist. *Pol.* 1257b; *Le dictionnaire de l'Académie françoise* (Paris, 1694), s.v. "caractère"; Ath. 524e.

56. *OED*, s.v. "character," n. See Aesch. *Supp.* 277–283, where a group of women are interrogated about their origin, their interlocutor sure they cannot be Argive because they appear to be stamped with the "character" of Cyprus.

57. Each of these terms is respectively used on 4 (*ethos*), 14 (*idios*), 405 (*phusis*), and 120 (*tropos*) occasions (across the corpus of texts: *Hist. pl.*, *Caus. pl.*, *Char.*, *On Odours*, and *On Weather Signs*). See Otto Thimme, "φύσις, τρόπος, ἦθος," (PhD diss., University of Göttingen, 1935).

58. Rusten, introduction, 7–8.

59. Theophr. *Char.* 14.1–12. I have made slight modifications to Rusten's translation here to stay closer to the Greek.

60. On the two exceptions to this rule (Characters 2 and 18), see William W. Fortenbaugh, Pamela M. Huby, Dimitri Gutas, and Robert W. Sharples, eds., *Theophrastus of Eresus: Commentary*, vol. 6.1, *Sources on Ethics* (Leiden, Netherlands: Brill, 2011), 139.

61. Shklar, *Ordinary Vices*, 1.

62. Shklar, *Ordinary Vices*, 247.

63. I use here a combination of the translated titles found in the editions by Rusten and Diggle. Diggle does not give the abstract nouns, and so in some cases, I have had to provide equivalents to the descriptions of types he delineates. I am indebted to both of their editions for the lists of intertextual echoes cited in the following paragraphs.

64. See Dilwyn Knox, *Ironia: Medieval and Renaissance Ideas on Irony* (Leiden, Netherlands: Brill, 1989), 139–140, for this derogatory understanding of irony in ancient Greece. For the consequence that this has of "avoiding all involvement," see Theophrastus, *Characters*, ed. Rusten, 146.

65. *Eth. Nic.* 1227a20; "Tractatus Coislinianus," in *"Poetics" with "Tractatus Coislinianus," Reconstruction of "Poetics II" and the Fragments of the "On Poets,"* ed. Richard Janko (Indianapolis: Hackett, 1987), 43–46. The question of the relationship between Aristotle's positive sense of irony as self-deprecation (exemplified by Socrates) and Theophrastus's negative portrait of irony as dissimulation is complex. Octave Navarre attempts to reconcile them in his *Caractères de Théophraste* (Paris: Belles-Lettres, 1924), 7. Knox, on the contrary, sees them as separate. For critical commentary on the sketch, see, as indicative, Otto Ribbeck, "Uber den Begriff des eiron," *Rheinisches Museum* 31 (1876): 381–400; Zoja Pavlovskis, "Aristotle, Horace, and the Ironic Man," *CPh* 63 (1968): 22–41.

66. *Eth. Nic.* 1108a. See also 1127a. Note that elsewhere, at 8.1, Aristotle says that friendship itself is either a virtue or involves virtue. See also Otto Ribbeck, *"Kolax": Eine ethologische Studie* (Leipzig, 1883).

67. *Eth. Nic.* 1117b35; *Rh.* 1390a9; "Tractatus Coislinianus," §5.

68. Theophrastus, *Characters,* ed. Diggle, 207; Theophrastus, *Characters,* ed. Rusten, 147. See also Otto Ribbeck, "*Agroikos,* eine ethologische Studie," *Abhandlungen der königlichen sächsischen Gesellschaft der Wissenschaften* 23 (1888): 1–68.

69. Aristotle does, however, use a different word—ἀναισθησία—to describe someone who is deficient in pleasures, which seems close to this Theophrastan figure: a man who cannot organize his life so that it will give him pleasure and so ends up doing menial labor and spending most of his time in jail. See *Eth. Nic.* 1107b.

70. *Rh.* 1383b22–30.

71. *Eth. Nic.* 1108a31–35; *Eth. Eud.* 1331a1; [*Mag. Mor.*] 1193a1. See also David Konstan, *The Emotions of the Ancient Greeks* (Toronto: University of Toronto Press, 2006), 99–100.

72. Theophrastus, *Characters,* ed. Rusten, 150–151. See also Men. fr. 106.

73. Theophrastus, *Characters,* ed. Diggle, 314; Dem. 25.27.

74. Theophrastus, *Characters,* ed. Diggle, 321. See J. R. Wilson, "*Kairos* as 'due measure,'" *Glotta* 58 (1980): 177–204.

75. Theophrastus, *Characters,* ed. Diggle, 327.

76. Theophrastus, *Characters,* ed. Rusten, 152; Thuc. 6.86; Dem. 21.153.

77. Theophrastus, *Characters,* ed. Diggle, 343–344; *Eth. Eud.* 1333b35–36.

78. Its position within the structure of the virtuous mean can be found in Stobaeus 2.7.52. See also W. R. Halliday, "The Superstitious Man of Theophrastus," *Folk-Lore* 41 (1930): 121–153; C. J. Babick, "De deisidaemonia veterum quaestiones" (PhD diss., University of Leipzig, 1891), 4–19.

79. Theophrastus, *Characters,* ed. Diggle, 376.

80. Arist. [*Ath. Pol.*] 12.5.

81. Theophrastus, *Characters,* ed. Diggle, 380.

82. Theophrastus, *Characters,* ed. Diggle, 386.

83. Theophrastus, *Characters,* ed. Diggle, 395.

84. Theophrastus, *Characters,* ed. Rusten, 154; *Eth. Nic.* 1124a10.

85. Theophrastus, *Characters,* ed. Diggle, 419; *Eth. Nic.* 1107b8–14.

86. Theophrastus, *Characters,* ed. Rusten, 155–156. See also Otto Ribbeck, *"Alazon": Ein Beitrag zur antiken Ethologie* (Leipzig: Teubner, 1886); D. M. MacDowell, "The Meaning of *alazon,*" in *Owls to Athens: Essays on Classical Subjects Presented to Sir Kenneth Dover,* ed. E. M. Craik (Oxford: Clarendon Press, 1990), 287–292.

87. Theophrastus, *Characters,* ed. Diggle, 445.

88. Theophrastus, *Characters,* ed. Diggle, 453. *Eth. Nic.* 1115b34–38; *Eth. Eud.* 1121a18.

89. Theophrastus, *Characters,* ed. Rusten, 157; *Resp.* 553a1–554b1; Andoc. 4.15; Lysias 25.8. Note that Theophrastus wrote an epitome of the *Republic* and so knew the text well. Here see Diog. Laert. 5.43.

90. Theophrastus, *Characters,* ed. Rusten, 157; Lane Fox, "Theophrastus," 132.

91. Theophrastus, *Characters,* ed. Rusten, 158; Theophrastus, *Characters,* ed. Diggle, 477; Ar. *Vesp.* 1112ff. See also Kenneth James Dover, *Greek Popular Morality* (Oxford: Blackwell, 1974), 103.

92. Theophrastus, *Characters,* ed. Rusten, 148; Theophrastus, *Characters,* ed. Diggle, 487.

93. Theophrastus, *Characters,* ed. Rusten, 159; Lane Fox, "Theophrastus," 132. I follow the latter in discounting the idea that this sketch satirizes someone with "popular politics."

94. Theophrastus, *Characters,* ed. Diggle, 507; *Eth. Nic.* 1122a3.

95. Paul Millett, *Lending and Borrowing in Ancient Athens* (Cambridge: Cambridge University Press, 1991), 6.

96. Lane Fox, "Theophrastus," 130.

97. Lane Fox, "Theophrastus," 132–133. For Lane Fox, this is perhaps explained by how "older men, as comedy recognised, were more set in their ways and therefore more apt for the one-sided types which Theophrastus isolated." See Arist. *Rh.* 1389a–b.

98. Rusten, introduction, 9.

99. The details in this paragraph are drawn from Lane Fox, "Theophrastus," 130–133. On class in Hellenistic Athens, see Michael Rostovtzeff, *The Social and Economic History of the Hellenistic World* (Oxford: Oxford University Press, 1941), 3:1352; G. E. M. de Sainte Croix, *The Class Struggle in the Ancient Greek World* (Ithaca, NY: Cornell University Press, 1981), 227, 505–506; Ellen Meiskins Wood, *Peasant-Citizen and Slave* (London: Verso, 1988), 64–80, 173–180.

100. Lane Fox, "Theophrastus," 131.

101. Lane Fox, "Theophrastus," 133.

102. The utility of the *Characters* for a social historian is indeed the driving argument of Lane Fox's article. See also Paul Millett, *Theophrastus and His World* (Cambridge: Cambridge University Press, 2007).

103. Rusten, introduction, 18–19. See Wilhelm Süss, *"Ethos": Studien zur älteren griechischen Rhetorik* (Leipzig: Teubner, 1910).

104. Cic. *Top.* 83, *De or.* 3.53.204; Quint. 1.9.3; Suet. *Gram. et rhet.* 4; *Rhet. Her.* 4.50–52. See also James J. Murphy, "The Key Role of Habit in Roman Rhetoric and Education, as Described by Quintilian," in *Quintiliano: Historia y actualidad de la retórica,* ed. Tomás Albaladejo, José Antonio Cabaellero López, and Emilio del Río (Logroño: Instituto de Estudios Riojanos, 1998), 141–150.

105. Rusten, introduction, 29. I dwell on this more in the following chapter.

106. FHS&G 671; *Rh.* 1358b6–8.

107. *Rh.* 1.3.

108. See Frédérique Woerther, *L' "éthos" aristotélicien: Genèse d'une notion rhétorique* (Paris: Vrin, 2007), which develops an understanding of *ethos* in relation to Aristotle's biological and rhetorical work. I follow in part her instinct and method in my approach to the *Characters.*

109. *Rh.* 2.1.5–9.

110. *Rh.* 2.12; 1.8.

111. See *Pol.* 5.1 on the development of different notions of justice arising from these two models, especially 1301a.

112. William W. Fortenbaugh, "Theophrastus, the *Characters* and Rhetoric," in *TS,* 224–243, at 239; Rusten, introduction, 18.

113. *Rh.* 2.13: "they are always suspicious owing to mistrust, and mistrustful"; "They are not generous"; "they are cowardly"; "they are rather shameless"; "This is the reason of their loquacity."

114. *Rh.* 2.16.

115. FHS&G 667, 670. See William W. Fortenbaugh, "Cicero as a Reporter of Aristotelian and Theophrastean Rhetorical Doctrine," *Rhetorica* 23 (2005): 37–64.

116. FHS&G 684; Arist. *Rh.* 3.2–12.

117. FHS&G 684. Based on Cicero's own report, this feature was present in Aristotle's lost dialogues.

118. R. G. Ussher, "Old Comedy and Character," *G&R* 24, no.1 (1977): 71–79. For a counterargument, see R. L. Hunter, *The New Comedy of Greece and Rome* (Cambridge: Cambridge University Press, 1985); Ranocchia, "Natura e fine," 69–91.

119. Ranocchia, "Natura e fine," 81; Arist. *Poet.* 1450a.

120. *Poet.* 1450b8–11. See William W. Fortenbaugh, "Theophrastus on Comic Character," in *TS,* 295–306, at 299, for a different argument that if Aristotle thought tragic character required choices, Theophrastus realized that comic character required behavioral regularities, which explains the lack of motives.

121. After Lane Fox, "Theophrastus," 139: "Orators did not need to turn to Theophrastus for their examples." If we think that it is the other way round, and that Theophrastus sketched figures that he had previously seen in the theater, we would need to confront the fact that not all thirty characters appear in (our necessarily limited knowledge of) Hellenistic plays.

122. FHS&G 708. For Diomedes, only the definition of tragedy is Theophrastan. Arguments have been made that the other definitions are too. Here see Antonietta Dosi, "Sulle tracce della poetica di Teofrasto," *Rendiconti* 94 (1960): 599–672, at 600, 620; Richard Janko, *Aristotle on Comedy: Toward a Reconstruction of "Poetics II"* (Berkeley: University of California Press, 1984), 48–49; Hermann Reich, *Der Mimus* (Berlin: Weidmann, 1903), 1:265; Augusto Rostagni, "Aristotele e aristotelismo nella storia dell'estetica antica," *Studi italichi di filologia classica* 2 (1922): 1–147, at 128. On the genre distinction, see Dosi, 619, 623; Rostagni, 126–127.

123. FHS&G 708.

124. *Poet.* 1448a4, 1448a16–18. For tragic reversals: 1450a33–35. Book 13 of the *Poetics* indicates that reversals in fortune can go from good to bad or bad to good, suggesting that "heroic" here refers to class status rather than good fortune.

125. FHS&G 708.

126. William W. Fortenbaugh, *Theophrastus of Eresus: Commentary,* vol. 8, *Sources on Rhetoric and Poetics (Texts 666–713)* (Leiden, Netherlands: Brill, 2005), 360.

127. FHS&G 708.

128. FHS&G 708.

129. FHS&G 701.

130. Gavin Lawrence, "Human Excellence in Character and Intellect," in *A Companion to Aristotle,* ed. Georgios Anagnostopoulos (Oxford: Blackwell, 2009), 419–441, at 420.

131. Balot, "The Virtue Politics of Democratic Athens," 274.

132. *Eth. Nic.* 1103a20.

133. *Eth. Nic.* 1103b1.

134. *Eth. Nic.* 1126b11–12.

135. *Eth. Nic.* 1115a6–1128b33.

136. *Eth. Nic.* 1125a34.

137. FHS&G 465. See Lawrence, "Human Excellence in Character and Intellect."

138. Ps. Aristotle, *The Athenian Constitution, The Eudemian Ethics, On Virtues and Vices,* trans. H. Rackham (Cambridge, MA: Harvard University Press, 1967). To take one example (1250b43–1251a1): "To folly belongs bad judgement of affairs, bad counsel, bad fellowship, bad use of one's resources, false opinions about what is fine and good in life."

139. It is important to note, however, that in books 3–5 of the *Ethics,* Aristotle does not always represent the mean but sometimes offers an indeterminate range between qualities in its place.

140. John Furley, "The Purpose of Theophrastus's *Characters,*" *SO* 30, no. 1 (1953): 56–60, at 59n122. Lane Fox, "Theophrastus," 140. Aristotle opens the possibility for this kind of negative reading in his *Rhetoric* 2.17: "We have spoken of the characters associated with different ages and fortunes; the opposite characters to those described, for instance, of the poor, of the unfortunate, and of the weak, are obvious." In J. H. Freese's translation (Cambridge, MA.: Harvard University Press, 1926).

141. FHS&G 711; FHS&G 453.

142. FHS&G 711.

143. Arist. *Rh.* 1371b; Pl. *Resp.* 452d.

144. Lane Fox, "Theophrastus," 141.

145. Theophrastus, *Metaphysics,* 8b24–27.

146. See Jacques Desautels, "La classification des végétaux dans la *Recherche sur les plantes* de Théophraste d'Erésos," *Phoenix* 42 (1988): 219–244.

147. Theophr. *Hist. pl.* 1.1.

148. Theophr. *Hist. pl.* 1.1.

149. Andrea Wulf, "The Unsung Hero of Western Science," *The Atlantic,* June 7, 2016.

150. FHS&G 143.

151. Theophrastus, *On Stones,* ed. Earle R. Caley and John F. C. Richards (Columbus: Ohio State University Press, 1956), §13–14.

152. Theophrastus, *On Stones,* §10. I borrow the edition's translation of *logos* here, which, due to the context, seems to have been chosen instead of "reasoning" (as I use prior).

153. Theophrastus, *On Winds,* ed. Robert Mayhew (Leiden: Brill, 2017), 85. Mayhew here refers to sections 10, 18, and 24 of *On Winds.*

154. Theophrastus, "On Fish," ed. Robert W. Sharples, in *Theophrastus. His Psychological, Doxographical and Scientific Writings,* ed. William W. Fortenbaugh and Dimitri Gutas (New Brunswick: Routledge, 1992), 347–385, at 358.

155. Theophrastus, *On Winds,* 85.

156. Theophrastus, *On Weather Signs,* §36–37. In David Sider and Carl Wolfram Brunschön's translation (Leiden, Netherlands: Brill, 2006).

157. Theophrastus, *On Weather Signs,* §16.

158. My sincere thanks go to Sarah Magagna for this example.

159. William W. Fortenbaugh, "The *Characters* of Theophrastus, Behavioral Regularities and Aristotelian Vices," in *TS,* 131–145.

160. Giovanni Reale, *The Concept of First Philosophy and the Unity of the "Metaphysics" of Aristotle,* trans. John R. Catan (Albany, NY: SUNY Press, 1980), 364.

161. Luciana Repici, "Limits of Teleology in Theophrastus' *Metaphysics*?," *AGPh* 72 (1990): 182–213, at 182. See also Mor Segev, "The Teleological Significance of Dreaming in Aristotle," *OSAPh* 43 (2012): 107–141, at 119n33. For the previous approach, see James G. Lennox, *Aristotle's Philosophy of Biology: Studies in the Origins of Life Science* (Cambridge: Cambridge University Press, 2001), 259–279.

162. See Boris Henning, "The Four Causes," *JPh* 106 (2009): 137–160. For an overview, see Monte Ransome Johnson, *Aristotle on Teleology* (Oxford: Oxford University Press, 2005).

163. See Arist. *Ph.* 2.3 and *Metaph.* V.2.

164. Arist. *Ph.* 2.8. Here see Mohan Matthen, "Teleology in Living Things," in *A Companion to Aristotle,* ed. Georgios Anagnostopoulos (Oxford: Blackwell, 2009), 335–347.

165. See, for example, Arist. *De An.* 434a31–32; *Pol.* 1256b20–21. On this principle, see Pamela M. Huby, "What Did Aristotle Mean by 'Nature Does Nothing in Vain'?," in *Logical Foundations: Essays in Honor of D.J. Connor,* ed. Indira Mattingham and Brian Carr (New York: Palgrave Macmillan, 1991), 158–165.

166. Arist. *Part. An.* 663b27–29, as quoted in Segev, "The Teleological Significance of Dreaming," 119n33.

167. For a view that highlights Aristotle's understanding of how nature makes mistakes, see Jill Frank, "Citizens, Slaves, and Foreigners: Aristotle on Human Nature," *APSR* 98, no. 1 (2004): 91–104. See also *Phys.* 2.8.

168. Repici, "Limits of Teleology in Theophrastus' *Metaphysics*?," 201. See *Part. An.* 677a7.

169. Theophrastus, *Metaphysics,* 7a19–21.

170. Theophrastus, *Metaphysics,* 10b7–16. See Segev, "The Teleological Significance of Dreaming," 119n33, on how "Theophrastus' remarks are intentionally based on Aristotle's own paradigm cases."

171. Theophrastus, *Metaphysics,* 11b12–17. The importance of this term in Theophrastus's *Metaphysics* suggests a possible link with Theophrastus's innovations to Aristotle's modal logic: the logical system that deals with notions of what is possible (*dunaton*) and what is necessary (*anagkaios ananke*). On Theophras-

tus's logic, see Pamela M. Huby, *Theophrastus of Eresus: Commentary,* vol. 2, *Logic* (Leiden, Netherlands: Brill, 2007).

172. Theophr. *Hist. pl.* 1.5. I borrow the translation by Arthur Hort Bart (Cambridge, MA: Harvard University Press, 1916–1926).

173. Repici lays out three Aristotelian approaches to teleology: something has a purpose, something follows by coincidence from something else that has a purpose, or something is a pure coincidence, like a physiological phenomenon. The *Characters* could be explained by either the second or third option. See Repici, "Limits of Teleology in Theophrastus' *Metaphysics?*," 201.

174. Theophr. *Hist. pl.* 1.2.5–6; FHS&G 531. Here see C. O. Brink, "*Oikeiōsis* and *oikeiotēs*: Theophrastus and Zeno on Nature in Moral Theory," *Phronesis* 1 (1956): 123–145; Anthony A. Long, "Theophrastus and the Stoa," in *Theophrastus: Reappraising the Sources,* ed. Johannes Max van Ophuijsen and Marlein van Raalte (New Brunswick, NJ: Transaction, 1998), 355–383.

175. Another way of approaching this issue would be to suggest that there *are* purposes to the typical behaviors in the *Characters* but that we simply do not see them. As Aristotle puts it, "It is absurd to suppose that purpose is not present because we do not observe the agent deliberating." *Phys.* 199b26–27, trans. R. P. Hardie and R. K. Gaye, in *The Basic Works of Aristotle* (New York: Modern Library, 2001). But, as deliberation seems so far beyond these sketches, this seems less likely.

176. FHS&G 590. Cicero describes how Theophrastus's twenty-four books of *Laws* collected the statues of "almost all political societies not only of Greece but also of the non-Greek world." He created what Ierodiakonou calls, in her "Theophrastus," "a practical guide or an encyclopedia," equivalent to the encyclopedic treatise in which Theophrastus listed his 550 species of plants. As Ierodiakonou puts it, in his politics, "Theophrastus used the same research methods as in the other disciplines."

177. Arist. *Pol.* 1321a.

178. On the custom of generosity in ancient Greece, see Dover, *Greek Popular Morality,* 230–231.

179. *Pol.* 1311a13–14.

180. Theophr. *Char.* 26.4.

181. Theophr. *Char.* 26.5-6.

182. Theophr. *Char.* 26.3.

183. Theophr. *Char.* 7.5.

184. Lane Fox, "Theophrastus," 134. See also Rusten, introduction, 10–11. In Ebner-Landy and de Nicolay, "Theophrastus's Oligarch and the Political Intention of the *Characters,*" we consider how the intentions of this character sketch would change in relation to different plausible composition dates.

185. *Rh.* 1.8.

186. FHS&G 725.

187. Theophr. *Char.* 26.3.

188. Theophr. *Char.* 26.4.

189. On radical democracy in the period, see Bayliss, *After Demosthenes,* 53; Lane Fox, "Theophrastus," 131–132.

190. Theophr. *Char.* 26.4.

191. T. W. Adorno, Else Frenkel-Brunswik, Daniel J. Levinson, and R. Nevitt Sanford, *The Authoritarian Personality* (New York: Harper & Brothers, 1950), 644–652.

192. What then, one might ask, about sketches of figures that represent other kinds of rule: why, for example, is there no sketch of the tyrant? Here I have worked from the assumption that Theophrastus followed Aristotle's own focus on democracy and oligarchy in the middle books of the *Politics,* in which, at 1301b, Aristotle claims that these are "the two principal forms of government." Translated by Benjamin Jowett, in *The Basic Works of Aristotle* (New York: The Modern Library, 2001).

193. Pl. *Resp.* 561e.

194. Pl. *Resp.* 561e.

195. Dietrich Boschung argues that the boy's adolescence is an additional sign of transience and points the reader to a reference to a razor in the *Iliad* 10.172–174, in which the question of whether the Achaeans will live, or be ruined, stands "on a razor's edge." See his *"Kairos" as a Figuration of Time: A Case Study* (Munich: Wilhelm Fink, 2013), 25, 11, 20.

196. Boschung, *"Kairos" as a Figuration of Time,* 28.

197. *Ant. Plan.* 275. I lightly modify the translation by W. R. Paton (Cambridge, MA: Harvard University Press, 1918).

198. Boschung, *"Kairos" as a Figuration of Time,* 9.

199. The political importance of *kairos* is recognized in Plato's *Statesman* (esp. 307b1–9), the Platonic *Ep.* 7 (326a), in Aristotle (*Eth. Nic.* 1104a8–9), and by Demetrius of Phalerum, who wrote a work entitled *Peri kairou* (Diog. Laert. 5.81). For the religious afterlife of *kairos,* see François Hartog, "*Chronos*, *Kairos*, *Krisis*: The Genesis of Western Time," *H&T* 60 (2021): 425–439.

200. FSH&G 590.

201. See Fragment B, lines 74–81, in Keaney and Szegedy-Maszak, "Theophrastus's *De eligendis magistratibus,*" 231.

202. FHS&G 449a.

203. In an Aristotelian framework, he too would lack the ability to deliberate: a quality that for Aristotle relies on acute perception. See *Eth. Nic.* 1114a10; John M. Cooper, *Reason and Human Good in Aristotle* (Cambridge, MA: Harvard University Press, 1971), 43–45; Pavel Gregorić, *Aristotle on the Common Sense* (Oxford: Oxford University Press, 2007), 121–123.

204. Theophr. *Char.* 27.10.

205. Millett, *Theophrastus and His World,* 87.

206. Theophr. *Char.* 1.3.

207. Theophr. *Char.* 3.2–3.

208. Theophr. *Char.* 4.2–3.

209. Theophr. *Char.* 7.7.

210. Theophr. *Char.* 8.7.

211. Theophr. *Char.* 24.8.

212. Mor Segev, "Fanaticism and Aristotelian Excessive Fear of the Divine," in *Fanaticism and the History of Philosophy,* ed. Paul Katsafanas (Abingdon, UK: Routledge, 2023), 33n34. See P. J. Koets, Δεισιδαιμονία: *A Contribution to the*

Knowledge of the Religious Terminology in Greek (Purmerend, Netherlands: Muusses, 1929), 36.

213. Segev, "Fanaticism and Aristotelian Excessive Fear of the Divine," 29.

214. Theophr. *Char.* 27.2–3.

215. Pl. *Resp.* 401b, 607a, my emphasis.

216. *Poet.* 1450a23–5.

217. Martha Nussbaum, *The Fragility of Goodness: Luck and Ethics in Greek Tragedy and Philosophy,* 2nd ed. (Cambridge: Cambridge University Press, 2001), xiii.

218. Nussbaum, *The Fragility of Goodness,* 322.

219. Nussbaum, *The Fragility of Goodness,* 323; *Eth. Nic.* 1.4.

220. Frank, *Poetic Justice,* 30–31.

221. See FHS&G 462.

222. Pl. *Leg.* 7 (816d–17a) leaves room for a different approach, allowing for an ethics of ridicule and comedy. Here see Martina Di Stefano, "The *pathos* of Ridicule (*to geloion*) in Plato's Dialogues," in *The Dark Side: Philosophical Reflections on the "Negative Emotions,"* ed. Paola Giacomoni, Nicolò Valentini, and Sara Dellantonio (Cham, Switzerland: Springer, 2021), 49–63.

2. Moral Instruction by Bad Example: The Latin Translations

1. On the *fortuna* of the Peripatetics, see David John Furley, "Peripatetic School," in *Oxford Classical Dictionary* (Oxford: Oxford University Press, 2016).

2. For Lyco's Drunkard, see Rutilius Lupus 2.7. For Aristo's Arrogant Man, see Phld. *On Vices,* book 10. For Satyrus, see Ath. 4.168c. For scholarship comparing Aristo's and Theophrastus's methods of character-writing in relation to one sketch, see Leopold Schmidt, *Commentatio de* εἴρωνος *notione apud Aristonem et Theophrastum* (Marburg, Germany, 1873); Graziano Ranocchia, "Natura e fine dei *Caratteri* di Teofrasto: Storia di un enigma," *Philologus* 155 (2011): 69–91.

3. Theoph. *Char.* 14.1. On the spurious nature of the definitions, see Friedrich Hanow, "De Theophrasti *characterum* libello commentatio philologica" (PhD diss., University of Bonn, 1858); Theodor Gomperz, *Über die "Charaktere" Theophrast's* (Vienna, 1889); Markus Stein, *Definition und Schilderung in den Theophrasts "Charaktaren"* (Stuttgart: Teubner, 1992).

4. See, respectively, Eiko Kondo, "I *caratteri* di Teofrasto nei papiri ercolanesi," *Cronache ercolanesi* 1 (1971): 73–86; M. Gronewald, "P.Hamb.143=Theophrastus, characters 7 and 8," *ZPE* 35 (1979): 21–22.

5. P.Oxy 699.

6. See Harry Caplan's account—in his edition of *Rhetorica ad Herennium* (Cambridge, MA: Harvard University Press, 1954), 387—of how far Roman comedy and oratory were inspired by character-writing.

7. Marc Fumaroli, *L'âge de l'éloquence*: *Rhetorique et "res literaria" de la Renaissance au seuil de l'époque classique* (Geneva: Droz, 2008), 381–382n395. On the differences between *ethopoeia, prosopographia,* and *prosopopeia,* see the entries in Henri Morier, *Dictionnaire de poétique et de rhétorique* (Paris: PUF, 1961), which presents *ethopoeia* as focused on a "moral portrait," *prosopographia* on the description of "physical appearances," and *prosopopoeia* on making an

"absent person" speak. See also Eugenio Amato and Jacques Schamp, eds., *"Ethopoiia": La représentation de caractères entre fiction scolaire et réalité vivante à l'époque impériale et tardive* (Salerno, Italy: Helios, 2005).

8. Jeffrey Rusten, introduction to *Characters,* in *Theophrastus "Characters," Herodas "Mimes," Sophron and Other Mime Fragments*, ed. and trans. Jeffrey Rusten and I. C. Cunningham, (Cambridge MA: Harvard University Press, 2002), 5–39, at 20.

9. For a fuller account of both the papyrus and manuscript transmission, see James Diggle, introduction to *Theophrastus: "Characters,"* ed. James Diggle (Cambridge: Cambridge University Press, 2004), 1–57, at 37–51. On the medieval manuscripts, see Charles B. Schmitt, "Theophrastus in the Middle Ages," *Viator* 2 (1971): 251–270; N. G. Wilson, "The Manuscripts of Theophrastus," *Scriptorium* 16 (1962): 96–102.

10. *Eustathii Archiepiscopi Thessalonicensis: Commentarii ad Homeri "Iliadem" Pertinentes,* ed. Marchinus van der Valk (Leiden, Netherlands: Brill, 1979), 3:469. Said in relation to Hom. *Il.* 13.276–287. Eustathius can easily be read here as comparing the two passages in terms of their form, as opposed to their content. This would resolve a difficulty for which N. G. Wilson hazards many explanations. See N. G. Wilson, *Scholars of Byzantium* (London: Duckworth, 1983), 200–201, and "The Manuscripts of Theophrastus," 99. I am grateful to Jeanne Capelle for her reading of this passage.

11. Tzetz. *Chil.* 9.941.

12. Here see Wilson, *Scholars of Byzantium,* 235.

13. Theophrastus, *Characters,* ed. Diggle, 161. Peter Steinmetz proposes that it was written in the fifth century CE, in *Theophrast: "Charaktere"* (Munich: Max Hueber, 1960), 1:55. Tzetzes refers to the Proem, making the twelfth century an upper bound. Karl Gottlieb Sonntag is often credited with proving the spurious nature of the Proem in his *Dissertatio,* but indications of this suspicion can be found as early as Leonhard Lycius's Leipzig edition of 1561, as I describe in the following.

14. Theophr. *Char.* 0.1. There are very few changes (and no substantive) to the Greek Proem over its history, and I therefore work from Rusten's modern edition. My English translation of the Proem borrows from Theophrastus, *Characters,* ed. Rusten, 49, and Theophrastus, *Characters,* ed. Diggle, 63.

15. Theophr. *Char.* 0.2.

16. Theophr. *Char.* 0.2.

17. Theophr. *Char.* 0.2.

18. Theophr. *Char.* 0.2.

19. Theophrastus, *Characters,* ed. Diggle, 161.

20. Theophr. *Char.* 3.5.

21. Between the ninth and eleventh centuries, the archetype of the medieval manuscripts, containing all thirty sketches, was divided into two halves, separating Characters 1–15 from 16–30, though the latter half was significantly less influential. From the thirteenth through fifteenth centuries, sixty-eight further manuscripts were produced. Here see Diggle, introduction, 38–39. Why the Proem did not also encourage the compilers of the medieval manuscripts to change the rhetorical classification of the text remains a mystery.

22. In French sixteenth-century theater, character sketches of types such as "the provincial" and the "old man in love" can be found in the Parisian farce *Femmes qui apprennent à parler latin* (c. 1515) and in *L'avare cornu* (Lyon, 1580). Across Reformation Germany, Austria, and Switzerland, there were translations and performances of Plautus, Terence, and Aristophanes; farces with stock characters including peasants; and a tradition of carnival drama with an interest in describing comic events from daily life. The Italian drama brought together translations of ancient comedy with the commedia tradition. See Jelle Koopmans, ed., *Le recueil de Florence: 53 farces imprimées à Paris vers 1515* (Orléans, France: Éditions Paradigme, 2011), chap. 17; Mariangela Miotti, Jean Balsamo, Charles Mazouer, Anna Bettoni, Nerina Clerici Balmas, Concetta Cavallini, and Eugenio Refini, eds., *La comédie à l'époque d'Henri III (1580–1589)* (Florence: Leo S. Olschki, 2017), 2–113; John Alexander, "Early Modern German Drama," in *Early Modern German Literature, 1350–1700*, ed. Max Reinhart (Rochester, NY: Boydell & Brewer, 2007), 357–394; T. F. Earle and Catarina Fouto, eds., *The Reinvention of Theatre in Sixteenth-Century Europe: Traditions, Texts and Performance* (Abingdon, UK: Routledge, 2015), chaps. 6 and 9.

23. "Inde praela fervere coeperunt ab opusculo quod Theophrastus Eresius, cum ad incultos et male dolatos mores instituendos, averruncandam e mentibus amentiam, tum ad virtutum et vitiorum indagandas naturas ʼΗΘΙΚΟΥΣ ΧΑΡΑΚΤΗΡΑΣ, quasi τῶν ἠθῶν εἰχονισμοὺς inscripsit," Pierre Matthieu, "Praefatio ad lectorem," in *Theophrasti notationes morum,* ed. and trans. Isaac Casaubon (Lyon, 1599), ā7r–ē2v, at ā7v–ā8r. The editions that preceded this are Johannes Gremper, ed., and Lapo da Castiglionchio, trans., *De Caracteribus, sive Notis libellus aureus* (Vienna, 1517); Willibald Pirckheimer, ed. and trans., Θεοφράστου χαρακτῆρες (Nuremberg, 1527); Θεοφράστου χαρακτῆρες: *Cum interpretatione latina* (Basel, 1531); Joannes Oporinus, ed., *Theophrasti* [. . .] *Opera* (Basel, 1541); Giambattista de Camozzi, ed., *Theophrasti historiam de plantis* [. . .] *et quosdam alios ipsius libros continens tomus VI* (Venice, 1552); Henri Estienne, ed., *Aristotelis et Theophrasti scripta quaedam* (Paris, 1557); Leonhard Lycius, ed. and trans., *Libellus Theophrasti continens notas atque descriptiones morum* (Leipzig, 1561); Claude Auberi, trans., "Theophrasti item Eressii Morum Characteres," in *Aristotelis Ethicorum Nicomachiorum libri decem,* ed. and trans. Denis Lambin (Basel, 1582), 2M1r–2N5v; Frédéric Morel, ed. and trans., *Theophrasti de notis morum liber* (Paris, 1583); Friedrich Sylburg, ed. and trans., *Aristotelis Ethicorum magnorum libri 2* [. . .] *Theophrasti Characteres Ethici* (Frankfurt, 1584); *Thesaurus philosophiae moralis quo continentur* [. . .] *Theophrasti Characteres* (Geneva, 1589); Isaac Casaubon, ed. and trans., *Theophrasti characteres ethici* (Lyon, 1592). I exclude from this list the many editions of Stobaeus's *Sententiae,* which contained a few Theophrastan figures.

24. Benjamin Boyce, *The Theophrastan Character in England to 1642* (Cambridge, MA: Harvard University Press, 1947), 16, 44, 53–54; J. W. Smeed, *The Theophrastan "Character": The History of a Literary Genre* (Oxford: Clarendon Press, 1985), 1–46.

25. Diggle, introduction, 52–54.

26. Donald Beecher, ed., *Characters: A Jacobean Miscellany* (Ottawa, Canada: Dovehouse, 2002), 33; Richard Squibbs, *Urban Enlightenment and the Eighteenth-*

Century Periodical Essay: Transatlantic Retrospects (London: Palgrave Macmillan, 2014), 201n12.

27. Daniel Furlanus and Adrien Turnèbe, eds. and trans., *Theophrasti Eresii Peripateticorum post Aristotelem principis pleraque antehac Latine nunquam, nunc Graece et Latine simul edita* (Hanover, 1605). On the reception of Theophrastus's other works, see Robert W. Sharples, "Some Medieval and Renaissance Citations of Theophrastus," *JWCI* 47 (1984): 186–190.

28. See David A. Lines, "Aristotle's *Ethics* in the Renaissance," in *The Reception of Aristotle's "Ethics,"* ed. Jon Miller (Cambridge: Cambridge University Press, 2012), 171–193.

29. For this manuscript date, see Charles B. Schmitt, "Theophrastus," in *"Catalogus translationum et commentariorum": Mediaeval and Renaissance Latin Translations and Commentaries,* ed. Paul Oskar Kristeller and F. Edward Kranz (Washington, DC: Catholic University of America Press, 1971), 2:239–322, 246. An earlier date of 1430 is given by Karl Müllner, "Zur humanistischen Übersetzungsliteratur: Fortsetzung," *Wiener Studien* 24 (1902): 216–230, 216–217. See Schmitt for the *Characters*' transmission to Italy. He notes that before Lapo's translation, one manuscript was in the possession of the Florentine humanist Antonio Corbinelli. Lapo's translation survives in a number of manuscripts, which predate the printed edition, including MS Vienna, Nationalbibliothek, cod. 199, ff. 4r–16v.

30. In line with the understanding of an *editio princeps* elaborated by Paul F. Grendler in his "Printing and Censorship," in *The Cambridge History of Renaissance Philosophy,* ed. Charles B. Schmitt, Quentin Skinner, Eckhard Kessler, and Jill Kraye (Cambridge: Cambridge University Press, 1988), 25–54, at 35n6. This edition's influence lies in how Lapo's translation served as the basis for two further sixteenth-century Latin translations in 1531 and 1583 (even if, in both cases, the editors mistook it for a translation by Angelo Poliziano). On the mistaken date, see Diggle, introduction, 52; Sonia Pertsinidis, *Theophrastus's "Characters": A New Introduction* (London: Routledge, 2018), 37; Jeffrey Ashcroft, *Albrecht Dürer: Documentary Biography* (New Haven, CT: Yale University Press, 2017), 2:828.

31. On Gremper's life see *MRFH* 0850 and Hans von Ankwiez, "Magister Johannes Gremper aus Rheinfelden: Ein Wiener Humanist und Bibliophile des XVI. Jahrhunderts," *ZBB* (1913): 197–216.

32. On Burgo see Michael J. Levin, *Agents of Empire: Spanish Ambassadors in Sixteenth-Century Italy* (Ithaca, NY: Cornell University Press, 2005), 47.

33. See Benedict Einarson, "The Manuscripts of Theophrastus's *Historia plantarum,*" *CPh* 71 (1976): 67–76.

34. "Sophorum Theophrastus ille Graium / Splendor, delitiaeque Palliati / Dulces eloquii, Latinitatis / Gaudens munere, prodit hic togatus / Nuper qui tenebris latens ab ipso est / Gremperi manibus revulsus orco, / Iam quamvis peregrinus, in Quirini / Sicut natus et institutus urbe, / Ipsi disserit invidenda Tullo"; "Ut quo iam virideis docente plantas / Recte conserimusque discimusque, / Hoc autore, animo nocens Lupinum, / Et foetus Lolii, piam prementeis / Virtutum segetem, graveisque Lappas, / Noscentes, celeri eruamus arte," Gremper, *De Caracteribus,* A1r.

35. Theophr. *Hist. pl.* 3.2, 8.7.

36. "Hunc ergo lege, quisquis es libellum, / Et fructus, novitas, stilus, placebit," Gremper, *De Caracteribus,* A1r.

37. I borrow this phrase from Richard Tuck, *Philosophy and Government, 1572–1651* (Cambridge: Cambridge University Press, 1993), 62. Tuck describes this being a feature of the "new humanism" of the mid-sixteenth century, one that combines influences from Stoicism, skepticism, and Tacitism. I come back to this later in the chapter.

38. "Quem cum ab auctore Graeco Peripateticorum eloquentissimo in nonagesimonono aetatis suae anno conscriptum, multoque rerum usu et experientia natum invenissem, mox dignum magnificentia tua opus existimavi. Cum enim sis vir in variis rebus expertissimus [. . .] tui statim sum admonitus," Gremper, *De Caracteribus,* A1v–A2r.

39. "Franciscum Patavinum, summi pontificis Cubicularium," Gremper, *De Caracteribus,* A2v. I thank Christopher Celenza for this indication. On dal Legname, see Alfred A. Strnad, "Dal Legname, Francesco," in *Dizionario biografico degli Italiani* (Rome: Instituto dell'Enciclopedia Italiana, 1986), 32:92–96, 93; Matteo Melchiorre, "L'afetto di Eugenio IV: Riforma e anatomia di un capitolo cattedrale (Padova, 1430–1439)," *RSCI* 65, no. 2 (2011): 471–512, at 474n12. Strnad's biography would date Lapo's translation to 1436. On Lapo and the Papal Curia, see Christopher Celenza, *Renaissance Humanism and the Papal Curia: Lapo da Castiglionchio the Younger's "De curiae commodis"* (Ann Arbor: University of Michigan Press, 1999).

40. "Tum quae ad regendam gubernandamque rempublicam ad administrandam rem domesticam spectant, et de educandis liberis, de sedandis cupiditatibus, instruendisque hominum moribus traduntur, et melius illi et copiosius prosecuti sunt quam nos," Gremper, *De Caracteribus,* A3r.

41. "Hunc igitur [*sc.* libellum] ille clarissimus philosophus de caracteribus nuncupavit," Gremper, *De Caracteribus,* A3v.

42. "In quo permulta colliguntur ab eo vicia, ac ita varie ac distincte ita urbane eleganterque exprimuntur, ut facile in eo Aristotelicae disciplinae (cuius sectator fuit) lumen appareat. Quare (ni forte contempseris) opinor te ex eo permultum utilitatis posse percipere; quod [*recte* quid] enim utilius aut accomodatius esse queat ei, qui amplissimis rebus, ut tu, administrandis praesit, et in eis cupiat cum dignitate versari, quam tenere signa quaedam et notas quibus animos hominum, varias multiplicesque naturas diiudicare possit, eisque suo consilio prudentiaque moderari?" Gremper, *De Caracteribus,* A3v.

43. In this edition, the *Nicomachean Ethics* and the *Characters* are brought even closer together by the editor choosing to respectively title the two works *De Moribus* and *Morum Characteres.* See Auberi, *Aristotelis Ethicorum Nicomachiorum,* a1r, title page.

44. In the sixteenth century, Cebes's *Table* was thought to have been written by Socrates's disciple Cebes. This text attracted Pirckheimer, too, with him providing the first German translation. See Reinhart Schleier, *"Tabula Cebetis": Studien zur Rezeption einer antiken Bildbeschreibung im 16 und 17 Jahrhundert* (Berlin: Mann, 1973). See also David A. Lines and Jill Kraye, "Sources for Ethics in the Renaissance: The Expanding Canon," in *Rethinking Virtue, Reforming Society:*

New Directions in Renaissance Ethics, c. 1350–c. 1650, ed. Sabrina Ebbersmeyer and David A. Lines (Turnhout, Belgium: Brepols, 2013), 29–56, 47–50.

45. "Suffurare igitur Laurenti tuis occupationibus ociolum aliquod (si potes) quod libelli huius lectioni impertias," *Epicteti Stoici Enchiridion, e Graeco interpretatum ab Angelo Politiano* (Paris, 1545), A2v. First published in 1497.

46. "Ut enim nec aliqua in arte excellere quis posset cui sit instrumentorum, quibus indigeat, usus incognitus, sic nec ab eo qui velit princeps inter homines esse, quicquam utiliter, aut magna laude dignum geri potest, qui non homines ipsos, quibus veluti instrumentis ad res gerendas utitur optime penitusque perspexerit," Gremper, *De Caracteribus,* A3v.

47. "Haec ex hoc libello probe colligi possunt," Gremper, *De Caracteribus,* A3v.

48. On the idea of the sixteenth-century "moral code as an economy of everyday life in interpersonal relationships," see Amedeo Quondam, *Forma del vivere: L'etica del gentiluomo e i moralisti italiani* (Bologna: Il Mulino, 2010), 23. Quondam, when listing the kinds of texts that provided this kind of moral instruction, does not mention characters. Here see *Forma del vivere,* 58.

49. Stephen Greenblatt, *Renaissance Self-Fashioning: From More to Shakespeare* (Chicago: University of Chicago Press, 1980), 2. Though contrary to Greenblatt's account of Renaissance self-fashioning, which shows writers concerned with balancing the demands of inwardness with those of self-presentation, these translators of Theophrastus's *Characters* were interested in instructing behavior alone. For them, as your actions indicate who you are, it is possible that by changing your actions, you can change yourself.

50. The Greek manuscript sent by Pico is "not identifiable," as noted by Diggle, introduction, 52.

51. "Salve. En tibi Theophrasti characteres exscriptos Graece. Relue iam debitum ex tua ephemeride," Gianfrancesco to Pirckheimer, September 8, 1515, in *V. illustris Bilibaldi Pirckheimeri,* ed. Melchior Goldast (Frankfurt, 1610), S4v. On Pirckheimer and Gianfrancesco's conversation over the draft, see Charles B. Schmitt, *Gianfrancesco Pico della Mirandola (1469–1533) and His Critique of Aristotle* (The Hague: Martinus Nijhoff, 1967), 194; *Willibald Pirckheimers Briefwechsel,* ed. Emil Reicke (Munich: Emil Reicke, 1940), 2:564–566. More broadly see Gian Mario Cao, "Pico della Mirandola Goes to Germany: With an Edition of Gianfrancesco Pico's 'De reformandis moribus oratio,'" *Annali dell'Istituto storico italo-germanico in Trento* 30 (2004): 463–525. I am grateful to Cao for his caution on overinterpreting the debt (personal correspondence).

52. See Corine Schleif, "Albrecht Dürer between Agnes Frey and Willibald Pirckheimer," in *The Essential Durer,* ed. Larry Silver and Jeffrey Chipps Smith (Philadelphia: University of Pennsylvania Press, 2010), 185–205, at 185.

53. Adam Smyth, "It Looks Nothing Like Me," *London Review of Books* 40, no. 13 (2018).

54. For the development of their relationship, see Marcel Brion, *Dürer: L'homme et son œuvre* (Paris: Somogy, 1960). For the two letters, see Hans Rupprich, ed., *Dürer: Schriftlicher Nachlass* (Berlin: Deutscher Verlag Für Kunstwissenschaft, 1956–1969), 1:43, 1:283–288.

55. This phrase is translated by Christopher S. Wood as "with a cock up the ass," in "This Strange Speech," *London Review of Books* 35, no. 14 (2013). For a

study of homosexuality in Dürer's art, see Bradley J. Cavallo, "Albrecht Dürer's *The Men's Bathhouse* of 1496–1497: Problems of Sexual Signification," *Journal for Early Modern Cultural Studies* 16, no. 4 (2016): 9–37.

56. Ashcroft, *Documentary,* 2:1177.

57. Despite several mentions of the dedication, for example, in Paul W. Eckert and Christoph von Imhoff's *Willibald Pirckheimer: Dürers Freund im Spiegel seines Lebens seiner Werke und seiner Umwelt* (Cologne: Wienand Verlag, 1971), there is no close investigation of its intention or textual detail.

58. Pirckheimer, *Characteres,* a1v–a2v. All citations of this text in Ashcroft's translation, *Documentary,* 2:827–828.

59. "humanas affectiones," Pirckheimer, *Characteres,* a1v.

60. "Quae quidem [*sc.* affectiones] legibus et institutione aliquantisper refrenatae, diutissime tamen aliquando se occulere solent, et non nisi data oportunitate ex altissimis cordium erumpere recessibus, ac si tum primum oriantur, et non potius legalis illius paedagogi timore, iam pridem constrictae delituerint, quo e medio sublato, tum demum palam in lucem prodire, et manifeste se ostendere audent," Pirckheimer, *Characteres,* a1v.

61. "Quod quidem verissimum esse, vel praesentia tempora prae caeteris declarant, quibus nimia libertas, nimium etiam procreat contemptum," Pirckheimer, *Characteres,* a1v.

62. "ita ut licet passim veritas praedicetur, nil minus tamen interim quam quod illa exigit peragitur, perinde ac regnum Dei in verbis potius nudis, quam operibus consistat peragendis," Pirckheimer, *Characteres,* a1v. Note that a later 1610 edition, by Melchior Goldast, deliberately added a "si" into the sentence.

63. Ashcroft, *Documentary,* 2:828.

64. Martin Luther, "Two Kinds of Righteousness," trans. Lowell J. Satre, in *Luther's Works,* ed. Harold J. Grimm (Philadelphia: Fortress Press, 1957), 31:293–306, at 299.

65. For differences on free will, see the letter from Pickheimer to Erasmus, about Luther, sent in March 1522, in *The Correspondence of Erasmus: Letters 1252 to 1355, 1522 to 1523,* trans. R. A. B. Mynors (Toronto: University of Toronto Press, 1989), 43. For differences on the Eucharist, see Erika Rummel, *The Confessionalization of Humanism in Reformation Germany* (Oxford: Oxford University Press, 2000), 97–101; on linking Lutheranism and radicalism, see Jeanne Peiffer, "Willibald Pirckheimer," in *"Centuriae Latinae" II: Cent une figures humanistes de la Renaissance aux Lumières,* ed. Colette Nativel (Geneva: Droz, 2006), 681–682.

66. Ashcroft, *Documentary,* 2:828.

67. Ashcroft, *Documentary,* 2:932.

68. Ashcroft, *Documentary,* 2:933.

69. For the causes of the Peasants' War and the contemporary perception that there was a relationship between Lutheranism and the rebellion, see Tom Scott, "The Peasants' War: A Historiographical Review," *The Historical Journal* 22, no. 3 (1979): 693–720; Thomas F. Sea, "Imperial Cities and the Peasants' War in Germany," *Central European History* 12, no. 1 (1979): 3–37.

70. Martin Luther, "Against the Robbing and Murdering Hordes of Peasants," in *Martin Luther: Documents of Modern History,* ed. E. G. Rupp and Benjamin

Drewery (London: Edward Arnold, 1970), 121–125, at 122; Friedrich Engels, *The Peasant War in Germany,* trans. Moissaye J. Olgin (Abingdon: Routledge, 2015), 48.

71. "Proinde quum omnes adeo teneri simus, ut nemo vitia sua libenter reprehendere audiat," Pirckheimer, *Characteres,* a1v.

72. "nihil utilius censeo, quam eos relegere libellos. . . . Ex quibus hunc vel praestantissimum iudico," Pirckheimer, *Characteres,* a1v–a2r.

73. "ita acri perlutus aceto, festivissime circa praecordia ludit," Pirckheimer, *Characteres,* a2r. In line with Pirckheimer's classicism, there is no contrast between moral instruction and delight. There is a similarity here with *Pers.* 1.116–118 (my emphasis): "omne vafer vitium ridenti Flaccus amico tangit et admissus *circum praecordia ludit,* callidus excusso populum suspendere naso." On this tag, see Phillips Salman, "Instruction and Delight in Medieval and Renaissance Criticism," *RenQ* 32, no. 3 (1979): 303–332.

74. Melchior Goldast, "Theophrasti characteres," in *V. illustris Bilibaldi Pirckheimeri* (Frankfurt, 1610), S4v–T1v.

75. "in quibus unusquisque proprii animi habitum tanquam in speculo quodam contemplari, ac contemplando emendare potest," Pirckheimer, *Characteres,* a1v–a2r.

76. For the sixteenth-century context of understanding mirrors as a kind of self-correction, see Paul Budra, *A Mirror for Magistrates and the De Casibus Tradition* (Toronto: University of Toronto Press, 2000).

77. To be sure, for Pirckheimer, and for the many other Renaissance readers considered in this chapter, Plato, Aristotle, and Theophrastus were aligned in many aspects of their philosophy, above all their ethics, which prioritized the cultivation of moral virtue. My attempt here is to highlight the differences in their aesthetics.

78. On the similar exemplarity of failure in female life-writing, see Martin Thompson, "Early Modern Exemplars: Reading Strategies in the Life-Writing of Mary Ward, Dionys Fitzherbert and Elizabeth Isham," *Sillages Critiques* 34 (2023).

79. Gerald Strauss, *Luther's House of Learning: Indoctrination of the Young in the German Reformation* (Baltimore: Johns Hopkins University Press, 1978), 135. For further comment on how it was "the unravelling of order in the early events of the Reformation" that provoked this urgency, see Gerald Strauss, "The Reformation and Its Public in an Age of Orthodoxy," in *The German People and the Reformation,* ed. R. Po-Chia Hsia (Ithaca, NY: Cornell University Press, 1988), 194–214, at 195; see also 201.

80. Martin Luther, "The Bondage of the Will," trans. Phillip S. Watson and Benjamin Drewery, in *Luther's Works,* ed. Philip S. Watson (Philadelphia: Fortress Press, 1972), 33:3–295, at 275. For Luther's ambitions to improve public morality, see Strauss, "The Reformation and Its Public in an Age of Orthodoxy," 198–201.

81. Strauss, *Luther's House of Learning,* 137. On printing and the Reformation, see Andrew Pettegree, *Brand Luther: 1517, Printing, and the Making of the Reformation* (New York: Penguin, 2015), chap. 6. For the many other forms moral indoctrination took, from drama to sermons and singing, see Pettegree, *Ref-*

ormation and the Culture of Persuasion (Cambridge: Cambridge University Press, 2005).

82. Strauss, *Luther's House of Learning,* 137, in reference to Simon Schaidenreisser's translation of *The Odyssey* (Augsburg, 1538).

83. Strauss, *Luther's House of Learning,* 149.

84. Strauss, *Luther's House of Learning,* 150.

85. I refer here to editions printed in Basel (1531, 1541, 1551, 1582), Antwerp (1551), Geneva (1557, 1589), Frankfurt (1584), and Lyon (1592, 1599). The first exception is the 1552 edition published in Venice by Giambattista de Camozzi, where Characters 16–23 were published for the first time. The second is the 1583 edition published in Paris by Frédéric Morel, considered in more detail in the following.

86. Here see Quentin Skinner, *The Foundations of Modern Political Thought* (Cambridge: Cambridge University Press, 2004), 2:29–30.

87. "tibi . . . dono dare constitui . . . quoniam pingendi arte admodum praecellis, cerneres etiam quam affabre senex ille et sapiens Theophrastus humanas affectiones depingere novisset," Pirckheimer, *Characteres,* a1r. Here I lightly modify Ashcroft's translation.

88. "si illam penicillo imitari nequis, mente saltem diligenter revolve," Pirckheimer, *Characteres,* a2v.

89. On the idea of accompanying images, see Patrizia Castelli, "'Theophrastus humanas affectiones depingere novisset.' La crisi della teoria delle proporzioni: fisiognomica, caratteri, affetti," *Critica letteraria* 117 (2017): 687–719, at 715.

90. The illustrations can be found reprinted in the edition by George Boas, *The Hieroglyphics of Horapollo* (New York: Pantheon Books, 1950).

91. A. Hyatt Mayor, *Prints and People: A Social History of Printed Pictures* (New York: Metropolitan Museum of Art, 1971), 14–18.

92. Albrecht Dürer, "Discourse on Aesthetics," in Ashcroft, *Documentary,* 2:872–884, at 877. Note Dürer's advice that "the character type (*art*) is consistent through the whole body, in all images, whether that type is harder or softer, fleshy or skinny" and that "it is proper for any image to be of one and the same type throughout."

93. On the relationship between this principle and the "Discourse on Aesthetics," see Jeffrey Ashcroft, "Art in German: Artistic Statements by Albrecht Dürer," *Forum for Modern Language Studies* 48, no. 4 (2012): 376–387, at 383.

94. Dürer, "Four Books on Human Proportion," in Ashcroft, *Documentary,* 2:878.

95. See Robert Scribner, *For the Sake of Simple Folk: Popular Propaganda for the German Reformation* (Cambridge: Cambridge University Press, 1981), on the political potential of images in the Reformation, in particular on how the woodcut was a chief form of propaganda. While I acknowledge Pettegree's recent questioning of how far the woodcut truly was a "popular medium of communication," my claim here is only that Pirckheimer might have thought this to be the case. See Pettegree, *Reformation and the Culture of Persuasion,* 102, and chap. 5 more generally.

96. Christiane Andersson, "The Censorship of Images in Nuremberg 1521–1527," in *Dürer and His Culture,* ed. Dagmar Eichberger and Charles Zika (Cambridge: Cambridge University Press, 1998), 164–178, at 165.

97. Ashcroft, *Documentary,* 1:375. This, as Ashcroft here notes, "anticipates Martin Luther's view of art as adiaphora, neither inherently good nor bad."

98. Ashcroft, *Documentary,* 2:867. On this see Joseph Leo Koerner, *The Reformation of the Image* (Chicago: University of Chicago Press, 2003).

99. Pirckheimer to Johann Tschertte, Nuremberg, October–December 1530, in Ashcroft, *Documentary,* 2:930–939, at 933.

100. "Ex vitio alterius sapiens emendat suum," Lycius, *Libellus Theophrasti,* A1r.

101. "Non enim dubium est, quin optime de Republica mereantur, quicunque ad erudiendam doctrina atque optimarum artium studiis pueritiam aliquid operae, studii, diligentiae, laboris, conferunt: cum liberi non solum parentibus, sed etiam patriae suscipiantur et educentur," Lycius, *Libellus Theophrasti,* A2r–v.

102. "neimini dubium esse potest, quin ad officium civium universorum maximopere hoc pertineat, ut ad ludos literarios, tanquam ad seminaria quaedam virorum praestantium et salutarium communitati hominum, singuli respectum habeant, et pro se quisque etiam atque etiam diligenter curet, ut et sui et aliorum liberi optimis institutionibus a pueris erudiantur," Lycius, *Libellus Theophrasti,* A2v.

103. "Quis enim non intelligit, quantum exempla valeant, et ad declarandum ea de quibus praecipitur, et ad afferendum motus auditoribus atque discipulis," Lycius, *Libellus Theophrasti,* A4r.

104. "et non illa quidem tantum exempla, quae rerum gestarum autoritate nituntur, sed etiam, quae, ut patent latius, ita vim non minorem habent, εἰκόνες et χαρακτῆρες earum praesertim rerum, quae res vulgo turpiter ac nequiter fieri solent, cuiusmodi in hoc libello tanquam in tabula expressae discentibus proponuntur"; "quid ad imbuendum teneros puerorum animos bonis opinionibus et honestis moribus accommodatius aut utilius?" Lycius, *Libellus Theophrasti,* A4r.

105. "Fieri enim mirabili quadam et divina mentis praescriptione consuevit, ut vitiositatis turpitudine conspecta, virtutis et honestatis ratio non modo melius intelligatur, sed ut animi etiam et voluntates ab illa alienatae, huic arctius adiungantur, et pluris hanc facere incipiant," Lycius, *Libellus Theophrasti,* A4r–v.

106. Mathias Roick, "Ethics and Social Relations," in *A Cultural History of Ideas in the Renaissance,* ed. Jill Kraye (London: Bloomsbury, 2023), chap. 3, 69. On emblem books, see John Manning, *The Emblem* (London: Reaktion Books, 2002); Peter M. Daly, ed., *Companion to Emblem Studies* (Brooklyn: AMS Press, 2008).

107. "Quam liberalis doctrinae rationem commendans Clemens Alexandrinus . . . in paedagogo suo, ubi docet, 'τὰς εἰκόνας καὶ τὰ ὑποδείγματα μέγιστον μέρος τῆς ὀρθῆς εἶναι παιδείας,'" Lycius, *Libellus Theophrasti,* A4v.

108. "utitur notissimo Lacedaemoniorum exemplo, qui cum institutionem puerilem magnae sibi curae esse paterentur, hanc illius esse partem quandam voluere, cum liberos ducerent ad spectandum servulos, qui vino se, iussu dominorum obruissent, ut conspecta ebrietatis deformitate, vitii huius odio imbuerentur, et magis continenter ac sobrie viverent," Lycius, *Libellus Theophrasti,* A4v.

109. On how instructing good customs worked to link the *studia humanitatis* with classical *paideia,* see Quondam, *Forma del vivere,* 40–42. Quondam quotes a passage from the 1528 *The Book of the Courtier* IV.3.16, which seems of partic-

ular relevance: "Good masters not only teach children their letters but also polite manners and correct bearing in eating, drinking, speaking and walking." In George Bull's translation (London: Penguin, 1976).

110. "Visum autem mihi est, libellum hunc ab autore vel Theophrasto, vel alio quopiam studiis puerilibus dedicatum . . . denuo conciliare ingenuis pueris, et tibi quidem Gottfride carissime in primis," Lycius, *Libellus Theophrasti,* A5v.

111. "Fieri potest ut sit Polyclis eius ad quem hunc libellum scripserat Theophrastus," Morel, *De notis,* c3v.

112. "At enim est, o Theophraste, difficile ab eiusmodi notarum labe puros, atque ab ea quae illis coniuncta est vitiositate castos, in hac quidem mortali vita conspicere," Morel, *De notis,* c3v.

113. "Aut igitur nos tibi obtemperantes hominum adspectum lucemque vitare oportet: aut, in sermonum et actionum communicatione, memoriam uniuscuiusque imitando tenere. Verum hac quidem ratione sequitur vitiorum examen, et alienatio a virtute: Illos autem inhumanitas et immane Timonis crimen comitabitur. Itaque facile non est hac in re quod melius est eligere: siquidem gravis est utrinque lapsus," Morel, *De notis,* c3v–c4r.

114. "Hexastichum apologeticum Theophrasti nomine," Morel, *De notis,* c4r.

115. "Praefatus monui quae te meminisse necesse est, / Has vitii iuvenes posse juuare Notas: / Profuit ut quondam pueris Lacedaemone natis / Ilotas madidos saepe videre mero. / Lumina nec vitare hominum, sed crimina quaevis / Consulo: non Timon sic eris, at sapies," Morel, *De notis,* c4r.

116. I discuss the relationship between contagion and social categorization in chapter 6 in my consideration of Hume.

117. "Risores valeant nulla gravitate dicaces: / Incolumis gravitas Lesbia mixta jocis," Morel, *De notis,* c4r.

118. Here see Anthony Grafton and Joanna Weinberg, *"I Have Always Loved the Holy Tongue": Isaac Casaubon, the Jews and a Forgotten Chapter in Renaissance Scholarship* (Cambridge, MA: Harvard University Press, 2011), 15.

119. Richard Calis, "Two Editors and Their Theophrastus," *JHI Blog,* October 12, 2015, https://jhiblog.org/2015/10/12/two-editors-and-their-theophrastus/.

120. Calis, "Two Editors and Their Theophrastus."

121. For further commentary, see Grafton and Weinberg, *Isaac Casaubon,* 27, who note the spelling error in the Hebrew.

122. Grafton and Weinberg, *Isaac Casaubon,* 6.

123. "Letter from Scaliger to Casaubon, May 7, 1594," in *The Correspondence of Joseph Justus Scaliger: January 1587 to December 1596,* ed. Paul Botley and Dirk van Miert (Geneva: Droz, 2012), 2:384–386.

124. Grafton and Weinberg, *Isaac Casaubon,* 8.

125. "Fuit vero et tertium quoddam tractandae morum disciplinae genus, e re χαρακτηριστικὸν ab iisdem illis nominatum. Hanc elegantissimam philosophandi viam, primus, ut videtur, facundissimi oris vir, (sic enim dicam, non divini) Theophrastus invenit: primus certe in eo se et elegantissimum illud ingenium suum exercuit," Casaubon, *Theophrasti characteres ethici,* *2v.

126. "descriptione constat eorum quae homines aut hac aut illa virtute vitiove praediti, facere ᾗ τοιοῦτοί εἰσι consueverunt," Isaac Casaubon, *ad Theophrasti characteres ethicos Liber commentarius* (Lyon, 1592), A5r.

127. "ad bene honesteque vitam degendam nobis hoc scripto praeire Theophrastus voluit: quo nihil est φιλοσοφικώτερον, nihil philosopho dignius," Casaubon, *Liber commentarius,* A4r.

128. Marc Escola, *La Bruyère* (Paris: Champion, 2001), 1:42n2.

129. Escola, *La Bruyère,* 1:42n2.

130. "Neque abest coniectura, summum virum cum a Platone didicisset, Virtutem, si oculis cerneretur mirabiles sui amores excitaturam: rationem et vestigasse prudenter, et pervestigasse sollerter, qua cum virtutis speciem pulcherrimam, tum etiam vitiorum dedecus ac turpitudinem ipsis pene dixerim corporis oculis spectandam exhiberet," Casaubon, *Theophrasti characteres ethici,* *2v.

131. "ut appararet libellum hunc, medii cuiusdam esse inter philosophorum et poetarum scripta generis," Casaubon, *Liber commentarius,* A4v.

132. "de virtute enim et vitio disputans [*sc.* philosophus], illam sequendam, hoc fugiendum nos docet," Casaubon, *Liber commentarius,* A4r.

133. "Historicus et poeta, non virtutes nec vitia in abstracto (ut loquuntur) nec eorum caussas naturamve . . . considerant," Casaubon, *Liber commentarius,* A4r–v.

134. "sed his praeditos homines considerant: factaque nobis et mores utrorumque explicantes, imitandorum atque fugiendorum exempla suppeditant: et tacite quodammodo nos inspicere in vitas hominum iubent, atque ex aliis sumere exemplum nobis," Casaubon, *Liber commentarius,* A4v. Translation influenced by Escola's French rendering of this passage, in *La Bruyère,* 1:42.

135. *Poet.* 1451a36–38, in Stephen Halliwell's translation (Cambridge, MA: Harvard University Press, 1995); "Rursus autem magna est lataque inter historicum et poetam differentia: ille res gestas, uti gestae sunt, simpliciter narrat: hic et gestas . . . et quae geri potuerunt . . . exequitur," Casaubon, *Liber commentarius,* A4v. On the period's consideration of history as furnishing exempla, see Jacques Amyot, *Les vies des hommes illustres grecs et romains* (Geneva, 1594), title page: "Enrichies en ceste derniere edition d'amples sommaires sur chacune vie: d'annotations morales en marge qui monstrent le profit qu'on peut faire en la lecture de ces histoires"; Timothy Hampton, *Writing from History: The Rhetoric of Exemplarity in Renaissance Literature* (Ithaca, NY: Cornell University Press, 1990); and on its fate, Reinhart Koselleck, "*Historia magistra vitae*: The Dissolution of the Topos into the Perspective of a Modernized Historical Process," in *Future's Past: On the Semantics of Historical Time,* trans. Keith Tribe (Cambridge, MA: MIT Press, 1990), 21–38.

136. "cum decenti imitatione. . . . Omnis enim poeta μιμητὴς, ait idem Plato," Casaubon, *Liber commentarius,* A4v.

137. "Itaque titulus hic Ἠθικοὶ χαρακτῆρες tantundem ferme valet, ac si dixisset Εἰκόνες ἠθῶν (sive εἰκονισμοὶ, ut appellat Seneca) hoc est, *Imagines morum*: sicut Cicero comicos appellat *imaginem vitae quotidianae,*" Casaubon, *Liber commentarius,* A5v. Comedy, Cicero was thought to have said, is "an imitation of life, a mirror of character, and an image of truth." The phrase does not exist in Cicero but comes from an attribution by Aelius Donatus. See "Donatus: On Comedy," in *Classical and Medieval Literary Criticism: Translations and Interpretations,* ed. Alex Preminger, O. B. Hardison Jr., and Kevin Kerrane (New York: Frederick Ungar, 1974), 305–309, at 305. Donatus also quotes Livius Andronicus's defini-

tion of comedy as a "mirror of daily life." Casaubon also points here to Seneca's *Ep.* 95.65–67, which describes the worth of exemplified description for the instruction of virtue.

138. "Mores igitur hominum ita hic olim erant descripti, ut liceret tanquam in speculo hinc virtutis splendorem et pulcherrimam intueri faciem: illinc vero vitiorum turpitudinem et dedecus animadvertere," Casaubon, *Liber commentarius,* A5r. Richard McCabe suggests that this remark of Casaubon's may have influenced Hamlet's advice to the players (3.2.20–24). See McCabe, "Refining Theophrastus: Ethical Concerns and Moral Paragons in the English Character Book," *Hermathena* 159 (1996): 33–50, at 34.

139. "Erat namque hoc tamquam exemplar et speculum quoddam morum, ubi virtutis et vitii cuiusque expressae notae cernebantur," Casaubon, *Liber commentarius,* A5r–v.

140. In highlighting the value of character in relation to the *Poetics,* Casaubon might have found a precedent in Joseph Scaliger's edition of the *Poetics* (1561), which, as Barbara Carnevali has pointed out, "takes an unexpectedly heterodox position, stating that the *mores* are even more important than the *fabula.*" See "Literary Mimesis and Moral Knowledge: The Tradition of *ethopoeia,*" *Annales (HSS)* 65 (2010): 291–322, at 305; Scaliger, *Poetices libri septem* (Stuttgart: Friedrich Frommann Verlag, 1964), book 3, chap. 12.

141. "Nunc, melior eius pars, proh dolor! intercidit: nam . . . ea pars quae erat de virtutibus tota hodie desideratur," Casaubon, *Liber commentarius,* A5r.

142. Here see Ingrid A. R. De Smet, "How the Sauce Got to be Better than the Fish: Scholarship and Rivalry in Isaac Casaubon's Studies of Ancient Satire," *Erudition and the Republic of Letters* 4 (2019): 275–315.

143. Casaubon, *Theophrasti characteres ethici,* f2r–f4v.

144. Quint. *Inst.* 5.10.20–53, 104; Hor. *Ars. P.* 361–365.

145. Joseph Hall, *Characters of Vertues and Vices* [. . .] (London, 1608). On the influence on English literature, see Boyce, *The Theophrastan Character,* 122–286; Smeed, *The Theophrastan "Character,"* 19–46. For French and German, see Smeed, 47–113.

146. Schmitt, "Theophrastus," 248.

147. "Praeterquam enim quod proprie ad moralem Philosophum pertinet eique in cognoscendis corrigendisve hominum vitiis insignem operam navat, non exiguum quoque usum praestat Rhetori, quatenus et ipse agit de moribus," *Theophrasti notationes morum* [. . .] (Braunschweig, Germany, 1659),):(6v [*sic*].

148. John T. Gilmore, *Satire* (Abingdon, UK: Routledge, 2017), 104.

149. John Healey, *Epictetus "Manual." Cebes "Table." Theophrastus "Characters"* (London, 1616), I3r.

150. On the presence of this contextualizing impulse in humanist scholarship, see Kathy Eden, *Hermeneutics and the Rhetorical Tradition: Chapters in the Ancient Legacy and Its Humanist Reception* (New Haven, CT: Yale University Press, 1997).

151. Lisa Jardine and Anthony Grafton, "'Studied for Action': How Gabriel Harvey Read His Livy," *P&P* 129 (1990): 30–78.

152. Enrica Zanin, "De l'éthique de la vertu au *self-help*: Parcours éthiques de la Renaissance au contemporain," in *Éthique et littérature aujourd'hui*, ed. Emil-

iano Cavaliere, Vincenza Perdichizzi, and Enrica Zanin (Paris: Éditions Hermann, 2025) chap. 12, 268. Zanin is here referencing Joannes Sambucus, "Usus, non lectio prudentes facit," in *Emblemata* (Antwerp, 1564), D7v.

153. David A. Lines, introduction to *Rethinking Virtue, Reforming Society: New Directions in Renaissance Ethics, c. 1350–c.1650,* ed. David Lines and Sabrina Ebbersmeyer (Turnhout, Belgium: Brepols, 2013), 1–26, at 7. See also Matthias Roick's account of the range of texts that were classified under the heading "Ethica" in the book collection of August the Younger (1579–1666), Duke of Braunschweig-Lüneburg, in "The *Ethica* Section in Wolfenbüttel and the Role of 'Academic' Writings in Early Modern Ethics," in *History of Universities,* vol. 34/2, *Teaching Ethics in Early Modern Europe,* ed. Valentina Lepri (Oxford: Oxford University Press, 2021), 65–81.

154. Ann Moss, "Morals Stored and Ready for Use," in *Rethinking Virtue, Reforming Society: New Directions in Renaissance Ethics, c. 1350–c.1650,* ed. David Lines and Sabrina Ebbersmeyer (Turnhout, Belgium: Brepols, 2013), 169–187.

155. As Hans-Georg Gadamer describes in *Truth and Method,* trans. Joel Weinsheimer and Donald G. Marshall (London: Continuum 1975), 306–310.

156. *Thesaurus philosophiae moralis,* *6r. This volume is a sextodecimo, smaller than the palm of your hand.

157. Colin Burrow, *Imitating Authors: Plato to Futurity* (Oxford: Oxford University Press, 2019), 10. For translation as an act of preserving the qualities that make the past imitable in the present, see G. W. Pigman III, "Imitation and the Renaissance Sense of the Past: The Reception of Erasmus' *Ciceronianus,*" *Journal of Medieval and Renaissance Studies* 9 (1979): 155–179.

158. François Rigolot, "The Renaissance Crisis of Exemplarity," *JHI* 59, no. 4 (1998): 557–563, at 558.

159. This quality further aligns the *Characters* with Cebes's *Table,* a text similarly repeatedly imagined and reimagined across the early modern period. The absent Table that is referred to in the text but never illustrated was taken up by some of the best artists in early modern Europe, with frontispieces by Hans Holbein the Younger (1522), Hendrik Goltizus (1592) and Matthaüs Merian (1638); in 1744, Giambattista Vico decided to open his *New Science* with these words: "Just as Cebes the Theban once made a Tablet of things moral, so I present here a Tableau of civil institutions." See Giambattista Vico, *New Science,* 3rd ed., trans. David Marsh (London: Penguin, 1999), 1. On the imagistic representation of the Table, see Schleier, *"Tabula Cebetis,"* chap. 4.

160. On Casaubon's use of Hebrew in his first working copy of Theophrastus, see Grafton and Weinberg, *Isaac Casaubon,* chap. 1; see also 150, where Grafton and Weinberg mention that Elijah Levita's Hebrew lexicon, his *Sefer haTishbi* (Isny, 1541), was "one of Casaubon's favorite sources." Levita gives two definitions of טבע: one related to money and the other to nature. The second is a gloss by Shlomo Yitzchaki (Rashi) on Genesis 12:1. See also "טבע" in Ludwig Köhler, Walter Baumgartner, and Johann Jakob Stamm, eds., *The Hebrew and Aramaic Lexicon of the Old Testament Online,* trans. M. E. J. Richardson (Leiden, Netherlands: Brill, 2017), which indicates a further link to something being impressed into the earth, or planted, which seems of particular

relevance. I am grateful to Jake Wiseman, Aron Landy, and Daniel Amir for their insight on these sources.

161. "Porro is verus est cuiusque rei χαρακτὴρ, ea vera imago, quae illius naturam optime exprimit. Ideo Hebraei sapientes naturam vocant טבע, quasi dicas χαρακτῆρα, aut σφραγῖδα. nam illis טבעת sigillum significat," Casaubon, *ad Theophrasti characteres ethicos Liber commentarius,* F5r.

162. Jennifer A. Herdt, *Putting on Virtue: The Legacy of the Splendid Vices* (Chicago: University of Chicago Press, 2008), 61.

163. Roick, "Ethics and Social Relations," 64.

164. Tuck, *Philosophy and Government,* xiv.

165. See Thornton C. Lockwood, "Habituation, Habit and Character in Aristotle's *Nicomachean Ethics,*" in *A History of Habit: From Aristotle to Bourdieu,* ed. Tom Sparrow and Adam Hutchinson (Lanham, MD: Lexington Books, 2013), 19–36. Though Luther critiques the notion of *habitus,* as Risto Saarinen and Roick have traced, he does not upturn the fundamental idea of a consistent moral character as much as the question of what it requires to obtain one. See Risto Saarinen, "Renaissance Ethics and the European Reformations," in *Rethinking Virtue, Reforming Society: New Directions in Renaissance Ethics, c. 1350–c.1650,* ed. Sabrina Ebbersmeyer and David A. Lines (Turnhout, Belgium: Brepols, 2013), 81–104, at 84; Roick, "Ethics and Social Relations," 76.

166. "Ad un Principe adunque non è necesario havere tutte le sopra scritte qualità; ma è ben necessario parere d'haverle," *Il Principe di Nicolo Machiavelli* (Florence, 1532), G3r.

167. See Machiavelli's comment: "ma è necessario questa natura saperla ben colorire, et essere gran simulatore, et dissimulatore," *Il Principe,* G3r; in Latin: "Verum hanc naturam plurimum refert, ut quis recte norit colore vestire, cum simulando, tum dissimulando," *Nicolai Machiavelli Princeps,* trans. Sylvestre Tellio (Basel [?], 1589), F7v. Casaubon does not use this translation for Theophrastus's first character but *cavillatione* instead. For commentary on this, see Dilwyn Knox, *Ironia: Medieval and Renaissance Ideas on Irony* (Leiden, Netherlands: Brill, 1989), 143–145.

168. Richard F. Hardin, "Encountering Plautus in the Renaissance: A Humanist Debate on Comedy," *Renaissance Quarterly* 60, no. 3 (2007): 789–818, at 800.

169. Ernst Cassirer, *The Platonic Renaissance in England,* trans. James P. Pettegrove (Austin: University of Texas Press, 1953), 170.

170. Mark Knights and Adam Morton, introduction to *The Power of Laughter and Satire in Early Modern Britain: Political and Religious Culture, 1500–1820,* ed. Mark Knights and Adam Morton (Woodbridge, UK: The Boydell Press, 2017), 1–26, at 3.

171. See Quentin Skinner, "Why Laughing Mattered in the Renaissance: The Second Henry Tudor Memorial Lecture," *History of Political Thought* 22 no. 3 (2001): 418–447, and his "Hobbes, Laughter and Civil Conversation," in *L'antidoto di Mercurio: La "civil conversazione" tra Rinascimento ed età moderna,* ed. Nicola Panichi (Florence: Leo S. Olschki Editore, 2013), 73–94. For a critique of Skinner's overemphasis on the Renaissance theory of laughter as mockery, see Cathy Shrank, "Mocking or Mirthful? Laughter in Early Modern Dialogue," in *The Power of Laughter and Satire in Early Modern Britain: Political*

and Religious Culture, 1500–1820, ed. Mark Knights and Adam Morton (Woodbridge, UK: The Boydell Press, 2017), 48–66.

172. See Mikhail Bakhtin, *Rabelais and His World,* trans. Helene Iswolsky (Cambridge, MA: MIT Press, 1968), 4.

173. Skinner, "Hobbes, Laughter and Civil Conversation," 87. Donatus mentions an early origin for Athenian comedy that runs along similar lines: "The original concept came in from foreign cities and with foreign customs. When the Athenians, the guardians of Attic propriety, wanted to rebuke anyone for an immoral life, they used to gather together from all sides, happily and eagerly, at the villages and crossroads. There they used to describe the vices of individuals publicly and with proper names. Comedy was named from this custom." In Preminger, Hardison, and Kerrane, eds., *Classical and Medieval Literary Criticism,* 309.

174. See Ar. *Rhet.* 1.11.28. Translated by John Henry Freese, revised by Gisela Striker (Cambridge, MA: Harvard University Press, 2020); Cic. *De or.* 2.58.237. Translated by E. W. Sutton and H. Rackham (Cambridge, MA: Harvard University Press, 1942).

175. Skinner, "Why Laughing Mattered," 431–434, and "Hobbes, Laughter and Civil Conversation," 80–84. *The Book of the Courtier, by Count Baldesar Castiglione,* trans. Leonard Eckstein Opdycke (New York: Charles Scribner's Sons, 1903), 131–132.

176. Giovanni Della Casa, *Galateo: A Renaissance Treatise on Manners,* trans. Konrad Eisenbichler and Kenneth R. Bartlett (Toronto: Centre for Reformation and Renaissance Studies, 2001), 32–33, translation lightly amended.

3. Early Modern Stoics: Two English Adaptations

1. Joseph Barnes, ed., [. . .] *Theoprasti* [*sic*] *notationes morum* (Oxford, 1604). Note that all first editions of sixteenth- and seventeenth-century texts in this chapter and the next were printed in London unless indicated otherwise.

2. Across this chapter, I use the same search constraints and database as elaborated in the introduction note 64.

3. J. W. Smeed, *The Theophrastan "Character": The History of a Literary Genre* (Oxford: Clarendon Press, 1985), 82. I come back to this later German reception in the epilogue, along with eighteenth-century translations of the *Characters* into Russian (1772) and Spanish (1787).

4. "non mi piacciono in esso alcune chiose, che tengono della satira; ne mi contentano cert'altre, che sentono della pompa," Ansaldo Cebà, *I charatteri morali di Theofrasto* (Genova, 1620), a1r [unpaginated]. It is only much later on, in his commentary, at D1r, that he frames the text as a tool to recognize customs.

5. My biographical account draws from Richard A. McCabe, "Hall, Joseph (1574–1656)," *ODNB*; Arnold Davenport, ed., *The Collected Poems of Joseph Hall* (Liverpool, UK: Liverpool University Press, 1949), xiii–xxiv. Casaubon's editions were known in early seventeenth-century England. The blank facing pages of the 1604 Oxford printing of the *Characters* include heavy manuscript additions to the text in both Latin and Greek, several of which refer to Casaubon's translation. See Barnes, [. . .] *Theoprasti* [*sic*] *notationes morum,* B4r, C1v.

6. John Hoskins, *Directions for Speech and Style,* ed. Hoyt H. Hudson (Princeton, NJ: Princeton University Press, 1935), 41–42. See John Buxton, "Sidney and Theophrastus," *English Literary Renaissance* 2, no. 1 (1972): 79–82, at 79. The current reappraisal of Sidney's Greek suggests that he may have had access to this text in the original. Here see Micha Lazarus, "Sidney's Greek *Poetics,*" *Studies in Philology* 112, no. 3 (2015): 504–536, and "Greek Literacy in Sixteenth-Century England," *Renaissance Studies* 29 (2015): 433–458. Sidney mentions Theophrastus's *Metaphysics* in his "Woorke concerning the trewness of the Christian Religion." In Philip Sidney, *The Defence of Poesie, Political Discourses, Correspondence, Translation,* ed. Albert Feuillerat (Cambridge: Cambridge University Press, 1962), 185–307, at 241.

7. William Scott, *The Model of Poesy,* ed. Gavin Alexander (Cambridge: Cambridge University Press, 2013), 35; Fraser Mcilwraith, "'Pictures of Every Posture in the Mind': Judging Sidney's Characters," *Sidney Journal* 37, nos. 1–2 (2019): 89–111, at 90.

8. Benjamin Boyce, *The Theophrastan Character in England to 1642* (Cambridge, MA: Harvard University Press, 1947), 44; Wendell Clausen, "The Beginnings of English Character-Writing in the Early Seventeenth Century," *PhQ* 25 (1946): 32–45, at 32–33. See also Edward Chauncey Baldwin, "Ben Jonson's Indebtedness to the Greek Character-Sketch," *Modern Language Notes* 16 (1901): 385–396, which argues that the first echo to Theophrastus in Jonson is in *Cynthia's Revels* (1600). Depending on the composition date of *All's Well That Ends Well,* the Theophrastan character sketch that James Berg argues inspired Parolles might be a rival first allusion. See his "Moral Agency as Readerly Subjectivity: Shakespeare's Parolles and the Theophrastan Character Sketch," *Shakespeare Studies* 40 (2012): 36–43.

9. Ben Jonson, *Volpone, or the Fox,* ed. Brian Parker (Manchester, UK: Manchester University Press, 1983), 4.1.136–138.

10. Theophr. *Char.* 16.3, in James Diggle's translation, *Theophrastus: "Characters"* (Cambridge: Cambridge University Press, 2004).

11. For a full account of this, see Boyce, *The Theophrastan Character,* 53–121; Smeed, *The Theophrastan "Character,"* 1–46.

12. On rhetoric, see, for example, Thomas Wilson, *The Arte of Rhetorique,* ed. G. H. Mair (Oxford: Clarendon Press, 1909), 187, and more broadly, Andrew Escobedo, "Premodern Literary Character," in *Edmund Spenser in Context,* ed. Andrew Escobedo (Cambridge: Cambridge University Press, 2016), 194–203; Heinrich F. Plett, *"Enargeia" in Classical Antiquity and the Early Modern Age: The Aesthetics of Evidence* (Leiden, Netherlands: Brill, 2012), chap. 15. For the medieval tradition, see Boyce, *The Theophrastan Character,* 88; Howard R. Patch, "Characters in Medieval Literature," *Modern Language Notes* 40 (1925): 1–14. For Bacon, [. . .] *Of the Proficience and Advancement of Learning* (1605), 2X2v.

13. See Ada Palmer, "The Recovery of Stoicism in the Renaissance," in *The Routledge Handbook of the Stoic Tradition,* ed. John Sellars (London: Routledge, 2016), 117–132.

14. Jill Kraye, "Stoicism in the Renaissance from Petrarch to Lipsius," *Grotiana* 22–23 (2001–2002): 23–46, at 23.

15. See Alexandre Tarrête, "Conclusion," in *Stoïcisme et christianisme à la Renaissance,* ed. Alexandre Tarrête (Paris: Rue d'Ulm, 2006), 197–201.

16. On the importance of constancy to Stoicism, see Jacqueline Lagrée, "Constancy and Coherence," in *Stoicism: Traditions and Transformations,* ed. Steven K. Strange and Jack Zupko (Cambridge: Cambridge University Press, 2004), 148–176.

17. Kraye, "Stoicism in the Renaissance," 45. On Stoicism as a response to political crisis, see Denise Carabin, *Les idées stoïciennes dans la littérature morale des XVIe et XVIIe siècles (1575–1642)* (Paris: Champion, 2004), 907–908. For the late coinage of "neo-Stoicism," see Jacqueline Lagrée, *Le néostoïcisme: Une philosophie par gros temps* (Paris: Vrin, 2010), 8. For scholarship on Lipsius, see Christopher Brooke, *Philosophic Pride: Stoicism and Political Thought from Lipsius to Rousseau* (Princeton, NJ: Princeton University Press, 2012), chap. 1.

18. Thomas James, *The Moral Philosophie of the Stoicks* (1598), A5v. On the influence of English neo-Stoicism, see Gilles D. Monserrat, *Light from the Porch: Stoicism and English Renaissance Literature* (Paris: Didier-Érudition, 1984); Reid Barbour, *English Epicures and Stoics: Ancient Legacies in Early Stuart Culture* (Amherst: University of Massachusetts Press, 1998); Andrew Shifflett, *Stoicism, Politics and Literature in the Age of Milton* (Cambridge: Cambridge University Press, 1998).

19. Here see Adriana McCrea, *Constant Minds: Political Virtue and the Lipsian Paradigm in England, 1584–1650* (Toronto: University of Toronto Press, 1997), chap. 5.

20. Joseph Hall, *Characters of Vertues and Vices* [. . .] (London, 1608), B3r.

21. Hall, *Characters,* C3r.

22. Andrew McRae, *Literature, Satire, and the Early Stuart State* (Cambridge: Cambridge University Press, 2004), 10; Alastair Bellany, *The Politics of Court Scandal in Early Modern England: News Culture and the Overbury Affair, 1603–1660* (Cambridge: Cambridge University Press, 2015), 8. On Overbury's life, see John Considine, "Overbury, Sir Thomas (*bap.* 1581, *d.* 1613)," *ODNB.*

23. My account of the book history of the characters is indebted to Bruce McIver, "'A Wife Now the Widdow': Lawrence Lisle and the Popularity of the Overburian Characters," *South Atlantic Review* 59, no. 1 (1994): 27–44. McIver notes that this first edition was possibly released in late 1613, Lisle having entered it for publication in the Stationers' Register on December 13. Here see Edward Arber, ed., *A Transcript of the Registers of the Company of Stationers of London 1554–1640 ad* (London, 1877), 3:584.

24. Thomas Overbury, *A Wife Now the Widdow* [. . .], 2nd ed. (1614), title page. The sketches in this edition, as Donald Beecher argues, were assigned to Overbury and his friends, the news to members of a different court circle. See Donald Allen Beecher, ed., *Characters* [. . .] *Based on the Eleventh Edition of "A Wife Now the Widow of Sir Thomas Overbury"* (Ottawa, Canada: Doverhouse Editions, 2003), 73.

25. Beecher, *Characters,* 73.

26. McIver, "'A Wife Now the Widdow,'" 27. For McIver's reasons for dismissing Hall, see 40n1.

27. *The "Conceited newes" of Sir Thomas Overbury* (1632), *3r [unpaginated], British Library Collection, 1078.a.15.

28. Cited in Beecher, *Characters,* 83.

29. Élisabeth Soubrenie, review of *Characters,* ed. Donald Beecher, Études Anglaises 58, no. 2 (2005): 202–204, at 203.

30. Beecher, *Characters,* 35; Eliane Cuvelier, "De l'allégorie à la personne: origines et développement du 'caractère' dans la littérature anglaise jusqu'en 1633," in *Vivante tradition, sources et racines: Évolution de quelques formes et forces en littérature et civilisation anglaises,* ed. Olivier Lutaud (Paris: Editions I.L.S. 1982), 15–23.

31. Richard A. McCabe, *Joseph Hall: A Study in Satire and Meditation* (Oxford: Oxford University Press, 1982), 128.

32. Richard A. McCabe, "Refining Theophrastus: Ethical Concerns and Moral Paragons in the English Character Book," *Hermathena* 159 (1996): 33–50, at 37.

33. Andrew Hadfield, *Shakespeare and Republicanism* (Cambridge: Cambridge University Press, 2005), 17. On the "monarchical republic," see Patrick Collinson, *"De republica anglorum": Or, History with the Politics Put Back* (Cambridge: Cambridge University Press, 1990), 23.

34. On the mixed constitution, see Thomas Smith, *"De Republica Anglorum": The Maner of Gouernement or Policie of the Realme of England* (London, 1583).

35. Mark Goldie, "The Unacknowledged Republic: Officeholding in Early Modern England," in *The Politics of the Excluded, c. 1500–1850,* ed. Tim Harris (New York: Palgrave, 2001), 153–194, at 154.

36. David Norbrook, *Writing the English Republic: Poetry, Rhetoric and Politics 1627–1660* (Cambridge: Cambridge University Press, 2000), 17.

37. Quentin Skinner, "A Third Concept of Liberty: Living in Servitude," *London Review of Books* 24, no. 7 (2002). See also Quentin Skinner, *Liberty before Liberalism* (Cambridge: Cambridge University Press, 1998); Martin van Gelderen and Quentin Skinner, eds., *Republicanism: A Shared European Heritage* (Cambridge: Cambridge University Press, 2002). On the presence of antimonarchical republicanism prior to the civil war, see Markku Peltonen, *Classical Humanism and Republicanism in English Political Thought 1570–1640* (Cambridge: Cambridge University Press, 1995); Hadfield, *Shakespeare and Republicanism*; Norbrook, *Writing the English Republic.*

38. Peltonen, *Classical Humanism,* 12.

39. Skinner, "A Third Concept of Liberty."

40. Isaiah Berlin, "Two Concepts of Liberty," in *Four Essays on Liberty* (Oxford: Oxford University Press, 1969), 118–172, at 135. Berlin saw this philosophy of retreat as perversely leading to totalitarian politics, in which a state would justify its interventions into individuals' lives by explaining that it was doing so in order to help them achieve self-mastery.

41. Felicity Green, *Montaigne and the Life of Freedom* (Cambridge: Cambridge University Press, 2012), 2.

42. See also Martha Nussbaum, *The Fragility of Goodness: Luck and Ethics in Greek Tragedy and Philosophy* (Cambridge: Cambridge University Press, 1986), xxii, for the claim that this means Stoicism lets distributive politics off the hook. If

external goods are of no relevance to individuals, it becomes of no relevance for the state to secure them for its citizens.

43. I follow Christopher Hill in my usage of "English Revolution." For a succinct argument on the importance of this description, see Hill, "Historians on the Rise of British Capitalism," *Science & Society* 14, no. 4 (1950): 307–321, at 321, where he argues that the lack of this description has meant that "for every Frenchman 1789 has a deep significance; but for most Englishmen 1640 means nothing." See also Christopher Hill, *The English Revolution 1640: An Essay* (London: Lawrence and Wishart, 1940).

44. Smeed, *The Theophrastan "Character,"* 6; Fumaroli, *L'âge de l'éloquence,* 725n137. Hall would have here found a precedent in the medieval exemplum, "a staple of Christian didacticism," as Alexander Gelly describes it, in his introduction to *Unruly Examples: On the Rhetoric of Exemplarity,* ed. Alexander Gelly (Stanford, CA: Stanford University Press, 1995), 1–26, at 4.

45. Philip A. Smith, "Bishop Hall, 'Our English Seneca,'" *PMLA* 63, no. 4 (1948): 1191–1204, at 1191, 1198; Audrey Chew, "Joseph Hall and Neo-Stoicism," *PMLA* 65, no. 6 (1950): 1130–1145.

46. McCabe, "Hall, Joseph." McCabe is here citing Thomas Fuller. In Hall's own lifetime, Henry Wotton called him "our spiritual Seneca."

47. Chew, "Joseph Hall and Neo-Stoicism," 1132.

48. Davenport, *The Collected Poems,* xvi.

49. McCabe, "Hall, Joseph"; Davenport, *The Collected Poems,* xvii.

50. Hall, *Virgidemiarum: Sixe Bookes* [. . .] *Of Tooth-lesse Satyrs* (1602), A8r; Francis Meres, *Treatise on Poetry,* ed. Donald Cameron Allen (Champaign: University of Illinois Press, 1933), 79; Francis Meres, *Palladis Tamia* (1598), 2O3v.

51. On the Bishops' Ban, see William R. Jones, "The Bishops' Ban of 1599 and the Ideology of English Satire," *Literature Compass* 7, no. 5 (2010): 332–346; Debora Shuger, *Censorship and Cultural Sensibility: The Regulation of Language in Tudor-Stuart England* (Philadelphia: University of Pennsylvania Press, 2006), 76; McCabe, *A Study in Satire and Meditation,* 71–72.

52. Jones, "The Bishops' Ban of 1599," 339.

53. Joseph Hall, *Meditations and Vowes* (London, 1606), B8v, J11r–K3v, G5v–G6r, K8v–K9v.

54. See Boyce, *The Theophrastan Character,* 122–123, for the comment that certain descriptions in this work may be considered "almost Characters."

55. McCabe, *A Study in Satire and Meditation,* 110. In 1614, Hall adds "The Penitent" and "He is a Happy Man."

56. John L. Lievsay, ed., *The Seventeenth-Century Resolve: A Historical Anthology of a Literary Form* (Lexington: University Press of Kentucky, 2014), 10.

57. Hall, *Characters,* A4r.

58. Hall, *Characters,* A4r–v.

59. *OED,* s.v. "inbred," adj., 1. On the broader context of this kind of elision, see Annabel S. Brett, *Changes of State: Nature and the Limits of the City in Early Modern Natural Law* (Princeton, NJ: Princeton University Press, 2011), chap. 3; Jan Schröder, "The Concept of (Natural) Law in the Doctrine of Law and Natural Law of the Early Modern Era," in *Natural Law and Laws of Nature in Early*

Modern Europe: Jurisprudence, Theology, Moral and Natural Philosophy, ed. Lorraine Daston and Michael Stolleis (Aldershot, UK: Ashgate, 2008), 57–71.

60. On the afterlife of this linkage between Sinai and nature, see Paul Franks, "Sinai since Spinoza: Reflections on Revelation in Modern Jewish Thought," in *The Significance of Sinai: Traditions about Sinai and Divine Revelation in Judaism and Christianity,* ed. George J. Brooke, Hindy Najman, and Loren T. Stuckenbruck (Leiden, Netherlands: Brill, 2008), 333–354.

61. See J. Bossy, "Moral Arithmetic: Seven Sins into Ten Commandments," in *Conscience and Casuistry in Early Modern Europe,* ed. Edmund Leites (Cambridge: Cambridge University Press, 1988), 214–234. Bossy argues that the move from Catholicism to Protestantism came with a shift from the heptad to the Decalogue, in part due to the Reformation's insistence on scripture.

62. Hall, *Characters,* A4v–A5r.

63. On the early modern uptake of *enargeia,* see Ruth Webb, *Ekphrasis, Imagination and Persuasion in Ancient Rhetorical Theory and Practice* (Farnham, UK: Ashgate, 2009), 87–94.

64. Isaac Casaubon, ed. and trans., *Theophrasti characteres ethici* (Lyon, 1592), *2r–v; Isaac Casaubon, *ad Theophrasti characteres ethicos liber commentarius* (Lyon, 1592), A5v.

65. See McCrea, *Constant Minds,* 192–195.

66. Anthony Grafton and Joanna Weinberg, *"I Have Always Loved the Holy Tongue": Isaac Casaubon, the Jews and a Forgotten Chapter in Renaissance Scholarship* (Cambridge, MA: Harvard University Press, 2011), 10.

67. Hall, *Characters,* A5v.

68. Hall, *Characters,* A5r–v.

69. Hall, *Characters,* A5r–v, B1v; McCabe, *A Study in Satire and Meditation,* 112.

70. Hall, *Characters,* B1v–B2r.

71. Hall, *Characters,* B1v–B2r.

72. Hall, *Characters,* B2r.

73. Melvin G. Williams, "The Bishop's Not a Preacher: A Reading of Joseph Hall's *Virgidemiarum,*" *Christianity and Literature* 24, no. 2 (1975): 36–41, at 38; McCabe, *A Study in Satire and Meditation,* 128. In *Doctor Faustus,* the sight of the vices rendered into satirical characters is not enough to direct Faustus away from sin but, on the contrary, works to forestall his repentance. After seeing the pageant, Faustus exclaims, "O, this feeds my soul!" See *Doctor Faustus* [. . .], ed. David Bevington and Eric Rasmussen (Manchester, UK: Manchester University Press, 1993), 2.3.166.

74. Fredson Bowers, ed., *The Dramatic Works in the Beaumont and Fletcher Canon* (Cambridge: Cambridge University Press, 1966), 1:147.

75. This suggests that Morton Bloomfield's idea that the tradition of the seven deadly sins ended in the early modern period is premature. Here see Richard G. Newhauser, "'These Seaven Devils': The Capital Vices on the Way to Modernity," in *Sin in Medieval and Early Modern Culture: The Tradition of the Seven Deadly Sins,* ed. Richard G. Newhauser and Susan J. Ridyard (New York: Boydell & Brewer, 2012), 157–188, at 157; Morton Bloomfield, *The Seven Deadly Sins* (East Lansing: Michigan State College Press, 1952). Note that there was also a major

tradition of depicting the vices on their own, as in Christopher Marlowe's *Doctor Faustus* (1604) and Thomas Dekker's *The Seven Deadly Sinnes of London* (1606).

76. See Sibylle Mähl, *"Quadriga virtutum": Die Kardinaltugenden in der Geistesgeschichte der Karolingerzeit* (Cologne: Böhlau, 1969); Jason Powell, "Thomas Wyatt and Francis Bryan: Plainness and Dissimulation," in *The Oxford Handbook of Tudor Literature, 1485–1603,* ed. Mike Pincome and Cathy Shrank (Oxford: Oxford University Press, 2009), 187–202.

77. Jill Kraye, "Moral Philosophy," in *The Cambridge History of Renaissance Philosophy,* ed. Charles Schmitt, Quentin Skinner, Eckhard Kessler, and Jill Kraye (Cambridge: Cambridge University Press, 1988), 303–386, at 320, and more generally 367–370. Kraye cites Erasmus's preface to his 1520 edition of Cicero's *De officiis* and Juan Luis Vives's complaint that Seneca taught the Christians what he should have learned from them.

78. McCabe, *A Study in Satire and Meditation,* x.

79. Smith, "Bishop Hall, 'Our English Seneca,'" 1191.

80. Kraye, "Moral Philosophy," 364, 372n413. The motto "bear and forbear" (*sustine et abstine*) is Angelo Poliziano's Latin translation of a Greek quotation present in Gell. *NA* XVII.xix.6: "Verba haec duo dicebat [*sc.* Epictetus]: ἀνέχου et ἀπέχου."

81. Nicholas Breton, *The Soules Immortal Crowne* [. . .] (1605), title page. For an analysis of the classical and Christian combination as part of a broader syncretizing trend in the period, see Sarah Hutton, *British Philosophy in the Seventeenth Century* (Oxford: Oxford University Press, 2015), 58.

82. Smith, "Bishop Hall, 'Our English Seneca,'" 1201.

83. Peltonen, *Classical Humanism,* 162; On the fifteenth-century background to this idea, see Albert Rabil Jr., ed., *Knowledge, Goodness, and Power: The Debate over Nobility among Quattrocento Italian Humanists* (Binghamton, NY: Medieval & Renaissance Texts & Studies, 1991), 22–23.

84. Boyce, *The Theophrastan Character,* 124. Another source could be Cicero's *De Amicitia.* On how Cicero's popular text linked friendship and republicanism, see Hadfield, *Shakespeare and Republicanism,* 170.

85. Hall, *Characters,* D1r–D3r.

86. Henry W. Sams, "Anti-Stoicism in Seventeenth- and Early Eighteenth-Century England," *Studies in Philology* 41, no. 1 (1944): 65–78, at 75.

87. Joshua Scodel, *Excess and the Mean in Early Modern English Literature* (Princeton, NJ: Princeton University Press, 2002), 3.

88. See Sen. *Ep.* 95.65–7 (indicated in Casaubon's Prolegomena), which describes the science of "characterization" as giving "the signs and marks which belong to each virtue or vice." In Richard M. Gummere's translation (Cambridge, MA: Harvard University Press, 1917–1925). The Stoic foundation to the whole collection led Rudolf Kirk to publish Hall's *Characters* as part of a trilogy of works of neo-Stoicism. See his *"Heaven upon Earth" and "Characters of Virtues and Vices"* (New Brunswick, NJ: Rutgers University Press, 1948).

89. Hall, *Characters,* B4r, D1v.

90. Hall, *Characters,* B5r, D4r.

91. Hall, *Characters,* C2r, C8r.

92. Peltonen, *Classical Humanism,* 131–132.

93. Hall, *Characters,* B4r, B5r–v. See also Peltonen, *Classical Humanism,* 132.

94. Hall, *Characters,* C7r–v.

95. Hall, *Characters,* B7v.

96. Hall, *Characters,* B3v. Here see Smeed, *The Theophrastan "Character,"* 21.

97. Hall, *Characters,* B7v, D1v. See Boyce, *The Theophrastan Character,* 128, on how Hall's *Salomons Divine Arts* (1609) invents a new kind of character sketch composed of "phrases and verses out of Proverbs and Ecclesiastes."

98. Casaubon's later edition includes sketches 24–28: arrogance (in Casaubon's translation: *superbia*), cowardice, oligarchy, late learning, and slander. Given that several of these would have been ripe for an adaptation on both Christian and Stoic lines but do not appear in Hall's work, it seems that Hall might have used the 1592 text. As there is a lack of evidence provided for the claim that "it seems quite evident that Casaubon's 1599 edition, and not, as commonly supposed, his 1592 edition, circulated in England," I find it hard to agree with Wendell Clausen that we should discount this earlier text. In his "The Beginnings of English Character-Writing," 38.

99. For a comparison of passages between Hall and Theophrastus across a number of these characters, see Edward Chauncey Baldwin, "The Relation of the English 'Character' to Its Greek Prototype," *PMLA* 18, no. 3 (1903): 412–423, at 418–420. Baldwin, in this piece to which Clausen refers, does not provide an argument for why the 1599 edition should be preferred, citing echoes that only pertain to the first twenty-three characters, in the ordering present in Casaubon's own text.

100. Hall, *Characters,* K3r. On the role of vainglory as a version of pride within the heptad of vices, see Carla Casagrande and Silvana Vecchio, *Histoire des péchés capitaux au Moyen Âge,* trans. Pierre-Emmanuel Dauzat (Paris: Aubier, 2002), 24–31.

101. Hall, *Characters,* K7r; Theophr. *Char.* 13.1–2, in Diggle's translation. I here depart from Boyce, who thinks that this character "seems new." In *The Theophrastan Character,* 126.

102. Hall, *Characters,* H2v, F8v.

103. If one follows Casagrande and Vecchio's elaboration of how each of the seven vices was thought to be "followed by a crowd of simple soldiers"—with pride incorporating hypocrisy and jabbering; anger including blasphemy; gluttony including verbosity and obscenity; and luxury including ambition—many further echoes with the heptad might be found across Hall's text. See Casagrande and Vecchio, *Histoire des péchés capitaux,* 8–9. McCabe goes as far to say that all of Hall's vices are "pervaded by the concept of sin" in *A Study in Satire and Meditation,* 119.

104. Hall, *Characters,* G7v–G8r.

105. Hall, *Characters,* H8r. For a list of occasions in which "self-knowledge" appears as a central quality across both vices and virtues, see Müller-Schwefe, "Joseph Hall's *Characters of Vertues and Vices*: Notes Toward a Revaluation," *Texas Studies in Literature and Language* 14 (1972–1973): 235–251, at 245n46.

106. Hall, *Meditations,* 2:30; McCabe, *A Study in Satire and Meditation,* 126.

107. See Max Weber, *The Protestant Ethic and the Spirit of Capitalism,* trans. Talcott Parsons (London: Routledge, 2010), 116. On Hall's Calvinism, see Jona-

than M. Atkins, "Calvinist Bishops, Church Unity, and the Rise of Arminianism," *Albion* 18, no. 3 (1986): 411–427; Kenneth Fincham and Peter Lake, "Popularity, Prelacy and Puritanism in the 1630s: Joseph Hall Explains Himself," *HER* 111 (1996): 856–881.

108. McCabe, *A Study in Satire and Meditation,* 119.

109. Hall, *Characters,* F2v.

110. Overbury, *A Wife Now the Widdow,* 2nd ed., C4r.

111. Overbury, *His Wife,* 11th ed. (1622), Q4r–v. The writer of this text dons a character to define a character, beginning, "If I must speake the Schoole-masters language." Here see Aaron Kunin, *Character as Form* (London: Bloomsbury, 2019), 48–49.

112. Peter Burke, "Seventeenth-Century London," in *Popular Culture in Seventeenth-Century England,* ed. Barry Reay (London: Routledge, 1985), 31–58.

113. Burke, "Seventeenth-Century London," 33–34.

114. Burke, "Seventeenth-Century London," 46. See K. J. Lindley, "Riot Prevention and Control in Early Stuart London," *RHS* 33 (1983): 109–126; R. M. Dunn, "The London Weavers' Riot of 1675," *Guildhall Studies in London History* 1 (1973–1974): 13–23; G. Holmes, "The Sacheverell Riots," *P&P* 72 (1976): 55–85.

115. Christopher Hill, *Change and Continuity in Seventeenth Century England* (London: Weidenfeld & Nicolson, 1974), 59.

116. Burke, "Seventeenth-Century London," 50.

117. Overbury, *A Wife Now the Widdow,* 2nd ed., E1v.

118. This first set of characters on women is thought to be by Overbury due to their echoes with *A Wife.*

119. Overbury, *A Wife Now the Widdow,* 7th ed. (1616), I8r–K1r, L7v–L8r, H5v–H6v.

120. Hall, *Characters,* A7r. The exception here is "Of the good Magistrate."

121. Overbury, *A Wife Now the Widdow,* 2nd ed., E2r; 11th ed., Q1v–Q2v; 4th ed. (1614), E4r.

122. Overbury, *A Wife Now the Widdow,* 2nd ed., E4r.

123. Hall, *Characters,* I1r–v; Overbury, *A Wife Now the Widdow,* 2nd ed., D3v.

124. Hall, *Characters,* I3v; Overbury, *A Wife Now the Widdow,* 2nd ed., D3v.

125. Overbury, *His Wife,* 11th ed., G6v.

126. Overbury, *His Wife,* 11th ed., E2v.

127. Overbury, *His Wife,* 11th ed., P3v–P4r. I look more closely at characters of place in the next chapter. A series of prison characters, including this one, were added to the 1622 edition by Thomas Dekker.

128. George Boas, *The History of Ideas* (New York: Charles Scribner's Sons, 1969), 216.

129. Overbury, *His Wife,* 11th ed., G1r.

130. Overbury, *His Wife,* H1v, H2r, H4v.

131. Overbury, *His Wife,* 8th ed. (1616), M7v. On her authorship, see Sarah C. E. Ross, "'Thou art the nursing father of all pietye': Sociality, Religion, and Politics in Anne Southwell's Verse," in *Women, Poetry, and Politics in Seventeenth-Century Britain* (Oxford: Oxford University Press, 2015), 63–99, at 68–69.

132. Overbury, *A Wife Now the Widdow,* 2nd ed., E4v, D4r.

133. Hall, *Characters,* G4r; Theophr. *Char.* 16.1–2.

134. Here see Beatrice White, *Cast of Ravens: The Strange Case of Sir Thomas Overbury* (London: John Murray, 1965), 40, 232. Note that in 1614, Lisle printed three books related to the marriage of Howard and Carr. In McIver, "'A Wife Now the Widdow,'" 29.

135. White, *Cast of Ravens,* 46. Edward Le Comte, *The Notorious Lady Essex* (New York: Dial Press, 1969), 53–55.

136. Bellany, *The Politics of Court Scandal,* 7, 9, 179. See also Alastair Bellany and Thomas Cogswell, *The Murder of King James I* (New Haven, CT: Yale University Press, 2015), 165, 180, 185, 331.

137. Here see Bellany, *The Politics of Court Scandal,* chap. 2; Bellany and Cogswell, *The Murder of King James I,* 470–480.

138. Bellany, *The Politics of Court Scandal,* 115.

139. *The Complete Poetry of Ben Jonson,* ed. William B. Hunter (New York: New York University Press, 1963), 363. As in my prior note, Lisle registered intent to publish *A Wife* in December 1613, suggesting either that Ben Jonson had access to the manuscript text or that the poem was published earlier than we think.

140. Overbury, *His Wife,* 11th ed., A6r.

141. Overbury, *His Wife,* 11th ed., B3r–v.

142. *OED*, s.v. "card," n., 2, 4b.

143. Overbury, *His Wife,* 11th ed., D2r.

144. David M. Bergeron, *King James and Letters of Homoerotic Desire* (Iowa City: University of Iowa Press, 1999), 73. On the scholarship about James's homosexuality, see Michael B. Young, "James VI and I: Time for a Reconsideration?," *Journal of British Studies* 51, no. 3 (2012): 540–567.

145. Bergeron, *King James,* 73.

146. Quoted in Bergeron, *King James,* 73.

147. Bergeron, *King James,* 138.

148. James VI, *Basilicon Doron* (Edinburgh, 1599), A2r, M3v–M4r. There are echoes of James's text in Overbury's poem. Both texts begin with a comparison with Adam and Eve, see marriage as a means to allay lust, and present three qualities in a wife as being no more than "accessories" or "additions"; "Beauty, Riches, & friendship by allie" for James, "Byrth, beauty, wealth" for Overbury. See Overbury, *His Wife,* 8th ed., B1r, B3v.

149. Overbury, *His Wife,* 11th ed., B2v.

150. Overbury, *His Wife,* 11th ed., B1v.

151. Overbury, *His Wife,* 11th ed., B4r.

152. This division can be found in Smeed, *The Theophrastan "Character,"* 25.

153. Overbury, *His Wife,* 11th ed., E1v.

154. Overbury, *His Wife,* 11th ed., F2v.

155. The Overburians, unlike Hall, do use ornament in their style, which Boyce calls "lavishly conceitful." In *The Theophrastan Character,* 143.

156. Overbury, *His Wife,* 11th ed., L4v.

157. Overbury, *His Wife,* 11th ed., F2r, G6v.

158. Overbury, *His Wife,* 11th ed., G4r, E7v.

159. Overbury, *His Wife,* 11th ed., F2r.

160. Overbury, *His Wife,* 11th ed., F2r.

161. Overbury, *His Wife,* 11th ed., F6r.

162. Overbury, *His Wife,* 11th ed., F8r, G3r.

163. Overbury, *His Wife,* 11th ed., G4r.

164. Overbury, *His Wife,* 11th ed., E7r–v.

165. Overbury, *His Wife,* 11th ed., E6v, E6v–E7r. Here see Georg Simmel's comments that fashion is a dialectic between the desire to conform and the desire to differentiate the self. The latter, he claims, can only happen in "highly civilized nations." See Simmel, "Fashion," in *On Individuality and Social Forms*, trans. and ed., Donald N. Levine (Chicago: Chicago University Press, 1971), 294–323, at 301.

166. Overbury, *His Wife,* 11th ed., F3v–F4r.

167. Overbury, *His Wife,* 11th ed., F2v.

168. See Hilary M. Larkin, *The Making of Englishmen: Debates on National Identity 1550–1650* (Leiden, Netherlands: Brill, 2014), 48–49, on how a neo-Roman perspective can be found in other character books' representation of travelers, who are often likened to slaves.

169. Overbury, *His Wife,* 11th ed., G1r, G2r.

170. Overbury, *His Wife,* 11th ed., E8r, E7v.

171. Overbury, *His Wife,* 8th ed., C5r.

172. Overbury, *His Wife,* 11th ed., S7v.

173. On the Dutch Republic, see Christopher W. Close, *State Formation and Shared Sovereignty: The Holy Roman Empire and the Dutch Republic, 1488–1696* (Cambridge: Cambridge University Press, 2021).

174. McRae, *Literature, Satire, and the Early Stuart State,* 11.

175. On Stoicism and masculinity, see Michael Goyette, "Insult to Injury: Senecan Stoicism, Misogyny, and the Semantics of 'Special Snowflake,'" in *Toxic Masculinity in the Ancient World,* ed. Melanie Racette-Campbell and Aven McMaster (Edinburgh: Edinburgh University Press, 2023), 199–215; on republicanism, Jamie A. Gianoutsos, *The Rule of Manhood: Tyranny, Gender, and Classical Republicanism in England 1603–1660* (Cambridge: Cambridge University Press, 2021).

176. Overbury, *His Wife,* 11th ed., E2r.

177. Overbury, *His Wife,* 11th ed., G5r.

178. For how Hall's sketch of the good magistrate is in fact part of his resistance to encouraging active political participation by suggesting that "society had its God-given magistrates to worry about the problems of politics," see McCrea, *Constant Minds,* 194–195.

179. Overbury, *His Wife,* 8th ed., M3v.

180. Overbury, *His Wife,* 8th ed., K6v.

181. Overbury, *His Wife,* 8th ed., L2v.

182. Overbury, *His Wife,* 11th ed., O5r–v.

183. Svetlana Alpers, *The Art of Describing: Dutch Art in the Seventeenth Century* (Chicago: University of Chicago Press, 1983). This is a transition that Brian W. Ogilvie has also found in approaches to natural history. See Brian W. Ogilvie, *The Science of Describing: Natural History in Renaissance Europe* (Chicago: University of Chicago Press, 2006).

4. Civil War Characters: How to Write Political Types

1. Thomas Hobbes, *Leviathan*, ed. Richard Tuck (Cambridge: Cambridge University Press, 1996), 10.

2. Historian Andrew McRae has in fact used the discussion of the Overbury affair as evidence for the presence of a public sphere at the beginning of the seventeenth century. See his *Literature, Satire, and the Early Stuart State* (Cambridge: Cambridge University Press, 2004), 13–14.

3. Here see Jürgen Habermas, *The Structural Transformation of the Public Sphere: An Inquiry into a Category of Bourgeois Society*, trans. Thomas Burger (Cambridge, MA: MIT Press, 1991), 22.

4. On the exchange of news in the cathedral, see Joad Raymond, *Pamphlets and Pamphleteering in Early Modern Britain* (Cambridge: Cambridge University Press, 2003), 1–3.

5. [John Earle], *Micro-cosmographie* (1628), J5r–v.

6. Using a sense of "map" as "a representation in abridged form; a summary or condensed account of a state of things; an epitome" (*OED*, s.v. "map," n., 5a), which lost currency after 1647.

7. Across this chapter, I use the same search constraints and database as elaborated in the introduction, at note 64. Note that these figures, however, exclude reprints of the Overburian volume.

8. Wilbur Samuel Howell, *Logic and Rhetoric in England, 1500–1700* (New York: Russell & Russell, 1961).

9. Wilbur Samuel Howell, *Eighteenth-Century British Logic and Rhetoric* (Princeton, NJ: Princeton University Press, 1971), 5–6.

10. Howell, *Logic and Rhetoric in England*, 9. On the importance of publicly communicating scientific knowledge, see Steven Shapin and Simon Schaffer, *Leviathan and the Air-Pump: Hobbes, Boyle, and the Experimental Life* (Princeton, NJ: Princeton University Press, 1985).

11. Thomas Sprat, *The History of the Royal Society of London, for the Improving of Natural Knowledge* (1667), O4r.

12. Sprat, *The History of the Royal Society*, P1r. Sprat's examples of the empirical method in practice come from a questionnaire submitted to Louis Philiberto Vernatti, an employee of the Dutch East India Company in Batavia, Indonesia. Both questions and answers suggest a proximity of empiricism to imperialism. Sprat includes questions like "Whether at Hermita, a Town in Ethiopia, there are Tortoises, so big, that Men may ride upon them?" See Sprat, *The History of the Royal Society*, X1v–Y1v.

13. For summaries, see Michel Foucault, "Foreword to the English Edition," in *The Order of Things: An Archaeology of the Human Sciences* (London: Routledge, 2002); Johan Heilbron, Lars Magnusson, and Björn Wittrock, eds., *The Rise of the Social Sciences and the Formation of Modernity: Conceptual Change in Context, 1750–1850* (Dordrecht, Netherlands: Kluwer, 1995), 6–7.

14. Foucault, *The Order of Things*, 19, 62.

15. Foucault, *The Order of Things*, 141.

16. Foucault, *The Order of Things*, 141.

17. Foucault, *The Order of Things*, 141.

18. Frances A. Yates, *The Occult Philosophy in the Elizabethan Age* (London: Routledge, 1979), 186; Ian Hacking, *The Emergence of Probability,* 2nd ed. (Cambridge: Cambridge University Press, 2006), xv–xvii.

19. Courtney Weiss Smith, *Empiricist Devotions: Science, Religion, and Poetry in Early Eighteenth-Century England* (Charlottesville: University of Virginia Press, 2016).

20. Ian Maclean, "Foucault's Renaissance Episteme Reassessed: An Aristotelian Counterblast," *Journal of the History of Ideas* 59, no. 1 (1998): 149–166.

21. A consideration of the politics of plain style sits alongside recent work on its religious backdrop. Here see Hilary Hinds, *God's Englishwomen: Seventeenth-Century Radical Sectarian Writing and Feminist Criticism* (Manchester, UK: Manchester University Press, 1996), 128–134; Peter Harrison, "Experimental Religion and Experimental Science in Early Modern England," *Intellectual History Review* 21, no. 4 (2011): 413–433.

22. Wye Saltonstall, *Picturae Loquentes* (1631), B5r–v.

23. Howell, *Logic and Rhetoric in England,* 10.

24. Howell, *Logic and Rhetoric in England,* 10.

25. Sprat, *The History of the Royal Society,* P1r.

26. A paradigmatic example here is Edward Chauncey Baldwin, "The Relation of the Seventeenth Century 'Character' to the Periodical Essay," *PMLA* 19, no. 1 (1904): 75–114, at 80. The more recent literary histories by Boyce and Smeed are similar in their internalized focus on the transformations of style.

27. L[ewis] G[riffin], *Overbury Revived* (1661).

28. Thomas Overbury, *A Wife Now the Widdow* [. . .], 2nd ed. (1614), E4r. On the relationship between the Overburian characters and Stephens's *Satyrical Essayes, Characters and Others,* see Gwendolen Murphy, *A Bibliography of English Character-Books 1608–1700* (Oxford: Oxford University Press, 1925), 19.

29. Often, after being printed on their own, characters made their way into a bigger volume. Tuke's *Character of a Painted Woman,* for example, reappeared a year later as part of *A Discourse against Painting and Tincturing of Women* (1616).

30. The numerous shorthand treatises published in the prewar seventeenth century include John Willis, *The Arte of Stenographie* (1602); Edmond Willis, *An Abreviation of Writing by Character* (1627); John Davies, *The Writing Schoolemaster* [. . .] *Wherein is Exactlie Expressed each Severall Character* (1631); Henry Dix, *A New Art of Brachygraphy; or, Short-writing by Characters* (1633). For a full bibliography across the period, see R. C. Alston, *A Bibliography of the English Language from the Invention of Printing to the Year 1800* (Leeds, 1966), 8:8–14.

31. This is also true in the inverse, where Edmond Willis, for example, comments, "And so commending these directions in all humble submission to thy favourable acceptation, and thy selfe with them to the gracious blessing of our God, whose Characters wee are all, I rest thine." In *Writing by Character,* A5v.

32. On these figures within Renaissance literature, see Russ McDonald, "Compar or Parison: Measure for Measure," in *Renaissance Figures of Speech,* ed. Sylvia Adamson, Gavin Alexander, and Katrin Ettenhuber (Cambridge: Cambridge University Press, 2007), 39–58; Brian Vickers, *Francis Bacon and Renais-*

sance Prose (Cambridge: Cambridge University Press, 1968), chap. 4. On *paradiastole* in early modern England, see Quentin Skinner, *Visions of Politics* (Cambridge: Cambridge University Press, 2002), 1:182–186, 2:264–85, 3:87–141. For a recent correction to this account, see Chenyu Tu, "Paradiastole as Distinction-Making," *International Journal of the Classical Tradition* 31, no. 2 (2024): 123–140.

33. *The Rich Cabinet* (1616), A2r.

34. *The Rich Cabinet,* N2v.

35. *The Rich Cabinet,* N2v. On the theological microcosm as metonym, see Samuel Shaw, *Words Made Visible: Or Grammar and Rhetorick Accommodated to the Lives and Manners of Men* (1678–1679), I3r, who describes how it "is by a real Metonimy that men of devout and refin'd minds discern the *Creator,* where others see nothing but the *Creature.*"

36. George Puttenham, *The Arte of English Poesie,* ed. Baxter Hathaway (Kent, OH: Kent State University Press, 1970), 222.

37. "Experientia est optimus magister," Geffray Mynshul, *Essayes and Characters* (1618), A1r.

38. Mynshul, *Essayes and Characters,* A2r.

39. Mynshul, *Essayes and Characters,* A4r.

40. Mynshul, *Essayes and Characters,* B1r.

41. Mynshul, *Essayes and Characters,* B3r.

42. Mynshul, *Essayes and Characters,* B2r–B3r.

43. Mynshul, *Essayes and Characters,* B3r.

44. Overbury, *A Wife* (1614), D1v; Mynshul, *Essayes and Characters,* B3v–B4r.

45. On the history of this concept, see Paolo d'Angelo, *Sprezzatura: Concealing the Effort of Art from Aristotle to Duchamp* (New York: Columbia University Press, 2018).

46. [Earle], *Micro-cosmographie,* A2v.

47. [Earle], *Micro-cosmographie,* H3r–v, B1r.

48. [Earle], *Micro-cosmographie,* C2v.

49. R. M., *Micrologia* (1629), B3r.

50. Richard Braithwaite, *Whimzies* (1631), G7v.

51. See R. M., *Micrologia,* D8r.

52. Donald Lupton, *London and the Country Carbonadoed* (1634), B3v.

53. See Henry Dix, *A New Art of Brachygraphy* (1633), B1r.

54. R. M., *Micrologia,* A3r–v.

55. R. M., *Micrologia,* A3r–v.

56. R. M., *Micrologia,* A3v.

57. R. M., *Micrologia,* A3v–A4r.

58. Wye Saltonstall, *Picturae Loquentes* (1631), A4r–v.

59. Saltonstall, *Picturae Loquentes,* A5r.

60. Braithwaite, *Whimzies,* A6r.

61. Braithwaite, *Whimzies,* A6r.

62. Braithwaite, *Whimzies,* A6v.

63. Braithwaite, *Whimzies,* A7r.

64. Braithwaite, *Whimzies,* A6v.

65. On this see Kathryn Murphy, "Of Sticks and Stones: The Essay, Experience, and Experiment," in *On Essays: Montaigne to the Present,* ed. Thomas Karshan and Kathryn Murphy (Oxford: Oxford University Press, 2020), chap. 3.

66. Mynshul, *Essayes and Characters,* D1v.

67. Its title, *Satyrical Essayes and Characters,* clearly announced its delineation into the two genres.

68. Saltonstall, *Picturae Loquentes,* A3v–A4r.

69. Thomas Jordan, *Pictures of Passions* (1641), B1r–v. On Jordan's politics, see Lynn Hulse, "Jordan, Thomas (*c.* 1614–1685)," *ODNB.*

70. Jordan, *Pictures of Passions,* B1r–v.

71. Kathryn Murphy and Anita Traninger, eds., *The Emergence of Impartiality* (Leiden, Netherlands: Brill, 2013), 2.

72. Murphy and Traninger, *The Emergence of Impartiality,* 2n4.

73. On *in utramque partem disserere* as between partiality and impartiality, see Anita Traninger, "Taking Sides and the Prehistory of Impartiality," in *The Emergence of Impartiality,* ed. Kathryn Murphy and Anita Traninger (Leiden, Netherlands: Brill, 2013), 31–63.

74. *The True Character of an Untrue Bishop* (1641), A2r.

75. *OED,* s.v. "true," adj., 1a, 3, 4.

76. *The True Character of an Untrue Bishop,* A2r.

77. See Jurgis Baltrušaitis, *Anamorphic Art,* trans. W. J. Strachn (New York: Harry N. Abrams, 1976).

78. See David Norbrook, "May, Thomas (*b.* in or after 1596, *d.* 1650)," *ODNB.*

79. Thomas May, *The Character of a Right Malignant* (1644), A1r–v.

80. In this, May's character unwittingly returns to a feature of Theophrastus's original set in emphasizing behavioral regularities and typical actions.

81. May, *The Character of a Right Malignant,* A4r.

82. *A True Character of Worsters Late Hurly-Burly* (1642), A2r.

83. *A True Character of Worsters Late Hurly-Burly,* A3v.

84. Murphy and Traninger, *Emergence of Impartiality,* 2.

85. On a different set of political uses for the language and "literature of discovery" in the period, see Andrew Fitzmaurice, "Classical Rhetoric and the Literature of Discovery 1570–1630" (PhD diss., University of Cambridge, 1996). The characters of discovery I describe move the genre away from rhetoric rather than employing it, as in the corpus of colonial texts that Fitzmaurice treats.

86. *The Jesuits Character* (1642), A1r.

87. *An Abstract of Some Late Characters* (1643), title page. See also Christopher Cob, *The Sect Every Where Spoken Against* [. . .] (*A Short Character, at Present, of Them and Their Way, Till an Opportunity of a Farther and Fuller Discovery*) (1651); George Hammon, [. . .] *A Discovery of the False and Corrupted Ministers by Ten Characters* [. . .]: *A Discovery of the True Ministers by Ten Characters* (1655).

88. *Englands Discoverer, or The Levellers Creed* (1649); John Canne, *The Discoverer: Wherein is Set Forth (To Undeceive the Nation) the Reall Plots and Stratagems of Lieut. Col. John Lilburn* (1649).

89. *The True Character of Such as are Malignants* (1643), A1r.

90. *OED,* s.v. "deceive," v., 1, 2.

91. *The True Character of Such as are Malignants,* A2r.

92. *The True Character of Such as are Malignants,* A2r.

93. *The True Character of Such as are Malignants,* A2v–A3r. The resonance of this number, with its echo of the cardinal sins, does not seem accidental.

94. *The True Character of Such as are Malignants,* A3r.

95. Here see John Wilkins, "Concerning an Universall Character, that May be Legible to All Nations and Languages," in *Mercury, or the Secret and Swift Messenger* (1641), chap. 13. His later treatise is entitled *An Essay Toward a Real Character, and a Philosophical Language* (1668). On Wilkins see M. M. Slaughter, *Universal Languages and Scientific Taxonomy in the Seventeenth Century* (Cambridge: Cambridge University Press, 1982), 112. For an overview of the movement of creating artificial languages, see Rhodri Lewis, *Language, Mind and Nature: Artificial Languages in England from Bacon to Locke* (Cambridge: Cambridge University Press, 2007).

96. Lia Formigari, *Language and Experience in 17th Century British Philosophy* (Amsterdam: John Benjamins, 1988), 61.

97. Francis Lodwick, *The Ground-work, or Foundation, Laid (or so Intended) for the Framing of a New Perfect Language and an Universal or Commonwriting* (1652), A4r; Cave Beck, *The Universal Character* (1657); Thomas Urquhart, *Logopandecteison, or an Introduction to the Universal Language* (1653), B1r.

98. R[ichard] W[ard], *The Character of Warre* (1643), A2r.

99. See also Thomas Ford, *The Times Anatomiz'd in Severall Characters* (1647)—one of the few political character books of the period; *An Agitator Anotomiz'd* [*sic*] (1648); Lionel Lockyer, *The Character of a Time-Serving Saint or, The Hypocrite Anatomized, and Thorowly Dissected* (1652).

100. *Character of a* [. . .] *Round-head,* A7v.

101. *Character of a* [. . .] *Round-head,* A8r.

102. *OED,* s.v. "anatomy," n., 1a., 10.

103. *The True Character of Mercurius Aulicus* (1645), A3r.

104. *The True Character of Mercurius Aulicus,* A3r.

105. *The True Character of Mercurius Aulicus,* A3r.

106. *The True Character of Mercurius Aulicus,* A3r.

107. See Quentin Skinner, "Hobbes and the Purely Artificial Person of the State," *The Journal of Political Philosophy* 7, no. 1 (1999): 1–29; Hobbes, *Leviathan,* 179.

108. *The King no Tyrant* (1643), A2r.

109. *The Rich Cabinet,* N2v.

110. *The King no Tyrant,* A2r.

111. *The King no Tyrant,* A2r–v.

112. Saltonstall, *Picturae Loquentes,* B5r–v.

113. *The King no Tyrant,* A2v.

114. John Cleveland, *A Character of a Diurnal-Maker* (1653), A2r.

115. Cleveland, *A Character of a Diurnal-Maker,* A2v.

116. Claire Labarbe, "*Mises en abyme,* and Satirical Descriptions: 'Characters' of Writing and Writers in Seventeenth-Century England," *Études Épistémè* 21 (2012), §60–61.

117. Labarbe, "*Mises en abyme,* and Satirical Descriptions," §60–61.

118. [John Cleveland], *The Character of a London Diurnall* (1644), A4v.

119. Labarbe, "*Mises en abyme,* and Satirical Descriptions," §62.

120. John Cleveland, "Of a Protector" [1654], in Verax Philobasileus [pseud.], *Confused Characters of Conceited Coxcombs* (1661), K1r–v, at K1r.

121. *The Martyr of the People* (1649), A2r–v.

122. *The Martyr of the People,* A2v–A3r.

123. *The Martyr of the People,* A2v.

124. *The Martyr of the People,* A2v.

125. For a variant on this commonplace, see also the entry for "Kings" in the *Rich Cabinet,* L2v: "Kings hearts are in the hands of God."

126. *The Martyr of the People,* A3r.

127. *The Martyr of the People,* A3r, A4r.

128. *The Martyr of the People,* A4v.

129. *The Martyr of the People,* A4v.

130. Balthazar Gerbier, *The None-such Charles his Character* (1650), B2r.

131. Gerbier, *The None-such Charles his Character,* A1r. Gerbier's position in the household of George Villiers, marquess of Buckingham, would have given him access to much firsthand information. See Jeremy Wood, "Gerbier, Sir Balthazar (1592–1663/1667)," *ODNB.*

132. Gerbier, *The None-such Charles his Character,* A3r–v.

133. Gerbier, *The None-such Charles his Character,* A3r–v.

134. Gerbier, *The None-such Charles his Character,* I1r, M4v, L2r.

135. Gerbier, *The None-such Charles his Character,* N3r.

136. Gerbier, *The None-such Charles his Character,* N4r.

137. Gerbier, *The None-such Charles his Character,* H2v.

138. For an example of how the "character" became a popular addition to an obituary in the 1650s, see *The Twelve Wonders of England, Being a Most Strange and Wonderful Relation of the Death of Mr. Parrey, an Inn-keeper* [. . .] *Together with a Narrative of his Life and Death, his Memento and Character* (1655).

139. T. L. W., *An Exact Character or, Narrative of* [. . .] *Oliver Cromwell* (1658), A2r.

140. I. S., *The Perfect Politician* (1659), A4r, A3r.

141. I. S., *The Perfect Politician,* A4r, A3r.

142. A curious connection between Evelyn, Casaubon, and Theophrastus is traced by Grafton and Weinberg. See their *Isaac Casaubon,* 19.

143. [John Evelyn], *A Character of England* (1659), A6r–v.

144. *A Character of England,* A7r.

145. *Cf.* Verg. *Aen.* III.164.

146. *A Character of England,* A7v–A8r.

147. *A Character of England,* A8r.

148. *A Character of England,* A8r.

149. *A Character of France* (1659), title page.

150. *A Character of France,* A2r–A3r.

151. *A Character of France,* B2v.

152. *A Character of France,* B11r.

153. *A Character of France,* B2r.

154. For their commitment to representing vices and virtues, see *Character of Spain* (1660), A4r; *Character of Italy* (1660), A5v.

155. *Character of Spain,* B1r–v.

156. *Character of Italy,* B1r. See *OED,* s.v. "clod," n., 1, 2.

157. *Character of Spain,* B2r; *Character of Italy,* B12r, C10v.

158. See Jacques Bos, *Reading the Soul: The Transformation of the Classical Discourse on Character 1550–1750* (Leiden, Netherlands: Brill, 2003), 216; Paola Gambarota, *Irresistible Signs: The Genius of Language and Italian National Identity* (Toronto: University of Toronto Press, 2011), 56; Jean Robertson, "Felltham's *Character* of the Low Countries," *Modern Language Notes* 58 (1943): 385–388, at 387.

159. G[riffin], *Overbury Revived,* B1r.

160. G[riffin], *Overbury Revived,* B5r.

161. G[riffin], *Overbury Revived,* B6r.

162. G[riffin], *Overbury Revived,* E5r–v.

163. Philobasileus, *Confused Characters,* A7r.

164. Philobasileus, *Confused Characters,* F6r–v.

165. On the simultaneous development of different forms of autobiography in the early modern period, see Adam Smyth, ed., *A History of English Autobiography* (Cambridge: Cambridge University Press, 2016), chaps. 4–7; Adam Smyth, *Autobiography in Early Modern England* (Cambridge: Cambridge University Press, 2010).

166. On Plutarch and Walton, see Jessica Martin, *Walton's Lives: Conformist Commemorations and the Rise of Biography* (Oxford: Oxford University Press, 2011), chap. 2.

167. Clement Barksdale, *Characters* (1662), B3r.

168. *The Cheating Sollicitor Cheated* (1665), B1v. On biography and funerary oration, see Martin, *Walton's Lives,* chap. 1.

169. M. P., *A Character of Coffee and Coffee-Houses,* A2r.

170. T. W., *The Poets Complaint* (1681), D1r. This is a reference to similar arguments about poetry's origin made by Aristotle in book 4 of the *Poetics* (1448b4–9): "It can be seen that poetry was broadly engendered by a pair of causes, both natural. For it is an instinct of human beings, from childhood, to engage in mimesis." In Stephen Halliwell's translation (Cambridge, MA: Harvard University Press, 1995).

171. George Alsop, *A Character of the Province of Mary-land* (1666), A3r–v. On this claim in the context of other promoters of New England, see E. Brooks Holifield, *Era of Persuasion: American Thought and Culture, 1521–1680,* 2nd ed. (Boston: Twayne, 2004), 18–38. My attempt here is to place Alsop in the context of the development of the character as a form alongside.

172. Alsop, *A Character of the Province of Mary-land,* E8r.

173. Alsop, *A Character of the Province of Mary-land,* A4v. If rendered similar to Mynshul in this promise to keep his text anchored in his own experience, Alsop is careful, unlike Mynshul, to write a significantly less rhetorical character.

174. *The Young Maids Character* (1677), A1v.

175. *The Young Maids Character,* title page.

176. *The Young Maids Character,* A1v. I am grateful to Lisa Shapiro for pointing out the context this text provides to some of Aphra Behn's work, as well

as to one of the scripted conversations from the Maison royale de Saint-Louis. Here see Shapiro, "On the Inseparability of Reasoning and Virtue: Madame de Maintenon's Maison Royale de Saint-Louis," *Metaphilosophy* 54 (2023): 254–267, at 261.

177. *The Young Maids Character,* A2v, A3r.

178. See, for example, Richard Baxter, *A Breviate of the Life of Margaret* (1681).

179. Samuell Person, *An Anatomical Lecture of Man* (1664), A4r.

180. Person, *An Anatomical Lecture of Man,* B1r.

181. Person, *An Anatomical Lecture of Man,* B1v.

182. Person, *An Anatomical Lecture of Man,* B2r.

183. Person, *An Anatomical Lecture of Man,* B2v.

5. Developing Moral Satire: The Character in France

1. *Dictionnaire de l'Académie françoise,* s.v. "*caracteriser,*" v.a.: "Marquer le caractere d'une personne, d'une passion, d'un vice, d'une vertu etc. Ce Poëte, cet Autheur caracterise bien les gens dont il parle, ou qu'il fait parler." For a similar definition, see also Antoine Furetière, *Dictionnaire universel* (The Hague, 1690), s.v. "caracteriser," verb. act. Note that unless indicated otherwise, first editions of all seventeenth- and eighteenth-century texts cited in this chapter were published in Paris.

2. For a good general account of the Fronde, see Orest Ranum, *The Fronde: A French Revolution, 1648–1652* (New York: W. W. Norton, 1993). On the role of popular revolt as a generating force, see Perry Anderson, *Lineages of the Absolutist State* (London: Verso, 1974), 98–99; Boris Porchnev, *Les soulèvements populaires en France de 1623 à 1648*, ed. Robert Mandrou (Paris: SEVPEN, 1963), 506–537.

3. Gerhard Müller-Schwefe, "Joseph Hall's *Characters of Vertues and Vices*: Notes toward a Revaluation," *Texas Studies in Literature and Language* 14 (1972–1973): 235–351, at 248.

4. For La Bruyère's notion that he is writing "remarks," see his *The Characters or the Manners of the Age* [. . .], 2nd ed. (London, 1700), B1v. I use the second edition of the English translation of La Bruyère's *Characters* due to acknowledged translation problems with the first. While these two volumes are published together, I henceforth refer to the adaptation as *Manners of the Age* and the translation as *Moral Characters,* as pagination is not continuous.

5. Christophe Schuwey, "L'organe des anciens? Retour sur les rééditions des *Caractères* de La Bruyère," *French Studies* 75, no. 1 (2020), 17–33, at 33.

6. Jon Elster, *Alchemies of the Mind: Rationality and the Emotions* (Cambridge: Cambridge University Press, 1999), 51; Johan Heilbron, *The Rise of Social Theory,* trans. Sheila Gogol (Cambridge: Polity Press, 1995), 71. On the lineage, see Michael Moriarty, *Fallen Nature, Fallen Selves: Early Modern French Thought II* (Oxford: Oxford University Press, 2006), 19.

7. Heilbron, *The Rise of Social Theory,* 71. This, for Heilbron, is why the French *moralistes* play an essential role in the emergence of the social sciences.

8. Friedrich Nietzsche, *Human, All Too Human,* trans. Marion Faber and Stephen Lehmann (London: Penguin, 1994), 40–41. For studies of Nietzsche and the *moralistes,* see Robert Pippin, "Nietzsche's Moral Psychology and the French Moralist Tradition," *Nietzscheforschung* 12 (2006): 313–321; Jiani Fan, "Pleasure as a First Principle? Nietzsche and the French Moralists on Morality and Religion" (PhD diss., Princeton University, 2021).

9. Damien Tricoire, "The Fabrication of the Philosophe: Catholicism, Court Culture, and the Origins of Enlightenment Moralism in France," *Eighteenth-Century Studies* 51, no. 4 (2018): 453–477, at 456.

10. Roland Barthes, "La Bruyère," in *Essais critiques* (Paris: Seuil, 1964), 229–245, at 239.

11. See François-Xavier Cuche, *Une pensée sociale catholique: Fleury, La Bruyere, Fénelon* (Paris: Cerf, 1991); François-Xavier Cuche, "La Bruyère et le Petit Concile," *Cahiers de l'Association internationale des études francaises* 44 (1992): 323–340; François-Xavier Cuche, *L'Absolu et le monde: Études sur les écrits du Petit Concile. Bossuet, La Bruyère, Fénelon et leurs amis* (Paris: Honoré Champion, 2017).

12. Cuche, "La Bruyère et le Petit Concile," 323.

13. Cuche, "La Bruyère et le Petit Concile," 326.

14. Cuche, *Une pensée sociale catholique,* 512.

15. The latter provides, as Michael Moriarty notes, one of the key differences with Calvinism. In "Augustinianism," in *The Cambridge History of French Thought,* ed. Michael Moriarty and Jeremy Jennings (Cambridge: Cambridge University Press, 2019), 135–140, at 139.

16. For a counterreading of Jansenism as a tendency that "redirected attention from the organizing activities of the monarchy to the energetic activities of all individuals within society," see Nannerl O. Keohane, *Philosophy and the State in France: The Renaissance to the Enlightenment* (Princeton, NJ: Princeton University Press, 1980), 21.

17. Cuche, *Une pensée sociale catholique,* 512.

18. Cuche, "La Bruyère et le Petit Concile," 334.

19. Jean de La Bruyère, "Discours de réception à l'Académie française," in *Les Caractères,* ed. Emmanuel Bury (Paris: Librarie Générale Française, 1995), 609–622, at 613–614.

20. Here see Moriarty, *Fallen Nature,* 19–20, after Louis van Delft, *Le Moraliste classique* (Geneva: Droz, 1982), 87–108. Moriarty has adopted Cuche's orientation to acknowledge the social and political work of La Bruyère's text. Here see *Fallen Nature,* 68–70; Michael Moriarty, "La Bruyère: Virtue and Disinterestedness," *French Studies* 68, no. 2 (2014): 164–179, at 177–179.

21. Larry Norman, *The Shock of the Ancient: Literature and History in Early Modern France* (Chicago: University of Chicago Press, 2011), 141.

22. Tricoire, "The Fabrication of the Philosophe," 454. This suggestion can also be found in the review by Michael Moriarty of François-Xavier Cuche's *L'Absolu et le monde* in *French Studies* 72, no. 3 (2018), 434. See also Julien Benda's earlier claim that "the precise role of La Bruyère, in terms of politics, seems to have been to be the first Cicero" in absolutist France, even if he should

not at all be associated with "our revolutionaries." In his introduction to *Œuvres complètes de La Bruyère* (Paris: Pléiade, 1951), ix–xxii, at xviii–xix.

23. Schuwey, "L'organe des anciens?," 25.

24. Cuche, "La Bruyère et le Petit Concile," 340.

25. La Bruyère, *Moral Characters,* 2A8v. He uses this phrase to likely refer to Pascal. I come back to this in more detail.

26. Here see Seyla Benhabib, *Critique, Norm, and Utopia: A Study of the Foundations of Critical Theory* (New York: Columbia University Press, 1986); Frederick Neuhouser, *Diagnosing Social Pathology: Rousseau, Hegel, Marx, and Durkheim* (Cambridge: Cambridge University Press, 2022).

27. For two excellent studies, see Susan James, *Passion and Action: The Emotions in Seventeenth-Century Philosophy* (Oxford: Oxford University Press, 1999), and the classic Anthony Levi, *French Moralists: The Theory of the Passions 1589 to 1649* (Oxford: Clarendon Press, 1964).

28. Adamantius, *La physionomie* [. . .], trans. Henry de Boyvin du Varoüy (1635), a4r–v. On the printing history, see William Alexander Greenhill, "Adamantius," in *Dictionary of Greek and Roman Biography and Mythology,* ed. William Smith (Boston: Little Brown, 1867), 1:18.

29. Adamantius, *La physionomie,* a4r–v.

30. Adamantius, *La physionomie,* d2r.

31. Marin Cureau de La Chambre, *Les characteres des passions* (1662), ¶4r.

32. La Chambre, *Les characteres des passions,* ¶4v.

33. La Chambre, *Les characteres des passions,* ¶4v.

34. La Chambre, *Les characteres des passions,* ¶4v.

35. La Chambre, *Les characteres des passions,* A1r.

36. René Descartes, *Les passions de l'âme* (1650), B6v–B7r. Here see James, *Passion and Action,* 255–268.

37. Descartes, *Les passions de l'âme,* C2r.

38. Descartes, *Les passions de l'âme,* D5v.

39. René Descartes, "Reponse a la seconde lettre," [August 14, 1649], in *Les passions de l'âme,* 3*7r–v.

40. On Descartes's targets here, see Josiane Boulad-Ayoub and Paule-Monique Vernes, *La révolution cartésienne* (Lévis, Quebec: Presses Université Laval, 2006), 176.

41. As Christopher Allen argues, this provoked major changes in the visual arts. Where before the passions were inner movements of the soul, "which might or might not manifest themselves adequately on the surface of the body; now the physical manifestation was the primary event, and the artist could expect, by concentrating on the measurable movements of the facial muscles, to grasp and convey the essential properties of the passions." See his "Painting the Passions: The *Passions de l'âme* as a Basis for Pictorial Expression," in *The Soft Underbelly of Reason: The Passions in the Seventeenth Century,* ed. Stephen Gaukroger (Abingdon: Routledge, 1998), 79–111, at 93. On Charles Le Brun's *Conférence sur l'expression des différents caractères des passions* (1668) as a major text in the uptake of this idea, see Stephanie Ross, "Painting the Passions: Charles Le Brun's *Conférence sur l'expression,*" *JHI* 45, no. 1 (1984): 25–47.

42. Note, however, that for Descartes the soul retains a separation from this mechanistic process. For a good summary of this, see Moriarty, *Fallen Nature,* 34–45.

43. Russell Goulbourne, "Satire in Seventeenth- and Eighteenth-Century France," in *A Companion to Satire: Ancient and Modern,* ed. Ruben Quintero (Malden, MA: Wiley, 2006), 139–169, at 143.

44. Hubert Carrier, *La presse et la Fronde (1648–1653)* (Geneva: Droz, 1989), 1:295.

45. Joël Cornette, "Les pamphlets de la Fronde," *RS,* nos. 1–2 (1992): 177–188, at 177–178. See also his list at 181.

46. See Mark Bannister, "Mazarinades, Manifestos and Mavericks: Political and Ideological Engagement during the Fronde," *French History* 30, no. 2 (2016): 165–180, at 165. For the figure see Cornette, "Les pamphlets de la Fronde," 177.

47. On Plutarch's early modern reception, see Sophia Xenophontos, ed., *Brill's Companion to the Reception of Plutarch* (Leiden, Netherlands: Brill, 2019), part IV.

48. *L'ambitieux ou le portraict d'Aelius Sejanus en la personne du Cardinal Mazarin* (1649), B2r.

49. *Le vray charactere du tyran* (1650), A2r, G2v.

50. On comparisons between the Fronde and the English Revolution, see Voltaire, *Siècle de Louis XIV,* ed. Émile Bourgeois (Paris: Hachette, 1906), 49–51; P. A. Knachel, *England and the Fronde: The Impact of the English Civil War and Revolution on France* (Ithaca, NY: Cornell University Press, 1967); Richard Bonney, "The English and French Civil Wars," *History* 65, no. 215 (1980): 365–382, at 371.

51. In Carrier's terms, "individual intimacies" played a large role in these civil wars, with the House of Condé pitted against the House of Vendôme and Cardinal Retz against La Rochefoucauld. See *La presse et la Fronde,* 1:300–301.

52. Here see Jacqueline Plantié, *La mode du portrait littéraire en France (1641–1681)* (Paris: Honoré Champion, 1994).

53. On how a religious dimension is "yet to be shown" for the Fronde and how "Local Huguenotism was studiously neutral in the South," see respectively Bonney, "The English and French Civil Wars," 373, and Anderson, *Lineages of the Absolutist State,* 99. But the emergence of the radical Ormée party in Bordeaux would have given character writers, in theory, an ample opportunity for pillorying a new faction. Here see Sal Alexander Westrich, *The Ormée of Bordeaux: A Revolution during the Fronde* (Baltimore: Johns Hopkins University Press, 1972); Hélène Sarrazin, *La Fronde en Gironde: l'Ormée, un movement révolutionnaire, 1648–1654* (Bordeaux: Les Dossiers d'Aquitaine, 1996).

54. Here see Lawrence Stone, "Social Mobility in England 1500–1700," *P&P* 33 (1966): 16–55; Richard Grassby, "Social Mobility and Business Enterprise in Seventeenth-Century England," in *Puritans and Revolutionaries: Essays in Seventeenth-Century History Presented to Christopher Hill,* ed. Donald Pennington and Keith Thomas (Oxford: Clarendon Press, 1978), 335–381. For different Marxist approaches to the Fronde, compare Karl Marx, "The Bourgeoisie and the Counter-Revolution I–IV," in *The Revolutions of 1848,* ed. David Fernbach (Harmondsworth: Penguin, 1973), 186–212, at 192–193; Porchnev, *Les soulèvements populaires en France,* 506–537.

55. See, for example, Tristan l'Hermite, *Le page disgracié, où l'on voit de vifs caractères d'hommes de tous temperamens et de toutes professions* (1667).

56. As Auerbach puts it, under its aegis, anyone "who wanted to be socially unexceptionable must not allow the economic basis of his life to be conspicuous, nor his professional specialty if he had one." In "The Faux Devot," in *Mimesis: The Representation of Reality in Western Literature,* trans. Willard Task (Princeton, NJ: Princeton University Press, 2003), 359–394, at 367–368. On *honnêteté* see Peter Brooks, *The Novel of Worldliness: Crébillon, Marivaux, Laclos, Stendhal* (Princeton, NJ: Princeton University Press, 1969), 54–55; Keith Thomas, *In Pursuit of Civility: Manners and Civilization in Early Modern England* (Waltham, MA: Brandeis University Press, 2018), 17, who claims that *honnêteté* was the ideal to which behavior tended in seventeenth-century France.

57. See Davis Bitton, *The French Nobility in Crisis, 1560–1640* (Stanford, CA: Stanford University Press, 1969); George Huppert, *Les Bourgeois Gentilshommes: An Essay on the Definition of Elites in Renaissance France* (Chicago: University of Chicago Press, 1977); André Devyver, *Le Sang épuré: Les préjugés de race chez les gentilhommes français de l'Ancien Régime (1560–1720)* (Brussels, Belgium: Éditions de l'Université de Bruxelles, 1973).

58. Auerbach, "The Faux Devot," 367.

59. See François duc de La Rochefoucauld, *Memoires de M.D.L.R.: Sur les brigues à la mort de Louys XIII* (Cologne [Brussels], 1663).

60. On the composition date, see Philippe Sellier, "La Rochefoucauld, Pascal, Saint Augustin," *Revue d'histoire littéraire de la France* 69, nos. 3–4 (1969): 551–575, at 552.

61. Quoted in Jean Rohou, introduction to *Réflexions ou sentences et maxims morales* by La Rochefoucauld, ed. Jean Rohou (Paris: Garnier, 1991), 5–61, at 47.

62. Rohou, introduction, 6.

63. Rohou, introduction, 36.

64. La Rochefoucauld, *Réflexions* [. . .], 5th ed. (1678), A1r, Q7r.

65. La Rochefoucauld, *Maximes* (1665), A1r. Other relevant causes to virtue may be purely physical, such as temperament.

66. Elster, *Alchemies of the Mind,* 32–33.

67. Here see Michael Moriarty, *Disguised Vices: Theories of Virtue in Early Modern French Thought* (Oxford: Oxford University Press, 2011), 2–3, and more generally chap. 14. See also Jean Starobinski, "La Rochefoucauld et les morales substitutives," *La Nouvelle Revue Française* 163–164 (1966): 16–34, and (1996): 211–229.

68. Skinner, *Visions of Politics,* 3:103, 2:280.

69. Skinner, *Visions of Politics,* 3:114, 3:122.

70. For the early medieval history of this concept, see Carla Casagrande and Silvana Vecchio, *Histoire des péchés capitaux au Moyen Âge,* trans. Pierre-Emmanuel Dauzat (Paris: Aubier, 2002), 293. See Moriarty, "Augustinianism," 135–136, for an account of why this concept was received with such fervor.

71. Rohou, introduction, 29. See 30–32 on the surge in the language of interest in the period and its relationship to financial speculation after the Franco-Spanish War (1635–1659) and the Fronde.

72. On de Tourval's other translations, see Alban Déléris, "Les vies françaises de l'*Arcadia*: Du roman de Sir Philip Sidney à ses adaptations dramatiques en France," *Renaissance and Reformation* 40, no. 3 (2017): 133–155. On the French reception of Hall, see Sidney Lee, "Beginnings of French Translation from the English," *Transactions of the Bibliographical Society* 8 (1907): 96–106.

73. During this time, Theophrastus's *Characters* itself was also translated into French. See Hierosme de Bénevent, trans., *Les charactères des mœurs* (1613).

74. For a composition date of around 1645, before its later publication, see Kirk, *"Heaven upon Earth" and "Characters of Virtues and Vices,"* 56.

75. Ulisse Paravicino, *La scuola del savio, tradotta (dal francese di U. Chevreau) in lingua italiana* (Basel, 1666).

76. Chevreau, *L'escole du sage,* K5v.

77. Chevreau, *L'escole du sage,* ā6r.

78. Chevreau, *L'escole du sage,* A6r.

79. For a good account of the changes in neo-Stoicism during the period, see Rohou, introduction, 8–9.

80. For other kinds of exemplary "characters," see Hippolyte-Jules Pilet de La Mesnardière's *Elegiac character* (1640), providing models of poems to be imitated, or the models of handwriting offered in Guy du Faur Pibrac's *Les quatrains du seigneur de Pibrac* [. . .] *Propres pour apprendre à lire et escrire aux Enfans* (Paris, 1645), a2r [my pagination].

81. La Rochefoucauld, "Réflexions diverses," [1673–1679], in *Réflexions ou sentences et maxims morales,* ed. Jean Rohou (Paris: Garnier, 1991), 199–263, at 214. For the composition date, see Rohou, introduction, 50.

82. La Rochefoucauld, "Réflexions diverses," in *Réflexions*, ed. Rohou, 214.

83. On the early stage of the portrait, see Brooks, *Novel of Worldliness,* 55–57.

84. La Rochefoucauld, "Portrait de La Rochefoucauld fait par lui-même" [1659], in *Réflexions,* ed. Rohou, 265–270.

85. Smeed, *The Theophrastan "Character,"* 48–49.

86. On the frontispiece in context, see Ian Maclean, "La Rochefoucauld, Little Learning and the Love of Truth," *JWCI* 75 (2012): 297–318.

87. La Rochefoucauld, "Réflexions diverses," in *Réflexions*, ed. Rohou, 202–203. On La Rochefoucauld as working within the tradition of treatises on conversation, see Oskar Roth, "La Rochefoucauld: De l'anthropologie pessimiste à la recherche d'un gout vrai et autonome," *Dix-septième siècle* 254 (2012): 59–71, at 60.

88. See Michael Moriarty, "Ethical, Political and Social Thought," in *The Cambridge History of French Thought,* ed. Michael Moriarty and Jeremy Jennings (Cambridge: Cambridge University Press, 2019), 169–182, at 172, for Esprit and de Sablé's connections with Augustinianism, and Moriarty, *Disguised Vices,* chap. 12, for a consideration of the collaboration. See "Lettre de La Rochefoucauld au Père Thomas Esprit. 6 février 1664," in *Réflexions*, ed. Rohou, 307–309, at 308.

89. La Rochefoucauld, "Lettre de La Rochefoucauld au Père Thomas Esprit. 6 février 1664," in *Réflexions,* ed. Rohou, 308.

90. For support of the Augustinian and specifically Jansenist inheritance, see Sellier, "La Rochefoucauld, Pascal, Saint Augustin"; Jean Lafond, *La Rochefou-*

cauld: Augustinisme et littérature (Paris: Klincksieck, 1977). For dissent from this thesis, see Corrado Rosso, "Un grande convertito: La Rochefoucauld (a proposito dell'interpretazione di Jean Lafond)," *Studi francesi* 18 (1979): 93–97; Henry C. Clark, *La Rochefoucauld and the Language of Unmasking in Seventeenth-Century France* (Geneva: Droz, 1994), chap. 6. Moriarty, *Disguised Vices,* 380, treads a path between these two approaches.

91. The letter coheres with the textual history of the *Maxims*, which was initially prefaced by a discourse by Henri de La Chapelle-Bessé explaining that La Rochefoucauld was following the path set out by Augustine. Even when this preface, and other Augustinian echoes, were removed from the second edition, thus severing an explicit link with religion, it remained an "exploration of human behaviour, which might nourish religious commitments," as Moriarty remarks in "Ethical, Political and Social Thought," 172–173.

92. In my citations of the *Pensées,* in-line I use the numbering in the edition by Michel Le Guern (Paris: Gallimard, 2004). I, however, borrow (and occasionally emend) the English translation by A. J. Krailsheimer (London: Penguin, 1995), in these notes. My emendations are marked by square brackets.

93. Pascal, *Pensées,* trans. Krailsheimer, 4.

94. Pascal, *Pensées,* trans. Krailsheimer, 4. For an evaluation of Pascal's success in carrying out these intentions, see Michael Moriarty, *Pascal: Reasoning and Belief* (Oxford: Oxford University Press, 2020).

95. Pascal, *Pensées,* trans. Krailsheimer, 5, 13.

96. Pascal, *Pensées,* trans. Krailsheimer, 12–13.

97. By not rendering "passions of the soul" here, but "passions" instead, Krailsheimer somewhat obfuscates the engagement with Descartes. See his *Pensées,* 13.

98. Blaise Pascal, "Entretien avec M. de Saci sur Épictète et Montaigne," in *Œuvres complètes de Blaise Pascal,* ed. Charles Lahure and Louis Hachette (Paris, 1871), 423–433, at 425: "J'ose dire qu'il [Épictète] méritoit d'être adoré, s'il avoit aussi bien connu son impuissance, puisqu'il falloit être Dieu pour apprendre l'un et l'autre aux hommes."

99. Pascal, *Pensées,* trans. Krailsheimer, 12.

100. Pascal, *Pensées,* trans. Krailsheimer, 69.

101. Moriarty, *Pascal,* 394.

102. For a good biography, from which these details are mostly taken, see Robert Garapon, Les caractères *de La Bruyère: La Bruyère au travail* (Paris: Société d'Édition d'Enseignement Supérieur, 1978), 11–28. See also Raymond Couallier, "Naissance et origines de La Bruyère," *Revue d'histoire littéraire de la France* (July-September 1963): 441–447.

103. Garapon, *La Bruyère au travail,* 22–23.

104. For the argument that La Bruyère's financial situation was actually fragile in this period, see Schuwey, "L'organe des anciens?," 20.

105. On the issue of accepting the ninth edition as La Bruyère's own work, see Benda, introduction, ix.

106. This figure is cited in Smeed, *The Theophrastan "Character,"* 50; Goulbourne, "Satire," 148. For a more detailed textual history, see P. Josserand, "Chronologie," in *Œuvres complètes de La Bruyère*, ed. Benda, xxiv–xxviii.

107. La Bruyère, *Moral Characters,* 2A2r.

108. La Bruyère, *Moral Characters,* 2A2r.

109. La Bruyère, *Moral Characters,* 2A2r.

110. Given that Casaubon's *Theophrasti characteres ethici,* *2–v, sees the second type as exhortatory paraenesis, I here disagree with Bury that La Bruyère's third type should be understood as "les ouvrages à vocation parénétique." See Emmanuel Bury, introduction to *Les Caractères* by La Bruyère ed. Emmanuel Bury (Paris: Librarie Générale Française, 1995), 9–42, at 14–15.

111. Bury, introduction, 15, also hazards two ancient possibilities for the first two categories: Aristotle and Hippocrates.

112. Benda proposes La Rochefoucauld, Descartes, La Bruyère in *Œuvres complètes de La Bruyère,* ed. Benda, 669; Bury, introduction, 15, suggests Nicolas Coëffeteau or Jean-François Senault, La Chambre, and La Bruyère. The latter seems more likely, given that La Bruyère seems to go on to praise La Rochefoucauld later in this preface.

113. La Bruyère, *Moral Characters,* 2A2r.

114. La Bruyère, *Moral Characters,* 2A2r. See "rebattu, ue," part. passé de "rebattre," senses 3–4: "Avoir les oreilles rebattues d'une chose, être las de l'entendre répéter"; "Répété à satiété," in Emile Littré, *Dictionnaire de français Littré* (Paris, 1863–1877), s.v.

115. La Bruyère, *Moral Characters,* 2A2r.

116. La Bruyère, *Moral Characters,* 2A2r. This is the translation used by the 1699 English edition, at 2G5r: "supposing the principles of Natural and Moral Philosophy left in a *controversial suspence* by the Antients and Moderns." The 1700 translation has only kept "controverted," which takes us away from the sense of *rebattu.* See La Bruyère, *The Moral Characters of Theophrastus* (London, 1699).

117. La Bruyère, *Moral Characters,* 2A1v.

118. Benda thinks that La Bruyère clearly prefers the second category of "Wit without Learning," but this seems to me hard to sustain considering the arguments that follow. See *Œuvres complètes de La Bruyère,*" ed. Benda, 669.

119. Schuwey, "L'organe des anciens?," 31.

120. La Bruyère, *Moral Characters,* 2A7r.

121. La Bruyère, *Moral Characters,* 2A7r.

122. La Bruyère, *Moral Characters,* 2A6r.

123. La Bruyère, *Moral Characters,* 2A5v.

124. La Bruyère, *Moral Characters,* 2A5v–6v.

125. Norman, *The Shock of the Ancient,* 132.

126. La Bruyère, *Manners of the Age,* S2r. The French original places La Bruyère's translation of Theophrastus before his own adaptation, but the English translation reverses this order.

127. Gloria Vivenza, *Adam Smith and the Classics: The Classical Heritage in Adam Smith's Thought* (Oxford: Oxford University Press, 2001), 179.

128. La Bruyère, *Moral Characters,* 2A6r–v.

129. La Bruyère, *Manners of the Age,* B3r

130. La Bruyère, *Manners of the Age,* H1r.

131. Heilbron, *The Rise of Social Theory,* 19.

132. La Bruyère, *Manners of the Age,* N3r.

133. La Bruyère, *Manners of the Age,* B7v, at K4v–K5r. See Schuwey, "L'organe des anciens?," 30–31, for the argument that La Bruyère is positioning *The Charac-*

ters or *Manners of the Age* as a rival to the *Mercure Galant* newspaper, a "veritable alternative" form of constantly reedited prose.

134. La Bruyère, *Moral Characters,* 2A8v.

135. La Bruyère, *Moral Characters,* 2A8v.

136. La Bruyère, *Moral Characters,* 2A8v.

137. Moriarty, *Fallen Nature,* 77. It should be noted that Moriarty is concerned here with exposing how the *Characters* is not *only* concerned with the internal but betrays a "social psychology."

138. La Chambre, *Les characteres des passions,* ¶iv,¶v.

139. Jacques Bos, "Individuality and Inwardness in the Literary Character Sketches of the Seventeenth Century," *JWCI* 61 (1998): 142–157, at 157.

140. See Moriarty, *Fallen Nature,* 77, for the qualification that this is not consistently true across the whole collection.

141. La Bruyère, *Manners of the Age,* Q1r.

142. La Bruyère, *Manners of the Age,* I8v–I9r.

143. For a formalist reading of the pair, see Serge Doubvrosky, "Lecture de la Bruyère," *Poétique: revue de théorie et d'analyse littéraire,* no. 2 (1970): 195–201.

144. For Elster, the French moralists deserve a major place in understanding the emotions, precisely because of their insights into how emotions affect behavior, generate other emotions, and shape judgment. See Elster, *Alchemies of the Mind,* 76.

145. La Bruyère, *Manners of the Age,* B4v.

146. La Bruyère, *Manners of the Age,* B6r. In terms of Theophrastus, see my Chapter 1.

147. Harald Wentzlaff-Eggebert, "Réflexion als Schlüsselwort in La Rochefoucaulds Réflexions ou Sentences et Maximes morales," *Zeitschrift für französische Sprache und Literatur* 82, no. 3 (1972): 217–242. Also see Rohou, introduction, 47.

148. Elster, *Alchemies of the Mind,* 107.

149. Auerbach, "The Faux Devot," 392.

150. La Bruyère, *Manners of the Age,* S5r [*sic*]. On the Cartesian influence, see Louis van Delft, "Clarté et cartésianisme de La Bruyère," *French Review* 44 (1970): 281–290; Jean Deprun, "La Bruyère entre Descartes et Pascal," in *La Bruyère: Le métier du moraliste,* ed. Jean Dagen, Elisabeth Bouguinat, and Marc Escola (Paris: Honoré Champion, 2001), 19–23; Cuche, "La Bruyère et le Petit Concile," 332.

151. La Bruyère, *Manners of the Age,* B1r.

152. La Bruyère, *Manners of the Age,* B1v.

153. La Bruyère, *Manners of the Age,* B1r; La Bruyère, *Moral Characters,* 2A2v.

154. Alvin Kernan, *The Cankered Muse: Satire of the English Renaissance* (New Haven, CT: Yale University Press, 1959), 35.

155. La Bruyère, *Manners of the Age,* O5v. See Moriarty, *Fallen Nature,* 68–69, on the Augustinian inheritance of this analogy.

156. La Bruyère, *Manners of the Age,* B1v.

157. Bernard Roukhomovsky, *Lire La Bruyère: Morale et littérature dans "Les Caractères"* (Rennes, France: PUR, 2019), 16.

158. La Bruyère, *Manners of the Age,* P2v, B6v.

159. La Bruyère, *Manners of the Age,* O5v.

160. La Bruyère, *Manners of the Age,* O5v.

161. La Bruyère, *Manners of the Age,* O5v–O6r.

162. La Bruyère, *Manners of the Age,* O6r.

163. La Bruyère's interest in Roman literature can be found from the *incipit* to his adaptation, which reworks a line by the Roman playwright Terence. See La Bruyère, *Manners of the Age,* B3r; Ter. *Eun.* 41.

164. Hor. *Sat.* 1.4.103–106. In H. Ruston Fairclough's translation (Cambridge, MA: Harvard University Press, 1926).

165. Juv. 1.87. In Susanna Morton Braund's translation (Cambridge, MA: Harvard University Press, 2004).

166. On this latter idea, see Paul Allen Miller, "Imperial Satire as Saturnalia," in *A Companion to Persius and Juvenal,* ed. Susanna Braund and Josiah Osgood (Malden, MA: Wiley, 2012), 312–333, at 312.

167. On the Christianized reception of Persius and Juvenal, see Dan Hooley, "Imperial Satire Revisited: Late Antiquity through the Twentieth Century," in *A Companion to Persius and Juvenal,* ed. Susanna Braund and Josiah Osgood (Malden, MA: Wiley, 2012), 337–362, at 339–340.

168. Hooley, "Imperial Satire Revisited," 339.

169. Goulbourne, "Satire," 148.

170. This intellectual history, tracing the Christianizing of satire, complicates the critic Alvin Kernan's idea that the satirist always acts as if God had "withdrawn and he stood alone in the lunatic world to stay its progressive degeneration." See Kernan, *The Cankered Muse,* 21.

171. La Bruyère, *Moral Characters,* 2A8r.

172. La Bruyère, *Moral Characters,* 2A8v. Maintained also by Bury. See La Bruyère, *Les Caractères,* ed. Bury, 71n2, n3.

173. La Bruyère, *Moral Characters,* 2A8v.

174. On his engagement with Pascal, see Deprun, "La Bruyère entre Descartes et Pascal." Note that in 1697, Pierre Brillon also drew Pascal and Descartes together in his *Ouvrage nouveau dans le gout des Caractères de Théophraste et des Pensées de Pascal.* For comparisons with La Rochefoucauld, see, for example, "Of the Heart," §72: "There is no Vice which has not the resemblance of some Virtue, or other, and which does not make its advantage of it."

175. Here see Louis van Delft, *La Bruyère moraliste: Quatre études sur les "Caractères"* (Geneva, Switzerland: Droz, 1971), 9: "For after all, in La Bruyère's own eyes, nothing is as important as moral instruction [*la morale*]."

176. On the link La Bruyère is making between atheists and libertines, see Moriarty, "La Bruyère: Virtue and Disinterestedness," 171.

177. La Bruyère, *Les caractères,* ed. Bury, 571. On La Bruyère's religious thought and specifically his critique of atheism, see also Alan Charles Kors, *Atheism in France, 1650–1729* (Princeton, NJ: Princeton University Press, 1990), 1:35.

178. La Bruyère, *Manners of the Age,* Z6r, Z8r, 2A3r.

179. La Bruyère, *Manners of the Age,* 2A4r.

180. La Bruyère, *Manners of the Age,* 2B3v.

181. La Bruyère, "Discours de réception à l'Académie française," ed. Bury, 613.

182. La Bruyère, "Discours de réception à l'Académie française," ed. Bury, 613–614. Punctuation lightly modified.

183. La Bruyère, "Discours de réception à l'Académie française," ed. Bury, 614.

184. La Bruyère, "Discours de réception à l'Académie française," ed. Bury, 614.

185. Cuche, "La Bruyère et le Petit Concile," 334–335.

186. Cuche, "La Bruyère et le Petit Concile," 334–335.

187. Roukhomovsky, *Lire La Bruyère,* 16.

188. La Bruyère, *Manners of the Age,* 2B6r.

189. La Bruyère, *Manners of the Age,* H5v.

190. La Bruyère, *Manners of the Age,* H5v–H6r.

191. La Bruyère, *Manners of the Age,* H8v–I1r.

192. La Bruyère, *Manners of the Age,* R1v.

193. See Eric Nelson, *Theology of Liberalism* (Cambridge, MA: Harvard University Press, 2019), for the argument that this Christian foundation still informs contemporary liberal approaches to economic distribution. This creates a problem, he argues, as unequal distribution is no longer incompatible with the justice of a God that does not exist. La Bruyère, an optimistic Augustinian, is situated somewhere in between the two legacies of religious thinking Nelson describes: those of the Pelagians, who highlight the possibility of choice and action (and therefore argue that we are free to sin), and the Augustinians, who believe in original sin and think that man alone cannot save himself.

194. La Bruyère, *Moral Characters,* 2A6v.

195. La Bruyère, *Moral Characters,* 2A6v.

196. Cuche, "La Bruyère et le Petit Concile," 338.

197. Prior scholarship has addressed the religious aspect of La Bruyère's *Characters,* although without reference to this form's involvement with moral philosophy. See Louis MacKenzie, "'Avec un style plus chrétien': Preaching, Philosophizing and Conversion in La Bruyère's *Caractères,*" *Religion and Literature* 22 (1990): 1–17; François Tavera, *L'idéal moral et l'idée religieuse dans les "Caractères," de la Bruyère* (Paris: Mellottée, 1940).

6. Turning Away from Theophrastus: David Hume in 1748

1. Jean de La Bruyère, *The Characters or the Manners of the Age* [. . .], 2nd ed. (London, 1700), 2A8v. This volume encompasses an adaptation and a translation of Theophrastus each of which has an accompanying preface. I henceforth refer to the adaptation as *Manners of the Age* and the translation as *Moral Characters,* as pagination is not continuous.

2. While the third Earl of Shaftesbury, Anthony Ashley Cooper, had recommended a move away from a kind of "mirror writing," replete with characters in his 1712 *Characteristics of Men, Manners, Opinions, Times*, by this he means dialogues, not sketches. Hume, on the other hand, is directly engaging with the adapters of Theophrastus. See Shaftesbury, *Characteristics of Men, Manners,*

Opinions, Times, ed. Lawrence E. Klein (Cambridge: Cambridge University Press, 2000), 90–92.

3. Annette C. Baier, *Death and Character: Further Reflections on Hume* (Cambridge, MA: Harvard University Press, 2008).

4. The earliest edition to include the title *The Enquiry concerning Human Understanding* (as opposed to *Philosophical Essays concerning Human Understanding*) is the 1758 collected *Essays and Treatises on Several Subjects.* Since I am tracing connections between the late 1740s and early 1750s texts, I am working from first editions, not, as is typical, from the 1777 collection of Hume's works.

5. As Kate Abramson underlines, Hume invokes this distinction twice beforehand, first in a 1739 letter to Hutcheson, then in some added paragraphs to the *Treatise* (1740). As she writes, in the eighteenth century, comparisons of these two kinds of philosophy to "painting" and "anatomy" were already "well-worn metaphors." See Kate Abramson, "Happy to Unite, or Not?," *Philosophy Compass* 1, no. 3 (2006): 290–302, at 290.

6. David Hume, *Philosophical Essays concerning Human Understanding* (London, 1748), A1v.

7. Hume, *Philosophical Essays,* A1v.

8. See Kate Abramson, "Hume's Distinction between Philosophical Anatomy and Painting," *Philosophy Compass* 2, no. 5 (2007): 680–698; Jacob Sider Jost, "David Hume, History Painter," *ELH* 81, no. 1 (2014): 143–165.

9. Abramson, "Happy to Unite, or Not?," 291.

10. For the literature on this question, see Abramson, "Happy to Unite, or Not?," 292.

11. David Hume, *Essays and Treatises on Several Subjects* (London, 1777), 2:A2r. See also Stephen Copley and Andrew Edgar, introduction to *Selected Essays* by David Hume (Oxford: Oxford University Press, 1996), vii–xxii, at viii.

12. James Moore, "Hume's Political Science and the Classical Republican Tradition," *Canadian Journal of Political Science* 10, no. 4 (1977): 809–839, at 810, 811.

13. Jeffrey Church, "Selfish and Moral Politics: David Hume on Stability and Cohesion in the Modern State," *The Journal of Politics* 69, no. 1 (2007): 161–181, at 174.

14. Even the scholars who have helped to nuance this picture, such as Church (who shows Hume's moral thought to be more ambivalent on the question of human selfishness than his political writings), similarly emphasize the role of institutions in Hume's solution to the problems provoked by passions. See Church, "Selfish and Moral Politics," 175, 178.

15. See *OED*, s.v. "literature," n., 3a.

16. Jost, "David Hume, History Painter," 145.

17. On the shifts in argument from the *Treatise* to the *Enquiry,* see Hsueh M. Qu, *Hume's Epistemological Evolution* (Oxford: Oxford University Press, 2020).

18. [David Hume], *The Life of David Hume, Esq. Written by Himself* (London, 1777), B4r–v. See Dennis C. Rasmussen, *The Infidel and the Professor: David Hume, Adam Smith, and the Friendship That Shaped Modern Thought* (Princeton, NJ: Princeton University Press, 2017), 21, for the note that this line comes from a poem by Alexander Pope.

19. For Hume's early biography and education, see M. A. Stewart, "Hume's Intellectual Development, 1711–52," in *Impressions of Hume,* ed. Marina Frasca-Spada and P. J. E. Kail (Oxford: Oxford University Press, 2005), 11–58; Annemarie Butler, "Hume's Early Biography and *A Treatise of Human Nature,*" in *The Cambridge Companion to Hume's "Treatise,"* ed. Donald C. Ainslie and Annemarie Butler (Cambridge: Cambridge University Press, 2015), 1–13.

20. Rasmussen, *The Infidel and the Professor,* 21. For the publication history of the *Treatise,* see Butler, "Hume's Early Biography."

21. Rasmussen, *The Infidel and the Professor,* 30.

22. [David Hume], *A Treatise of Human Nature* [. . .], (London, 1739), 1:B3r.

23. [Hume], *Treatise,* 1:B3v.

24. [David Hume], *Abstract* [. . .], (London, 1740), A3v.

25. [Hume], *Abstract,* A3v.

26. [Hume], *Treatise,* 1:B3v, B3r. For a good account of Hume's understanding of "moral subjects," see J. A. Passmore, *Hume's Intentions* (Cambridge: Cambridge University Press, 1952), 1–18.

27. [Hume], *Treatise,* B3r.

28. [Hume], *Treatise,* B3v.

29. [Hume], *Abstract,* A3v.

30. [Hume], *Abstract,* A3r–v.

31. [Hume], *Abstract,* A3v.

32. [Hume], *Abstract,* A3v.

33. [Hume], *Abstract,* A3v; [Hume], *Treatise,* 1:B2r.

34. Here see Jill Kraye, "Conceptions of Moral Philosophy," in *The Cambridge History of Seventeenth-Century Philosophy,* ed. Daniel Garber and Michael Ayers (Cambridge: Cambridge University Press, 1998), 2:1279–1316.

35. See Thomas Hobbes, *On the Citizen,* trans. and ed. Richard Tuck and Michael Silverthorne (Cambridge: Cambridge University Press, 2003), 5. As Skinner shows in *Reason and Rhetoric,* Hobbes's eventual position was one that combined the two methods, having understood the difficulty of convincing warring factions exclusively with reason.

36. [Hume], *Abstract,* B1r.

37. [Hume], *Abstract,* B1r. Where Locke faltered in Hume's view is that "he comprehends all our perceptions under the term of idea, in which sense it is false that we have no innate ideas."

38. [Hume], *Abstract,* B4v.

39. [Hume], *Abstract,* B4v. For Hume's theory of causation, see Martin Bell, "Hume on Causation," in *The Cambridge Companion to Hume,* ed. David Fate Norton and Jacqueline Taylor, 2nd ed. (Cambridge: Cambridge University Press, 2009), 147–176; Don Garrett, "Hume's Theory of Causation: Inference, Judgment, and the Causal Sense," in *The Cambridge Companion to Hume's "Treatise,"* ed. Donald C. Ainslie and Annemarie Butler (Cambridge: Cambridge University Press, 2015) 69–100.

40. [Hume], *Abstract,* C4v–D1r.

41. [Hume], *Abstract,* D1r.

42. [Hume], *Abstract,* D1r.

43. [Hume], *Abstract,* D4r.
44. [Hume], *Abstract,* D4r.
45. [Hume], *Abstract,* D4v.
46. [Hume], *Treatise,* 3:H7v.
47. David Fate Norton, "An Introduction to Hume's Thought," in *The Cambridge Companion to Hume,* ed. Norton and Taylor, 1–39, at 35. For Hume, this reform would predominantly happen in moral philosophy through people practicing his four moral principles. For Hume as a reformer, see John B. Stewart, *Opinion and Reform in Hume's Political Philosophy* (Princeton, NJ: Princeton University Press, 1992).
48. The role of character and personal identity in Hume is the subject of much debate, to which this short summary cannot do justice. For further discussion, see as indicative John Bricke, "Hume's Conception of Character," *The Southwestern Journal of Philosophy* 5, no. 1 (1974): 107–113; Jane L. McIntyre, "Character: A Humean Account," *HPhQ* 7, no. 2 (1990): 193–206; Timothy M. Costelloe, "Beauty, Morals, and Hume's Conception of Character," *HPhQ* 21, no. 4 (2004): 397–415; Constantine Sandis, *Character and Causation: Hume's Philosophy of Action* (London: Routledge, 2019).
49. [Hume], *Treatise,* 1:2G3r.
50. [Hume], *Treatise,* 1:2G3r–v.
51. [Hume], *Treatise,* 1:2G3v.
52. [Hume], *Treatise,* 1:2G3v.
53. [Hume], *Treatise,* 1:2G3v.
54. [Hume], *Treatise,* 1:2G3v.
55. [Hume], *Treatise,* 1:2G4r.
56. [Hume], *Treatise,* 1:2G4v.
57. [Hume], *Treatise,* 1:2G4v.
58. [Hume], *Treatise,* 2:K1v.
59. Here see Donald Ainslie, "Character Traits and the Humean Approach to Ethics," in *Moral Psychology,* ed. Sergio Tenenbaum (Amsterdam: Rodpi, 2008), 79–110; "Scepticism about Person in Book II of Hume's *Treatise,*" *Journal of the History of Philosophy* 37, no. 3 (1999) 469–492.
60. [Hume], *Treatise,* 3:C6r.
61. [Hume], *Treatise,* 3:C6r–v.
62. [Hume], *Treatise,* 3:C6v.
63. Hume, *Philosophical Essays,* A1r.
64. Hume, *Philosophical Essays,* A1v.
65. Hume, *Philosophical Essays,* A1v. On the French inheritance to Hume's adoption of the language of taste and sentiment, and especially the role of the Abbé J.-B. du Bos, see Peter Jones, *Hume's Sentiments: Their Ciceronian and French Context* (Edinburgh: Edinburgh University Press, 1982), chap. 3.
66. Hume, *Philosophical Essays,* A1v.
67. Hume, *Philosophical Essays,* A1v.
68. Hume, *Philosophical Essays,* A1v.
69. Hume, *Philosophical Essays,* A1v.
70. Hume, *Philosophical Essays,* A1v.

71. La Bruyère, *Manners of the Age*, B1v.

72. "medii cuiusdam esse inter philosophorum et poetarum scripta generis," Isaac Casaubon, *ad Theophrasti characteres ethicos liber commentarius* (Lyon, 1592), A4v.

73. "Itaque titulus hic Ἠθικοὶ χαρακτῆρες tantundem ferme valet, ac si dixisset Εἰκόνες ἠθῶν (sive εἰκονιομοὶ, ut appellat Seneca) hoc est, *Imagines morum*: sicut Cicero comicos apppellat *imaginem vitae quotidianae*," Casaubon, *Liber commentarius*, A5v.

74. Joseph Hall, *Characters of Vertues and Vices* [. . .] (London, 1608), B1v.

75. Thomas Ahnert and Susan Manning, introduction to *Character, Self and Sociability in the Scottish Enlightenment*, ed. Thomas Ahnert and Susan Manning (New York: Palgrave-Macmillan, 2011), 1–31, at 1. The Theophrastan tradition also had an impact on Adam Smith's philosophy. Here see Charles L. Griswold, *Adam Smith and the Virtues of Enlightenment* (Cambridge: Cambridge University Press, 1999), 59, 205; Damien Tricoire, "The Fabrication of the Philosophe: Catholicism, Court Culture, and the Origins of Enlightenment Moralism in France," *Eighteenth-Century Studies* 51, no. 4 (2018): 453–477, at 469; Michaël Biziou, "Commerce et caractère chez La Bruyère et Adam Smith: la préhistoire de l'*homo œconomicus*," *Revue d'Histoire des Sciences Humaines* 5 no. 1 (2001): 11–36.

76. Here see Timothy John Stuart-Buttle, "An Authority from Which There Can Be No Appeal," *Journal of Scottish Philosophy* 18, no. 3 (2020): 289–309; Aaron Garrett, "Hume, Cicero, and the Ancients," in *Hume's "An Enquiry Concerning the Principles of Morals": A Critical Guide*, ed. Esther Engels Kroeker and Willem Lemmens (Cambridge: Cambridge University Press, 2021), 192–218.

77. It is Annette C. Baier, *A Progress of Sentiments: Reflections on Hume's "Treatise"* (Cambridge, MA: Harvard University Press, 1991), 312n17, that led me to the edition. This copy is at McGill University Library.

78. Henry Gally, *The Moral Characters of Theophrastus* (London, 1725).

79. Hume, *Philosophical Essays*, A2v–A3r.

80. The technique of *notatio*, the Latin for *ethopoeia*, or the description of character, is present in the *Rhetorica ad Herennium*, a work that was attributed to Cicero until recently. There is, for example, a 1748–1749 collection of Cicero's complete works in Latin printed in Glasgow that includes this text (as well as earlier Oxford editions from the 1710s and later editions from the 1760s and onward, printed in Paris, Naples, and Lyon, that do the same).

81. Theresa Schön, "Moral Curiosity Cabinets: Listing and the Character Sketch in Addison and Steele's Periodicals," in *Forms of List-Making: Epistemic, Literary, and Visual Enumeration*, ed. Roman Alexander Barton, Julia Böckling, Sarah Link, and Anne Rüggemeier (Cham, Switzerland: Palgrave Macmillan, 2022), 81–100, at 81. See also Theresa Schön, *A Cosmography of Man: Character Sketches in "The Tatler" and "The Spectator"* (Berlin: de Gruyter, 2020).

82. Margaret Turner, "The Influence of La Bruyère on the 'Tatler' and the 'Spectator,'" *The Modern Language Review* 48 (1953): 10–16, at 10.

83. *The Tatler*, no. 158 (April 11–13, 1710); *The Tatler*, no. 155 (April 5, 1710), both in Daniel McDonald, ed., *Selected Essays from "The Tatler," "The Spectator," and "The Guardian"* (Indianapolis: Bobbs-Merrill, 1973), 59–62, 54–59, 54.

84. *The Tatler,* no. 155 (April 5, 1710), in McDonald, *Selected Essays,* 54.
85. *The Tatler,* no. 155 (April 5, 1710), in McDonald, *Selected Essays,* 58.
86. Hume, *Philosophical Essays,* A1v.
87. Hume, *Philosophical Essays,* A1v.
88. Hume, *Philosophical Essays,* A1v.
89. Hume, *Philosophical Essays,* A2r.
90. Hume, *Philosophical Essays,* A2r.
91. Isaac Casaubon, *Theophrasti characteres ethici* (Lyon, 1592), *2v.
92. Hall, *Characters of Vertues and Vices,* A4v–A5r.
93. La Bruyère, *Moral Characters,* 2A2r.
94. I am indebted in this account to Peter Millican, *Reading Hume on Human Understanding* (Oxford: Oxford University Press, 2002), 20. On Hume and Malebranche, see Passmore, *Hume's Intentions.*
95. "La Bruyère, Jean de (1645–96)," in *The Oxford Dictionary of Philosophy,* ed. Simon Blackburn (Oxford: Oxford University Press, 2008).
96. In this, I agree with Abramson that Hume's "synthetic work constitutes a third species of philosophy altogether." This is all the more striking once we consider that character-writing had historically been positioned here. See Abramson, "Hume's Distinction between Philosophical Anatomy and Painting," 689.
97. Hume, *Philosophical Essays,* A3r. As we saw, these titles were common in seventeenth-century character-writing. Recall the Overburians "A mere common Lawyer," "A mere Scholler," "A meere Fellow of an House," and "A mere Pettyfogger" in Overbury, *His Wife,* 12th ed. (London, 1627), H5v–I1v, M6v–M8v.
98. Hume, *Philosophical Essays,* A3r.
99. David Hume, *Essays, Moral and Political* (Edinburgh, 1742), 2:A1r–A4v, A1r; 2:F2r–G2v, F3r.
100. Hume, *Philosophical Essays,* A3v.
101. Ernest Campbell Mossner, *The Life of David Hume* (Austin: University of Texas Press, 1954), 140.
102. Hume, *Philosophical Essays,* A4r.
103. Hume, *Philosophical Essays,* A4r.
104. Hume, *Philosophical Essays,* A4r–v.
105. Hume, *Philosophical Essays,* A4v. On the arrival of this metaphorical language in the early modern period, aligning philosophy with the enquiry into "inner space," see Richard Rorty, *Philosophy and the Mirror of Nature* (Princeton, NJ: Princeton University Press, 2018), chap. 3, especially 136–139.
106. Hume, *Philosophical Essays,* A4v.
107. Hume, *Philosophical Essays,* A4v.
108. Hume, *Philosophical Essays,* A5v.
109. Hume, *Philosophical Essays,* A5r.
110. Hume, *Philosophical Essays,* A6v.
111. Hume, *Philosophical Essays,* A6r–v.
112. Hume, *Philosophical Essays,* A7r.
113. Hume, *Philosophical Essays,* A7v.
114. Hume, *Philosophical Essays,* A8r. For Newton's influence on Hume, see as indicative Nicholas Capaldi, *David Hume: The Newtonian Philosopher* (Boston: Twayne Publishers, 1975), 29–70; Yoram Hazony and Eric Schliesser, "Newton

and Hume," in *The Oxford Handbook of Hume,* ed. Paul Russell (Oxford: Oxford University Press, 2014), 673–707; Matias Slavov, "Newtonian and Non-Newtonian Elements in Hume," *Journal of Scottish Philosophy* 14, no. 3 (2016): 275–296.

115. Hume, *Philosophical Essays,* A8v.

116. Although Hume does not mention it here, one further discipline looking for principles—and in which Hume was to become a major participant—was political economy. Here see Andrew S. Skinner, "Hume's Principles of Political Economy," in *The Cambridge Companion to Hume*, ed. David Fate Norton and Jacqueline Taylor, 2nd ed. (Cambridge: Cambridge University Press, 2009), 381–413.

117. Hume, *Philosophical Essays,* A9v–A10r.

118. For an example of going beyond our faculties, consider the question of *why* the fundamental principles of resemblance, contiguity, cause, and effect produce their respective consequences. I owe this point to John Biro, "Hume's New Science of the Mind," in *The Cambridge Companion to Hume*, ed. David Fate Norton and Jacqueline Taylor, 2nd ed. (Cambridge: Cambridge University Press, 2009), 40–70, 42–43.

119. Despite how this form animates Hume's many works, he is rarely seen as an important figure in histories of philosophy focused on the development of the "principle" as a philosophical tool and concept, which often skip from Descartes to Kant. See, for example, Bernard Mabille, ed., *Le principe* (Paris: Vrin, 2006), and Alexandre Feron and Elena Partene, eds., *Le principe* (Limoges: Lambert-Lucas, 2021), which contain only passing discussion of Hume unrelated to the development of the "principle."

120. Letter from Hume to Hutcheson, September 17, 1739, in Francis Hutcheson, *Correspondence and Occasional Writings,* ed. M. A. Stewart and James Moore (Carmel, IN: Liberty Fund, 2022), 71–74, at 72.

121. *Three Essays* was not the first of Hume's works to appear publicly under his name, as has been claimed, but was preceded by the earlier essay collection, dating from 1741 to 1742. See Aaron Garrett, "Hume's 'Original Difference': Race, National Character and the Human Sciences," in *David Hume (International Library of Essays in the History of Social and Political Thought),* ed. Richard Whatmore and Knud Haakonssen (Farnham, UK: Ashgate, 2013), 241–266, at 248. For a good editorial history of Hume's essays, see Amyas Merivale, "Editorial Notes: *Essays, Moral, and Political, and Literary* (1741, 1777)," accessed February 18, 2022, https://davidhume.org/texts/emp/notes. The title page of *Three Essays* indeed claims that this collection "compleats the former Edition, in two Volumes, Octavo."

122. While this text seems to have been composed in 1748, perhaps in response to Hume's naval travels the year before, his interest in national characters can be traced all the way back to 1734. Here see J. Y. T. Grieg, ed., *The Letters of David Hume* (Oxford: Oxford University Press, 1933), 1:21. I owe this point to Silvia Sebastiani, "National Characters and Race: A Scottish Enlightenment Debate," in *Character, Self and Sociability in the Scottish Enlightenment,* ed. Thomas Ahnert and Susan Manning (New York: Palgrave-Macmillan, 2011), 187–205, at 201n12.

123. See, for example, James R. Fleming, "Climate and Culture in Enlightenment Thought," in *Historical Perspectives on Climate Change,* ed. James R.

Fleming (Oxford: Oxford University Press, 1998), chap. 1. For a notable example that pays some attention to the Theophrastan precedent, see John G. Hayman, "Notions on National Character in the Eighteenth Century," *HLQ* 35, no. 1 (1971): 1–17.

124. For printing history, and the supposition that this character could have been written earlier, see Jean Robertson, "Felltham's *Character of the Low Countries*," in *Modern Language Notes* 58, no. 5 (1943): 385–388. Where there had been sketches previously written about people who come from a particular country—such as the Overburians' "A Welchman"—as well as numerous travel accounts and histories of nations written that were not characters, Felltham seems to have been the first to bring these two genres together.

125. Felltham, *Character of the Low-Countreyes,* A3r.

126. Felltham, *Character of the Low-Countreyes,* A3r.

127. William Petty, *The Political Anatomy of Ireland* (London, 1691), A5r.

128. See Garrett, "Hume's 'Original Difference,'" 248, on the link between this essay and "Of National Characters." For Hume's indebtedness to Petty in his economic writings, see Istvan Hont, "The 'Rich Country–Poor Country' Debate Revisited: The Irish Origins and French Reception of the Hume Paradox," in *David Hume's Political Economy,* ed. Carl Wennerlind and Margaret Schabas (Abingdon, UK: Routledge, 2008), 243–323, at 250–257.

129. The idea of tabulating national mores would arrive with the *Völkertafel,* "Table of Nations," an oil painting created in Austria in the eighteenth century that compared European nations on the bases of different attributes of character. This borrows both from the rhetorical tradition of analogical comparison as well as from the tabulations of demographic qualities.

130. Petty, *The Political Anatomy of Ireland,* H1v.

131. David Hume, "Of National Characters," in *Three Essays: Moral and Political* (London, 1748), B1r–C6v, at B1r.

132. [Hume], *Treatise,* 1:Q4v–Q5r.

133. Isaac Newton, "Scholium generale," in *Philosophiæ naturalis principia mathematica,* 2nd ed. (Cambridge, 1713), 3Q1r–3Q2v, at 3Q2v. For how this comes into play, not only in the *Abstract* but in the *Second Enquiry,* see R. I. G. Hughes, "Hume's *Second Enquiry*: Ethics as Natural Science," *HPhQ* 2, no. 3 (1985): 291–307. See Hughes, "Hume's *Second Enquiry,*" 305n11, for more detail on Newton's attitude toward hypotheses.

134. Hume, "Of National Characters," B1r–v.

135. Garrett makes a case for Hume borrowing these terms from du Bos's *Réflexions critiques sur la poësie et sur la peinture* (1719). See Garrett, "Hume's 'Original Difference,'" 250. This is intended as a riposte against arguments that Hume was here influenced by Montesquieu, in particular as articulated by Paul Chamley, "The Conflict between Montesquieu and Hume: A Study of the Origins of Adam Smith's Universalism," in *Essays on Adam Smith,* ed. Andrew Skinner and Thomas Wilson (Oxford: Oxford University Press, 1975), 274–305.

136. Hume, "Of National Characters," B1v.

137. Hume, "Of National Characters," B1v.

138. Hume, "Of National Characters," B2r.

139. Hume, "Of National Characters," B2r.

140. Hume, "Of National Characters," B2r.

141. Hume, "Of National Characters," B4v.

142. Hume, "Of National Characters," B5r.

143. Hume, "Of National Characters," B5r.

144. Hume, "Of the Rise and Progress of the Arts and Sciences," in *Essays, Moral and Political,* 2:G3r–N2v, at G4r. While Garrett in "Hume's 'Original Difference,'" 250, points to the continuation of this discussion of causation, he does not pick up on the shared language of "contagion."

145. Hume, "Of the Rise and Progress of the Arts and Sciences," G3v.

146. Hume, *Treatise,* 2:F5r–v.

147. Hume, *Treatise,* 2:F5v.

148. Hume, "Of National Characters," B5v.

149. Hume, "Of National Characters," B5v.

150. Hume, "Of National Characters," B5v.

151. Hume, *Treatise,* B6r.

152. Hume, *Treatise,* C1r.

153. Hume, *Treatise,* C1r.

154. For the revision, see Hume, "Note [M]," in *Essays and Treatises on Several Subjects,* 1:2N3v–2N4r. There is an enormous literature on the footnote. See, as indicative, Richard Popkin, "The Philosophical Bases of Modern Racism," in *The High Road to Pyrrhonism,* ed. R. A. Watson and J. E. Force (San Diego: Austin Hill Press, 1980), 79–102; John Immerwahr, "Hume's Revised Racism," *JHI* 53 (1992): 481–486; Robert Palter, "Hume and Prejudice," *Hume Studies* 21, no. 1 (1995): 3–23; Robert Mankin, "Hume et les races humaines," *Corpus: Revue de Philosophie* 57 (2009): 75–99.

155. Hume, "Note [M]," 1:2N3v–2N4r.

156. Hume, "Note [M]," 1:2N4r.

157. This reading draws on Garrett's interpretation of this passage in his "Hume's 'Original Difference,'" 257–261. Garrett does not, however, make sense of the connection with the previous sentence, or with Hume's arguments about plants and animals earlier, and therefore does not point to the recall to the physical cause.

158. Hume, "Note [M]," 2N4r.

159. Here see Londa Schiebinger, "The Anatomy of Difference: Race and Sex in Eighteenth-Century Science," *Eighteenth-Century Studies* 23, no. 4 (1990): 387–405; Nicholas Hudson, "From 'Nation' to 'Race': The Origin of Racial Classification in Eighteenth-Century Thought," *Eighteenth-Century Studies* 29, no. 3 (1996): 247–264; Thierry Hoquet, "Biologization of Race and Racialization of the Human: Bernier, Buffon, Linnaeus," in *The Invention of Race: Scientific and Popular Representations,* ed. Nicolas Bancel, Thomas David, and Dominic Thomas (New York: Routledge, 2014), 17–32; Justin E. H. Smith, *Nature, Human Nature, and Human Difference: Race in Early Modern Philosophy* (Princeton, NJ: Princeton University Press, 2015).

160. Londa Schiebinger, "Medical Experimentation and Race in the Eighteenth-Century Atlantic World," *Social History of Medicine* 26, no. 3 (2013): 364–382, at 381.

161. Garrett, "Hume's 'Original Difference,'" 265. It does seem, however, that Hume could have used a thicker theory of his own moral causes, extending to the

prejudices held by institutions, to explain why it was comparatively harder for black people to integrate into predominantly white European societies. I am grateful to Gautham Shiralagi for this point.

162. David Olusoga, "The Roots of European Racism Lie in the Slave Trade, Colonialism—and Edward Long," *The Guardian*, September 8, 2015.

163. Edward Long, *The History of Jamaica* (London, 1774), 2:475–485, at 477.

164. Robert Bernasconi and Tommy Lott, introduction to *The Idea of Race*, ed. Robert Bernasconi and Tommy Lott (Indianapolis: Hackett, 2000), vi–xviii, at xiii.

165. See, for example, Stella Sandford, "Kant, Race, and Natural History," *Philosophy & Social Criticism* 44, no. 9 (2018): 950–977, which does not once mention the influence of Hume. See also Huaping Lu-Adler, *Kant, Race, and Racism: Views from Somewhere* (Oxford: Oxford University Press, 2023), which argues that Kant's own system can help clarify his approach to race. Kant's full comment runs (my emphasis), "The Negroes of Africa have by *nature* no feeling that rises above the ridiculous. Mr. Hume challenges anyone to adduce a single example where a Negro has demonstrated talents, and asserts that among the hundreds of thousands of blacks who have been transported elsewhere from their countries, although very many of them have been set free, nevertheless not a single one has ever been found who has accomplished something great in art or science or shown any other praiseworthy quality, while among the whites there are always those who rise up from the lowest rabble and through extraordinary gifts earn respect in the world. So *essential* is the difference between these two human kinds, and it seems to be just as great with regard to the *capacities of mind* as it is with respect to colour." In Kant, *Observations on the Feeling of the Beautiful and Sublime and Other Writings*, ed. Patrick Frierson and Paul Guyer (Cambridge: Cambridge University Press, 2011), 58–59.

166. Hudson, "From 'Nation' to 'Race,'" 256.

167. Here see Evelynn M. Hammonds and Rebecca M. Herzig, eds., *The Nature of Difference: Sciences of Race in the United States from Jefferson to Genomics* (Cambridge, MA: MIT Press, 2008).

168. See here Hume, *Essays, Moral and Political*, 2:N3r–X3v; [Hume], *The Life of David Hume*, C8v–D2r; David Hume, "A Character of Sir Robert Walpole," in *Essays, Moral and Political*, 2:2C1v–2C2v. Hume's *History of England* often includes sections entitled "Death and Character."

169. On the idea of impersonation, see the "Advertisement" to vol. 2 of *Essays, Moral and Political* informing the reader that "in those Essays, intitled, *The Epicurean, Stoic*, etc., a certain Character is personated; and therefore, no Offence ought to be taken at any Sentiments contain'd in them."

170. Donald T. Siebert, review of *Society and Sentiment: Genres of Historical Writing in Britain, 1740–1820*, by Mark Salber Phillips, *Eighteenth-Century Scotland* 15 (2001): 26–27.

171. Baier, *Death and Character*, 218.

172. Baier, *A Progress of Sentiments*, 218–219.

173. [Hume], *Treatise*, 3:O5r.

174. [Hume], *Treatise*, 3:O6r.

175. [Hume], *Treatise*, 3:O6v.

176. Hall, *Characters*, G4r–G6r; *A Brief Description or Character of the Religion and Manners of the Phanatiques in Generall* (London, 1660); David Hume, "Of Superstition and Enthusiasm," in *Essays, Moral and Political* (Edinburgh, 1741), 1:S3r–T4r, at S4r–v, S3r, T1r.

177. Hume, "Of Superstition and Enthusiasm," S3r.

178. Hume, "Of Superstition and Enthusiasm," S4v.

179. Francis Bacon, "Of Superstition," in *The Essayes* (London, 1625), N4v–O2r, at O1v.

180. Hume, "Of Superstition and Enthusiasm," T3r.

181. Hume, "Of Superstition and Enthusiasm," T2r–v.

182. Hume, "Of Superstition and Enthusiasm," T3v.

183. Hume, "Of Superstition and Enthusiasm," T2r.

184. Hume, "Of Essay-Writing," A1r.

185. Hume, "Of Essay-Writing," A1v.

186. Hume, "Of Essay-Writing," A1v. This essay thus replicates the argument of the opening of the *First Enquiry*, with the "easy and obvious philosophy" representing "conversation and common Life" and "the abstruse philosophy" representing learning.

187. David Hume, "Of Commerce," in *Political Discourses* (Edinburgh, 1752), A1r–C3v, at A1r.

188. David Hume, "Of Commerce," A1v–A2r.

189. David Hume, "Of Commerce," A2r.

190. David Hume, "Of Commerce," A2r.

191. Due to their proliferation in Hume's works, the characters of the "shallow" and the "abstruse" seem to attain the status of essential "conceptual personae" in his philosophy. On this as a methodological approach to the history of philosophy, see Gilles Deleuze and Félix Guattari, *What Is Philosophy?*, trans. Hugh Tomlinson and Graham Burchell (New York: Columbia University Press, 1994), 61–84.

192. David Hume, "That Politicks May be Reduc'd to a Science," in *Essays, Moral and Political,* 1:D2r–F4v, at D2r.

193. Hume, "That Politicks May be Reduc'd to a Science," D3r.

194. Hume, "That Politicks May be Reduc'd to a Science," E1v.

195. Hume, "That Politicks May be Reduc'd to a Science," E1v.

196. Hume, "Of the Delicacy of Taste and Passion," in *Essays, Moral and Political,* 1:A1r–A4v, at A3r.

197. Hume, "Of the Delicacy of Taste and Passion," A3r.

198. Hume, "Of the Delicacy of Taste and Passion," A3r.

199. Several of these arguments are further developed in Hume's later "Of the Standard of Taste" (1757). See Hume, "Of the Standard of Taste," in *Four Dissertations* (Edinburgh, 1757), L2r–M8v, at M3r, M2v, L4r.

200. David Hume, "A Dialogue," in *An Enquiry concerning the Principles of Morals* (London, 1751), L4r–M7r, at L11r–v.

201. Hume, "A Dialogue," L11r–v.

202. We can draw a parallel here to the split between continental and analytic philosophy, which Simon Critchley understands in these terms and sees as originating with Kant. See Critchley, *Continental Philosophy: A Very Short Introduction* (Oxford: Oxford University Press, 2001), chaps. 1 and 2. Michael Dummett,

who places this split between Frege and Husserl, also uses the metaphor of the divergence between the Rhine and the Danube to describe it. See Michael Dummett, *Origins of Analytical Philosophy* (London: Duckworth, 1993), 24–25.

203. Immanuel Kant, *Critique of Pure Reason,* ed. Paul Guyer and Allen W. Wood (Cambridge: Cambridge University Press, 1998), 156, §A21/B35, note.

204. Guido Mazzoni, *Theory of the Novel,* trans. Zakiya Hanafi (Cambridge, MA: Harvard University Press, 2017), 114.

205. Mazzoni, *Theory of the Novel,* 114.

206. Rorty, *Philosophy and the Mirror of Nature,* 134.

207. Rorty, *Philosophy and the Mirror of Nature,* 136, 140.

208. Rorty, *Philosophy and the Mirror of Nature,* 132.

209. Rorty, *Philosophy and the Mirror of Nature,* 132.

210. Rorty, *Philosophy and the Mirror of Nature,* 11–13. See, more generally, chap. 8. It is striking that each of these philosophers makes significant room for the aesthetic.

211. Rorty, *Philosophy and the Mirror of Nature,* 136, for Rorty's retelling of an anecdote about William James, who bemoaned the bald-headed young PhDs boring each other to death at seminars and "never confounding *Aesthetik* with *Erkenntnistheorie.*"

212. Rorty, *Philosophy and the Mirror of Nature,* 319.

213. Rorty, *Philosophy and the Mirror of Nature,* 359. See Hans-Georg Gadamer, *Truth and Method,* trans. Joel Weinsheimer and Donald G. Marshall (London: Continuum, 1975), especially 11–14, where Gadamer moves this concept away from Hegel's philosophy of absolute spirit.

214. Rorty, *Philosophy and the Mirror of Nature,* 369.

215. Rorty, *Philosophy and the Mirror of Nature,* 379.

Epilogue

1. J. W. Smeed, *The Theophrastan "Character": The History of a Literary Genre* (Oxford: Clarendon Press, 1985), 82. The Russian and Spanish cases may well have produced intriguing reception stories of their own.

2. Smeed, *The Theophrastan "Character,"* 91; cited in Smeed, *The Theophrastan "Character,"* 84.

3. Smeed, *The Theophrastan "Character,"* 103, 113.

4. Helen Small, "Artificial Intelligence: George Eliot, Ernst Kapp, and the Projections of Character," *19: Interdisciplinary Studies in the Long Nineteenth Century* 29 (2020): 1–16, at 1. On the character in Victorian England, see Stefan Collini, "The Idea of 'Character' in Victorian Political Thought," *RHS* 35 (1985): 29–50.

5. Roger Hargreaves, *Little Miss Late* (New York: HarperCollins, 2018), unpaginated.

6. For this angle on Spinhirny's *Les caractères aujourd'hui: Ce qui résisté et ce qui cede* (Paris: Payot, 2022), see Apolline Guillot, "Can We Still Have Character at Work? Interview with Frédéric Spinhirny," *Philonomist,* March 22, 2023. On the related industry of personality tests and their current use in corporate environments, see Emma Goldberg, "The $2 Billion Question of Who You Are at Work,"

New York Times, March 5, 2023. For a history of one of the most popular tests, see Merve Emre, *What's Your Type: The Strange History of Myers-Briggs and the Birth of Personality Testing* (London: William Collins, 2018).

7. Theorizing about the creation of particular types, as Owen Jones does in his *Chavs: The Demonization of the Working Class* (London: Verso, 2011), though not Theophrastan, is worth mentioning as a splinter genre. See also Penelope Eckert, *Jocks and Burnouts: Social Categories and Identity in the High School* (New York: Teachers College Press, 1990), and my "The Politically Wandering Jew," *La revue K,* November 7, 2024.

8. On how these cases should be read as a continuation of an earlier practice of *ethopoeia,* see Barbara Carnevali, "Literary Mimesis and Moral Knowledge: The Tradition of *ethopoeia,*" *Annales (HSS)* 65 (2010): 291–322. Stendhal, "Projet d'article sur *Le Rouge et le Noir,*" [1832], in *Œuvres romanesques complètes* (Paris: Gallimard, 2005), 1:822–838, at 827. On Flaubert and the *roman de mœurs,* see Philippe Dufour, preface to *Madame Bovary,* in *Gustave Flaubert: Œuvres completes,* ed. Gisèle Séginger (Paris: Honoré Champion, 2021), 9–36, at 17. See Peter Brooks, *The Novel of Worldliness: Crébillon, Marivaux, Laclos, Stendhal* (Princeton, NJ: Princeton University Press, 1969), 88–89, for French character-writing and the novel.

9. English Victorian novels also include Theophrastan types, from the many unnamed professional figures who populate Dickens's novels to named characters like Mr. Collins, a transformed Obsequious Man, who walks his way into Jane Austen's 1813 *Pride and Prejudice.* On unnamed (and unspeaking) characters in the Victorian novel, see Tara Menon, *Spoken Words: Direct Speech in the Nineteenth-Century British Novel* (Princeton, NJ: Princeton University Press, forthcoming).

10. Christopher Ricks, "The Art of Lydia Davis," in *The Collected Stories of Lydia Davis* (New York: Penguin, 2014), xii–xxii, at xiii.

11. Davis also typifies and distances by using mathematical symbols. Here see "Problem," in *The Collected Stories of Lydia Davis* (New York: Penguin, 2014), 124. On literary distancing, see Carlo Ginzburg, *Wooden Eyes: Nine Reflections on Distance,* trans. Martin Ryle and Kate Sopher (New York: Verso, 2002).

12. For a theorization of how recognizing the "conceptual personae" in a given philosopher's notions can serve as a method of understanding the history of philosophy (where the ancient Greek notion of "philosophy," for example, holds the persona of the "friend"), see Gilles Deleuze and Félix Guattari, *What Is Philosophy?,* trans. Hugh Tomlinson and Graham Burchell (New York: Columbia University Press, 1994), chap. 3.

13. Richard Rorty, *Contingency, Irony, and Solidarity* (Cambridge: Cambridge University Press, 1989), xv. For a more recent example of a philosopher who uses types, see Liam Kofi Bright, "White Psychodrama," *Journal of Political Philosophy* 31 (2023): 198–221.

14. Rorty, *Contingency, Irony, and Solidarity,* xv.

15. Rorty, *Contingency, Irony, and Solidarity,* xv.

16. One might also argue that Richard Rorty uses this character type to embody the kind of philosophy he had celebrated in his earlier *Philosophy and the Mirror of Nature* (Princeton, NJ: Princeton University Press, 2018): one that imagines

philosophy "in the conversation of mankind," as an exchange between different kinds of people. See chap. 8, §5.

17. Sianne Ngai, *Our Aesthetic Categories: Zany, Cute, Interesting* (Cambridge, MA: Harvard University Press, 2012), 9.

18. Barbara Carnevali, "Commentaire: Habilitation à diriger des recherches d'Enrica Zanin," presentation at the University of Strasbourg, December 17, 2021.

19. See, for example, Friedrich von Schlegel, *On the Study of Greek Poetry*, trans. S. Barnett (Albany: State University of New York Press, 2001); Martin Heidegger, *Poetry, Language, Thought*, trans. Albert Hofstadter (New York: HarperCollins, 1971).

20. See Alasdair MacIntyre, *After Virtue: A Study in Moral Theory* (Notre Dame, IN: University of Notre Dame Press, 1981); Martha Nussbaum, *Love's Knowledge: Essays on Philosophy and Literature* (Oxford: Oxford University Press, 1992); Cora Diamond, *The Realistic Spirit: Wittgenstein, Philosophy, and the Mind* (Cambridge, MA: MIT Press, 1995); Vincent Descombes, *Proust: Philosophie du roman* (Paris: Minuit, 1987); Rorty, *Contingency, Irony, and Solidarity*; Jacques Bouveresse, *La connaissance de l'écrivain: Sur la littérature, la vérite et la vie* (Marseille, France: Agone, 2008).

21. Martha Nussbaum, *Poetic Justice: The Literary Imagination and Public Life* (Boston: Beacon Press, 1996), 6. Note that the ethical impact of the novel has been claimed in other, earlier contexts, such as the eighteenth century. For Lynn Hunt, the epistolary novel is foundational in understanding the development of human rights. See her *Inventing Human Rights: A History* (New York: W. W. Norton, 2007).

22. Carnevali, "Literary Mimesis"; Engel, "Literature and Practical Knowledge," *Argumenta* 2 (2016): 55–76.

23. Enrica Zanin, "Éthique et nouvel du récit: Le cas des nouvelles de la Renaissance," in *En deçà du bien et du mal: Morales de la littérature de la Renaissance à l'âge contemporain* (Paris: Hermann, 2024), 25–45, at 26–27.

24. Amit Pinchevski, "Bartleby's Autism: Wandering along Incommunicabiltiy," *Cultural Critique* 78 (2011): 27–59, at 30. This means that Melville's story "is taken as empirical evidence to support the existence of autism almost a century before it was formally recorded." Note also the conference presentation by Nicholas Manning, "L'autisme de Bartleby: Le diagnostic des personnages comme question éthique," Éthique et littérature aujourd'hui: *l'état de la question, l'héritage du passé*, University of Strasbourg, March 22–23, 2023.

25. Here see Stephen Halliwell, *The Aesthetics of Mimesis: Ancient Texts and Modern Problems* (Princeton, NJ: Princeton University Press, 2002).

26. For a discussion about the ethics of rewriting Roald Dahl, see Hayden Vernon, "Roald Dahl Books Rewritten to Remove Language Deemed Offensive," *The Guardian*, February 18, 2023; "Roald Dahl, Ian Fleming, Godard . . . Faut-il adapter les classiques à leur époque?," in *L'Invité des Matins*, presented by Guillaume Erner, *France Culture*, March 10, 2023. On the Florida bill, see Jessica Winter, "The Queer Children's Books Targeted by the 'Don't Say Gay' Bill," *The New Yorker: The Political Scene Podcast*, July 15, 2022, https://www.newyorker.com/podcast/politics-and-more/the-queer-childrens-books-targeted-by-the-dont-say-gay-bill.

27. For critiques of neo-Platonic approaches as they pertain to pornography (and that can be applied beyond), see, for example, Ronald Dworkin, "Women and Pornography," *New York Review of Books,* October 21, 1993; Bernard Williams, ed., *Obscenity and Film Censorship: An Abridgement of the Williams Report* (Cambridge: Cambridge University Press, 2015), chap. 6. On contemporary censorship, see Carole Talon-Hugon, *L'art sous contrôle: Nouvel agenda sociétal et censures militantes* (Paris: Presses universitaires de France, 2019). Communitarian Aristotelian approaches may be subject to some of these same issues. Here see Martha Nussbaum's review of Alasdair MacIntyre's *Whose Justice? Which Rationality?* (Notre Dame, IN: University of Notre Dame Press, 1989) in "Recoiling from Reason," *New York Review of Books,* December 7, 1989.

28. I deal with these concerns in my "A Critique of Martha Nussbaum's Liberal Aesthetics," *Political Theory* 52, no. 3 (2023): 374–403. See also David Bromwich, "Rat Poison," *London Review of Books,* October 17, 1996; Daniel A. Bell, "The Limits of Liberal Justice," *Political Theory* 26, no. 4 (1998): 557–582.

29. *Curb Your Enthusiasm,* season 8, episode 3, "Palestinian Chicken," directed by Robert B. Weide, written by Larry David, Alec Berg, and David Mandel, aired July 24, 2011, on HBO, https://www.imdb.com/title/tt1640882/; Fiona Spence, "Tár: A Guide to How a Female Narcissist Behaves," *Fiona Spence: Blog,* March 14, 2023, https://fionaspence.com.au/narcissistic-female-behaviour-tar/.

30. Merve Emre, "What's Your Type?," *New York Review of Books,* March 7, 2024. She writes this in relation to Eleanor Catton's bestselling *Birnam Wood* (2023).

31. These latter two examples of the moralization of everyday life are taken from the introduction to Enrica Zanin, *Fiction et vérité, l'éthique du récit de Boccace à Madame de Lafayette* (Geneva: Droz, 2024).

32. For a rich comparison on the similarities between humanist strategies of reading with those present in the contemporary, see Zanin, "De l'éthique de la vertu au *self-help*: parcours éthiques de la Reniassance au contemporain," in *Éthique et littérature aujourd'hui,* ed. Emiliano Cavaliere, Vincenza Perdichizzi, and Enrica Zanin (Paris: Éditions Hermann, 2025) chap. 12.

33. On the ethical turn in the United States, see Todd F. Davis and Kenneth Womack, eds., *Mapping the Ethical Turn* (Charlottesville: Virginia University Press, 2001); Stephen K. George, ed., *Ethics, Literature, and Theory: An Introductory Reader* (Oxford: Oxford University Press, 2005). For the arrival of the ethical turn in France, see Sandra Laugier, *Éthique, littérature, vie humaine* (Paris: Presses Universitaires de France, 2006); Alexandre Gefen, *Réparer le monde, la littérature française face au XXIe siècle* (Paris: Corti, 2017). For the Italian reception, one might point to the rebuttal found in Walter Siti, *Contro l'impegno: Riflessioni sul Bene in letteratura* (Milan: Rizzoli, 2021). And, for the reception in China, see the Call for Papers for the Ninth Convention of the International Association for Ethical Literary Criticism, held at Zhejiang University, Hangzhou, China, November 8–10, 2019, https://www.ae-info.org/attach/Acad_Main/Past_Events/2011-present/The%20Ethico-Political%20Turn%20in%20Literary%20Studies/Hangzhou%20Conference%2001-08-2019.pdf. Time will tell whether the ethical turn in Chinese academia will lead to similar public polemics as those concerning the

Roald Dahl rewrite or the Florida ban (on the presumption, too difficult to substantiate here, that the two have been linked in these other contexts).

34. In his *Visions of Politics,* Quentin Skinner traces an important shift in the history of Western political thought from duties into rights: a move away from a Renaissance model of virtue politics, which believes that sovereignty is a property of the people, something that gives centrality to the notion of the virtuous citizen and comes with theories about citizens' duties, toward a Hobbesian model, which thinks that sovereignty is a property of the state, something that gives centrality to the sovereign as a representative of the state and comes with theories about the rights citizens have against it. It would be interesting to examine whether certain literary genres suit these different political visions and whether the link between virtuous politics and character-writing might be compared to an association between rights and the epistolary novel. Here see Quentin Skinner, *Visions of Politics* (Cambridge: Cambridge University Press, 2002), 1:viii; Hunt, *Inventing Human Rights.*

35. Here see Chad Levin, "Solidarity and the Ethical Turn," *Cultural Critique* 117 (2022): 88–108, at 88. The ethical turn in political theory is here seen to come, on the one hand, from an impetus to care for the self, inspired by Foucault, and, on the other, an imperative to care for the other, inspired by Levinas.

36. Katrina Forrester, *In the Shadow of Justice: Postwar Liberalism and the Remaking of Political Philosophy* (Princeton, NJ: Princeton University Press, 2019), xvi–xvii, 246.

37. Marin Cogan, "The Mittsplainer: An Alternate Theory of Mitt Romney's Gaffes," *GQ,* August 1, 2012, https://www.gq.com/story/the-mittsplainer-an-alternate-theory-of-mitt-romneys-gaffes.

38. This involves a presumption that they would be worried about someone like Cogan ridiculing them, that they would take seriously her approval or reprobation and wish to some extent to be part of her in-group.

39. Rebecca Solnit, *Men Explain Things to Me* (Chicago: Haymarket, 2014), 13.

40. Miranda Fricker, *Epistemic Injustice: Power and the Ethics of Knowing* (Oxford: Oxford University Press, 2007), 2.

41. Fricker, *Epistemic Injustice,* 1.

42. Fricker, *Epistemic Injustice,* 154.

43. Fricker, *Epistemic Injustice,* 2, 154.

44. Fricker, *Epistemic Injustice,* 152. See here for how hermeneutical injustice differs from epistemic bad luck.

45. As quoted in Elster, *Alchemies of the Mind,* 101, in relation to how "some emotions are not consciously acknowledged as such because the culture lacks the concept of those specific emotional states."

46. Pierre Bourdieu, *Distinction: A Social Critique of the Judgement of Taste,* trans. Richard Nice (Cambridge, MA: Harvard University Press, 1984), 481.

47. Fricker, *Epistemic Justice,* 164–165.

48. Here see Solnit, *Men Explain Things to Me,* 14, on the term: "I have doubts about the word ['mansplainer'] and don't use it myself much; it seems to me to go a little heavy on the idea that men are inherently flawed this way, rather than that some men explain things they shouldn't and don't hear things they should."

49. See Pierre Bourdieu, *The Logic of Practice,* trans. Richard Nice (Stanford, CA: Stanford University Press, 1990), 52.

50. One cannot, as my colleague Jason Ferguson noted, mansplain to a child.

51. Carnevali, "Literary Mimesis," 298.

52. While I use the term "character sketch," by the mid-nineteenth century, the genre of the character has been transformed once again, with Thackeray's collection reading more like a series of anecdotes: written in the first person, taking place in the past tense, and including people's proper names.

53. Barbara Carnevali, "Snobbery: A Passion for Nobility," in *Navigatio vitae: Saggi per i settant'anni di Remo Bodei,* ed. Luigi Ballerini, Andrea Borsari, and Massimo Ciavolella (New York: Agincourt, 2010), 384–406, at 387. Though Carnevali's "Literary Mimesis" brims with examples, I turn to her work on snobbery, published the same year: both to give us a sense of a nineteenth-century character sketch and because it clarifies important differences between the character as a tool for moral knowledge and for epistemic justice.

54. William Makepeace Thackeray, *Book of Snobs: By One of Themselves* (Auckland, New Zealand: Floating Press, 2011), 254.

55. Thackeray, *Book of Snobs,* 254.

56. This validation seems that it will rely on other features that the individuals doing the recognizing must share. If Thackeray and his interlocutor, both invited to this dinner, find Jawkins to be a snob, the waiters serving the dinner might think this true of Thackeray himself.

57. See John Gibson, "Literature and Knowledge," in *The Oxford Handbook of Philosophy and Literature,* ed. Richard Eldridge (Oxford: Oxford University Press, 2009), 468–485, at 471.

58. Gibson, "Literature and Knowledge," 471.

59. Carnevali, "Literary Mimesis," 291. While Carnevali focuses on a realist canon in literature, see 315 for how this might extend into modernism.

60. Engel, "Literature and Practical Knowledge," 70.

61. Engel, "Literature and Practical Knowledge," 63.

62. Engel, "Literature and Practical Knowledge," 72.

63. Engel, "Literature and Practical Knowledge," 72–73. This is what makes Engel's version of practical knowledge "propositional": with literary works having a truth value that can be justified by reasons.

64. This 1848 collection was previously titled *The Snobs of England* (1846–1847).

65. From *kata-* ("against") and *agoreuein* ("to speak in assembly"), perhaps gaining its classificatory meaning from its status in logic, "to predicate of a person or thing."

66. As Proust puts it, how do we handle the fact that, even if the term "snob" seems to perfectly fit a character like Legrandin, it is clear that he himself "could not, from his own knowledge, at least, be aware that he was one also." See Marcel Proust, *In Search of Lost Time, Volume I. Swann's Way,* ed. William C. Carter (New Haven: Yale University Press, 2013), 147.

67. Cogan, "The Mittsplainer."

68. Here one might productively draw on standpoint epistemology, a heterogenous set of theories about the epistemic limitations that emerge from one's par-

ticular sociopolitical standpoint. See, for example, Donna Haraway, "Situated Knowledges: The Science Question in Feminism and the Privilege of Partial Perspectives," *Feminist Studies* 14, no. 3 (1988): 575–599; Sandra Harding, ed., "Standpoint Theory as a Site of Political, Philosophic, and Scientific Debate," in *The Feminist Standpoint Theory Reader: Intellectual and Political Controversies* (New York: Routledge, 2003), 1–16. My thanks go to Keidrick Roy for pointing me to this literature.

69. Here see Samia Hesni, "How to Disrupt a Social Script," *Journal of the American Philosophical Association* 10, no. 1 (2024): 24–45.

70. Hesni, "How to Disrupt a Social Script," 29, 32.

71. My account here is drawn from Irina Kalinka's "The Politics of Appearance on Digital Platforms: Personalisation and Censorship," *Z Politikwiss* 32 (2022): 531–549.

72. See also Dale Zhou, Shubhankar Patankar, David M. Lydon-Staley, Perry Zurn, Martin Gerlach, and Dani S. Bassett, "Architectural Styles of Curiosity in Global Wikipedia Mobile App Readership," *Science Advances* 10, no. 43 (2024), which classifies Wikipedia use into different styles of curiosity: "the busybody," "the hunter," and "the dancer."

73. See Fricker, *Epistemic Justice,* 4, and more fully chap. 1.

74. For a recent critique of the former, see Lidal Dror, "Is There an Epistemic Advantage to Being Oppressed?," *Noûs* 57, no. 3 (2023): 618–640.

75. Ian Hacking, "Making Up People," in *Forms of Desire: Sexual Orientation and the Social Constructionist Controversy,* ed. Edward Stein (New York: Routledge, 1992), 69–88, at 70. There is a tension here between social constructionism and Fricker's approach, which aims to discover shared realities.

76. There is a plausible Platonic argument that the creation of this category could force some people to purposefully mansplain as a way of signaling their rejections of the norms of an "in-group." On this as a kind of "vice signaling," see Olúfẹ́mi O. Táíwò, "Vice Signaling," *Journal of Ethics and Social Philosophy* 22, no. 3 (2022): 295–316.

77. Jean-Paul Sartre, *Anti-Semite and Jew: An Exploration of the Etiology of Hate,* trans. George J. Becker (New York: Schocken, 1976), 4. Excluding titles, I amend the spelling of "anti-Semite" to "antisemite," given that the former presupposes an idea of the "Semite," which, as the International Holocaust Remembrance Alliance describes, "legitimizes a form of pseudo-scientific racial classification that was thoroughly discredited by association with Nazi ideology," https://www.holocaustremembrance.com/antisemitism/spelling-antisemitism. This also happens to follow the original French (*antisémite*).

78. Sartre, *Anti-Semite and Jew,* 4.

79. Sartre, *Anti-Semite and Jew,* 5.

80. Sartre, *Anti-Semite and Jew,* 6, 11.

81. Sartre, *Anti-Semite and Jew,* 23, 36.

82. Sartre, *Anti-Semite and Jew,* 38.

83. Sartre, *Anti-Semite and Jew,* 5. Bourdieu's attempt in *Distinction* to later do the same for aesthetic judgment might, in this respect, be seen as a continuation of Sartre's project. Bourdieu does later make inroads in thinking of politics as part of a *habitus,* arguing that "campus radicalism," for example, is a feature of "the

effects of enclosure, compounded by those of scholastic election and the prolonged cohabitation of a socially very homogeneous group." See Pierre Bourdieu, *Sketch for a Self-Analysis,* trans. Richard Nice (Chicago: University of Chicago Press, 2007), 8–9.

84. Sartre, *Anti-Semite and Jew,* 33, 7, 31, 18; see 20 for Sartre's note on how this pertains to Proust's description of snobbery: "Proust has shown, for example, how antisemitism brought the duke closer to his coachman, how, thanks to their hatred of Dreyfus, bourgeois families forced the doors of the aristocracy."

85. T. W. Adorno, Else Frenkel-Brunswik, Daniel J. Levinson, and R. Nevitt Sanford, *The Authoritarian Personality* (New York: Harper & Brothers, 1950), ix.

86. Adorno et al., *The Authoritarian Personality,* 971n1.

87. Adorno et al., *The Authoritarian Personality,* 2–3, 5.

88. Adorno et al., *The Authoritarian Personality,* 971.

89. Adorno et al., *The Authoritarian Personality,* 973.

90. Adorno et al., *The Authoritarian Personality,* 975–976.

91. Adorno et al., *The Authoritarian Personality,* 975–976.

92. See Sartre, *Anti-Semite and Jew,* 106.

93. Sartre, *Anti-Semite and Jew,* 106. For Bourdieu, too, changing someone's *habitus* involves changing their situation, the field in which they operate.

94. Joan Didion, "Comrade Laski, C.P.U.S.A. (M.-L.)," in *Slouching toward Bethlehem* (New York: Farrar, Straus and Giroux, 1968), 68–73, at 69. See also Tom Wolfe, "Radical Chic: That Party at Lenny's," *New York Magazine,* June 8, 1970; David Brooks, *Bobos in Paradise: The New Upper Class and How They Got There* (New York: Simon & Schuster, 2020).

95. The proliferation of types in the Brexit years led journalist John Crace to write "a new political glossary," explaining a number of terms, many of which are written as characters. See his "Brexit Means Brexit, Corbynistas and 'Facts'—The New Political Glossary," *The Guardian,* September 6, 2016. "The conspiracy theorist" has recently been subjected to a similar analysis to those conducted by Adorno and Sartre on authoritarians and antisemites. Here see Joseph E. Uscinski and Joseph M. Parent, *American Conspiracy Theories* (Oxford: Oxford University Press, 2014).

96. I borrow this terminology from Georgina Ramsay, who makes this argument in relation to the framing of two modern types, "the refugee" and "the homeless veteran." See her "Displacement and the Capitalist Order of Things," *Humanity: An International Journal of Human Rights, Humanitarianism, and Development* 12, no. 3 (2021): 368–379.

97. Bernard Williams, *Moral Luck: Philosophical Papers 1973–1980* (Cambridge: Cambridge University Press, 1982), 26–27.

98. Cited in Georg Lukács, "Tolstoy and the Development of Realism," in *Studies in European Realism,* ed. Alfred Kazin (New York: Grosset & Dunlap, 1964), 126–205, at 167.

99. Overbury, "An Host," in *His Wife,* 12th ed. (London, 1627), G2r.

100. Leo Tolstoy, *War and Peace,* trans. Richard Pevear and Larissa Volokhonsky (London: Vintage, 2007), 10.

101. Leo Tolstoy, *Anna Karenina,* trans. Constance Garnett (Minneapolis: Lerner, 2015), 574.

102. Tolstoy, *Anna Karenina,* 575.

103. Tolstoy, *Anna Karenina,* 575.

104. Tolstoy, *Anna Karenina,* 587–588.

105. See Lukács, "Tolstoy and the Development of Realism." For a clear account of the role of the type in Marxist literary criticism after Lukács, see Raymond Williams, *Marxism and Literature* (Oxford: Oxford University Press, 1977), 101–107.

106. Lukács, preface to *Studies in European Realism,* ed. Alfred Kazin (New York: Grosset & Dunlap, 1964), 1–19, at 6.

107. Georg Lukács, "The Intellectual Physiognomy in Characterization," in *Writer and Critic and Other Essays,* trans. and ed. Arthur D. Kahn (New York: Grosset & Dunlap, 1971), 149–188, at 158. For this as a development of Hegel's "concrete universal," see Lukács, "Art and Objective Truth," in *Writer and Critic,* 25–60, at 35. For the Marxist understanding of "concrete" on which Lukács relies, see Karl Marx, "Introduction to the Critique of Political Economy," in *A Contribution to the Critique of Political Economy,* trans. S. W. Ryazanskaya (London: Lawrence and Wishart, 1971), app. 1.

108. See Isaiah Berlin, "The Hedgehog and the Fox: An Essay on Tolstoy's View of History," in *The Proper Study of Mankind: An Anthology of Essays,* ed. Henry Hardy (New York: Farrar, Straus and Giroux, 1999), 436–498; Isaiah Berlin, "Political Judgement," in *The Sense of Reality: Studies in Ideas and Their History,* ed. Henry Hardy (New York: Farrar, Straus and Giroux, 1996), 40–53.

109. Berlin, "The Hedgehog and the Fox," 436.

110. Berlin, "The Hedgehog and the Fox," 451.

111. Berlin, "The Hedgehog and the Fox," 489, 487.

112. Berlin, "Political Judgement," 46.

113. Berlin, "Political Judgement," 52.

114. Joseph North, *Literary Criticism: A Concise Political History* (Cambridge, MA: Harvard University Press, 2017), xi.

Acknowledgments

Someone once said to me that the best reason to write a book is the chance to write the acknowledgments. Over the course of these years, I have often imagined writing this page, ever accruing new debts of gratitude and friendships. I began this book in London, continued it in Paris, and finished it in Cambridge, Massachusetts, and my thanks go to people and institutions in these three places I have been lucky enough to call home.

Thanks are first due to my teachers. In London, I must first thank the co-supervisors of the dissertation that became this book: Quentin Skinner and David Colclough. To Quentin, whose patience and responsiveness have been unparalleled and matched with an ability to always quietly be one step ahead. I am grateful to him for letting me run while unfailingly providing the incisive comment that would help me see things differently. To David, for his editor's eagle eye, for helping me find the shape of my enquiry, and for providing the first line of this book. I must next thank my judicious examiners, Andrew Fitzmaurice and Michael Moriarty, who provided a springboard from which to jump away from the thesis and into something bigger. In Paris Barbara Carnevali set me on the right track and understood my project before I understood it myself. It is under her guidance that I found my voice as a scholar and have started a life's project of finding ways to balance the abstract and the concrete. So many of the ideas in this book were nurtured in our seminar *Littérature, philosophie, sciences sociales*, and I am deeply appreciative of the community of colleagues and friends that this brought, from whom I have learnt so much. At the École Normale Supérieure, I hold a great debt of gratitude not only to the voluminous and cosy library but to my excellent teachers, Dimitri El Murr, Florent Guénard, and Elena Partene.

My thanks secondly go to organizations and interlocutors. At Harvard, where I am finishing this book, on one of Boston's bright days of cold sun,

I cannot thank the Society of Fellows enough, and especially Noah Feldman, for believing in this book and creating an extraordinary environment in which to think and write. My conversations at the Society with Jason Ferguson, Peter Galison, Gregory Nagy, Keidrick Roy, Elaine Scarry, Harmon Siegel, Christopher Spaide, and Spencer Weinreich have all shaped this book and have sparked many new ideas that will stay with me for years to come. In Cambridge, I must also thank the brilliant Scott Walker at the Harvard Map Collection, who created the historical map in chapter 2. On a material level, I am very grateful to the Center for Hellenic Studies in Greece, where I spent an unforgettable summer thinking about Theophrastus's biography, a short sail away from his birthplace, and Queen Mary University of London's Arts and Humanities Research Studentship, which made my initial research possible. So too did the indefatigable staff at the Universität Wien Library, the Bayerische StaatsBibliothek, the Widener Library, the McGill University Library, and the British Library. In consulting the resources housed in their rich collections, I further owe a curious debt to Keith Thomas. Chancing upon his illustration of his arcane working methods in a *London Review of Books* diary post was a rare gift, as these methods soon became something of an inspiration to my own.

Parts of this book found their initial formulations elsewhere. Chapter 1 builds on ideas first presented in an article coauthored with René de Nicolay, "Theophrastus' 'Oligarch' and the Political Intention of the *Characters*," *The Cambridge Classical Journal*, no. 69 (2023): 1–21. Portions of chapter 2 were first published as "Moral Instruction by Bad Example: The First Latin Translations of Theophrastus' Characters," *Renaissance Studies* 36, no. 5 (2022): 668–685. Chapter 4 includes text first published in "The Study of National Character in Seventeenth-Century London: From Satire to Social Science," *Intersezioni* 43, no. 1 (2023): 39–59. I have also presented parts of the book in front of a number of kind audiences, at the Renaissance Studies Association, the American Philosophy Association, the American Historical Association, the Sorbonne's Séminaire Locke, Harvard's Early Modern Workshop, Princeton's Department of Politics, the Hume Society, the Annual Southwest Graduate Philosophy Conference, the Annual Conference of the Interdisciplinary Center for Hellenic Studies, Queen Mary University of London's Postgraduate Colloquium, and the Britain & Ireland Association for Political Thought. Special thanks, among the many generous respondents, readers, hosts, audience members, and email correspondents, go to David Armitage, Emma Bartel, Ann Blair, Emiliano Cavaliere, Jill Frank, Angus Gowland, Melissa Lane, Kathryn Murphy, Mor Segev, Martina Di Stefano, Georgios

Varouxakis, Jordan Walters, Jake Wiseman, Ming Wong, Bernardo Zacka, and Enrica Zanin.

Now, to my friends and family, with whom I have discussed many angles of this book, and (just as importantly) so much else. In Cambridge, I am grateful to Jordan Cotler, whose endless curiosity and easy laugh have kept me happy; to Ana Novak, for making me always feel at home; to Ida Assefa, whose generous spirit of adventure has helped me remember the world beyond the university; and to Jensen Suther, for helping me understand what it is to live a thinking life. My long transatlantic phone calls with Haziran Zeller, with his bright and surprising mind, showed me new ways of approaching the questions in this book, just when I thought I had finished it. In Paris, I must thank Marion Krafft, for her careful listening and insight; René de Nicolay, for the joy of thinking together about ancient political thought; Micol Bez, whose open mind always brings so much new light; and both Octave Boczkowski and Mark Thakkar (back in England) for precious help on all matters linguistic. In London, Barnaby Raine has kept my thinking political, Elie Jesner has kept me grounded, and I could not have asked for a better makeshift doctoral cohort than Gautham Shiralagi, Peter Huhne, and Saul Nelson. My siblings, Rebecca and Sam, are my emotional foundation, and my parents, Joanna Ebner and Aron Landy, have supported me in countless ways: making what I do seem possible (and even sometimes interesting), which I know is a luxury.

My final word of thanks is to the team at Harvard University Press—Sana Mohtadi, Jillian Quigley, and Stephanie Vyce—and, of course, to my editor, Emily Silk. Having never done this before, I had no idea what it would be to write a book. Emily has made this process a complete joy: I have learned things about my work, my writing, and myself that will last a lifetime, along with my awe at her capacity for crystal-clear thinking and her commitment to getting something right.

This book is dedicated to my late grandparents, Ann and Henry Ebner, neither of whom were able to do the postgraduate study that they, in another world, might have, and who never stopped asking me what exactly it was I was writing about.

Index